Grammatical Voice

The grammatical category of voice covers a wide range of phenomena, including causatives, applicatives, passives, antipassives, middles, and others. Drawing on data from over 200 languages, Fernando Zúñiga and Seppo Kittilä illustrate the semantic, morphological, and syntactic variation of voice across languages from a range of families and regions. They approach the topic from a broad and explicit perspective, and discuss a variety of topics that are not always regarded as voice, in order to make a clear and useful conceptual delimitation. Clearly organized and accessibly written, the book will be welcomed by students and scholars of linguistics, especially those interested in how grammatical categories work.

FERNANDO ZÚÑIGA is professor of linguistics at the University of Bern. His research focuses on the qualitative typology of voice and alignment, as well as on benefaction and wordhood issues. He has co-edited numerous books including *Typological Hierarchies in Synchrony and Diachrony* (2018) with Sonia Cristofaro.

SEPPO KITTILÄ works as a senior lecturer in linguistics at the University of Helsinki. He has published extensively on transitivity and argument marking, and also causatives. He has co-edited numerous books on these topics including *Benefactives and Malefactives* (2010) with Fernando Zúñiga.

T0349847

CAMBRIDGE TEXTBOOKS IN LINGUISTICS

General editors: P. AUSTIN, J. BRESNAN, B. COMRIE, S. CRAIN, W. DRESSLER,
C. EWEN, R. LASS, D. LIGHTFOOT, K. RICE, I. ROBERTS, S. ROMAINE, N. V. SMITH.

Grammatical Voice

In this series

Earlier issues not listed are also available.

Grammatical Voice

FERNANDO ZÚÑIGA

University of Bern

SEPPO KITTILÄ

University of Helsinki

CAMBRIDGE
UNIVERSITY PRESS

University Printing House, Cambridge CB2 8BS, United Kingdom

One Liberty Plaza, 20th Floor, New York, NY 10006, USA

477 Williamstown Road, Port Melbourne, VIC 3207, Australia

314–321, 3rd Floor, Plot 3, Splendor Forum, Jasola District Centre, New Delhi – 110025, India

79 Anson Road, #06–04/06, Singapore 079906

Cambridge University Press is part of the University of Cambridge.

It furthers the University's mission by disseminating knowledge in the pursuit of
education, learning, and research at the highest international levels of excellence.

www.cambridge.org
Information on this title: www.cambridge.org/9781107159242
DOI: 10.1017/9781316671399

First published 2019

Printed and bound in Great Britain by Clays Ltd, Elcograf S.p.A.

A catalogue record for this publication is available from the British Library.

Library of Congress Cataloging-in-Publication Data
Names: Zúñiga, Fernando, author. | Kittilä, Seppo, author.
Title: Grammatical voice / Fernando Zúñiga, Seppo Kittilä.
Description: First edition. | Cambridge, United Kingdom ; New York, NY : Cambridge University Press,
    2019. | Series: Cambridge textbooks in linguistics | Includes bibliographical references and index.
Identifiers: LCCN 2018042532 | ISBN 9781107159242 (hardback : alk. paper) |
    ISBN 9781316612125 (paperback : alk. paper)
Subjects: LCSH: Grammar, Comparative and general–Grammatical categories. |
    Grammar, Comparative and general–Voice.
Classification: LCC P240.5 .Z86 2019 | DDC 415–dc23
LC record available at https://lccn.loc.gov/2018042532

ISBN 978-1-107-15924-2 Hardback
ISBN 978-1-316-61212-5 Paperback

Contents

Figures

Tables

Acknowledgments

First, Seppo Kittilä would like to thank the Academy of Finland (grant number 265951) and the University of Helsinki for funding several parts of this study. Second, we would like to express our heartfelt gratitude to Peter Austin, who was the clearance reader assigned by Cambridge University Press, for his insightful comments on the first version of the manuscript. Third, we are grateful to Nikolaus Himmelmann and Katharina Haude for their valuable feedback on some sections of Chapter 4. Fourth, Fernando Zúñiga is grateful to Spike Gildea, Doris Payne, and Tom Payne for very stimulating conversations on voice-related topics during his stay in Oregon in 2017. Last, but definitely not least, we would like to thank Florian Matter and Jean Rohleder for their help with hard-to-find references and sources; Kirsi Kauppinen and Lucy Zuberbühler for their help with practical things related to finalizing the book for submission and publication; and Gordon Lee, as well as Grace Morris and everybody else at Cambridge University Press, for their careful and diligent work during production.

Abbreviations

A	agent-like argument of bivalent predicate
AFC	agent focus construction
DOC	double object construction
DOM	differential object marking
EPC	external possession construction
G	goal-like argument of trivalent predicate
IAC	involuntary agent construction
ICC	inanimate causer construction
IOC	indefinite object construction
ISC	indefinite subject construction
NIC	nominal incorporation construction
NP	noun phrase
P	patient-like argument of bivalent predicate
R	referent
S	single argument of monovalent predicate
T	theme-like argument of trivalent predicate
TDC	transitivity discord construction
w/	with
X^0	extra-thematic argument

Abbreviations Used in the Glosses

ABL	ablative
ABS	absolutive
ABSNT	absential
ACC	accusative
ACT	active
ADD	additional
ADEL	adelative
ADESS	adessive
ADJ	adjunct
AF	agent focus
AFF	affectedness, affirmative
AGT	agentive
AI	animate intransitive
ALL	allative

ANIM	animate
ANT	anterior
ANTIC	anticausative
ANTIP	antipassive
AOBJ	applied object
AOR	aorist
APPL	applicative
ART	article
ASP	aspect
ASS	assertive
ATTR	attributive
AUG	augmented
AUX	auxiliary
AV	agent voice
BARE	bare
BEN	benefactive
CAUS	causative
CNJ	conjunct
CNSTR	construct state
COM	comitative
COMPL	completive
CONJ	conjunction
CONT	continuous, continuative
CONV	conveyance
CORE	core
CSEE	causee
CTRL	control
CV	conveyance voice
CVB	converb
CVRS	conversive
DAT	dative
DECL	declarative
DEF	definite
DEIC	deictic
DEM	demonstrative
DET	determiner
DETR	detransitive
DIR	direct
DISJ	disjunctive
DIST	distal
DOBJ	direct object
DRCT	directional
DS	different-subject

DU	dual
DYN	dynamic
EMPH	emphatic
ENUNC	enunciative
EPE	epenthetical segment(s)
ERG	ergative
EVID	evidential
EXCL	exclusive
F	feminine
FIN	finite
FOC	focus
FUT	future
GEN	genitive
GER	gerund
HAB	habitual
HON	honorific
HUM	human
II	inanimate intransitive
ILL	illative
IMPER	imperative
IMPRS	impersonal
INAN	inanimate
INCEP	inceptive
INCL	inclusive
INCOMPL	incompletive
IND	indicative
INDF	indefinite
INF	infinitive
INESS	inessive
INS	instrumental
INST	instigation
INTR	intransitive
INV	inverse
IOBJ	indirect object
IPFV	imperfective
IRR	irrealis
ITER	iterative
IV	instrument(al) voice
LAT	lative
LD	locative-directional
LNK	linker
LOC	locative
LOCUT	locutor

LT	low-tone form
LV	locative voice
M	masculine
MAL	malefactive
MID	middle
N	neuter
ND	nondirect
NEG	negative
NFIN	nonfinite
NFUT	nonfuture
NHUM	nonhuman
NMLZ	nominalizer
NOM	nominative
NPST	nonpast
NSBJ	nonsubject
NSG	nonsingular
NTH	nontheme
NTOP	nontopic
NVIS	nonvisual
OBJ	object
OBL	oblique
OBV	obviative
PARAG	paragoge
PASS	passive
PAT	patient
PART	particle
PERF	perfect
PFV	perfective
PL	plural
POBJ	primary object
POS	positive
POSS	possessive
POSTP	postposition
POT	potential
PRED	predicative
PREF	prefix
PREP	preposition
PREPOBJ	prepositional object
PRIOR	prioritive
PROG	progressive
PROX	proximate
PROP	proprietive
PRS	present

PRSNT	presential
PS	pseudo-
PSR	possessor
PST	past
PTCL	particle
PTCP	participle
PTV	partitive
PURP	purposive
PV	patient voice
PVB	preverb
REAL	realis
REC	recipient
RECP	reciprocal
REFL	reflexive
REL	relative
RELINQ	relinquitive
RPST	recent past
SAF	stem affix
SAP	speech-act participant
SBJ	subject
SG	singular
SOBJ	secondary object
SOCIAT	sociative
SPONT	spontaneous
STAT	stative
SUB	subordinate
SUNUCL	subjective undergoer nucleative
SUPERESS	superessive
TA	transitive animate
TAM	tense-aspect-mood
TI	transitive inanimate
TH	thematic
TNS	tense
TOP	topic
TR	transitive
TRANSL	translative
UV	undergoer voice
VIS	visual
VN	verbal noun
VOC	vocative
VOL	volitionality
WIT	witnessed

Other Symbols Used in the Glosses

I, II, …	nominal classes; inflectional sets
x→y	*x* acting on *y*
-	default morpheme boundary
=	(internal) clitic morpheme boundary
≡	external clitic morpheme boundary
~	reduplicative morpheme boundary
< >	infix
#	phonological word boundary

1   Introduction

1.1   Preliminaries

The term VOICE can refer to several different things in the study of human language. In literary-linguistic studies, it is used to describe an author's style – the formal qualities that make his/her writing unique. In phonetics, the term refers to the articulatory process in which the vocal cords vibrate. In morphosyntax, where it is sometimes specified as GRAMMATICAL VOICE, it denotes a particular relationship between the meaning and the form of clauses.

For instance, the following English sentences are usually thought of as conveying propositions with the same truth values, but they are used in different conditions or contexts of use on the one hand and have a different formal make-up on the other:

(1)   English (Germanic, world language)[1]
        a.   *The paparazzi saw Zelda at the party.*
        b.   *Zelda was seen by the paparazzi at the party.*

The first sentence – an example of the active voice – is more naturally used when talking about paparazzi and what they did, whereas the second, passive-voice, sentence appears to be more commonly used when talking or writing about Zelda (especially in formal registers of the language). Several formal features distinguish both sentences, namely constituent order, verb morphology, and the syntactic status of the main participants (*the paparazzi* and *Zelda*), in addition to intonational patterns. The study of grammatical voice deals precisely with such conditions or contexts of use and with such formal differences, not only in English active–passive pairs but also in similar or related oppositions found in virtually every natural language.

Grammatical voice is one of the oldest topics in descriptive linguistics. In his *Aṣṭādhyāyī* 'Eight Chapters', Pāṇini (c. sixth–fourth century BCE) describes the inflectional paradigms of Sanskrit verbs, which show what we nowadays call a voice opposition between *parasmaipada* 'word for another' and *ātmanepada* 'word for oneself' (e.g., *bharati* 's/he bears' vs. *bharate* 's/he is borne').

---

[1] Most examples in this study come from published sources, which are acknowledged in the text or the indented examples. Where no source is given, the examples are based on the authors' personal knowledge.

The treatise on Greek grammar called *Téchnē Grammatikḗ* 'Art of Grammar' – customarily attributed to Dionysius Thrax (170–90 BCE) – uses the term *diáthesis* 'state, condition, disposition' to describe the three-way opposition found with Greek verbs between *enérgeia* 'activity, vigor', *páthos* 'suffering', and *mesótēs* 'intermediate, middle' (e.g., *etúptēsa* 'I struck' vs. *etúphthēn* 'I was struck' vs. *etuptēsámēn* 'I struck for myself').[2] Later grammarians use the Latin terms *verborum genus / genus verbi* 'genus/gender of verb(s)' and *vox* 'voice' for the analogous grammatical category of Latin. The latter language has a two-way opposition between *vox activa* 'active voice' and *vox passiva* 'passive voice' (e.g., *ferō* 'I bear' vs. *feror* 'I am borne'), which are the origins of the present-day English terms used to refer to the verb forms in (1) above, as well as of similar terms used in other European languages.

The present study of grammatical voice, written in the functional-typological tradition, has two objectives. First, it is intended to provide an overview of the manifestations of the category grammatical voice in the grammars of the world's languages. Second, it seeks to lend clarity to the current understanding of the category by proposing a model of voice that is not only broad enough to cover numerous grammatical facts but also strict enough to draw meaningful lines between voice phenomena, voice-like phenomena, and categories that are related to voice but best seen as different from it. In particular, we include in our treatment selected phenomena that some earlier approaches choose to exclude from their voice models (e.g., applicatives), and we exclude some phenomena that at least one recent approach subsumes under the term voice (e.g., formally unmarked diathetical alternations). Another hallmark of the present study is that we present voice phenomena according to semantic criteria first – alteration vs. maintenance of semantic argument structure and increase vs. decrease of number of arguments – followed by a presentation of morphological and syntactic features of the constructions under scrutiny.

We hope that these choices contribute to balancing the literature on grammatical voice, which for many years tended to focus on interesting syntactic aspects of passive(-like) constructions but comparatively neglected other aspects of many different constructions in the world's languages that were equally important. After three decades of descriptive work of unprecedented depth, detail, and breadth in Western linguistics, as well as four decades of stimulating theoretical and typological studies addressing issues related to voice, we have found a daunting but exhilarating amount of material at our disposal. We have tried to present the readers of this book with a study intended

---

[2] The earliest use of the term *diáthesis* to mean 'grammatical voice' seems to be found in Aristotle's *Categories*, which predates the *Art of Grammar* by approximately two centuries. Apollonius Dyscolus (second century CE) employs the term more broadly in *Perì Syntáxeōs* 'On Syntax': he distinguishes between three kinds of diatheses, namely *sōmatikḗ* 'relative to the body' (i.e., voice), *psychikḗ* 'relative to the soul' (i.e., mood), and *chronikḗ* 'relative to time' (i.e., tense and aspect).

to deepen their understanding and broaden their horizons, rather than merely classify grammatical facts.

1.2   Terminological and Analytical Prerequisites

Several related concepts are important for the study of grammatical voice, namely valency, transitivity, and diathesis. VALENCY is the number of arguments a predicate takes: semantically, syntactically, or morphologically. The first refers to the number of arguments in semantic structure; predicates can be semantically avalent (e.g., English *rain*), monovalent (e.g., *weep*), bivalent (e.g., *kill*), or trivalent (e.g., *give*) (Tesnière 1959). The other two kinds of valency refer to the number of arguments instantiated in the syntactic structure of the clause and the morphological structure of a predicate, respectively. For instance, in English *she gives the beggar her coat*, the semantically trivalent verb *give* appears in a clause with three arguments, and the verb marks one argument, its subject.

TRANSITIVITY is a multi-parameter notion that comprises different facets of clauses, including semantic and syntactic valency, but also agentivity, affectedness, and referentiality of different arguments (see, e.g., Hopper & Thompson 1980 and Næss 2007). Clauses can thus occupy an intermediate zone between intransitive and transitive poles. For example, inanimate, indefinite, or nonspecific patients may appear as unmarked objects vis-à-vis more "transitive" constructions with animate and highly individuated patients that are expressed as case- or adposition-marked objects – a well-known and much-studied phenomenon called differential object marking (see the literature from Bossong 1985 to Iemmolo 2011). Similarly, events instigated by non-prototypical agents (which may, e.g., act involuntarily or be inanimate) can be expressed by constructions encoding lower transitivity (Fauconnier 2012). Descriptive studies occasionally deal with some specific phenomena that belong to this intermediate zone using the label "detransitive constructions." These may comprise different instances of voice, but also different instances of differential argument marking.

Many studies do not distinguish between valency and transitivity as strictly. It is common to find the following labels referring to predicate valency values of 0, 1, 2, and 3, respectively: atransitive, intransitive, (mono-)transitive, and ditransitive. In recent years, the term "ambitransitive" has also been used in typological studies to refer to labile predicates like English *eat*, which have a syntactic valency value of 1 (e.g., *he ate too late last night*) or 2 (e.g., *she ate her supper*). In this book, transitivity is understood as in the studies mentioned in the preceding paragraph. Instead of using the potentially ambiguous terms "intransitive verb" and "transitive verb," however, we will specify whether predicates are semantically or syntactically (or morphologically) monovalent or bivalent, and we will characterize clauses that have subjects only as one-argument, those that have a subject and an object as two-argument, and those with a subject and two objects as three-argument clauses. (The two objects of three-argument clauses are seldom identical: they are usually either direct and indirect or primary and secondary objects. See Dryer 1986.)

DIATHESIS refers to any specific mapping of semantic roles (SRs) onto grammatical roles (GRs). The former include notions like agent, patient, theme, recipient, experiencer, stimulus, source, goal, etc., which are usually conceived of as low-level abstractions over predicate classes (Bickel 2011). We work with the following generalized roles here: A and P for the agent-like and patient-like argument of bivalent predicates, respectively; A, T, and G for the agent-like, the theme-like, and the goal-like argument of trivalent predicates, respectively;[3] and S for the single argument of monovalent predicates.[4] (We specify the S further as S_A and S_P when necessary. The distinctions made in functional studies on the one hand between agentive 'dance' and patientive 'break' predicates and on the other between active 'come' and stative 'be cold' predicates basically corresponds to what the literature in the Chomskyan tradition labels the unergative-unaccusative distinction; see, e.g., Levin & Rappaport Hovav 1994: 59f.) Grammatical roles include notions like subject, object, other complements, and adjunct. At the center of attention in this book are DIATHETICAL OPERATIONS, that is, strategies used by natural languages to alter diathetical structure. The mechanisms employed in such operations relate to semantic argument structure, such as argument INSTALLMENT or REMOVAL; syntactic structure, such as argument PROMOTION or DEMOTION (and the latter's extreme case, viz., SUPPRESSION); or both.

GRAMMATICAL VOICE is defined here as a grammatical category whose values correspond to particular diatheses marked on the form of predicates. Diathesis refers to the number of semantic arguments involved in a state of affairs, to how they are involved in it, and to how they are assigned to GRs of varying salience and flexibility. Voice refers to the way a specific diathesis is formally marked on functional or lexical verbs in the predicate complex. For instance, the English examples in (1) above show a difference in verb morphology: while the active verb appears in a simple, unmarked, form (*saw*), the passive verb form is especially marked as an auxiliary-cum-participle construction (*was seen*). Thus, the English passive diathesis is expressed by a passive voice. By contrast, the examples in (2) from Palu'e show that the only formal difference between the active and passive diatheses may concern

---

[3] We follow common practice in not distinguishing between the agent-like argument of bivalent predicates and the agent-like argument of trivalent predicates. Unlike split intransitivity, which is hardly a marginal phenomenon, languages that distinguish between agent-like arguments of higher-valency predicates in their grammar appear to be extremely rare (Bickel 2011).

[4] The symbols S, A, P, etc. are widely used in functional-typological studies, but different authors understand them differently (Haspelmath 2011). Unlike Dixon (1994) and Comrie (1981), who employ them as syntactic notions orbiting semantic cores, we use them as generalized semantic roles (like in Bickel 2011).

constituent order. In such a language, the diathetical opposition is not expressed by a voice opposition: there is simply no voice, due to the lack of any kind of (argument-related) verbal morphology.

(2)   Palu'e (Austronesian, Indonesia; Donohue 2005: 60)
   a. *Ia   cube   vavi   va'a.*
      3SG   shoot   pig   DEM
      'He shot the pig.' (active diathesis)
   b. *Vavi   va'a   ia   cube.*
      pig   DEM   3SG   shoot
      'That pig was shot by him.' (passive diathesis)

Among the several hallmarks of the definition of voice employed in this book, the one regarding morphological marking deserves special attention, for two reasons. First, natural languages frequently have several alternative grammatical structures that can be used to portray the same, or nearly the same, state of affairs. More often than not, however, only some of these structures have an overt marking that identifies them as particular voices. There is usually one construction that is formally unmarked vis-à-vis the others, and linguistic studies have traditionally not only chosen such unmarked structures as the vantage point from which the other structures are characterized, but have also labeled them as voice despite their lack of formal marking, like the English active voice in (1) above. Second, many languages do not have a formally unmarked construction; all related structures are equally marked – although they may differ as to the exact means of marking. Some languages have contrasting sets of argument markers, like active *-mus* vs. mediopassive *-mur* for the 1PL in Latin *monē-mus* 'we admonish' vs. *monē-mur* 'we are admonished'. Others show active and passive morphemes, like *men-* and *di-* in Standard Indonesian:

(3)   Standard Indonesian (Austronesian, Indonesia; Sneddon 1996: 247–248)
   a. *Dia   men-jemput   saya.*
      3SG   ACT-meet   1SG
      'He met me.' (active voice)
   b. *Saya   di-jemput   oleh   dia.*
      1SG   PASS-meet   by   3SG
      'I was met by him.' (passive voice)

Even though the requirement that only coded diatheses be labeled voices may strike some readers as unnecessarily Eurocentric, such predicate-marking patterns are not only found outside Europe but are also quite widespread, both areally and genealogically. The obvious alternative would consist in calling both coded and uncoded diatheses "voices" (thereby dispensing with the distinction between diathesis and voice), but we have followed current mainstream studies here in taking a conservative tack.

Another hallmark of the present study is that we deliberately keep the modeling of both semantic and syntactic structure rather abstract and vague in order to facilitate its cross-linguistic and (almost) frame-neutral application. On the semantic side, even though there are a number of proposals as to how to best handle the semantic relations between predicates and their arguments, there is still no universally accepted General Theory of them (Kittilä & Zúñiga 2014). Some authors regard SRs as impressionistic labels and model the causal chain in formal terms resorting to other notions (e.g., Van Valin & LaPolla 1997, Croft 2012). Others regard SRs as definable based on semantic features (e.g., Rozwadowska 1989, Næss 2007). Most authors nowadays simply work with SRs acknowledging the relevance of both causal-chain considerations and specific features, but this has not yet resulted in a principled and comprehensive theory encompassing all that we know about SRs. In the present book, we assume that semantic arguments are identified by the authors of descriptive studies (i) on a language-specific basis and (ii) based on formal (i.e., morphosyntactic, albeit perhaps indirect) diagnostics. The former means, for instance, that rough translational equivalents of English *shout*, *beat*, or *give* in other languages do not necessarily have the same argument structures (Kittilä 2006, 2007). The latter means that a reasonable effort has been undertaken to make claims regarding the semantic characterization of the relevant predicates falsifiable.

On the syntactic side, different theories work with slightly different inventories of GRs, and even theories that have superficially equivalent inventories define the notions differently (e.g., via structural configuration, as primitives of different kinds, or as sets of arguments selected by specific constructions for particular syntactic purposes). In addition, GRs may be seen as universal (i.e., the same for all human languages) or not. We work here with an array of non-primitive and language-specific GRs that makes use of the received terminology (subject, direct and indirect objects, primary and secondary objects, complements, adjuncts). We agree that GRs are best seen as construction-specific but have chosen to assume at least some uniformity or clustering in how the diagnostic properties of GRs pattern language-internally, solely in order to use the received terms in an uncomplicated way. Consequently, even though our approach to syntactic issues is not theory-neutral, it is easily translatable into the approaches employed in formal frameworks. We do not claim here that GRs defined based on clustering of diagnostic morphosyntactic properties are the best or only option, or that the resulting constructs are universal. We merely claim that cross-linguistic comparison of voice phenomena based on such unsophisticated SRs and GRs is still a feasible and a worthwhile endeavor.

It is important to mention that we do not regard voice, or any other structural category of grammar, as the expression of a pre-established category (Haspelmath 2007b). This has three important analytical consequences. First, we arrive at the voice prototypes mentioned above by distilling shared traits from disparate language-specific constructions. These particular constructions may instantiate the prototypes to varying degrees, deviating from them, as they often do, in ways that are complex, subtle, or both. Second, we do not believe that a specific grammatical phenomenon must express *either* voice *or* another grammatical category; a particular pattern or marker might well express *both* voice *and* another category (e.g., aspect) in any given language. Pure and hybrid voices are interesting phenomena in their own right, but our definition is independent of this dimension. Lastly, voice may develop in a given language from either another, already existing, grammatical category or a lexical element. Nevertheless, we do not regard only some final point in the development path as voice, thereby relegating all previous stages to pre-voice, incomplete voice, or the like. As they grammaticalize further, particular constructions typically become more general and more productive, and we simply see the prototype as involving the highest possible level of applicability to all suitable clauses for the specific value at hand. This means, for instance, that we see both causatives and anticausatives as voices, even though the latter are consistently less widely applicable than the former (which is partly due to how they alter diathetical structure, as we discuss in Chapter 2).

Finally, we use some other expressions in this book that are not exclusively related to the study of voice. *Flagging* is an umbrella term that covers case morphology and adpositional marking, and *indexing* denotes the marking of features related to arguments or adjuncts by means of bound elements. We say that a particular phenomenon is *typical* if it occurs frequently, either language-specifically or cross-linguistically. By contrast, we say that a particular phenomenon is *prototypical* if it conforms to a prototype, which we have defined striking a balance between capturing cross-linguistic regularities and departing from mainstream terminology as little as possible – at least in the many cases where there is reasonable consensus on how the term in question is used. We have chosen not to employ the word *canonical* here, in order to avoid confusion with the term as employed either in general, to refer to (orthodox) rules, or in particular, in the Canonical Typology literature (e.g., in Brown et al. 2013). Lastly, we follow a practice that gained a foothold in functional-typological studies written in English in the late twentieth century in using grammatical labels with an initial capital to refer to language-particular descriptive categories (e.g., "the Tagalog Patient Voice") and ordinary lower-case spelling to refer to comparative concepts (e.g., "the patient voice"), especially when the relation between the two categories is at the center of attention.

1.3   The Study of Grammatical Voice

1.3.1   Previous Studies

Studies of grammatical voice can be classified into two groups according to whether the notion of voice is defined structurally or functionally. Both the functional-typological mainstream and the generative literature belong to the former group. Neither the terminology nor the theoretical apparatus of studies belonging to the latter group have been widely adopted – with one notable exception we mention below.

Structural studies define voices based on the assignment of SRs to GRs. The original conceptualization of the category as applied in antiquity to the descriptions of Classical Sanskrit, Classical Greek, and Classical Latin focuses on the subject. Recent studies also cover some kinds of objects, albeit seldom in a comprehensive and systematic fashion. This corresponds to the view many functional-typologically minded scholars work with nowadays (e.g., Haspelmath & Müller-Bardey 2004, Mel'čuk 2006, Dryer 2007, Kulikov 2011a, and Siewierska 2013), which is the view we espouse in the present book.

Functional studies concentrate on the fact that specific predicate forms and the clauses they head denote particular meanings and are used in particular ways in discourse. The most prominent example of this tradition is a series of studies published in the 1980s and 1990s by Ann Cooreman, Talmy Givón, and several other scholars; we outline the essential features presented in Givón's (2001) synthesis here. This author works with what he calls functional deviations from the "prototype transitive event," distinguishing between primarily semantic detransitive voices on the one hand and primarily pragmatic detransitive voices on the other. The former include reflexives, reciprocals, middles, and adjectival-resultatives. Such operations are said to "tamper with transitivity" in terms of three semantic parameters, namely the decreased agentivity of the agent or subject, the decreased affectedness of the patient or object, and the decreased telicity or perfectivity of the predicate. These operations are defined via coreference conditions (Givón's reflexives and reciprocals) or by a focus on the change undergone by the patient (his middles). Givón's pragmatic voices are the passive, the antipassive, and the inverse; such operations are said to "render the same semantically-transitive event from different pragmatic *perspectives*" (2001: 93, emphasis original). These operations are defined based on relative topicality values of the A and P: the values are said to correlate clearly but variably with specific morphosyntactic structures. In mainstream terminology, these values roughly correspond to strong A-backgrounding and strong P-backgrounding, as well as weak P-backgrounding and weak A-backgrounding, respectively.[5]

Klaiman (1991) stands apart in that she postulates different kinds of voices, not only different values for the same kind of voice. Two of her four voice types are structurally defined: her "basic voice" essentially corresponds to the original notion developed for the classical languages (albeit with some additions and changes in emphasis), and her "derived voice" covers passives and antipassives (and explicitly excludes causatives and applicatives). The other two types, subsumed under the cover term "pragmatic voice," are functionally defined – in fact, they can be seen partly as functional counterparts of her two structural voice types. Her "informational-salience voice" is based on the semantic role of

---

[5] Givón sees the topic as a pragmatic function related to the cognitive dimension, "having to do with the focus of attention on one or two important events-or-state participants during the processing of multi-participant clauses" (2001: I: 198).

the topic rather than the subject,[6] and her "ontological-salience voice" corresponds to mappings between semantic roles and referents (which are categorized according to person, animacy, and/or topicality or topic-worthiness) rather than grammatical relations.

Klaiman's "pragmatic voice" should not be confused with Givón's "pragmatic de-transitive voices." First, the latter author distinguishes four predetermined values of relative topicality for the arguments of semantically bivalent clauses in general, whereas Klaiman leaves this question open. Second, Klaiman's ontological-salience subtype conflates several dimensions within pragmatics (one related to topicality and the other to the speech act) and semantics (animacy). Most importantly, Klaiman sees her pragmatic voice, which she claims is not syntactically remapping, as structurally opposed to her derived voice, which is remapping by definition. Unlike Givón, for whom inverse and passive are two different values on a scale, Klaiman sees both the inverse in ontological-salience systems and the patient voice in informational-salience systems as structurally active, and therefore as qualitatively, not quantitatively, different from the passive.

Unlike Givón's and Klaiman's voice models, which are not widely employed, Shibatani's (2006) almost exclusively semantic definition of voice has met with some acceptance from several scholars currently working on Austronesian. Since this language family plays an important role in the conceptualization of grammatical voice, it is in order to take a closer look at how it is handled in this part of the linguistic literature. We find the following wording by Arka and Wouk (2014: 314) particularly clear:

> [Voice is] a language-specific system of grammatical opposition pertaining to stages of event realization and the conceptual-pragmatic relevance of the participants of the event (cf. Shibatani 2006). The opposition may be coded by at least one of the following strategies: different verbal marking [...], different argument marking [...], and different linear order [...]. Voice alternation often, but not necessarily always, involves a change of grammatical relations. The active-middle opposition in Sanskrit given below, for example, involves no change in linking of the [agent and patient] arguments.

"Events" are actions, processes, or states, and the "stages of realization" include "linguistically important phases of initiation, development, and extension and/or termination" (Arka & Wouk 2014: 315). The relevant parameters here are – and Arka and Wouk follow Shibatani (2006) rather closely – control, volitionality, and instigation of the agent, affectedness and individuation of the patient, and the existence of an additional affected participant.

According to Shibatani (2006), what defines the different voices is the number and kind of semantic arguments, as well as the kind of states of affairs they are involved in, rather than morphosyntactic features. Although this author labels his

---

[6] Klaiman defines her topic loosely but explicitly by referring to referential continuity and activation/known status in unfolding discourse (1991: 252).

voices using the traditional terms, namely passive, antipassive, causative, etc., the latter refer to related but crucially different notions when compared to mainstream functional-typological studies. Shibatani says that "voice oppositions are typically based on conceptual – as opposed to pragmatic – meanings, may not alter argument alignment patterns, may not change verbal valency, and may not even trigger verbal marking" (2006: 217). Consequently, for instance, he sees passives as constructions that express "actions that originate with an agent extremely low in discourse relevance, or at least lower relative to the patient" (2006: 248), and as merely orbiting a passive prototype with specific morpho-syntactic features (Shibatani 1985), rather than limited to it.

1.3.2   Voice as Understood and Presented in This Book

Voice as understood in the present study is based on semantics and syntax. It defines diatheses as mappings of the roles of the semantic arguments of predicates onto grammatical relations in clauses, and voices as diatheses formally marked on predicates. This view is similar in spirit to Comrie's (1985) structured survey of relatively few but nonetheless fairly varied valency-changing oper-ations, and it is particularly close to the influential work by Soviet and Russian scholars since Mel'čuk and Xolodovič's (1970) seminal study. The reader is referred to Mel'čuk's (1993, 2006: Ch. 3) argument in favor of his framework and his terminology, and to Kulikov (2011a) for a recent synthesis and application.

The present book consists of this introductory chapter, seven chapters devoted to different manifestations of phenomena related to grammatical voice focusing on main clauses and only occasionally addressing dependent clauses or nomin-alizations, and a final chapter with concluding summaries and remarks.

Chapter 2 surveys ARGUMENT-STRUCTURE MODIFYING operations that alter the number of semantic arguments by either installing new ones in the clause or removing original ones from it. We cover causatives, applicatives, anticausatives, and antiapplicatives, all of which normally differ syntactically from the base constructions. Many of these voices have been treated as something different from voice by earlier studies – with the notable exception of Croft (1994), which integrates them into a causal-chain analysis in a natural way, and Kulikov (2011a), which labels them "voices *sensu latiore.*"

Chapter 3 surveys ARGUMENT-STRUCTURE PRESERVING operations that do not alter the number of semantic arguments but modify the kinds, and potentially the numbers, of their assigned core and/or adjunct arguments. (Subjects and objects are core arguments; other arguments like oblique objects, as well as adjuncts, do not belong to the clause core.) We cover passives, antipassives, and related constructions. Most of these operations have been addressed by earlier studies of voice (Klaiman's 1991 "derived voice," Kroeger's 2005 "meaning-preserving alternations," Haspelmath and Müller-Bardey's 2004 and Mel'čuk's 2006 "voice," and Kulikov's 2011a "voices *sensu stricto*").

Chapter 4 surveys instances of argument-structure preserving and argument-structure modifying operations that have been explored by former studies under labels as diverse as "Philippine-type voices," "symmetrical voice oppositions," and "inverse voice." We follow earlier studies in centering the discussion on the semantic and pragmatic factors that inform voice alternations in languages both from the Austronesian family and from indigenous South and North America. Unlike several previous studies (e.g., Klaiman 1991), however, we do not see either Philippine-type or American-type voices as instantiating fundamentally different kinds of voices. We also emphasize the heterogeneity of such language groups, particularly from the perspective of grammatical voice.

Chapter 5 surveys what we do see, not entirely unlike Klaiman (1991), as a qualitatively different kind of voice: a double, rather than single, assignment of semantic roles to grammatical relations (we label this DUPLEX VOICE), focusing on "affected subjects." We cover reflexives, reciprocals, and middles, which have received a disparate treatment in the previous literature, and hope that our view of these phenomena proves useful.

Chapter 6 surveys what we call VOICE-LIKE PHENOMENA or COVERT DIATHESES. These diathetical operations are not overtly coded on the predicate complex and show both syntactic and functional parallels to their voice counterparts, but they signal quite a different make-up of both the grammar and the lexicon of the languages that make ample use of such uncoded alternations.

Chapter 7 addresses what we call VOICE-RELATED PHENOMENA, which consist in operations that show neither morphological nor syntactic signs of diathetical change but are nonetheless conceptually, and occasionally also morphosyntactically, connected to diathetical operations. We focus on selected constructions that merely denote reduced or increased transitivity when compared to other constructions with which they may alternate.

Chapter 8 addresses the diachrony of voice. We first discuss the sources for different voice categories and then examine voice syncretisms in some detail.

2 Changing Semantic Valency: Causatives, Applicatives, and Related Constructions

There are five common kinds of basic semantic argument structures, which are presented in Table 2.1 below: one kind of predicate is avalent, two are monovalent, one is bivalent, and one is trivalent.[1] These argument structures are then mapped onto syntactic structures of clauses – thereby configuring diatheses, which in turn might be expressed morphologically via voices – according to the (ir)regularities of the lexicon and the grammar of specific constructions in individual languages.[2]

The present chapter deals with operations that alter the morphosyntactic structure of the clause in varied ways but crucially alter its semantic structure as well. Roughly, CAUSATIVES turn those structures of Type II into those of Type IV (increasing semantic valency by installing an A), and ANTICAUSA-TIVES turn those of Type IV into those of Type II (reducing semantic valency by removing an A); both terms are well established in linguistic studies and cover a variety of operations compatible with, or extended from, this core characteriza-tion. We deal with these operations in Sections 2.1 and 2.2, respectively. Similarly, APPLICATIVES turn argument structures of Type III into those of Type IV (increasing semantic valency by installing a P) or those of Type IV into those of Type V (also increasing semantic valency). (As we will see, however, causatives and applicatives are not mirror images of each other; the former typically install an A, but the latter install or promote an object.) We deal with the applicative domain in Section 2.3. The term ANTIAPPLICATIVE could, in principle, cover operations that turn argument structures of Type IV into those of Type III (reducing semantic valency by removing a P), but operations understood in this strict sense seem to be very rare. If this label is used at all in descriptive studies, it denotes operations that do not alter semantic structure. We deal with these issues in Section 2.4. Operations that turn argument structures of the Type I into other argument structures in

---

[1] We are glossing over many complications here for the sake of expository ease (e.g., the fact that the A should logically distinguish bivalent and trivalent predicates).

[2] We are claiming neither that these five argument structure types are universal (e.g., not all languages distinguish two monovalent types, and some languages appear to lack non-derived trivalent predicates – see Bowden 2001 for Taba), nor that they are the only possible or attested types. We are only claiming that they are widespread and suffice to model a significant number of the observed phenomena under scrutiny in this study.

Table 2.1 *Argument structure types*

	Name	Arguments		
I	Avalent	—		
II	Patientive monovalent			S_P
III	Agentive monovalent	S_A		
IV	Bivalent	A		P
V	Trivalent	A	G	T

Table 2.1 are possible and attested as well, and the labels introduced above are also used in such cases.

Typical argument-installing and argument-removing operations are schematically summarized in Table 2.2 below. (The symbol $X°$ stands for extra-thematic participants, that is, those semantic roles not licensed to the arguments of the base predicate.) We call diathetical operations that install a new argument to the semantic structure of the clause as syntactic core argument (subjects or primary/direct objects) NUCLEATIVIZING.[3] Analogously, DENUCLEATIVIZING operations remove an argument from the semantic structure and from the syntactic core of the clause.

ACTOR NUCLEATIVES, that is, clauses where an agentive argument has been installed, can introduce the latter as a subject or an object; we use the terms (SUBJECTIVE) CAUSATIVE and OBJECTIVE CAUSATIVE for these two cases, respectively. Analogously, UNDERGOER NUCLEATIVES are the result of non-agentive arguments being installed; the latter can be introduced as objects or subjects, and we use the terms (OBJECTIVE) APPLICATIVE and SUBJECTIVE APPLICATIVE here, respectively. Undergoer nucleatives have received some attention but a rather disparate treatment in the literature.[4] Since they play an important role in theoretical and typological accounts of voice and voice systems, we deal with them from the viewpoint of individual constructions in Section 2.5 and from the viewpoint of voice systems in Chapter 4. In the present chapter, we focus on subjective causatives, objective applicatives, and their argument-removing counterparts.

[3] Despite the use of the term *nucleus* in some syntactic theories, the term *nucleative* is not widely used in linguistics. Payne (2000) suggests using it for something much more limited in scope, namely what we label NONDIRECT APPLICATIVES (Margetts & Austin's 2007 "oblique applicatives") (see Section 2.2). Klaiman (1988, 1991) uses *nucleonic* to denote a semantic subtype of her middle, namely when "the object of an action belongs to, moves into, or moves from the 'sphere' of the source-subject" (1988: 43).

[4] Trask (1992: 42–43) uses the term CIRCUMSTANTIAL for undergoer nucleatives of the subjective subtype.

Table 2.2 *Typical operations on argument and clause structure*

		ARGUMENT-INSTALLING (NUCLEATIVIZATION)		ARGUMENT-REMOVING (DENUCLEATIVIZATION)	
		SBJ	OBJ	SBJ	OBJ
A	agent	(subjective) causativization	objective causativization	(subjective) anticausativization	objective anticausativization
P/T	patient theme				
G	recipient				
X°	beneficiary maleficiary possessor	subjective applicativization	(objective) applicativization	subjective antiapplicativization	(objective) antiapplicativization
	instrument co-agent				
	location goal				
	others				

2.1   Causatives

Causatives are the most common valency-increasing operation, and the literature on them is vast. Suffice it to mention here references like Comrie (1975, 1976, 1981, 1985), Comrie and Polinsky (1993), Song (1996), Dixon (2000b), and Shibatani (2002).

Causatives increase the semantic valency of predicates by introducing a new agent to their argument structure, as in English *I went* ➔ *he made me go*. The events coded by causatives differ semantically from their non-causative counterparts in that the caused event includes a causer/agent that is lacking in the non-caused event. Speakers use causatives when they need, or want, to introduce to the clause an external agent, the CAUSER. The latter can either be a prototypical agent (e.g., in *the child broke the vase*) or instigate the event without being responsible for its performance (e.g., in *John made Bill wash the car*). In the latter case, a different agent (the CAUSEE) is "internally" responsible for the event (e.g., in *John made Bill wash the car*, it is Bill who actually performs the denoted action).

Causatives differ from some other instances of voice, most notably from passives and antipassives, in that the reasons for their use are usually semantic: events such as 'I went' and 'he made me go' are different extra-linguistically. Consequently, and also because the literature on causatives has paid much attention to semantic issues, we devote considerable space to the semantics of causatives in the following subsections.

2.1.1   Prototypical Causatives

Since causatives constitute a popular topic in both formal and typological-functional linguistics, and given that they display a wide range of variation, it is perhaps unsurprising that they have been given many different definitions. This also has the consequence that the prototype of causatives may be defined in different ways. In this book, we use a rather broad prototype in order to cover most causatives (see, e.g., Dixon & Aikhenvald 2000: 13 for a different prototype). The definition used in this book is given in (4) (Examples (5) to (7) illustrate different particular instantiations of the prototype from Turkish, and schematic representations of the corresponding diathetical structures are given in Figures 2.1–2.3).

(4)   Characteristics of the causative voice
   a.   The syntactic valency of a causative clause is one higher than that of the base, non-causativized, clause (e.g., it is bivalent when its non-causative counterpart is monovalent, and trivalent when the base clause is bivalent).
   b.   A new A (the causer) is installed into the semantic argument structure.

c.   The new A (the causer) is introduced as the subject of the causative clause; the base subject of the non-causative clause (the causee) may be a core argument or an adjunct in the causative clause.[5]

d.   Causativization is formally coded on the predicate complex.

As noted above, the proposed definition is meant to cover most constructions that we wish to label as causative. The definition thus considers those features that most causative constructions have in common. If any of these is missing, the given construction cannot be viewed as a prototypical causative construction. In other words, most causatives in the world's languages correspond to the prototype proposed above despite their formal differences. There is massive variation, for instance, in the morphological status of the marker employed for causativization, and in the formal treatment of the base subject of the original clause. Semantics plays an important role here, as shown below (see, e.g., the semantic definition of the narrow prototype). In addition, causatives have an array of other functions that are labeled as non-prototypical in this book. In this book, only those causatives that lack any of the features above are labeled as non-prototypical (see Section 2.1.2).

Example (5a) illustrates the basic one-argument clause of Turkish, schematically represented in Figure 2.1 below. The verb is unmarked for voice and the S (here: an S_P) appears in the (default) nominative case. In (5b), the causative morpheme *-dUr* has been added to the verb (feature 4d), which has increased the syntactic valency of the predicate by one, producing a two-argument clause (feature 4a). The introduced causer appears in A function (feature 4b) and as the new subject (feature 4c), and the base patient is a direct object (feature 4c):

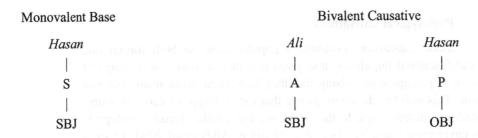

Monovalent Base   Bivalent Causative

Figure 2.1 *Causative diathesis I*

(5)   Turkish (Turkic, Turkey; based on Comrie 1976: 263): Causative with monovalent base

a.   *Hasan   öl-dü.*
     H.[NOM]   die-PST
     'Hasan died.'

---

[5]   If a voice operation introduces the causer as the object of the causative clause but shows the other three characteristics, we call the construction OBJECTIVE CAUSATIVE. This is found, for instance, in cases where the default two-argument clause of the language has a subject P and an object A (i.e., it shows "ergative syntax") and the causative clause follows the same pattern, so that the causer is an object while the causee retains its subject status.

b. *Ali   Hasan-ı   öl-dür-dü.*
A.[NOM]   H.-ACC   die-CAUS-PST
'Ali killed Hasan.'

By contrast, the result of causativizing a two-argument base clause (6a) is a three-argument clause (6b), in which the base A bears dative coding (Figure 2.2).[6]

(6)   Turkish (Comrie 1976: 263): Causative with bivalent base
a. *Müdür   mektub-u   imzala-dı.*
director[NOM]   letter-ACC   sign-PST
'The director signed the letter.'
b. *Dişçi   mektub-u   müdür-e   imzala-t-tı.*
dentist[NOM]   letter-ACC   director-DAT   sign-CAUS-PST
'The dentist made the director sign the letter.'

Bivalent Base		Trivalent Causative		
müdür	*mektub*	*dişçi*	*müdür*	*mektub*
'director'	'letter'	'dentist'	'director'	'letter'
|	|	|	|	|
A	P	A	G	T
|	|	|	|	|
SBJ	OBJ	SBJ	NSBJ=IOBJ	OBJ

Figure 2.2 *Causative diathesis II*

Lastly, the result of causativizing a three-argument base clause (7a) is a three-argument clause with an adjunct (7b), with the base A (represented here as *bA*) as adjunct, because the indirect object slot (i.e, the slot the causee takes with bivalent bases) is already occupied (Figure 2.3):

Trivalent Base			Trivalent + Adjunct Causative			
müdür	*Hasan*	*mektub*	*dişçi*	*müdür*	*Hasan*	*mektub*
'director'		'letter'	'dentist'	'director'		'letter'
|	|	|	|	|	|	|
A	G	T	A	bA	G	T
|	|	|	|	|	|	|
SBJ	IOBJ	DOBJ	SBJ	ADJ	NSBJ=IOBJ	DOBJ

Figure 2.3 *Causative diathesis III*

---

[6] In other languages (like Finnish), the base A can be expressed as an adjunct instead. Moreover, it is not uncommon for the base A to be the new direct object in the causative construction, and the base P is either an indirect object or an adjunct, like in several Bantu languages (Alsina 1992: 518).

(7)   Turkish (Comrie 1976: 263): Causative with trivalent base
        a. *Müdür   Hasan-a mektub-u göster-di.*
           director[NOM] H.-DAT letter-ACC show-PST
           'The director showed the letter to Hasan.'
        b. *Dişçi   Hasan-a mektub-u müdür   tarafından göster-t-ti.*
           dentist[NOM] H.-DAT letter-ACC director[NOM] by   show-CAUS-PST
           'The dentist made the director show the letter to Hasan.'

The operation of introducing an agent to the argument structure of the predicate is clearest conceptually, and least restricted empirically, in what we call AGENT-RELATED CAUSATION here. This is a narrow causative prototype: the causativization of one-argument clauses headed by monovalent (patientive) predicates (a special case of Figure 2.1 above, which corresponds to the examples in (5) from Turkish). Such causatives can be characterized as follows (see Kittilä 2009 for details):

(8)   Semantic characterization of the narrow causative prototype
        a. An external agent (the causer) is added to a one-argument base clause
            headed by a semantically monovalent predicate.
        b. All features of agency are introduced into the causativized clause. The
            agent's participation in the resulting state of affairs is volitional,
            purposeful, and controlled. It is the primary cause of the event or state in
            question; the latter does not occur if the agent does not induce it. Lastly,
            the agent targets its action directly at the patient (the causee), aiming at
            bringing about a change in the latter's state.
        c. The introduction of the argument produces a transitive event involving a
            salient cause (the agent) and a salient effect (the patient). The agent is
            completely unaffected by the event, while the patient is thoroughly
            affected and thus registers the effect of the described event.
            Causativization does not have any necessary consequences for the
            specific kind of affectedness of the patient.

In principle, the only difference between the caused and the non-caused state of affairs lies in the presence of an external agent: the patient is equally affected in both. This means that the resulting construction resembles clauses denoting highly transitive events, such as 'the teacher painted the house' (Givón 1995: 76; Næss 2007). Nevertheless, these two event types – transitive causatives and base transitive events – can and need to be distinguished. Predicates like English *break* can be used to portray either events brought about by an agent (e.g., *the child broke the vase*) or events in which the patient's change of state occurs spontaneously, without the participation of an agent (e.g., *the vase broke*). By contrast, predicates like English *paint* or *wash* cannot head clauses of the latter type (e.g., *the teacher painted the house* vs. **the house painted*). Consequently, the causative prototype is semantically characterized by agent installment, whereas inherently transitive events, such as those portrayed by English *paint* and *wash*, always involve both an agent and a patient. Thus, clauses expressing inherently transitive events do not bear causative coding, since this is not needed for introducing an agent to the clause. In terms of Hopper and Thompson's (1980: 252) transitivity parameters, causativized and inherently transitive events can both be viewed as equally highly transitive, but they are distinguished based on whether the agent is inherently a part of the denoted event or not.

Agent-related causation can also be schematically described as follows (using Næss's 2007 version of semantic role decomposition in the features volitionality, instigation, and affectedness):

(9)   Agent-related causation
         a.   Uncaused event
              'the vase broke'
                  the vase   [−VOL]   [−INST]   [+AFF]
         b.   Caused event
              'the child broke the vase (on purpose)'
                  the child   [+VOL]   [+INST]   [−AFF]
                  the vase   [−VOL]   [−INST]   [+AFF]

The base event 'the vase broke' (a) has only a patient, and thus only the feature of affectedness is present, because prototypical patients are not volitionally involved in events, nor are they instigating participants. The caused event 'the child broke the vase' (b), in turn, involves a prototypical agent who is acting volitionally and is responsible for the denoted event. Complete agent introduction is rendered possible by all features of agency being lacking in the base event: there is no competition for the agent slot, as it were. Moreover, 'break' denotes an event that may either happen spontaneously or be caused externally. The mere lack of an agent does not suffice for an event to be causativized, however. For example, weather phenomena are typically characterized by the total lack of an agent, but despite this, meteorological verbs do not usually allow causativization (see Eriksen et al. 2010 for details).[7] In other words, the introduced agent must be able to exercise control over the event (or the causee) that it causes to happen in agent-related causation.

Formulating the prototype in this way explains part of the distribution of morphological causatives in the world's languages: if a language has any kind of morphological causative, it applies at least to the kind of event defined above. Nevertheless, a morpheme does not have to be able to apply to the type of event described above in order to be considered a causative morpheme. Many languages have multiple causatives, some of which are employed (only) for less prototypical instances of causation, which means that they may not be used to causativize prototypical patientive monovalent verbs.

Finally, causation can be described in more general and formal terms as the result of predicate fusion (Austin 2005, from Alsina 1992: 521): a trivalent functional predicate CAUSE takes an agent (the causer), a patient (the causee), and a clause that represents the caused event portrayed by a lexical predicate:[8]

---

[7] In some societies, meteorological phenomena are seen as controllable by spirits or gods and as potentially controlled by shamans, for instance. Peter Austin (personal communication) drew our attention to the grammaticality of examples like *unkiyali ngankarna warrayi thalara kurdar-nanthu* 'the clever-man made it rain' in Diyari.

[8] Austin (2005) actually proposes a general transitivizing predicate AFFECT, of which CAUSE is a special case. See Section 2.3.1 for the functional predicate of prototypical applicatives.

(10)   Predicate fusion with prototypical causatives
        CAUSE [A, P, *predicate* [. . .]]

Different coreference conditions in specific causatives lead to part of the observable cross-linguistic variation. If the base, lexical, predicate is semantically monovalent, as in agent-related causation, its only argument is coreferential with the patient of CAUSE. If it is bivalent, its agentive argument is coreferential with the patient of CAUSE.

2.1.2   Non-Prototypical Causatives and Lookalikes

There are at least three kinds of non-prototypical causativization, namely covert causativization, valency-neutral transitivization, and detransitivizing causativization.[9] We address them in turn in what follows.

COVERT CAUSATIVIZATION consists in causativized predicates having a higher number of semantic arguments than, but the same number of syntactic arguments as, the corresponding base predicates (Kittilä 2009). This is attested, at least in the languages we have data for, for trivalent verbs, which suggests that the phenomenon is conditioned by language-specific restrictions on the highest number of syntactic arguments per clause.

Examples from Songhai and Finnish follow (see also (37) from Awa Pit). In Songhai, trivalent verbs may also be causativized, as shown in (b). The number of syntactic arguments does not increase, however; both (a) and (b) are three-argument clauses:

(11)   Songhai (Nilo-Saharan, West Africa; Comrie 1976: 9f, cited from Shopen and Konaré 1970: 215)
        a. *Ali   nga-ndi   tasu   di   Musa   se.*
            A.   eat-CAUS   rice   the   M.   IOBJ
            'Ali made Mousa eat the rice.'
        b. *Garba   neere-ndi   bari   di   Musa   se   (*Ali se).*
            G.   sell-CAUS   horse   the   M.   IOBJ   A.   IOBJ
            'Garba had Mousa sell the horse.' / 'Garba had the horse sold to Mousa.'

Finnish allows multiple causativization, and there is no formal limit to how many causative affixes a verb may take, at least in principle, but only the first causative is valency-increasing – so, unlike in Songhai, this is not real covert causativization. For instance, in all three clauses in (12), the number of arguments is the same (viz., three), even though the number of causative affixes on the verb would suggest otherwise. In case more than one causer/causee needs to be added, periphrastic causativization must be used.

---

[9] Malchukov (2017: 8–9) labels the use of Balinese causative *-ang* in pairs like *anak=e luh ento mandus* (person=DEF female that AV.wash) 'the girl washed (herself)' vs. *anak=e luh ento mandus-ang anak cenit ento* (person=DEF female that AV.wash-CAUS person small that) 'the girl washed the child' as "antireflexive." The causative simply introduces an agent/causer semantically and syntactically in such instances, however; see Section 6.5.1 for the phenomenon of implicit reflexives.

(12)   Finnish (Uralic, Finland and Sweden)
   a. *Rakennu-t-i-n*   *talo-n*   *Kalle-lla.*
      build-CAUS-PST-1SG   house-ACC   K.-ADESS
   b. *Rakennu-ta-t-i-n*   *talo-n*   *Kalle-lla.*
      build-CAUS-CAUS-PST-1SG   house-ACC   K.-ADESS
   c. *Rakennu-tu-ta-t-i-n*   *talo-n*   *Kalle-lla.*
      build-CAUS-CAUS-CAUS-PST-1SG   house-ACC   K.-ADESS
   All three: 'I made Kalle build the house.'

With VALENCY-NEUTRAL TRANSITIVIZATION, the number of both semantic and syntactic arguments remains unaltered, but the causative-like marking
denotes an increase in transitivity. A special case of this is AGENTIVE
CAUSATIVIZATION, which consists in causativized verbs encoding the high
degree of agency associated with the instigator of the event (Kittilä 2009). The
following example from Godoberi shows that the only formal difference between
the two two-argument clauses might be the transitivizing morphology on the verb
with the verb *čib-* 'splash' (*-al* is the default causative in the language):

(13)   Godoberi (Northeast Caucasian, Russia; Kibrik 1996: 128)
   a. *Mak'i-di*   *łeni*   *čib-i.*
      child-ERG   water   splash-PST
      'The child splashed the water (perhaps involuntarily).'
   b. *Mak'i-di*   *łeni*   *čib-al-i.*
      child-ERG   water   splash-TR-PST
      'The child splashed the water (purposefully and repeatedly).'

In another subtype of valency-neutral transitivization, causative-like morphology
denotes higher transitivity based on aspectuality features. In Mari (14), for instance,
the suffix *-alt* signals either prototypical causativization (a) or a punctual, as
opposed to iterative and therefore durative, event (b). Example (15) from Cora
shows a similarly dual function of *-re* with the same verb, which expresses
causativization in (a) but telicity/dynamicity, as opposed to atelicity/stativity, in (b):

(14)   Mari (Uralic, Russia; Kalinina et al. 2006: 444–445)
   a. *Jüšö*   *jeŋ*   *pört-š-əm*   *jül-alt-əš.*
      drunk   man   house-3SG.PSR-ACC   burn-CAUS-PST[3SG]
      'A drunk man set the house on fire.' (causativization)
   b. *Meče*   *küškö*   *töršt-alt-ən.*
      ball   high   bounce-TR-PST[3SG]
      'The ball bounced high up.' (transitivization)

(15)   Cora (Uto-Aztecan, Mexico; Vázquez Soto 2002: 212)
   a. *ɨ*   *siká*   *hám^{w}eʔi*   *pú*   *ţɨʔ-u-ȼeʔi-re.*
      DET   sun   tortilla   3SG   PL-COMPL-hard-CAUS
      'As for the sun, it hardened the tortillas.' (causativization)
   b. *ɨ*   *hám^{w}eʔi*   *ţíʔi-ȼeʔi.*
      DET   tortilla   PL-hard
      'The tortillas are hard.'
   c. *ɨ*   *hám^{w}eʔi*   *ţíʔ-u-ȼeʔi-re-kaʔa.*
      DET   tortilla   PL-COMPL-hard-TR-PST
      'The tortillas got hard.' (transitivization)

Causative-like morphology can also denote higher transitivity based on event-specificity, as in Example (16) below, which is possibly related to the aspectuality-conditioned cases just mentioned. The otherwise causativizing suffix -*tja* of Kwaza merely signals that the event is both a specific occurrence (as opposed to repeated, general occurrences) and more concrete and particularized:

(16)   Kwaza (unclassified, Brazil; Van der Voort 2004: 362)

    a. *'We-da-ki   jere'xwa.*
        fear-1SG-DECL   jaguar/dog
        'I am afraid of dogs (in general).'

    b. *We-'tja-da-ki   jerexwa-'wã.*
        fear-TR-1SG-DECL   jaguar/dog-OBJ
        'I am afraid of (this) dog.'

Example (17) from Kambera seems to show yet another similar phenomenon. The otherwise causative prefix *pa-* denotes that the direction of motion is specific and the event has a definite result in (b):

(17)   Kambera (Austronesian, Indonesia; Klamer 1998: 182)

    a. *Mài-ma-ki-a-danya-ka*   *uda.*
        come-EMPH-TAM-TAM-3PL.CONT-PERF   EMPH.3PL
        'They just came.' (i.e., direction/purpose not important)

    b. *Pa-mài-ng-ma-ki-a-danya-ka*   *uda.*
        TR-come-?-EMPH-TAM-TAM-3PL.CONT-PERF   EMPH.3PL
        'They just came.' (to stay, i.e., they just moved here)

Valency-neutral transitivization may also be used to convey intensity. For instance, the pairs in Examples (18)–(19) below portray the same events, but the use of *ha-* in Taba and -*ets* in Chichewa (which are the default causativizers in the languages, respectively) express that the events in question were performed more intensely, occasionally with the implication of higher patient affectedness:

(18)   Taba (Austronesian, Indonesia; Bowden 2001: 202)

    a. *Tit*   *t=wonga*   *maliling* *ya.*
        1PL.INCL   1PL.INCL=stay.awake.all.night   night   up

    b. *Tit*   *t=ha-wonga*   *maliling* *ya.*
        1PL.INCL   1PL.INCL=TR-stay.awake.all.night   night   up
    Both: 'We stayed awake all last night.'

(19)   Chichewa (Bantu, Southeast Africa; Hopper & Thompson 1980: 264)

    a. *Mwana-'yu*   *w-a-dy-a.*
        child-this   he-TNS-eat-IND
        'The child has eaten.'

    b. *Mwana-'yu*   *w-a-dy-ets-a.*
        child-this   he-TNS-eat-TR-IND
        'This child has eaten too much.'

A particularly noteworthy instance of causative-like constructions consists in cases of reduced, rather than increased, transitivity. Such DETRANSITIVIZING CAUSATIVES can be divided into two subtypes, depending on whether the number of arguments is reduced or not. The former is illustrated by the following Korean example, where -i may either install an agent, as in (b), or demote it, as in (c):

(20)   Korean (Koreanic, Korea; Soon Mi Hong-Schunka, pers. comm.)
    a. *Ku   saram-i   na-rul   po-ass-ta.*
        DET   person-NOM   1SG-ACC   see-PST-DECL
        'The man saw me.'
    b. *Ku   saram-i   na-eykey   kurim-ul   po-i-ess-ta.*
        DET   man-NOM   1SG-DAT   picture-ACC see-CAUS-PST-DECL
        'The man showed me the picture.' (causative)
    c. *Ku   saram-i   po-i-ess-ta.*
        DET   man-NOM   see-PASS-PST-DECL
        'The man was seen.' (passive)

This kind of polysemy may appear counter-intuitive at first, since in such cases causative morphemes express a function that can be considered the exact opposite of their typical function. Nevertheless, the grammaticalization path from causative to passive is not uncommon (see Chapter 8).

With the second subtype of detransitivizing causative, the number of arguments is not altered. In Finnish and Mangap-Mbula, for instance, transitivity is decreased based on reduced control on the A's part. In the clause headed by the otherwise causative *tt*-form in (21), Aino feels an urge to sing, which means that she cannot fully control whether she intends to perform the denoted act or not. In this case, the lack of control is also related to volitionality: Aino's action is intentional in (a), while it is more probably unintentional in (b).

(21)   Finnish
    a. *Aino   laulaa.*
        A.[NOM]   sing.3SG.PRS
        'Aino is singing.'
    b. *Aino-a   laula-tt-aa.*
        A.-PTV   sing-DETR-3SG.PRS
        'Aino feels like singing.'

In the clause headed by the otherwise causative *pa*-form in (22), the lack of control concerns the completion of the event. In (a), the A is in full control and able to complete the event as s/he intends to, while in (b), the A probably controls the instigation of the event only, since s/he has to make a special effort in order to finish the event in the desired way:

(22)   Mangap-Mbula (Austronesian, Papua New Guinea; Bugenhagen 1995: 175)
    a. *Aŋ-kaaga   kataama.*
        1SG-open   door
        'I opened the door.'

b. *Aŋ-pa-kaaga*   *kataama.*
    1SG-DETR-open   door
    'I managed to get the door open.'

Lastly, transitivity is decreased by causative-like morphology in Kambera based on aspectuality. As seen above, habitual events are comparatively low in transitivity: their P is often indefinite, and they do not denote a specific instance of an event (see, e.g., Gerstner-Link 1998 and Kittilä 2002: 226–227). In (23), causative-like morphology (*pa-*) denotes a habitual event:

(23)   Kambera (Klamer 1998: 180, 186)
    a. *Tila-nanya*   *na*   *njara.*
        kick-3SG.CONT   the   horse
        'The horse is kicking (now).'
    b. *Rimang,*   *na-pa-tila*   *na*   *njara.*
        look.out   3SG.NOM-DETR-kick   the   horse
        'Be careful, the horse kicks.' (i.e., it is her character)

Finally, there are some other intriguing uses of causative-like morphology that are neither well documented nor well understood yet. For instance, an implicit causee may be installed – rather than an explicit causee, as in prototypical causatives. In Chechen (24), for example, the default case is that the agent buys a book to read him/ herself (a). By contrast, the verb takes causative-like morphology in (b), where there is an implicit causee of disjoint reference, and therefore the clause can be understood as being more transitive in the sense of having an additional, distinct argument.

(24)   Chechen (Northeast Caucasian, Russia; Nichols 1994a: 68)
    a. *As*   *kni:ga*   *yecna*   *jieša^n.*
        1SG.ERG   book.NOM   bought   read.INF
        'I bought a book to read.'
    b. *As*   *kni:ga*   *yecna*   *jieši:ta^n.*
        1SG.ERG   book.NOM   bought   read.TR.INF
        'I bought a book for someone else to read.'

Something similar is reported for Diyari (25), where the causative *-ipa* can be added to bivalent or trivalent predicates to indicate that someone other than the A benefits from the event (Austin 2011: 79–84). Even though the exact reference of this beneficiary is typically determined from contextual clues, the participant can be expressed by a constituent in the clause. In the latter case, since the constituent is not a primary/direct object, we are not dealing with the causative-applicative isomorphism addressed in Section 8.2.1. (Compare the related but different pseudo-applicatives mentioned in Section 2.3.2.)

(25)   Diyari (Pama-Nyungan, Australia; Austin 2005: 7)
    a. *Karna-li*   *wilha*   *nandra-ipa-yi*   *(ngakarni).*
        man-ERG   woman   hit-TR-PRS   1SG.DAT
        'The man hit the woman for me.'

> b. *Kupa*   *tharka-ipa-ipa-mayi*   *(ngakarni)!*
>   child   stand-CAUS-TR-IMPER.EMPH   1SG.DAT
>   'Stand up the child for me!'

By contrast, the following example from Latvian shows that the use of the causative morpheme may have formal consequences – compare the difference in flagging and syntactic status of the experiencer in (a) and (b) – without any apparent semantic correlates:

(26)   Latvian (Baltic, Latvia; Holvoet 2015: 162–163)
> a. *Mun*   *sāp*   *tav-a*   *nodevīb-a.*
>   1SG.DAT   hurt.3.PRS   your-NOM.SG.F   betrayal-NOM
> b. *Mani*   *sāpina*   *tav-a*   *nodevīb-a.*
>   1SG.ACC   hurt.CAUS.3.PRS   your-NOM.SG.F   betrayal-NOM
> Both: 'Your (SG) betrayal hurts me.'

To sum up, the atypical functions of causatives can be seen as extensions of the typical ones. This is clearest for agentivization, where the relevant difference between prototypical and non-prototypical causatives is found in the starting point. The result is a two-argument construction in both cases. The relation between prototypical and non-prototypical cases is also rather straightforward in the case of valency-neutral transitivization. Covert causativization, in turn, is best explained by restrictions on the number of syntactic arguments in a clause: many languages disfavor or even exclude constructions with four syntactic arguments, an exclusion which blocks the explicit reference to all semantic arguments present with causativized trivalent predicates. By contrast, detransitivizing causatives are not best explained by resorting to features of prototypical causativization or causation but by considering the opposition between direct and indirect causation; the decreased agency of the agent (yielding lower overall transitivity) in the latter is relevant in this regard (see Section 2.1.4.2).

2.1.3   Formal Variation of Causatives

2.1.3.1   Morphological Variation of Causatives

Causatives show variation with respect to the marking of the predicate, the flagging of the constituent denoting the causee, and possible syncretisms with other voice markers.

The typological literature customarily divides causatives into three formal types according to the locus of the voice marker, namely LEXICAL, MORPHOLOGICAL/SYNTHETIC, and SYNTACTIC/PERIPHRASTIC. Lexical causatives are those in which no specific morpheme denotes causation; instead, there is a typically unproductive and (quasi-)suppletive opposition between a non-causative verb and its causative counterpart, like in English *die* vs. *kill*, or *sit* vs. *set*. The two verbs are semantically related in the same way as spontaneous and caused *break*. Further examples of lexical causatives are found in Yimas:

(27)   Yimas (Ramu-Lower Sepik, Papua New Guinea; Dixon 2000b: 39)

mal	'die'	*tu*	'kill'
awa	'burn'	*ampu*	'burn'
aypu	'lie down'	*ti*	'lay down'

In morphological causatives, some morphological process productively causativizes the predicate. Several linear and nonlinear processes are attested, namely segmental mutation (Lithuanian), consonant gemination (Gulf Arabic), vowel lengthening (Kashmiri), tonal change (Lahu), and affixation (Dixon 2000b: 34). Affixation is perhaps the most common process cross-linguistically; such affixes can be suffixes, like *-kam* in K'iche', circumfixes, like *a-...-ev* in Georgian, or prefixes, like *pa-* in Kambera (see (23) above). Lastly, syntactic/periphrastic causatives resort to some kind of complex predicate to encode causation. In (28) from Lao, the verbs *hêt1* 'make' (a) and *haj5* 'give' (b) act as causativizers. In (c), the combination of both auxiliaries is responsible for introducing the causer. The English translations of (b) and (c) are further examples of periphrastic causatives.

(28)   Lao (Tai-Kadai, Laos; Enfield 2007: 423f)

    a. *Man2   hêt1   còòk5   tèèk5.*
        3.BARE make   cup   break
        'He broke the cup.'

    b. *Man2   haj5   nòòj4   paj3   talaat5.*
        3.BARE give   N.   go   market
        'He had/let/made/got Noi go to the market.'

    c. *Man2   hêt1-haj5   còòk5   tèèk5.*
        3.BARE make-give cup   break
        'He caused the cup to break.'

A special case of morphological causativization is found in languages where causative two-argument clauses and non-causative one-argument clauses use different auxiliaries, which in turn index either two arguments or only one, respectively. In the quite productive Basque alternation illustrated in (29), for instance, the participle *hil* can take either the "transitive" auxiliary **edun* 'have' in a bipersonal form, in which case it is the translational equivalent of English 'kill' (a), or the "intransitive" auxiliary *izan* 'be' in a monopersonal form, in which case it corresponds to 'die' (b):

(29)   Basque (Oyharçabal 2003: 224)

    a. *Haurra-k   katua   hil   du.*
        child.DET-ERG cat.DET[ABS] die/kill.PFV have.3SG→3SG
        'The child (has) killed the cat.'

    b. *Katua   hil   da.*
        cat.DET[ABS] die/kill.PFV be.3SG
        'The cat (has) died.'

Even though such examples are sometimes said to illustrate the (uncoded) causative alternation in the literature (e.g., Oyharçabal 2003, Creissels 2014), we have followed our broad definition of (4) above strictly and treated these causative diatheses like those where the formal difference is a causative morpheme (see Section 6.2.1).

Periphrastic causatives can be further classified depending on how tightly connected the individual verbs of the construction are (Dixon 2000b, Shibatani 2002).[10] Verbs are granted most autonomy in the biclausal expression of causation, where there is no complex predicate. If there is one, however, it may be a serial verb construction, where the individual verbs still retain some formal autonomy, like *-a* 'make' and *-hɲa* 'eat' in Tariana:

(30)   Tariana (Arawakan, Brazil; Aikhenvald 2000: 160)
        Nu-inipe-nuku   *kwaka-mhade* *nu-a*   *nu-hɲa.*
        1SG-children-TOP.NSBJ how-FUT   1SG-make   1SG-eat
        'How will I get my children to eat?'

Alternatively, the causative may be a converbal construction, where the functional verb denoting the CAUSE predicate bears finite morphology and the lexical verb denoting the base predicate appears in some kind of dependent form; cases with strongly grammaticalized functional verbs are usually analyzed as auxiliary verb constructions. Shibatani and Pardeshi (2002: 103f) note that there is a continuum of integration of the two predicates, argument structures, and clauses. In Korean (31), for example, the default causative with *hay-* 'do' shows dative/accusative flagging of the causee, but nominative flagging is also possible – suggesting at least vestigial formal autonomy of the base clause – and the unit consisting of the converb and the finite verb can be interrupted by the negation *an* or the topic marker *nun*:

(31)   Korean (Shibatani & Pardeshi 2002: 103)
        a. *Ai-ka*   *chaek-ul*   *ilk-etta.*
            child-NOM   book-ACC   read-PST.IND
            'The child read the book.'
        b. *Emeni-ka*   *ai-eykey/lul/ka*   *chaek-ul* *ilk-key*   *hay-etta.*
            mother-NOM   child-DAT/ACC/NOM   book-ACC   read-CVB   do-PST.IND
            'Mother made the child read the book.'

By contrast, the German causative with *lassen* 'let' in (32) does not allow nominative marking of the causee but expresses it as some kind of object – accusative-marked and immediately post-verbal, like a direct object, but unpassivizable (unlike the causee of a less grammaticalized verb like *zwingen* 'force', which is passivizable):

---

[10] Song's (1996) three types divide the formal space differently: "COMPACT" (subsuming lexical and morphological causatives), and "AND" and "PURP" (representing two subtypes of periphrastic causatives, viz., one featuring a coordinating element between two complete clauses and the other like the Korean converbal construction shown further down in the text). This typology has not found wide acceptance yet.

(32)   German (Germanic, Central Europe; Shibatani & Pardeshi 2002: 103)
Hans ließ   seinen   Sohn den   Brief abtippen.
H.   let.PST[3SG] his.ACC son   ART.ACC letter type.INF
'Hans made his son type the letter.'

Lastly, the French causative with *faire* 'do, make' in (33) shows a high degree of integration. Finite *faire* and its base verb in the infinitive cannot be separated by clitic indexes, and therefore behaves like underived trivalent verbs like *donner* 'give' (and unlike less grammaticalized auxiliaries like *laisser* 'let', which can be separated from its infinitival complement):

(33)   French (Romance, world language; Shibatani & Pardeshi 2002: 104)
J'ai   fait   préparer   la   mayonnaise à Jean.
1SG.have make.PTCP prepare.INF ART mayonnaise to J.
'I made Jean prepare the mayonnaise.'

A different source of variation is the coding of the causee. Typically, this argument is an object or adjunct that takes the same morphology as other objects or adjuncts in any given language. Nivkh is one of the comparatively rare languages in which the causee takes dedicated marking – even though it is obligatory only with trivalent base verbs:

(34)   Nivkh (unclassified, Russia; Nedjalkov et al 1995: 78)
a. *Ətək   ola(-ax)   vigud'.*
    father   child-CSEE   go.CAUS.FIN
    'The father made/let the child go.'
b. *Ətək   ola(-ax)   lep   n'igud'.*
    father   child-CSEE   bread eat.CAUS.FIN
    'The father made/let the child eat the bread.'
c. *Ətək   ola-ax   lep   pʰnanak   ximgud'.*
    father   child-CSEE bread his.older.sister give.CAUS.FIN
    'The father made/let the child give the bread to his older sister.'

The causee may show different flagging within a given language; see Section 2.1.3.2.

Lastly, causative constructions can show the same structural make-up as applicatives; we deal with this "causative-applicative syncretism" in Section 8.2.1. In addition, causatives may receive the same formal coding as passives (see (394) in Section 8.2.2.2), and what we have labeled as malefactive nucleative (Section 2.5.2).

2.1.3.2   Syntactic Variation of Causatives

The sources of syntactic variation we survey here are some restrictions related to syntactic valency and the syntactic status of the causee (and, albeit less frequently, the base P).

It is common for languages to limit the number of overtly expressed arguments per clause, which in turn has consequences for causativization. Two different subtypes will be distinguished here, namely (i) languages that allow causativization of predicates of higher semantic valency only after reducing their syntactic valency and (ii) languages that do not require a valency-reduction operation but simply fail to accommodate all arguments in the causativized clause. The former subtype is illustrated by Halkomelem (35) and Southern Tiwa (36), where the syntactic valency of a bivalent base verb needs to be reduced before causativization. This is achieved via antipassivization in Halkomelem and via nominal incorporation in Southern Tiwa:[11]

(35)   Halkomelem (Salishan, Canada; Gerdts 1984: 195)
        Ni   cən q̓ʷəl-əm-stəxʷ   θə   sɬéniʔ   ʔə   kʷθə səplíl.
        AUX 1SG bake-ANTIP-CAUS DET woman   OBL DET bread
        'I had the woman bake the bread.'

(36)   Southern Tiwa (Kiowa-Tanoan, USA; Baker 1988: 194)
        I-'u'u-kur-'am-ban.
        1SG→2SG-baby-hold-CAUS-PST
        'I made you (SG) hold the baby.'

The second subtype is illustrated by Awa Pit (37), where the causative suffix *-nin* is productively attached to verbs of different semantic valency. With monovalent and bivalent verbs, this yields an increase in syntactic valency, as is typical of causatives. Nevertheless, in (c), the verb has been causativized, but the number of syntactic arguments is unaltered due to the overall restriction on syntactic valency. Causativization is thus not a syntactic valency-increasing operation for causativized trivalent verbs.[12]

(37)   Awa Pit (Barbacoan, Colombia; Curnow 1997: 74, 162, 165)
        a. *Tinta   awa   uk   man   ki-nin-tu.*
            strong   person   stone   move$_1$ move$_2$-CAUS-IPFV.PTCP
            'The strong man moved the stone.'
        b. *Na=na   kuzhu   piya   kwa-nin-ta-w.*
            1SG.NOM=TOP   pig   corn   eat-CAUS-PST-LOCUT.SBJ
            'I let the pig eat corn.'
        c. *Na=na   Demetrio=ta pala   kwin-nin-ta-w.*
            1SG.NOM=TOP   D.=ACC   plantain give-CAUS-PST-LOCUT.SBJ
            'I made Demetrio give a plantain.' (or: 'I had a plantain given to Demetrio.')

Such a phenomenon is not at all uncommon across languages. In Finnish, for example, the causee can be left out with many causativized bivalent verbs, leading to readings like 'I had the house built (by someone)'. In languages like Awa Pit, however, the omission of the causee or the recipient from clauses like the one in (c) above is obligatory.

Another important parameter of syntactic variation of causatives is the status of the causee. In languages where the default two-argument clause instantiates an agent diathesis, i.e., a clause with a subject A and a patient P, the installed agent

---

[11] Something similar to the Tiwa phenomenon is found in Paumarí and Bandjalang (Dixon 2000b: 44). By a different token, some Australian languages have to reduce the syntactic valency of the clause (e.g., via antipassivization) in order to applicativize it (Austin 2005).

[12] See also Example (11) from Songhai.

is introduced as a subject and any base object retains its object status in the causativized clause. Causees, however, may be granted core argument status as direct/primary or indirect/secondary objects, or be demoted to adjuncts.[13] This variation in grammatical relation correlates with variation in the flagging of the NP expressing the causee.

It is common for the causee to lose syntactic prominence along with an increase of the semantic valency of the base predicate. Remember that, in the Turkish examples in (7) above, the causee is an accusative-marked direct object with base monovalent verbs, a dative-marked indirect object with base bivalent verbs, and a postposition-marked low object or adjunct with trivalent verbs. Something analogous occurs in Finnish (see Example (42) below) and Bote (with the proviso that core arguments take absolutive and ergative cases in this language). In Tsez (38), the causee appears in the absolutive with a monovalent base verb (a) but takes possessive case with a bivalent verb (b). (Since the argument in G function has different flagging in three-argument clauses, this possessive marking is to be considered oblique.)

(38)   Tsez (Northeast Caucasian, Russia; Comrie 2000: 365, 368)
   a. *Už-ā*   *č'ikay*   *y-exu-r-si.*
       boy-ERG   glass.ABS   II-break-CAUS-PST.WIT
       'The boy broke the glass.'
   b. *Aħ-ā*   *čanagˤan-qo* *zey*   *žek'-er-si.*
       shepherd-ERG   hunter-POSS   bear.ABS   hit-CAUS-PST.WIT
       'The shepherd made the hunter hit the bear.'

Notably, in Finnish, Tsez, and Agul (Daniel et al. 2012), causativized bivalent verbs do not yield default three-argument clauses. By contrast, the causee is granted higher syntactic prominence than the base patient in some languages. Examples of this include Evenki (Nedjalkov 1997: 231–232), Kammu (Svantesson 1983: 103–105), and Amharic (39). In the last language, the base patient loses its definiteness, appears unmarked, and is optional in the causative voice – even though there are double object constructions available in the language:

(39)   Amharic (Semitic, Ethiopia; Amberber 2000: 320)
   a. *Aster*   *siga-w-in*   *k'orrət'ə-čč.*
       A.   meat-DEF-ACC   cut.PERF-3F
       'Aster cut the meat.'
   b. *Ləmma* *Aster-in* *(siga)* *as-k'orrət'-at.*
       L.   A.-ACC   meat   CAUS-cut.PERF.3M-3F.P
       'Lemma made Aster cut (some meat).'

---

[13] In languages with default two-argument clauses instantiating a patient diathesis, i.e., clauses with a subject P and an object A, the causer is introduced as object; we call this objective causative here. Moreover, languages may have not only agent but also patient non-causative diatheses (see Chapter 4), allowing the installed causer to be introduced as either subject or object.

Yet other languages have double object construction causatives, like Purépecha (40), where several objects are flagged alike (observe that the story, a secondary object, is in an unmarked form in (c) below).

(40)   Purépecha (Maldonado & Nava 2002: 168–169)
    a. *Valeria   ura-pe-ra-s-Ø-ti*   *takusï-ni.*
        V.   be.white-PRED-CAUS-PERF-PRS-IND.3   cloth-OBJ
        'Valeria whitened the cloth.'
    b. *Valeria   urhu-ra-s-Ø-ti*   *tsíri-ni*   *Yuyani-ni.*
        V.   grind-CAUS-PERF-PRS-IND.3   corn-OBJ   Y.-OBJ
        'Valeria made Yuyani grind the corn.'
    c. *Ricardo   arhi-ra-s-Ø-ti*   *ma*   *wantantskwa*   *Valeria-ni*
        R.   tell-CAUS-PERF-PRS-IND.3   a   story   V.-OBJ
        Yuyani-ni.
        Y.-OBJ
        'Ricardo made Valeria tell Yuyani a story.'

Crucially, equivalent morphology does not imply equivalent syntax. It is unclear to us whether all Purépecha *ni*-NPs have the same syntactic prominence (Maldonado & Nava 2002: 162 mentions that *ni*-NPs are different kinds of nonsubjects, and their exact syntactic properties are yet to be determined). In Korean and Dutch, however, double-accusative constructions are syntactically asymmetrical: there is only one direct object in the clause, according to syntactic tests (Kozinsky & Polinsky 1993, Shibatani 2002). The available evidence suggests that Panoan languages like Matsés and Shipibo-Konibo do have such symmetrical causatives (Fleck 2002, Valenzuela 2002).

2.1.4   Semantic Variation of Causatives

The two main parameters of variation of causatives are the semantic valency of the base predicate (which is usually, but not always, reflected in the syntactic valency of the clause) and other details concerning the event structure of the base and causativized events (which ultimately lead to the popular, traditional, and often somewhat vague distinction between direct and indirect causatives).

2.1.4.1   Sensitivity to Semantic Valency

Some languages use the same verbal make-up for the causative voice irrespective of the semantic valency of the predicate. Examples of this include the English periphrastic *make*-causative and the Purépecha morphological *ra*-causative in (40) above. Nevertheless, it is not uncommon for languages to causativize predicates of different semantic (and syntactic) valency using different formal strategies. Tukang Besi (41), for instance, has a morphological causative *pa-* for monovalent and bivalent predicates, but trivalent predicates like *-hu'u* 'give' must be causativized via a periphrastic construction:

(41)   Tukang Besi (Austronesian, Indonesia; Donohue 1999: 220)
      a. *No-pa-hu'u   te   ana   te   iai-no   te
          3.SBJ.REAL-CAUS-give   CORE   child   CORE   younger.sibling-3.PSR   CORE
          ana   u   riirii.
          child   GEN   duck
          (Intended: 'She made the child give the duckling to his brother.')
      b. *No-tumpu-'e*   na   ana   oko   namo'u   te
          3.SBJ.REAL-order-3.OBJ   NOM   child   COMP   3.SBJ.IRR.give   CORE
          iai-no   te   ana   u   riirii.
          younger.sibling-3.PSR   CORE   child   GEN   duck
          'She told the child to give the duckling to his brother.'

Similar phenomena are found in Basque (Saltarelli 1988: 220f, as cited in Dixon 2000b: 57) and Dulong/Rawang (LaPolla 2000). According to Næss (2007: 63), in Amharic, Palauan, Kolami, Sinhalese, and Maricopa, only monovalent verbs can be causativized morphologically, while all other verbs must be causativized periphrastically; only monovalent verbs can be causativized in most Pama-Nyungan languages (Austin 2005).

   In yet other languages, it is not the voice marker but case marking that shows sensitivity to semantic valency – although syntactic status may correlate with flagging specifics. The Finnish morphological *tt*-causative is a case in point: it applies to all verbs, but the causee is in the accusative with base monovalent verbs (a–b) and in the adessive with base bivalent (c) or trivalent (d) verbs:[14]

(42)   Finnish
      a. *Kalle*   *sula-tt-i*   *lume-n.*
          K.[NOM]   melt-CAUS-3SG.PST   snow-ACC
          'Kalle melted the snow.'
      b. *Kalle*   *pudo-tt-i*   *kissanpennu-n.*
          K.[NOM]   drop-CAUS-3SG.PST   kitten-ACC
          'Kalle dropped a/the kitten.'
      c. *Kalle*   *rakennu-tt-i*   *talo-n*   *Ville-llä.*
          K.[NOM]   build-CAUS-3SG.PST   house-ACC   V.-ADESS
          'Kalle made Ville build the house.'
      d. *Kalle*   *lähety-tt-i*   *kirjee-n*   *Liisa-lle*   *Ville-llä.*
          K.[NOM]   send-CAUS-3SG.PST   letter-ACC   L.-ALL   V.-ADESS
          'Kalle made Ville send the letter to Liisa.'

Further note that it is patientive monovalent verbs that co-occur with accusative-marked causees in Finnish, like in (a) above and (a) below; agentive monovalent verbs have partitive-marked causees (b):

(43)   Finnish
      a. *Ville*   *pudo-tt-i*   *pallo-n.*
          V.[NOM]   fall-CAUS-3SG.PST   ball-ACC
          'Ville dropped the ball.'

---

[14] See Section 2.1.3 for variation in the status of the causee.

b. *Kenraali   juoksu-tt-i   sotila-i-ta.*
   general[NOM] run-CAUS-3SG.PST soldier-PL-PTV
   'The general made the soldiers run.'

Patientive monovalent verbs like *pudota* 'fall' (a) lack an agent altogether, which means that agent installment is easy: the causative construction features an agent and a patient and thus qualifies as a prototypical transitive construction (Næss 2007). By contrast, agentive monovalent verbs like *juosta* 'run' (b) have an agent as their only argument, which has the consequence that its causative has two agentive arguments. One of these instigates the event, while the other is responsible for performing it.

If languages allow some causatives to apply rather liberally but restrict others to some valency classes, monovalent predicates, particularly those with a patientive subject, seem to be universally causativizable. It appears that avalent predicates (e.g., meteorological verbs) and trivalent predicates (e.g., verbs of giving and saying) are the most commonly excluded, or at least dispreferred, classes (Kittilä 2007, Eriksen et al. 2010). Nevertheless, it is not uncommon to find exceptions to such generalizations. Even though Finnish allows morphological causatives of most trivalent verbs, *antaa* 'give' can only be causativized periphrastically. Similarly, most bivalent verbs are causativized periphrastically in Amharic (Amberber 2002), Palauan (Josephs 1975: 206–207), and Sinhalese (Gair 1970: 67), but a small number of them, most notably 'eat' and 'drink' may be causativized morphologically as well, in all three languages. Lastly, there exist cases like Marathi, in which periphrastic causativization may be unavailable to express indirect causation due to the nature of the non-caused event:

(44)   Marathi (Indo-Aryan, India; Shibatani & Pardeshi 2002: 93)
    a. *Shaam   buḍ-l-aa.*
       Sh.   drown-PERF-M
       'Sham drowned.'
    b. *Raam-ne   Shaam-laa   buḍ-aw-l-a.*
       R.-ERG   Sh.-DAT   drown-CAUS-PERF-M
       'Ram drowned Sham.'
    c. **Raam-ne Shaam-laa   buḍ-aaylaa   laaw-l-a.*
       R.-ERG   Sh.-DAT   drown-PTCP   make-PERF-N
       (Intended: 'Ram made Sham drown.')

On the other hand, periphrastic causativization is possible in other cases where indirect causation is possible. This is attested, for instance, with the verb 'give' and an agentive causer and an agentive causee (Shibatani & Pardeshi 2002: 92).[15]

---

[15] In Diyari, there is a special causative affix *-ma* for verbs like 'drown' (as opposed to *-ipa*, which occurs on other monovalent verbs (Austin 2011: 78)).

2.1.4.2   Sensitivity to Other Aspects of Event Structure

Most kinds of semantic variation found with causatives are frequently captured in the descriptive and typological literature by positing two event prototypes, usually called DIRECT and INDIRECT CAUSATION.[16] We follow Shibatani and Pardeshi (2002) here in regarding these prototypes (i) as opposite ends of a multi-dimensional causation continuum and (ii) as best defined in terms of single-event causation and two-event causation, respectively.

With respect to the continuum, consider the following triplet from Alamblak, which shows a direct (a) and indirect (c) pair, as well as a construction occupying a semantically intermediate zone, namely the SOCIA-TIVE causative (b):

(45)   Alamblak (Sepik, Papua New Guinea; Bruce 1984: 155–156)
      a. *Ka-fkne-më-r-m.*
         CAUS₁-enter-RPST-3SG.M-3PL
         'He caused them to enter (sthg.) by physically taking   (direct) them.'
      b. *Ha-fkne-më-r-m.*
         CAUS₂-enter-RPST-3SG.M-3PL
         'He caused them to enter (sthg.) by entering with them.'   (sociative)
      c. *Yima-r   fĕrpam   hay-noh-më-r-a.*
         person-3SG.M   potion   give-be.unconscious-RPST-3SG.M-1SG
         'A man gave me a potion, causing me to become   (indirect) unconscious.'

The direct and sociative causatives are marked alike (by prefixing *ka-* and *ha-* to the verb, respectively), whereas the indirect causative employs a complex predicate with *hay-* 'give'. Shibatani and Pardeshi (2002: 100) note that the sociative causative has at least three subtypes (viz., joint-action, assistive, and supervision); as we will see below, the direct and indirect poles are best thought of as areas (rather than points).

With respect to how these poles are best defined, Shibatani and Pardeshi propose to use spatial, temporal, and actional "profiles" of events – parameters that admittedly correlate with some features of the arguments involved, but these authors do not see such features as criterial. Direct causation corresponds to a single event in space and time, while indirect causation consists of two sub-events that are linked in a causal chain; Shibatani (1976, 2002) calls the latter "causing event" and "caused event."[17] In more formal terms (46), direct causation corresponds to a functional predicate CAUSE that takes three arguments (viz., an agent, a patient, and a clause) and is a reduced and condensed semantic representation of the causal chain (a). Indirect causation, by contrast, corresponds

---

[16] Dixon's (2000b) admittedly "tentative and preliminary" study works with nine semantic parameters and postulates two possible prototypes as well (based not only on semantic considerations but also on morphosyntactic correlations), but these differ from the received notions.

[17] Frawley (1992: 159) labels them "precipitating event" and "result," respectively.

to two sub-events linked by a causal connector. Each sub-event is in principle characterized by autonomous argument structures, and is an open and uncondensed representation of the causal chain (b):[18]

(46)   Semantic structure of causation prototypes
        a.   Direct: CAUSE [A, P, *predicate* [. . .]]
        b.   Indirect: *predicate*$_1$ [A, . . .] CAUSAL.LINK *predicate*$_2$ [. . .]

Earlier studies typically focus on selected aspects of this opposition that appear to be especially prominent in the data they address for the characterization of the prototypes. For instance, Masica (1976: Ch. 3) distinguishes between "contactive" and "distant" causation: the causer does something to the object directly in the former (e.g., 'Ram broke the mirror'), but brings about the result through an intermediate agent in the latter (e.g., 'Shyam made Ram break the mirror'). Similarly, Shibatani (1973, 1976) distinguishes between "manipulative" and "directive" causation: the causer physically manipulates a (typically inanimate) causee in the former but employs a speech act to manipulate a (typically human) causee in the latter. Example (47) from Yimas illustrates Shibatani's distinction in an elegant way; both causatives are built on complex predicates, but the direct type uses *tar*- 'hold' (a) while the indirect type uses *tmi*- 'say' (b):

(47)   Yimas (Foley 1991: 291)
        a.   *Na-na-tar-kwalca-t.*   (direct causative)
              3SG.A-1SG.P-hold-rise-PERF
        b.   *Na-na-tmi-kwalca-t.*   (indirect causative)
              3SG.A-1SG.P-say-rise-PERF
        Both: 'She woke me up.'

Analogous examples can be found in Ingush with 'make' and 'take' (Nichols 1994b) and in Lao with 'make' and 'give' (see (28) above).

In many languages, causatives follow an iconic pattern: if there are multiple causative strategies and they differ along the complex direct–indirect parameter, formally more integrated constructions will tend to express semantically more integrated causal chains, rather than vice versa. With lexical and morphological causatives, the causing sub-event and the caused sub-event are usually integrated into one single event (e.g., in Hopi *tootim saaqa-t leepek-na-ya* [boys ladder-OBJ fall-CAUS-PL] 'the boys made the ladder fall', Kalectaca 1978: 75). With periphrastic causatives, the two sub-events are separable, at least in principle (e.g., in English *John made Bill build the house*). Speakers may actually choose to portray the same state of affairs in different ways, however. We may, for example, say *I killed my friend* when it is clear that we have not purposely caused our friend to die, but we blame ourselves for his/her death (for example, when we have told our friend to travel to Africa where s/he is attacked by a lion and dies).

---

[18] Direct causatives are often monoclausal constructions, whereas many indirect causatives are often biclausal.

The following examples from Nivkh (48), Finnish (49), and Buru (50) illustrate this distinction:

(48)   Nivkh (Nedjalkov et al. 1995: 64)
    a. *If   lep   seu-d'.*
         he   bread   dry(TR)-FIN
         'He dried the bread.'
         (direct causation, lexical causative)
    b. *If   lep   če-gu-d'.*
         he   bread   dry(INTR)-CAUS-FIN
         'He caused the bread to dry.'
         (indirect causation, morphological causative)

(49)   Finnish
    a. *Kalle   tappo-i   Ville-n.*
         K.[NOM]   kill-3SG.PST   V.-ACC
         'Kalle killed Ville.'
    b. *Kalle   pol-tt-i   talo-n.*
         K.[NOM]   burn-CAUS-3SG.PST   house-ACC
         'Kalle burnt the house.'
         (direct causation, lexical causative)
    c. *Kalle   anto-i   Ville-n   kuolla.*
         K.[NOM]   give/let-3SG.PST V.-ACC   die
         'Kalle let Ville die / Kalled caused Ville to die.'
    d. *Kalle   anto-i   talo-n   palaa.*
         K.[NOM]   give/let-3SG.PST house-ACC   burn
         'Kalle let the house burn / Kalle caused the house to burn.'
         (indirect causation, periphrastic causative)

(50)   Buru (Austronesian, Indonesia; Dixon 2000b: 69, from Grimes 1991: 211)
    a. *Da   pe-gosa   ringe.*
         3SG.A $CAUS_1$-be.good   3SG.P
         'He healed her (directly, with spiritual power).'
         (direct causation, morphological causative)
    b. *Da   puna   ringe   gosa.*
         3SG.A $CAUS_2$ 3SG.P   be.good
         'He (did something which indirectly) made her well.'
         (indirect causation, periphrastic causative)

Languages may distinguish between direct and indirect causation (as defined in Shibatani and Pardeshi 2001: 89) by formally resorting to means other than voice marker allomorphy. Finnish, for instance, can do so via the marking of the causee, namely accusative (a) vs. partitive (b):

(51)   Finnish
    a. *Eversti   sula-tt-i   lume-n.*
         colonel[NOM]   melt-CAUS-3SG.PST   snow-ACC
         'The colonel melted the snow.' (direct causative)

b. *Eversti*   *juoksu-tt-i*   *sotila-i-ta.*
   colonel[NOM] run-CAUS-3SG.PST   soldier-PL-PTV
   'The colonel made the soldiers run.' (indirect causative)

Compare the following examples from Tukang Besi, where direct and indirect causation are distinguished not only by different verbal marking (*pa-* vs. *hepe-*) but also by flagging and grammatical relation assignment:

(52)   Tukang Besi (Donohue 1999: 212, 217)

a. *No-wila*   *na*   *ana.*
   3.SBJ.REAL-go   NOM   child
   'The child goes.' (non-causative)

b. *No-pa-wila*   *te*   *anabou* *i*   *jambata* *na*   *ana.*
   3.SBJ.REAL-CAUS$_1$-go   CORE   father   OBL   jetty   NOM   child
   'The father sends the child to the jetty.' (direct causative)

c. *Ku-hepe-wila*   *(na*   *iaku)* *di*   *ana.*
   1SG.SBJ-CAUS$_2$-go   NOM   1SG   OBL   child
   'I ask the child to go.' (indirect causative)

Sometimes, direct causation is seen as prototypically applying to patientive monovalent predicates – what we call agent-related causation here – and indirect causation as applying to predicates that have an agent irrespective of their semantic valency. Shibatani and Pardeshi (2002) themselves present such an impressionistic analysis at the outset of their study, and even though such a distribution is frequently found in natural languages, they emphasize that the two polar prototypes are not defined by such an account.

As mentioned above, the direct–indirect opposition does correlate with particular argument features. With an indirect causative, the causee is explicitly characterized as less volitional than with the non-causative counterpart, and the causee may also be conceived of as somewhat affected by the event in that s/he is made to behave in a certain way. (In order to capture such nuances, Dixon (2000b) works with a ternary distinction for affectedness, viz., non-affected, partially affected, completely affected.) Control is usually seen as an essential property of a prototypical agent and is also relevant to the distinction between causer and causee in indirect causation. The causer instigates the event as a whole and is possibly in control of the beginning of the caused event, but after that the causee typically takes over control and is responsible for the successful completion of the caused event. This also underlines the division of agentive features in indirect causation.

Consider in this context the following examples from Japanese, which express different kinds of indirect causation. The causee has much more control in (b) (a subtype occasionally called "permissive causation") than in (a); verbal marking is identical (-*(s)ase*) but case marking (accusative vs. dative) disambiguates:

(53)   Japanese (Japonic, Japan; Nobufumi Inaba, pers. comm.)

a. *Hanako=ga*   *Kozue=o*   *konsaato=e*   *ik-ase-ta.*
   H.=NOM   K.=ACC   concert=LAT   go-CAUS-PST

    b. *Hanako=ga   Kozue=ni   baa=e   ik-ase-ta.*
       H.=NOM   K.=DAT   bar=LAT   go-CAUS-PST
       'Hanako let Kozue go to a bar.'

Something analogous occurs in Korean and Even (accusative vs. dative), as well as in Bolivian Quechua (accusative vs. instrumental). In Purépecha (54), by contrast, the causee marker is constant, but the voice marker distinguishes between volitional (*-ta*) and non-volitional agents (*-ku*):

(54)   Purépecha (Maldonado & Nava 2002: 175)
        a. *Valeria   umi-rhu-ku-s-Ø-ti*   *chríri-ni.*
          V.   suffocate-TOP-CAUS$_1$-PERF-PRS-IND.3   fire-OBJ
          'Valeria suffocated the fire (unintentionally).'
        b. *Valeria   umi-rhu-ta-s-Ø-ti*   *chríri-ni.*
          V.   suffocate-TOP-CAUS$_2$-PERF-PRS-IND.3   fire-OBJ
          'Valeria suffocated the fire (intentionally).'

By a similar token, Chrau (55) normally encodes direct and indirect causation via the prefix *ta-* and the verb *ôp*, respectively, but an opposition in purpose can be denoted within indirect causation via *ta*-prefixation:

(55)   Chrau (Austroasiatic, Vietnam; Dixon 2000b: 70, from Thomas 1969: 100)
        a. *Ănh   ôp   dăq   khlâyh.*
          1SG   CAUS$_2$ trap   escape
          'I made the trap spring (on purpose).'
         b. *Ănh   ôp   dăq   ta-khlâyh.*
          1SG   CAUS$_2$ trap   CAUS$_1$-escape
          'I made the trap spring (accidentally).'

Guugu Yimidhirr (56) draws a sharper line between causation types in that non-volitional causation (where the causer can also be viewed as a source/reason only) has to be expressed by a one-argument clause with an optional oblique causer (b):

(56)   Guugu Yimidhirr (Pama-Nyungan, Australia; Haviland 1979: 125)
        a. *Ngayu   nhanu   minha   gundil   bulii=ma-ni.*
          1SG.NOM   2SG.GEN.ABS   meat.ABS   egg.ABS   fall=CAUS-PST
          'I dropped (lit. caused to fall) your (SG) egg.'
        b. *Nhanu   minha   gundil   buli   (ngadhun.gal).*
          2SG.GEN.ABS   meat.ABS   egg.ABS   fall.PST   1SG.ADESS
          'I dropped your (SG) egg by accident / your (SG) egg fell.'

    Data from Kammu (57) show that the animacy of the causer can play a role as well. Causativization is possible with animate causers (a) but excluded with inanimate ones (b):

(57)   Kammu (Austroasiatic, Laos; Svantesson 1983: 104)
        a. *Rwàay   p-háan   tráak.*
          tiger   CAUS-die   buffalo
          'The tiger killed the buffalo.'

b. *Mìit   p-háan   tráak.
    knife   CAUS-die   buffalo
    (Intended: 'The knife killed the buffalo.')

In the following examples from Korean (58) and Finnish (59), it is features of the causee with particular predicates that play a central role. Since the events denoted (i.e., running and digging a hole) require the active participation of the causee, the latter must be animate, which in turn makes the Korean (b)-clause ungrammatical and the Finnish (b)-clause ungrammatical at least with the intended causative reading:[19]

(58)   Korean (Hak-Soo Kim, pers. comm.)
    a. Kɨ-ka   ku   namcha-eykey   talli-ke   ha-yəss-ta.
        3SG-NOM   DET   man-DAT   run-CAUS   do-PST-DECL
        'He let the man run.'
    b. *Kɨ-ka   ku   tol-eykey   ttele   ha-yəss-ta.
        3SG-NOM   DET   stone-DAT   fall.PASS.CAUS   do-PST-DECL
        (Intended: 'He made/let the stone fall.')

(59)   Finnish
    a. Opettaja   kaivau-tt-i   kuopa-n   laulaja-lla.
        teacher[NOM]   dig-CAUS-3SG.PST   hole-ACC   singer-ADESS
        'A/the teacher made a/the singer dig a/the hole.'
    b. *Opettaja   kaivau-tt-i   kuopa-n   lapio-lla.
        teacher[NOM]   dig-CAUS-3SG.PST   hole-ACC   shovel-ADESS
        (Intended: 'A/the teacher made a/the shovel dig a/the hole.')
        (Possible: 'The teacher made someone dig a/the hole with a shovel.')

Finally, a number of semantic features, such as dynamicity, naturalness, and expectedness, have not been discussed extensively in the literature on causatives, but appear to play a role as well, so we will mention some pertinent examples.[20] For instance, Amharic has two causative morphemes, a- and as-; the former attaches only to change-of-state verbs (which are dynamic), while the latter may be used with either dynamic or stative verbs (Amberber 2000). In Mohawk, only stative verbs may be causativized (Baker 1988: 348–352). Naturalness plays a role in Russian causativization (60). In (b) the causer must use more energy, and probably has less control, than in (a):

(60)   Russian (Slavic, Russia; Dixon 2000b: 72)
    a. On   na-poi-l   menja   vinom.
        3SG.M   PVB-drink.CAUS₁-PST.SG.M   1SG.ACC   wine.INS.SG
        'He got me to drink wine (and I didn't resist).'

[19] The only possible reading of lapiolla in (b) is as instrument. Animacy of the causee is not a general requirement of causativization for Finnish, however; the causee of causativized patientive monovalent verbs is often inanimate.
[20] Shibatani and Pardeshi's (2002) broad subtypes of causation can easily accommodate the latter two features. Dixon (2000b) sees at least the former two features as basic parameters of causation in their own right.

b. *On   za-stavi-l   menja   pitj   vino.*
   3SG.M   PVB-CAUS$_2$-PST.SG.M   1SG.ACC drink   wine.ACC.SG
   'He forced me to drink wine (e.g., by threats or blows).'

Just how expected the result is plays a role in Caodeng Gyalrong causativization (61). It is more likely for Sonam to be the A and the tiger to be the P. If this is the case, a lexical causative is used, and the causer bears no explicit coding (a). If the roles are reversed, however, causation is less expected and morphological causativization is used instead (b):

(61)   Caodeng Gyalrong (Sino-Tibetan, China; Sun 1998: 130f)
       a. *Sonəm   qəɟje   ne-ntʃʰez.*
          S.   tiger   PFV.TR -kill.PFV
          'Sonam killed the tiger.'
       b. *Qəɟje-ke   Sonəm   ne-sə-set.*
          tiger-ERG   S.   PFV.TR-CAUS-die.PFV
          'The tiger killed Sonam.'

2.1.5   Distribution of Causatives

Given that many events may be externally caused or not, and that languages need to be able to capture this difference somehow, causation can be regarded as a universally attested meaning – which in turn makes it unsurprising to find causative diatheses in all natural languages known to date. While the causative voice is common, however, not all languages have it. For example, some languages only have labile verbs for the (anti-)causative diathesis (which is the case for some English alternating predicates, like *break*) (see Section 6.2.1). Moreover, Dixon (1972) claims that Dyirbal has no causative diatheses (only lexically unrelated monovalent and bivalent verbs).

Since either coded or uncoded causatives seem to be universal, it is not very useful to discuss the geographical distribution of causatives per se in general. Song (2005a, 2005b, 2008a, 2008b) discusses the distribution of lexical and morphological vs. periphrastic causatives in the world's languages. He finds no relevant geographical tendencies for non-periphrastic causatives, but there are some tendencies for the latter; for example, Song's purposive type is much more common than his sequential type in southern Africa. Nevertheless, this author notes himself that previous studies of causatives have focused more on morphological causatives, thereby neglecting periphrastic causatives. It also seems that sociative causation is attested mostly in South American languages (Guillaume & Rose 2010).

According to Song (2008a, 2008b), non-periphrastic causatives are more frequent than periphrastic ones. This is an interesting finding on at least two grounds. First, languages with analytic morphology tend to show comparatively scarce (inflectional) morphology, which in many (yet not all) languages leads to these languages also lacking morphological causatives. Second, if we extend the notion of periphrastic causatives to any construction that denotes causation regardless of its formal expression, it becomes rather likely that periphrastic causatives are attested in all languages.[21] For example, verbs like 'order', 'make', 'allow', 'tell' etc. may be used to denote manipulative causation, and in case these are all included into the definition of causatives, periphrastic causatives probably become a universal category. Be this as it may, more studies are needed in order to say more about the areal distribution of causatives.

2.2   Anticausatives

2.2.1   Prototypical Anticausatives

The term was introduced by Nedjalkov and Sil'nickij (1973) (in the 1969 Russian original) and suggests that anticausatives constitute the opposite of causatives (see also Haspelmath 1993b).[22] This indeed applies to the prototypes of both notions in that the former removes an agent from the verbal semantics, while the latter installs an external causer to the denoted event. Nevertheless, the two notions are far from being symmetrical opposites of each other. For instance, formal and functional variation is less significant for anticausatives. Moreover, causativization usually applies to most verbs in natural languages, while anticausativization is usually available for only those bivalent verbs that allow agents to be omitted altogether. It does not apply to monovalent verbs and trivalent verbs, which usually allow some kind of causativization (even though the mechanisms may vary) in most languages.

The anticausative voice is defined here as follows:

(62)   Characteristics of the anticausative voice
   a.   Its semantic and syntactic valency is one less than that of the base.
   b.   The A is removed from argument structure, both semantically and syntactically.
   c.   Its subject corresponds to the P of the non-anticausative voice.[23]
   d.   Anticausativization is formally coded on the predicate complex.

---

[21] An analogy is provided by evidentiality: it is attested as an obligatory morphological category only in some languages, but all languages may refer to the source of information in some way, if only via lexical verbs.

[22] There are a number of alternative terms in the literature: "middle" (Keenan 1985), "inchoative" (Everaert 1986), and "spontaneous" (Shibatani 1985), as well as, albeit more marginally, "pseudo-passive" (Derbyshire 1985: 90), "derived intransitive" (Cranmer 1976), and others. See Haspelmath (1987: 9–10) for an early critique and additional references.

[23] In languages where the non-anticausative clause has a subject P and an object A (i.e., it instantiates the patient diatheses or shows "ergative syntax"), we label the counterpart of the (subjective) anticausative OBJECTIVE ANTICAUSATIVE.

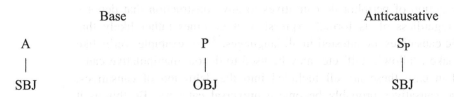

Figure 2.4 *Anticausative diathesis*

The following example from Turkish illustrates this prototype:

(63)   Turkish (Haspelmath 1987: 2)

    a. *Annem*   *kapı-yı*   *aç-tı.*
        mother.1SG.PSR[NOM]   door-ACC   open-PST
        'My mother opened the door.'

    b. *Kapı*   *aç-ıl-dı.*
        door[NOM]   open-ANTIC-PST
        'The door opened.'

In (a), a subject A is targeting his/her action at an object P that is directly affected by the given event. In (b), an anticausative marker has been suffixed to the verb, which has decreased the valency of the predicate by one, yielding a monovalent predicate. In addition, the case marking of the P has also changed from accusative to nominative. The S_P argument of (b) is coreferential with the P of (a). The event denoted by an anticausative occurs completely spontaneously, which distinguishes anticausatives from passives, where the argument in A function can be omitted from the clause but is still a semantic argument.

What distinguishes the anticausative from the active diathesis expressing a transitive event is that the former is not caused intentionally and purposefully by a salient A. More precisely, anticausatives make the causer non-salient and remove the A from argument structure, without completely omitting the cause. This has the consequence that anticausatives usually block an overt reference to an A, but they may include different kinds of causers, as for example, 'wind' or 'fire', as shown in Section 2.2.2.

The central semantic motivation for the use of anticausatives appears to be related to pragmatics. Anticausatives may be used to escape one's own responsibility for a given event, or they may be employed to avoid accusing someone else directly for something that has happened. For example, in Finnish, it is very common to use anticausatives whenever the speaker thinks that s/he is not responsible for the denoted event, or at least s/he has not acted volitionally. Constructions such as *it just broke* are common in these kinds of situations in English also. This underlines the similarities between passives and anticausatives, both of which can be used when it is important to downplay the contribution of an A to the occurrence of the given event. This pragmatic motivation is also seen in cases where a given event cannot happen spontaneously (as is the case with 'paint' and 'build', for example), but it is described as such (see Section 2.2.3.2).

Finally, unlike passives, anticausatives do not seem to have syntactic motivations in any language we have data for. This may seem somewhat unexpected due to the functional similarities between the two constructions, but the nature and motivation of A-omission is probably relevant here. Passive and active voices may be used to describe the same event from different perspectives, while the anticausative denotes a different event altogether. From this it follows that passives may have syntactic functions, because passivization has no drastic semantic consequences. The denoted event thus remains semantically unchanged, and passivization may, for example, be used to promote P to subject to make relativization possible. On the other hand, anticausativization always affects the nature of the denoted event as well, which seems to exclude the use of anticausatives for purely syntactic purposes.

2.2.2   Non-Prototypical Anticausatives and Lookalikes

We survey three kinds of constructions here that show not only important similarities to but also crucial differences with anticausatives. Agentless resultatives are not marked like anticausatives but can instantiate that diathesis. Involuntary agent constructions and inanimate causer constructions, by contrast, are marked like anticausatives but differ from the latter's prototype in important ways.

AGENTLESS RESULTATIVES resemble anticausatives in that both decrease the syntactic valency of the predicate. Consider the following Russian examples:

(64)   Russian (Haspelmath & Müller-Bardey 2004: 1134–1135)
    a.   *Mira*   *zakryvaet*   *dver'*.
        M.[NOM]   close.3SG   door[NOM/ACC]
        'Mira is closing the door.'
    b.   *Dver'*   *zakryvaet-sja*.
        door[NOM/ACC]   close.3SG-ANTIC
        'The door is closing.' (anticausative)
    c.   *Dver'*   *zakry-ta*.
        door[NOM/ACC]   close-PTCP
        'The door is closed.' (resultative)

The two constructions differ, however, regarding aspectuality and the exact nature of omission of the agent. As to the former, anticausatives are aspectually neutral and can therefore be dynamic (see (b) above); resultatives are strictly static (c). As to the latter, anticausatives denote events that occur spontaneously without any kind of (salient) agent. Agentless resultatives, in turn, simply denote the result of an event; the agent may have been a part of the semantics of the event in question but is completely backgrounded, since the focus is solely on the result. Just as anticausatives have a particular diathesis while being aspect-neutral, agentless resultatives have a particular aspect while being diathesis-neutral: they usually allow both a passive and an anticausative reading. In other words, their semantic argument structure is usually ambiguous between

[A P] and [S$_P$] – which explains the fact that such resultatives are possible with a wider range of predicates than anticausatives.[24]

Agentless resultatives rule out the expression of an A, as in German and Finnish (see Nedjalkov & Otaina 1988: 135 for a similar note on Nivkh):

(65)   German
        *Das   Fenster ist von mir   / durch den   Wind
        ART.NOM window is by 1SG.DAT through ART.ACC wind
        geöffnet.
        open.PST.PTCP
        (Intended: 'The window is open by me / in the wind.')

(66)   Finnish
        *Ovi   on   avattu   tuule-ssa   / tuule-lta
        door   be.3SG.PRS open.PST.PTCP   wind-INESS   wind-ABL
        / tuule-n   toimesta.
        wind-GEN   by
        (Intended: 'The door is open(ed) by the wind.')

Nevertheless, Finnish and German allow the A to be expressed in other non-prototypical anticausatives; the agent expression is, for instance, possible, in IACs in both languages (see below). In Finnish, *tuulessa* 'wind.INESS' cannot express an agent/causer in this case; it would refer to the circumstances instead, and the reading of the clause would be 'the door was open(ed) in windy weather'.

Unsurprisingly, agentless resultative constructions show formal variation. In Evenki, for instance, the P object is in the accusative in (a) and turns into the S$_P$ subject in the nominative in (b); the base A subject is removed in (b):

(67)   Evenki (Tungusic, China/Russia; Nedjalkov & Nedjalkov 1988: 242)
        a. Nuŋan   tadū   kalan-me   loko-d'oro-n.
            he.NOM there   pot-ACC   hang-PRES-3SG
            'He is hanging a pot there.'
        b. Tadū   kalan   lokū-ča-d'ara-n.
            there   pot.NOM hang-RES-PRES-3SG
            'A pot is hanging (hangs) there.'

In Mandarin Chinese, the equivalent removal and promotion can be seen from constituent order instead of case morphology; subjects are preverbal and objects postverbal:

(68)   Mandarin Chinese (Sino-Tibetan, China; Jaxontov 1988: 113)
        a. Tā   kāi   mén.
            3[SG]   open   door
            'S/he opens the door.'

---

[24] Agentless resultatives are a special case of resultative constructions, which in principle need not alter diathetical structure. See Nedjalkov and Jaxontov (1988) for a general characterization and typology.

b. *Mén   kāi-zhe.*
door   open-RES
'The door is open.'

In German, case morphology behaves like in Evenki, and position relative to the finite verb is like in Mandarin; unlike in these languages, however, the resultative consists of a copula and a participle (69). The expression of the resulting state of an action resembles constructions denoting properties, which easily accounts for the use of adjectives in resultatives.

(69)   German
a. *Jutta   öffne-t   ihr-en   Mund.*
J.   open-3SG   her-SG.M.ACC   mouth
'Jutta opens her mouth.'
b. *Ihr   Mund   ist   weit   geöffnet.*
her[SG.M.NOM]   mouth   is   wide   open.PST.PTCP
'Her mouth is wide open.'

Another source of cross-linguistic variation of resultatives is related to the reference of their subject. The most common constructions fall into two types: the resultative subject is coreferential with either the subject or the object of the clause that expresses how the result came about (Nedjalkov & Jaxontov 1988: 8). The first type is exemplified by English *John's eyes have inflamed → John's eyes are inflamed*, and by the following Russian pair:

(70)   Russian (Nedjalkov & Jaxontov 1988: 10)
a. *On   pomer.*
he[NOM]   died
'He has died.'
b. *On   pomer-ši.*
he[NOM]   die-PST.GER
'He is dead.' (subjective resultative)

The second type is exemplified by the following Russian pair:

(71)   Russian (Nedjalkov & Jaxontov 1988: 9)
a. *Oni   pomyli   pol.*
they[NOM]   washed   floor
'They have washed the floor.'
b. *Pol   pomy-vši.*
floor   wash-PST.GER
'The floor is washed.' (objective resultative)

We follow Haspelmath (1993a: 292) in using the term INVOLUNTARY AGENT CONSTRUCTIONS (IACs) to refer to clauses that denote events occurring without a volitionally acting agent, which very well accounts for the use of anticausative voice as their coding. IACs express transitivity values intermediate between intransitivity and full transitivity.

Formally, they differ from prototypical anticausatives in the presence of an explicit causer, as shown in the following examples:

(72)   Finnish
    a. *Mies*   *rikko-i*   *maljako-n.*
        man[NOM]   break-3SG.PST   vase-ACC
        'The man broke the vase.'
    b. *Miehe-ltä*   *rikko-utu-i*   *maljakko.*
        man-ABL   break-ANTIC-3SG.PST   vase[NOM]
        'The man accidentally broke a vase / the vase broke on the man.'

(73)   Guugu Yimidhirr (Haviland 1979: 125)
    a. *Ngayu*   *galga*   *nhanu*   *dumbi.*
        1SG.NOM   spear.ABS   2SG.GEN.ABS   break.PST
        'I broke your (SG) spear (on purpose).'
    b. *Ngadhun-gal* *galga*   *nhanu*   *dumbi-:dhi.*
        1SG-ADESS   spear.ABS   2SG.GEN.ABS   break-ANTIC.PST
        'I broke your (SG) spear (by accident).'

IACs also differ from prototypical two-argument constructions in the coding of the A (ablative in Finnish and adessive in Guugu Yimidhirr). IACs thus resemble anticausatives in their verbal morphology and default two-argument constructions in the number of overt syntactic arguments (see Kittilä 2005 and Fauconnier 2012 for a discussion of IACs across languages).

In (72) and (73) above, the use of the anticausative marker in (b) is determined by lack of control and volitionality, whereas events denoted by (a) do involve a typical agent (see Dixon 1977: 275 for a similar case in Yidiny). Put another way, causers in the (b)-clauses above lack part of feature 1 ("volitional involvement in the event or state") of Dowty's proto-agent (Dowty 1991: 572). If the expression of such a meaning is seen as the primary function of IACs, it comes as no surprise that these constructions can usually be formed only from predicates denoting events that may occur spontaneously, without any kind of intervention by an agent. Verbs like English *paint, wash,* and *eat* do not normally appear in IACs. Another consequence of the semantics of IACs is that they are usually possible only with animate causers.[25]

In addition to this semantic motivation, IACs are sometimes used for (socio-) pragmatic reasons. This follows, since IACs underline the lack of control and volitionality, which makes it possible for speakers to escape responsibility for their actions, as in English *the phone just broke on me.* Moreover, in some languages, such as Samoan and Tongan, the use of two-argument constructions with an A in the ergative is seen as an ascription of responsibility, possibly even as an accusation (Duranti & Ochs 1990). This means that ergative case marking on the agent is avoided under certain but frequent circumstances, which in turn

---

[25] Kittilä (2005) suggests that one of the reasons for this is that the differences in agency between base clauses and IACs need to be significant enough in order for an IAC to be licensed.

makes IACs natural in cases where we are not sure whether the agent has actually acted volitionally or not.

INANIMATE CAUSER CONSTRUCTIONS (ICCs) formally resemble IACs in that both clause types involve anticausative voice marking and an obliquely coded causer. In Yidiny, for instance, the only difference between a default two-argument construction and an ICC lies in the verbal morphology. In (74), the verb bears anticausative coding, but the argument flagging is the same as in the two-argument clause (i.e., the 3rd-person A occurs in the ergative and the 1st-person P in the accusative):

(74)   Yidiny (Pama-Nyungan, Australia; Dixon 1977: 275)
        Ɖaɲaɲ   ginga-:ŋ   giba-:dyi-ɲu.
        1SG.ACC   prickle-ERG   scratch-ANTIC-PST
        'A prickle scratched me.'

In Sinhalese, the differences also concern the coding of the arguments; the causer is in the dative, while the P occurs in the unmarked nominative:

(75)   Sinhalese (Indo-Aryan, Sri Lanka; Chandralal 2010: 105)
        Kaɖuə-ʈə   atə   kæpe-nəwa.
        sword-DAT   hand[NOM]   cut.ANTIC-IND
        'The sword is cutting his hand.'

Semantically, ICCs can be divided into two major groups. First, the explicit expression of an agent can have significant consequences for the reading of a given clause. Examples (74) and (75) above, as well as the following Finnish example, illustrate this:

(76)   Finnish
        a.   *Talo*   *tuho-utu-i*   *soda-ssa.*
              house[NOM]   destroy-ANTIC-3SG.PST   war-INESS
              'The house was destroyed in the war.'
        b.   *Maljakko*   *rikko-utu-i*   *maanjäristykse-ssä.*
              vase[NOM]   break-ANTIC-3SG.PST   earthquake-INESS
              'The vase broke in an earthquake.'

Since the change of state in the patientive argument may have several different reasons, omitting the causer would lead to the loss of some potentially relevant information. In (76), in turn, the denoted event needs some kind of salient cause that is made explicit by adding an agent phrase to the construction. Unlike with prototypical transitive events, the causer is inanimate here and therefore cannot act volitionally. The second type consists in a natural causer simply being made explicit, as in the following Spanish example:

(77)   Spanish (Romance, world language)
        La   puerta   se   abrió   por   el   viento.
        ART   door   ANTIC   open.PST.3SG   by   ART   wind
        'The door opened due to the wind.'

Opening may occur spontaneously or be externally caused. In the former case, natural causes for it include, for instance, a breeze of wind or a draft. In other words, the expression of the causer merely makes a natural causer explicit in (77), and the omission of the agent would not have any major consequences for the reading of the clause.

Even though both IACs and ICCs include a non-prototypical agent/causer, the motivation for this inclusion is different: in ICCs, the non-prototypicality follows from the inherent nature of the causer; inanimate causers cannot instigate events volitionally. A formal distinction between both constructions is made in languages like Guugu Yimidhirr, for instance, where the involuntary agent takes the adessive in IACs while the inanimate causer takes instrumental/ergative coding in ICCs:

(78)   Guugu Yimidhirr (Haviland 1979: 125, 123)
    a.   *Ngadhun-gal   galga   nhanu*   *dumbi-:dhi.*
        1SG-ADESS   spear.ABS 2SG.GEN.ABS   break-ANTIC.PST
        'I broke your spear (by accident).' (IAC)
    b.   *Nganhi   wagi-:dhi*   *naaybu-unh.*
        1SG.ACC   cut-ANTIC.PST   knife-INST/ERG
        'I got cut on the knife.' (ICC)

The differences in the coding of IACs and ICCs can also be approached from a (socio-)pragmatic viewpoint. As noted above, in some languages, the use of two-argument clauses with an A in the ergative may be construed as an accusation, which makes IACs and the use of one-argument clauses in general more frequent. Note that the accidental nature of causation is not directly inferable from the semantics of the given agent; agents of IACs are animate entities that are expected to act volitionally, which makes it important to highlight their non-prototypicality. By contrast, inanimate causers are inherently non-prototypical, and there is thus no need for highlighting this. For instance, English clauses such as *the storm destroyed the city* are normal, while the accidental nature of causation with animate agents needs to made clear, for example, by an adverb, as in *the child accidentally broke the vase*.

2.2.3   Variation of Anticausatives

While causatives display substantial variation, both semantically and formally, variation in anticausatives is comparatively modest. One obvious reason for this may simply be that anticausatives are less frequent than causatives, but we will see below that semantics may also be a relevant factor in this respect.

2.2.3.1   Formal Variation of Anticausatives

Typical anticausatives are morphological, like the prefix *hm-* in Kammu:

(79) Kammu (Svantesson 1983: 111)
 a. *ʔòʔ pìr tóʔ.*
  I shake table
  'I shake the table.'
 b. *Tóʔ hm-pìr.*
  table ANTIC-shake
  'The table is shaking.'

Periphrastic anticausatives are rare but do exist:

(80) Swedish (Germanic, Sweden and Finland)
 Bil-en gick sönder.
 car-DEF went broken
 'The car broke down.'

The [*go* + adjective]-construction in (80) from Swedish is not a fully productive anticausative, but it has such a reading with some verbs. Moreover, similarly to English, where a non-grammaticalized anticausative may be formed with *become*, Lezgian can use the equivalent verb in some cases (e.g., in *alčax* 'low' vs. *alčax xun* 'become lower', Haspelmath 1993a: 166). Interestingly enough, such periphrastic strategies do not seem to constitute the default anticausativizing mechanism in any natural language.

The morphological variation of anticausatives seems to be largely cross-linguistic rather than language-internal. In other words, languages usually have only one anticausativizing mechanism at their disposal, or at least only one mechanism is clearly the primary one. Finnish is an example of a language with two mechanisms:

(81) Finnish
 a. *Henkilö rikko-i maljako-n.*
  person[NOM] break-3SG.PST vase-ACC
  'A/the person broke the vase.'
 b. *Maljakko rikko-utu-i.*
  vase[NOM] break-ANTIC-3SG.PST
  'A/the vase broke.'
 c. *Maljakko men-i rikki.*
  vase[NOM] go-3SG.PST broken
  'The vase broke.'

The (a)-clause exemplifies the default two-argument clause of Finnish, while (b) and (c) are its morphological and periphrastic anticausative counterparts, respectively. Two important caveats are in order, however. First, in contrast to the morphological and periphrastic causatives of the language, the variation illustrated above is not semantically motivated: both constructions may denote the same spontaneous breaking of a vase. The only difference between (b) and (c) is stylistic: the latter is more colloquial than the former. Second, the [*go* + adjective]-construction seems to be possible only with verbs of breaking. Even though the morphological anticausative illustrated in (b) is also far from being very productive, it is possible with a higher number of verbs (e.g., with *avata* 'open' and *tuhota* 'destroy').

The central syntactic effects of anticausativization are invariable: the P object of the base clause becomes the S$_P$ subject of the anticausative, and the base A subject is omitted. Even though anticausatives are usually agentless constructions, clauses headed by anticausativized verbs may include an explicit reference to the causer, and languages vary according to the form the latter takes, which in turn may often correlate with some variation in syntactic status. First, there are languages where the anticausativized verb may have transitive argument marking (e.g., in Yidiny, (74)). Second, and much more frequently, causers take adjunct-like marking – which can be inessive, illative, or ablative flagging, as in Finnish, or dative, instrumental, or postpositional, as in Sinhalese (see (75), Chandralal 2010: 106, and Gair 1990: 16).

Lastly, languages differ according to whether the coding of the causer in anticausatives coincide with the coding of agents of passives. In German, for instance, the coding of causers in anticausatives and agents in passives may coincide: see the use of *durch* 'through' in both clauses of (82). The default coding of the passive agent, namely the preposition *von* 'by', is possible in (b), but it leads to a "personifying" reading in which the wind has animate-like qualities:

(82)   German
    a. *Die Tür öffne-te   sich   durch   den   Wind.*
        ART door open-PST[3SG] ANTIC through ART wind
        'The door opened in the wind.'
    b. *Die Tür wurde   durch   den   Wind   geöffnet.*
        ART door became[3SG] through ART wind open.PST.PTCP
        'The door was opened by the wind.'

In Finnish, in turn, the coding of causers and agents never coincides (83). The expression of the agent with anticausatives is marginal, if at all possible (a); the expression of the agent with passives is possible, albeit in the colloquial register (b). A causer in the inessive case, however, is ungrammatical in the passive.

(83)   Finnish
    a. *Ovi   ava-utu-i   tuule-ssa   ($^{??/}$*tuule-n toimesta).*
        door[NOM] open-ANTIC-3SG.PST wind-INESS wind-GEN by
        'The door opened in the wind ($^{??/}$*by the wind).'
    b. *Ovi   ava-ttiin   Kalle-n   toimesta / *Kalle-ssa.*
        door[NOM] open-PASS.PST K.-GEN   by   Kalle-INESS
        'The door was opened by Kalle (*in Kalle).'

Finally, the same marker *por* 'by' may occur in both passives and anticausatives in Spanish, but it denotes agents in the former and reasons/causes in the latter.

2.2.3.2   Semantic Variation of Anticausatives

Anticausatives are attested only for bivalent predicates, which also restricts their semantic variation. For example, the differences between direct and less direct "anti-causation" seem not to be relevant; this probably accounts for the rare occurrence of differences between lexical, morphological, and periphrastic anti-causatives in a single language, at least to some extent. Thus, the semantic variation of anticausatives concerns their applicability (i.e., which verbs allow anticausativization and under which circumstances), the readings they may receive, and the motivation of their use in cases where the genuine omission of agent is not possible.

All languages with any type of anticausatives allow the complete removal of the agent, which is in accordance with our definition of prototypical anticausatives. A-removal is complete in cases that correspond to what Haspelmath (2017) labels "automatic." This applies, for example, to events such as freezing, melting, and opening, which may, and often do, occur without any kind of salient causation. In addition, many of the events of the "costly"-type (e.g., 'break', 'cut', etc., where spontaneous causation is somewhat less natural) exemplify A-removal. Note, however, that even these events are always somehow caused. For example, snow melts whenever the temperature rises above zero degrees Celsius, but what distinguishes *the snow melted* from *John melted the snow* is that in the former the denoted change of state follows automatically and always happens if we do not actively prevent it. Furthermore, anticausativization occurs naturally and frequently in cases such as *the city got destroyed in an earthquake*. In contrast to, for instance, melting of snow in the spring, causation is salient in the case of destruction, even though control is lacking and the consequences of an earthquake also follow spontaneously.

Anticausativization is blocked whenever a given predicate denotes an event that requires some kind of volitionality and control; only semantically bivalent predicates whose A is not necessarily a prototypical agent (i.e., with a "thematically underspecified causer") can be anticausativized (Haspelmath 1987: 15, Koontz-Garboden 2009: 80f). Thus, for example, the equivalents of 'murder', and 'assassinate' usually cannot anticausativize, while those of 'break' and 'open' can. Control is closely related to whether a given predicate has lexicalized the use of a specific instrument as part of its semantics. Only predicates that do not imply specific instruments or methods, or that lexicalize a manner component rather than simply a final state/result (Haspelmath 1993b: 93, Rappaport Hovav & Levin 2008), may be anticausativized. Thus, 'bite', 'cut', 'dig', 'paint' usually fail to anticausativize. The following examples from Amharic are illustrative in this regard:

(84)   Amharic (Amberber 2000: 314–315)

    a. *Ber-u*   *tə-kəffətə.*
           door-DEF   ANTIC/PASS-open.PERF.3M
           'The door (was) opened.'

    b. *Gəmad-u*   *(bə-Aster)*   *tə-k'rrət'ə.*
           rope-DEF   by-A.   PASS-cut.PERF.3M
           'The rope was cut (by Aster).' (Not: 'The rope cut.')

In this language, the same marker codes both passives and anticausatives; in (a), both readings are possible, because 'open' allows A-removal, but it is also possible that the A is only omitted from the syntax, which results in a passive structure and reading. The verb 'cut', in turn, requires the use of an instrument, which excludes anticausativization, and the only available reading is passive in (b). Closely related to the use of instruments, adverbs such as 'with care' also exclude anticausative readings in Amharic (Amberber 2000: 315).

Nevertheless, not all languages block the anticausativization of roughly equivalent verbs. Spanish, for example, allows constructions such as *se cortó* [ANTIC/REFL cut.3SG.PFV.PST]. With an animate subject, the reading is reflexive (e.g., 's/he cut him/herself'), while with an inanimate subject, the reading is always (and unproblematically) anticausative (e.g., 'the connection / the rope got cut off'). The anticausativization of 'cut' is possible in Finnish as well. The difference between English and Amharic on the one hand and Spanish and Finnish on the other is, at least to some extent, accounted for by the fact that different languages have lexicalized different properties of events to different degrees. As such, something can get into two pieces without an instrument (i.e., 'become cut'), or a patient may become clean without any kind of action by a volitionally acting agent (i.e., 'get washed').

Finally, anticausativization is sometimes found where the objective is not to remove the A from argument structure but to convey that an action can be performed *as though* there were no A. Consider in this context data from Finnish. Unlike cleaning / becoming clean, washing and building require both an A and a P when linguistically expressed in this language. Despite this, (non-prototypical) anticausativization is possible in (85) below:

(85)   Finnish
        a. *Tä-llä   ainee-lla   tiski-t   pese-yty-vät   itsestään.*
           this-ADESS dish.soap-ADESS   dish-PL wash-ANTIC-3PL by.themselves
           'With this dish soap the dishes (practically) wash themselves.'
        b. *Näi-llä   väline-i-llä   talo   raken-tuu*
           DEM.PL-ADESS equipment-PL-ADESS house   build-ANTIC.3SG
           silmä-n-räpäykse-ssä.
           eye-GEN-blink-INESS
           'With this equipment a house can be built in the blink of an eye.'

In (a), the washing can be carried out without considerable effort on the A's part. In (b), the equipment in question is viewed as so superior that anyone can build a house with it, which makes the A's contribution to a successful completion of the event marginal, and the A is thus backgrounded. An explicit reference to an agent is restricted in (85), even though an A in the ablative may be added to both clauses under favorable conditions.

2.2.4   Distribution of Anticausatives

Anticausatives have been less comprehensively studied than causatives, but we can make two general comments on their relative occurrence. First, the anticausative voice seems to be much less frequent than the causative voice. Even though the distinction between caused and non-caused events is arguably universal in that humans conceptualize many events in the extra-linguistic world as either caused or non-caused, languages do not necessarily reflect this by providing formally symmetrical means of expression for such events. Alternatively, labile verbs may be used, such as *break* in English. Second, in well-studied languages, the number of verbs that allow anticausativization is lower than the number of verbs that may be causativized. While A-removal is possible only for a limited set of verbs, most events may be caused externally – meteorological events being one notable exception.

2.3   Applicatives

2.3.1   Prototypical Applicatives

The term APPLICATIVE seems to have been first used in Rincón's (1595) description of particular patterns of verb derivation in Classical Nahuatl. It now covers a number of operations that allow the applicativized predicate to take a direct or primary object (called the "applied object") bearing a semantic role different from the one the base predicate would normally take (if any), for instance, a beneficiary, instrument, or location instead of a patient or theme. The applicative construction can be defined as follows:

(86)   Characteristics of the applicative voice
    a.   Its syntactic valency is one more than that of the non-applicative diathesis (e.g., the predicate is bivalent when its counterpart is monovalent, and trivalent when its counterpart is bivalent).
    b.   Its subject corresponds to the subject of the non-applicative diathesis.
    c.   Its primary/direct object corresponds to an adjunct or non-core argument in the non-applicative voice, or to a participant that is introduced to the clause as primary/direct object.
    d.   Applicativization is formally coded on the predicate complex.

Example (87) from Halkomelem illustrates an applicative that introduces a participant as an NP expressing the goal of motion with the monovalent verb *nem̓* 'go' (Figure 2.4 graphically represents both voices). This new argument in a P function is a direct object, the S of the monovalent becomes the A, and the bivalent verb takes the applicative suffix -*nəs*:

(87)   Halkomelem (Gerdts 2004: 191)
    a.   *Niʔ   nem̓   kʷθə   sʷiw̓ləs.*
         AUX go   DET   boy
         'The boy went.' (non-applicative)
    b.   *Niʔ   nəm-nəs-əs   kʷθə   sʷiw̓ləs   kʷθə   John.*
         AUX go-APPL-3.A   DET   boy   DET   J.
         'The boy went up to John.' (applicative)

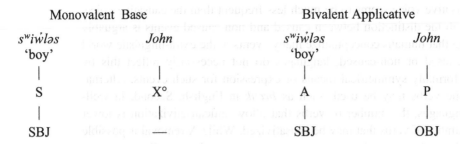

Figure 2.5 *Applicative diathesis I*

Example (88) from German illustrates the participant-promoting use of the *be*-applicative:

(88)   German
     a. *Kann   man   (in   diesem   Fluss)   frei   angeln?*
        can.3SG IMPRS in   this.DAT river   freely fish.INF
     b. *Kann   man   diesen   Fluss   frei   be-angeln?*
        can.3SG IMPRS this.ACC river   freely APPL-fish.INF
     Both: 'Can one fish in this river?'

In the non-applicative voice (a), the (optional) location is expressed as an oblique (*in diesem Fluss* 'in this river', with the preposition *in* and dative case) and the monovalent verb shows no voice marker. In the applicative voice (b), the location is the direct object and appears in the accusative (*der Fluss* 'the river'), and the verb takes the voice marker *be-* and is bivalent. The subject status and nominative morphology of the A is the same in both constructions (see Figure 2.6).

Example (89) illustrates the alternation between the two voices in Ndendeule:

(89)   Ndendeule (Bantu, Tanzania; Ngonyani 2000: 62)
     a. *Nyɛni   a-ki-hɛmɛl-a   hiteβo.*
        guest.I I.SBJ-PST-buy-ASP   chair.VIII
        'The guest bought chairs.' (non-applicative)
     b. *Nyɛni   a-ki-yi-hɛmɛl-ɛl-a   shuli   hiteβo.*
        guest.I I.SBJ-PST-IX.OBJ-buy-APPL-ASP school.IX chair.VIII
        'The guest bought chairs for the school.' (applicative)

In the non-applicative construction (a), the beneficiary *shuli* 'school' does not occur at all and the bivalent verb shows no voice marker. In the applicative (b), by contrast, the beneficiary occurs as an object without an adposition or case marker, the verb indexes this argument via the prefix *yi-*, and the trivalent verb takes the voice marker *-ɛl*. The subject status and nominative morphology of the A is the same in both constructions. Figure 2.7 graphically represents these voices. (The exact nature of the two objects may vary both from language to language and from one applicative to another in the same language; see Section 2.3.3.2.)

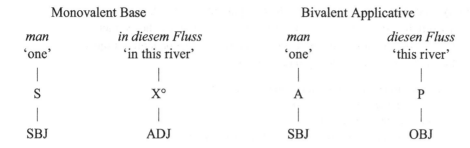

Figure 2.6 *Applicative diathesis II*

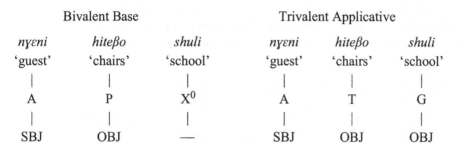

Figure 2.7 *Applicative diathesis III*

Applicativization can be described in more general and formal terms as the result of predicate fusion (Austin 2005): a trivalent functional predicate APPLY takes an agent, a patient (the applied object), and a clause that represents the event portrayed by a lexical predicate:[26]

(90)   Predicate fusion with prototypical applicatives
        APPLY [A, P, *predicate* [...]]

Different coreference conditions in specific applicatives lead to part of the observable cross-linguistic variation. If the base, lexical, predicate is semantically monovalent, its only argument is coreferential with the agent of APPLY. If it is bivalent, the agents of both predicates are coreferential; the two patients have disjoint reference.

2.3.2   Applicative Types and Lookalikes

With respect to whether applicatives contrast with other monoclausal constructions in a given language, consider the *e*-operation in Tolai (91), which,

---

[26] Austin (2005) actually proposes a general transitivizing predicate AFFECT, of which APPLY (our term) is a special case. See Section 2.1.1 for the functional predicate of prototypical causatives.

unlike prototypical applicatives, can introduce a patient to the clause. Rather unexpectedly from the perspective of western European languages, the syntactically monovalent predicate *momo* 'drink' cannot accommodate a patientive object unless the latter is licensed via valency increase (b):[27]

(91)   Tolai (Austronesian, Papua New Guinea; Mosel 1991: 248)

    a. *A   vavina   i   momo.*
       ART woman 3.SBJ drink
      'The woman drank (something).' (non-applicative)

    b. *A   vavina   i   mom=e   ra   tava.*
       ART woman 3.SBJ drink=APPL ART water
      'The woman drank the water.' (applicative)

Something similar happens in Lauje (92), where the *a'e*-operation has to be used in order to denote an event involving a beneficiary (with undergoer (a) and agent voice (b) forms), since there is no non-applicative version of such clauses:

(92)   Lauje (Austronesian, Indonesia; Himmelmann 2002: 135)

    a. *setela   p<in>o-gutu-a'e   balung   e   e'e*
       after   GER<UV.REAL>-make-APPL provisions PARAG DIST
      'when those provisions had been made (for him)'

    b. *Tuai-'u   moN-'oni-a'e   lia'e.*
       younger.sibling-1SG.GEN AV.IRR-carry-APPL 1SG
      'My brother is going to carry (it) for me.'

In other words, applicatives like the Halkomelem, Ndendeule, Tolai, and Lauje operations in (87) and (89)–(92) are the only way to express those particular states of affairs with a single clause in those languages. By contrast, other applicatives – like the German operations in (88) and (94) – stand in opposition to monoclausal constructions that express a similar meaning. A further case in point is the Indonesian *kan*-operation (93); the beneficiary *saya* 'I' is an adjunct in (a) but a core argument in (b):[28]

(93)   Standard Indonesian (Shibatani 1996: 160)

    a. *Dia mem-buat   kursi   itu   untuk saya.*
       3SG AV-make   chair   DEIC for   1SG
      'He made this chair for me.'

---

[27] Lehmann and Verhoeven (2006) call such an operation "extraversive" and see it as an unproductive lexical process that (i) has syntactic consequences similar to the ones found with the real applicative and (ii) introduces arguments whose roles are determined by the base predicate (unlike with their "applicative," which introduces recipients, beneficiaries, instruments, or comitatives irrespective of the base predicate).

[28] Kulikov (2011a) distinguishes his (more restrictive) applicatives from his "2/3 permutations" along these lines: Example (90) qualifies as an instance of the former, while (92) illustrates the latter.

    b. *Dia mem-buat-kan   saya kursi itu.*
       3SG AV-make-APPL 1SG chair DEIC
       'He made me this chair.'

In the spirit of mainstream terminology, which favors using APPLICATIVE for a variety of constructions and further qualifying the term if needed, Donohue (2003) suggests using NONDYNAMIC and DYNAMIC APPLICATIVES for these two prototypical types. The latter stand in "dynamic and productive" opposition to non-applicative clauses where the extra-thematic participant is coded "with some form of oblique marker" in a given language, whereas for the former there is no such alternative strategy.[29]

The applicatives presented in (87)–(89) above increase syntactic valency by introducing an object to the clause. It is common to find a different operation marked by the same morphology; such REMAPPING APPLICATIVES merely re-allocate grammatical relations without either increasing the overall syntactic valency or altering the semantic valency. Some German *be*-applicatives actually belong to this non-prototypical type:

(94)   German
      a. *Er   lud   das   Heu   auf   den   Wagen.*
         he.NOM loaded[3SG] ART   hay   on   ART   wagon
         'He loaded the hay onto the wagon.' (non-applicative)
      b. *Er   be-lud   den   Wagen mit   dem Heu.*
         he.NOM APPL-loaded[3SG]   ART   wagon with ART hay
         'He loaded the wagon with the hay.' (applicative)

In the non-applicative voice (a), the theme is the direct object (*das Heu* 'the hay') and the location is expressed as a prepositional object (*auf den Wagen* 'onto the wagon'). In the applicative voice (b), the location appears as the direct object (*den Wagen* 'the wagon') and the theme is expressed by a prepositional object (*mit dem Heu* 'with the hay').

Turning to the question of grammatical relations, the applied object may not be a primary or direct object but have a less prominent grammatical relation instead. Consider the data from Dulong/Rawang in (95) below; the verbal suffix *-ā* introduces a new participant (usually a beneficiary) to the clause, but, instead of being a zero-marked direct or primary object, the NP corresponding to this participant appears either with the postposition *dvpvt* 'for' (a) or the oblique ("locative/dative") marker *-svng* (b):

---

[29] Consider in this context also Beck's (2009: 536–537) definition, which is parallel to his characterization of the causative (a "morpheme that adds a new actant to the semantic valency of the verb, that actant being expressed as a syntactic object"), and his very brief but interesting comments ("applicatives sometimes allow the expression of implicit participants, and there are also applicatives that, for certain verbs, merely promote an oblique object that is already part of the base's semantic valency. Clearly, there is room for a more nuanced discussion of the issue beyond the scope of this paper").

(95)   Dulong (Sino-Tibetan, India and Burma; LaPolla 2000: 305)
    a. *Ngà-í   àng dvpvt shǿng rí-ng-ā-ng-ò-ē.*
       1SG-AGT 3SG for   wood carry-1SG-ND.APPL-1SG-3.TR.NPST-NPST
    b. *Ngà-í   àng-sv̀ng shǿng rí-ng-ā-ng-ò-ē.*
       1SG-AGT 3SG-OBL wood carry-1SG-ND.APPL-1SG-3.TR.NPST-NPST
    Both: 'I am carrying wood for him.'

Beck (2009) proposes the terms DIRECT and NONDIRECT APPLICATIVES in his work on Lushootseed, and this is the terminology we recommend using for the Rawang phenomena as well.[30] Direct applicatives are characterized by the introduced participant having direct object status, like *tiʔəʔ c'ixč'ix̆* '(this) Fish Hawk' in (a) from Lushootseed, while the latter's applied objects are nondirect or obliques (illustrated with data from Georgian in (b) below):[31]

(96)   Direct (prototypical) vs. nondirect (oblique) applicatives
    a. Lushootseed (Salishan, USA; Hess 1995: 153)
        łal   čəd   gʷə=bə=ʔuləx̆-yi-d   tiʔəʔ čixč'ix̆
        also 1SG.SBJ SBJ=ADD=forage-APPL-CAUS DEIC Fish.Hawk
        ʔə   kʷi   sʔuladxʷ.
        OBL DEIC salmon
        'I too can get salmon for Fish Hawk.'
    b. Georgian (Kartvelian, Georgia; Kulikov 2011a: 391)
        Sandro-m bavšv-s ǩoǩa ga-Ø-u-ṭexa.
        S.-ERG   boy-DAT jug PREF-3SG.IOBJ-3.ND.APPL-break.PERF[32]
        'Sandro broke the jug for the boy.'

Similarly, Abaza verbs can take specialized oblique applicative prefixes like *z-* 'benefactive', *čʷ-* 'malefactive', and others, as illustrated in (97) below. The A is indexed on the verb via morphemes that form the ergative series (e.g., *l-* for 3rd person singular feminine), whereas the S/P is indexed by means of markers taken from the absolutive series (*y-* for 3rd person singular neuter or nonhuman). Nevertheless, even though the arguments introduced by the nondirect applicative prefix are allowed to appear as unmarked NPs in the clause – they would take postpositional marking in the non-applicative version – they do not appear as absolutive, but as ergative, prefixes on the verb.[33]

---

[30] Margetts and Austin (2007) call such constructions "oblique applicatives."
[31] Beck (2009) mentions that his direct applicatives demote the original direct object. He allows for the possibility of a third type, however, which creates trivalent predicates with equally ranked or symmetrical objects, like in Upper Necaxa Totonac and Chaga respectively (2009: 540).
[32] The prefixes *i-* for 1st and 2nd person and *u-* for 3rd person are values of the OBJECTIVE VERSION in Kartvelian studies.
[33] O'Herin (2001) does not provide many relevant examples that are suitable for this brief outline, and the 1st-person plural prefix *ħə-* has the disadvantage of covering both absolutive and ergative (as well as the arguments introduced by the applicative). Note, however, that all 3rd-person singular prefixes distinguish these functions: absolutive *d(ə)-* 'human' and *y(ə)-* 'nonhuman' contrast with ergative *l(ə)-* 'feminine', *y(ə)-* 'masculine' and *a-* 'nonhuman'.

(97)   Abaza (Northwest Caucasian, Russia and Turkey; O'Herin 2001: 481)

    a. *Y-ħə-z-ʕa-kʷə-l-c'a-t'.*
       3SG.N.ABS-1PL.AOBJ-ND.APPL:BEN-DRCT-PREF-3SG.F.ERG-put-TAM
       'She put it (here) for us.'

    b. *Y-ħə-čʷ-ʕa-kʷə-l-c'a-t'.*
       3SG.N.ABS-1PL.AOBJ-ND.APPL:MAL-DRCT-PREF-3SG.F.ERG-put-TAM
       'She put it (here) against our will.'

Nondirect applicatives may be more widespread than the language-specific and typically opaque terminology used to label them suggests; in-depth research on such constructions would possibly uncover not only more of them but also different subtypes. The last case in point to be mentioned here is the grammatical relation introduced by some preverbal elements in Algonquian languages – something Rhodes (2010) labels "relative root complements" in his study of the construction as found in Ottawa Ojibwa (98). (Note that this language has primary and secondary, rather than direct and indirect, objects.)

(98)   Ojibwa (Algonquian, Canada and USA; Rhodes 2010: 306–307)

    a. *Od-ozhit-amaw-aa-an*   *wii=agwi-ini-d.*
       3A-make-APPL-3OBJ.ANIM-OBV   FUT=wear-OBV-3.CNJ
       'She is making it for her so she can wear it.' (primary applicative)

    b. *Aniniw-ing=sh*   *go*   *naa*   *o-gii=iN-aabam-aa-an*
       man-LOC=PTCL   PTCL   PTCL 3A-PST=ND.APPL-see-3OBJ.ANIM-OBV
       aniwi   *manidoo-an.*
       this.OBV spirit-OBV
       'He saw the spirit in the form of a man.' (nonprimary applicative)

The primary applicative characterized by the element *-amaw* in (a) introduces a beneficiary and grants it primary object status (even though there is no corresponding lexical NP in this particular clause). By contrast, the nondirect applicative characterized by the "relative root" *iN-* 'like, in a certain way' in (b) introduces the participant *aniniw* 'man', which has a grammatical relation that clearly differs from primary objects; in fact, several morphosyntactic diagnostics place it after secondary objects and before adjuncts. Note that this nondirect applicative introduces an argument with a semantic role that is cross-linguistically uncommon.

Some kinds of NOMINAL INCORPORATION are a special case of applicativization. In some types of such constructions, as illustrated in (99), a syntactically bivalent verb can accommodate a different participant in the clause which is now a semantic argument thanks to the operation; the object is the P (*soβá* 'his face') in (a), while it is the G in (b), which has the T (*-oβá* 'face') as incorporate. (See 7.3 for other types of this operation.)

(99)   Tupinambá (Tupí-Guaraní, Brazil; Mithun 1984: 857)

    a. *S-oβá*   *a-yos-éy.*
       his-face   1SG.A-it-wash

    b. *A-s-oβá-éy.*
       1SG.A-him-face-wash
       Both: 'I washed his face.'

A different kind of situation can be seen in (100) from Amharic (Afro-Asiatic, Ethiopia). We have labeled this construction PSEUDO-APPLICATIVE here:[34]

(100)   Amharic (Amberber 2000: 321)
          a. *Aster mət'rəgiya-w-in   dəǰǰ   t'ərrəgə-čč-ibb-ət.*
             A.(F) broom(M)-DEF-ACC doorway sweep.PFV-3F.SBJ-PS.APPL-3M.OBJ
          b. *Aster bə-mət'rəgiya-w   dəǰǰ   t'ərrəgə-čč(-ibb-ət).*
             A.(F) OBL-broom(M)-DEF doorway sweep.PFV-3F.SBJ-PS.APPL-3M.OBJ
          Both: 'Aster swept a doorway with the broom.'

The suffix *-(i)bb* allows the instrument *mət'rəgiyaw* 'the broom' to appear with the accusative suffix in (a) – instead of the oblique marker *bə-* it takes in the (b)-sentence, which has a number of possible English translations (including 'with', 'by', 'at', 'on'). Nevertheless, *-(i)bb* is invariably accompanied by personal morphology (here: *-ət* '3M.OBJ'), and it is a necessary, rather than a sufficient, condition for prototypical object marking on the lexical NP. (Note that prototypical applicativization is both necessary and sufficient for object status and prototypical object marking.) It might be argued that the function of some of these pseudo-applicatives, rather than introducing new participants to a clause or promoting adjunct participants to objecthood, is to express explicitly that the direct/primary object is not a patient of the verb.[35]

Finally, there are two construction-independent ways in which a diathetical operation can introduce a new non-agentive subject to the clause – thus failing to meet the criteria to be called OBJECTIVE APPLICATIVIZATION and justifying the use of the term SUBJECTIVE APPLICATIVIZATION. First, such a result can be the by-product of the basic syntactic organization of languages with a patient voice (see the introduction to Chapter 3) as the sole two-argument clause (like Dyirbal). Second, it can be the by-product of the syntactic organization of languages with both an agent voice and a patient voice as two-argument clauses (like Mapudungun).

The definition in (86) above has object status as criterial, and since it is arguably the A rather than the P that bears that grammatical relation in Dyirbal two-argument clauses, the *lma*-operation illustrated in (101) below does not alter the assignment of objecthood; 'the man' is the object in both sentences, and it is the subject that switches from 'the woman' in (a) to 'the stick' in (b):

---

[34] Amberber (2000: 321–322), obviously using a much broader definition of the term, says it "can be described as applicative [. . .] [since it allows] an erstwhile peripheral argument [to occur] as a core argument."

[35] Some recent studies use the term in a slightly different way, namely for lexicalized applicatives that no longer introduce arguments to the clauses headed by their predicate stems (Good 2007, Pacchiarotti 2017).

(101)   Dyirbal (Pama-Nyungan, Australia; Dixon 1972: 93, 95)

    a.   *Balan*   *dyugumbil*   *baŋgul*   *yaṟa-ŋgu*

        ART.II.ABS   woman(II)[ABS]   ART.I.ERG   man(I)-ERG

        baŋgu   *yugu-ŋgu*   *balga-n.*

        ART.III.ERG   stick(III)-INS   hit-NFUT

    b.   *Bala*   *yugu*   *baŋgul*   *yaṟa-ŋgu*

        ART.III.ABS   stick(III)[ABS]   ART.I.ERG   man(I)-ERG

        balga-lma-n   *bagun*   *dyugumbil-gu.*

        hit-APPL-NFUT   ART.II.DAT   woman(II)-DAT

    Both: 'The man is hitting the woman with a stick.'

Undergoer nucleativization covers operations allowing non-agentive participants to become core arguments in general (objects or subjects), and objective
applicatives that target direct/primary objects are a special case thereof. The
lma-operation of Dyirbal constitutes the other case: subjective applicativization. Other than the "ergative syntax" basis, such constructions, found in some
Australian languages like Dyirbal, are analogous to their Bantu or Salishan
counterparts – they typically allow a non-patient to become a core argument –
even though they alter subject, rather than object, assignment. (See Austin 2005
for a discussion of applicative-antipassive interactions in Kalkatungu, Yidiny,
and Dyirbal.)

    The applicatives of Mapudungun present a similar problem when the state
of affairs involves a speech act participant (102). In all SAP↔3 interactions
expressed by two- or three-argument clauses, the 1st or 2nd person is the subject,
and the 3rd person is the primary object (or some kind of objective core
argument), irrespective of agentivity and affectedness. Consequently, *-(l)el* qualifies as objective applicative in the (direct) agent voice (a), where the subject
A is 1SG and the primary object G is a 3rd person, but as subjective applicative
in the (inverse) patient voice (b), where the primary object A is a 3rd person
and the subject G is 1SG (the T, *kuram* 'egg(s)', is a secondary object in both
clauses):

(102)   Mapudungun (unclassified, Chile and Argentina)

    a.   *Küpal-el-fi-n*   *kuram.*

        bring-APPL-3.P-1SG.IND   egg

        'I brought her/him some eggs.' (objective applicative)

    b.   *Küpal-el-e-n-mew*   *kuram.*

        bring-APPL-INV-1SG.IND-3.A   egg

        'S/he brought me some eggs.' (subjective applicative)

Note that the subject-object alternation in Mapudungun is governed by factors
that are not related to applicativization; the syntactic alternation reveals a general
sensitiveness to a nominal hierarchy where 1st and 2nd persons outrank 3rd
persons. (Something similar happens in Northern Sasak and Balinese, albeit with
several of the characteristic features of western Austronesian languages; see
Section 4.1.)

2.3.3   Variation of Applicatives

2.3.3.1   Morphological Variation of Applicatives

Part of the morphological variation of applicatives is related to the origins of the markers involved. Some are affixes – possibly with some specific semantics but basically the finished product of some grammaticalization process, fully integrated as they arguably are into the predicate word or predicate complex. Such affixes may, however, have developed from erstwhile independent verbs occurring in complex predicates.[36] We follow Creissels (2010) in calling constructions in which a verb introduces a non-agentive participant as a nonsubject argument into a monoclausal structure APPLICATIVE PERIPHRASES.

The three basic formal types of such periphrases can be seen from the benefactive examples in (103) below. A serial verb construction, where each of the serialized elements could appear as sole matrix-clause predicate in its own right, is shown in (a). Ranking constructions in which there is a formal asymmetry between a finite verb and a nonfinite one follow; (b) illustrates what Creissels calls a "marked lexical verb" construction and corresponds to the widespread strategy in which the functional or operator verb (here: *di-* 'give') is finite while the lexical one is nonfinite (here: as *ūn*-converb); (c) illustrates the much rarer "marked operator verb" subtype, in which it is the lexical verb that is finite. (Within Type (b), verbs of giving are cross-linguistically the most frequent operator choice for benefactive applicatives; verbs of taking are common for instrumental applicatives.)

(103)   Applicative periphrases
    a. Serial verb construction: Baule (Kwa, Ivory Coast; Creissels 2010: 34)
        Ákísí   *à-tɔ̀n*   *duô*   *à-màn*   *Kòfí.*
        A.   PERF-cook   yam   PERF-give   K.
        'Akissi has cooked yam for Kofi.'
    b. Marked lexical verb: Marathi (Pardeshi 1998: 147–148)
        Rām-ne   *Sitā-lā*   *bāg*   *zāḍ-ūn*   *di-l-ī.*
        R.-ERG   S.-DAT   garden(F)   sweep-CVB   give-PST-SG.F
        'Ram swept the garden for Sita.'
    c. Marked operator verb: Mankon (Grassfields Bantu, Cameroon; Leroy 2003: 459)
        Mà   *m↑ɨ́*   *fàʔá*   *ɣ↑á*   *mbó*   *zúɔ́.*
        1SG   FUT   work   give.NFIN   to   3SG.ENUNC
        'I will work for him.'

It is not uncommon for applicatives and causatives to share a common form – a fact generally referred to in the typological literature as the "causative/applicative syncretism" (Shibatani & Pardeshi 2002) or "causative/applicative isomorphism" (Peterson 2007).[37] The descriptive literature occasionally labels such

---

[36] Applicative markers can also originate as adpositions that migrate towards the clause head (see Chapter 8).

[37] See also Austin (2005) for similar instances of such syncretism in Pama-Nyungan languages.

applicative-cum-causative markers (GENERAL) TRANSITIVIZERS. We address the diachrony of this phenomenon in Chapter 8.

2.3.3.2 Syntactic Variation of Applicatives

Most formal variation with applicatives stems from the fact that not all applied objects acquire all properties associated with direct/primary objects (and base objects retain some of their original properties). This distinction is usually labeled as SYMMETRIC versus ASYMMETRIC APPLICATIVES. With the former (104), both applied and base objects show direct/primary object properties like agreement type and the possibility of passivization:

(104)   Kinyarwanda (Bantu, Rwanda; Kimenyi 1980: 32)
  a.   *Umukoôbwa   a-ra-som-er-a*   *umuhuûngu   igitabo.*
       girl.I   I.SBJ-PRES-read-APPL-ASP   boy.I   book.IX
       'The girl is reading a book for the boy.'
  b.   *Umugóre   a-rá-kor-er-a*   *umugabo.*
       man.I   I.SBJ-PRES-read-APPL-ASP   woman.I
       'The woman is working for the man.'

With asymmetric applicatives like the ones in (105)–(106), only the applied object shows these properties:

(105)   Kinyarwanda (Kimenyi 1980: 92)
  a.   *Umuhuûngu   á-r-íig-ir-á-ho*   *ishuûri   imibáre.*
       boy.I   I.SBJ-PRS-study-APPL-ASP-LOC   school   mathematics
       'The boy is studying mathematics at school.'
  b.   **Umuhuûngu á-r-íig-ir-á-ho*   *ishuûri.*
       boy.I   I.SBJ-PRS-study-APPL-ASP-LOC   school
       Intended: 'The boy is studying at school.'

(106)   Lunda (Bantu, Zambia; Givón and Kawasha 2006: 24–25)[38]
  a.   *W-a-tuuñ-il*   *Mari   itala.*
       3SG.SBJ-PST-build-APPL   M.   house
       'S/he built Mary a house.'
  b.   *Itala   a-a-di-tuuñ*   *kudi-Mari.*
       house   3PL.SBJ-PST-NHUM.OBJ-build   DAT-M.
       'The house was built for Mary.'
  c.   *Taata   a-a-mu-tuuñ-ila*   *itala   kudi-Mari.*
       father   3PL.SBJ-PST-3SG.OBJ-build-APPL   house DAT-M.
       'Father was built a house by Mary.'
  d.   **Itala   a-a-di-tuuñ-ila*   *taata   kudi-Mari.*
       house   3PL.SBJ-PST-NHUM.OBJ-build-APPL   father DAT-M.
       (Intended: 'The house was built for father by Mary.')

---

[38] The Lunda passive is described by the authors as non-prototypical in that it is non-promotional in the morphology (hence the 3rd person plural marking *a-* on the passive) but promotional in the syntax.

Symmetric applicatives are reported to apply indistinctly to base predicates of either valency; asymmetric ones appear not to allow unergatives or static predicates.[39]

Pylkkänen's (2008: 12f) distinction between HIGH and LOW APPLICATIVES addresses the question of base predicate valency and some of the issues raised by the symmetric–asymmetric distinction.[40] High applicatives like those in the Vunjo variety of Chaga (107) "denote a relation between an event and an individual," that is, they add a participant – in this case, a beneficiary – to the base event portrayed by the verb, which may be bivalent (a) or monovalent (b):

(107)   Chaga (Bantu, Tanzania; Bresnan & Moshi 1990: 148–149)
    a. *N-ǎ-í-lyì-í-à*   *mkà*   *kélyà.*
        FOC-I.SBJ-PRS-eat-APPL-ASP wife.I   food.VII
        'He is eating food for/on his wife.'
    b. *N-ǎ-í-zrìc-í-à*   *mbùyà.*
        FOC-I.SBJ-PRS-run-APPL-ASP friend.IX
        'He is running for a friend.'

By contrast, low applicatives like the one in Chimwiini (108) "denote a relation between two individuals," that is, their applied objects bear no semantic relation to the verb but there is merely "a transfer of possession relation between the new participant and the direct object":[41]

(108)   Chimwiini (Bantu, Somalia; Kisseberth & Abasheikh 1974: 123)
    Ni-mw-andik-il̵-il-e   *Nu:ru xati.*
    1SG.SBJ-I.OBJ-write-APPL-ASP-ASP N.   letter
    'I wrote Nuru a letter.'

While high applicatives apply to base predicates of either valency, low applicatives are said to be redirective only. The high–low distinction also helps to distinguish Japanese so-called gapless malefactives on the one hand (which are high applicatives) from Hebrew external possessive constructions and Japanese gapped malefactives on the other (which are low applicatives). Note that Pylkkänen further distinguishes between two subtypes of low applicatives, namely "recipient" or *to*-applicatives (like the English double object construction just

---

[39] See Baker (1988: Ch. 5), Bresnan & Moshi (1990), Marantz (1993), Alsina & Mchombo (1993), Ngonyani (2000), Ngonyani & Githinji (2006), Marten et al. (2007), and Marten & Kula (2012) for more details on this and related distinctions in Bantu languages.

[40] The terms *high* and *low* stem from where, in Pylkkänen's view, the "Applicative Head" that introduces the new argument is placed in a given phrase structure (viz., higher and lower than the verb and its direct object, respectively).

[41] Pylkkänen models the high–low distinction in terms of semantics, as well as configuration: an applicative head introduces the applied objects, but while with high applicatives this functional head is a sister of the verb phrase, with low applicatives the applicative head is verb phrase internal. See Pylkkänen (2008: Ch. 2) and Jeong (2007) for more details.

illustrated) and "source" or *from*-applicatives (where the transfer of possession takes place from, not to, the new participant).[42]

Finally, note that some remapping applicatives may actually reduce the syntactic valency of the clause (Malchukov 2017; see also Austin 2005 for similar phenomena in Yidiny, Kalkatungu, and Dyirbal). A case in point is the German *be*-applicative with a semantically trivalent like *schenken* 'give as a gift':

(109) German
   a. *Ich*   *schenk-te*   *den*   *Kinder-n*   *Kleidung.*
      1SG.NOM give-PST[3SG] ART.PL.DAT child.PL-DAT clothes
   b. *Ich*   *be-schenk-te*   *die*   *Kinder*   *mit*
      1SG.NOM APPL-give-PST[3SG] ART.PL.ACC child.PL[ACC] with
      Kleidung.
      clothes
   Both: 'I gave clothes to the children as a gift.'

In (a), the T is a direct object in the accusative and the G is an indirect object in the dative. In (b), however, the G is the direct object in the accusative, but the T appears as a prepositional oblique (which is frequently omitted in spontaneous discourse).[43]

2.3.3.3 Semantic Variation of Applicatives

Some applicatives indistinctly derive verbs from either monovalent or bivalent predicates, like German *be-*; consider monovalent *wohnen* 'dwell' vs. bivalent *bewohnen* 'inhabit' vis-à-vis bivalent *rühren* 'move, stir' vs. bivalent *berühren* 'touch'. Nevertheless, it is not uncommon to find markers that are syntactically specialized: in her study of applicatives in Salishan languages, Kiyosawa (2006) distinguishes between a RELATIONAL and a REDIRECTIVE type along these lines. The former typically enables monovalent predicates to accommodate stimuli, goals, or topics of *verba dicendi* (110):

(110) Okanagan (Salishan, Canada; Kiyosawa 2006: 1–2)
   a. *Kən*   *n-x̌íɬ.*
      1SG.SBJ   LOC-afraid
      'I got scared.' (non-applicative)
   b. *N-x̌íɬ-mə-nt-s-ən.*
      LOC-afraid-APPL-TR-2SG.OBJ-1SG.SBJ
      'I got scared of you (SG).' (relational applicative)

---

[42] Some studies have proposed reducing the symmetric–asymmetric and the high–low oppositions to only one basic opposition – see, e.g., McGinnis (2005) and McGinnis and Gerdts (2004). According to Jeong (2007), however, these two distinctions cannot be collapsed into one another, nor can they be reduced to some other distinction: the symmetric–asymmetric opposition is best seen as a function of several variables that include the high–low distinction and the difference between structural and inherent case, among others (2007: 86–87). Such an analytical move allows Jeong to account for cases not predicted by the reductionist approach, namely high asymmetric and low symmetric applicatives, in an elegant way.

[43] Peter Austin (pers. comm.) aptly pointed out that an alternative analysis of the (b)-construction would be as a two-argument clause with an adjunct. In either case, syntactic valency is reduced by the applicative operation.

By contrast, the redirective type enables bivalent predicates to accommodate recipients, beneficiaries, possessors, or sources (111):[44]

(111)   Shuswap (Salishan, Canada; Kiyosawa 2006: 3)
    a. *M-k̓úl-n-s*   *γ*   *mim̓x.*
        PERF-make-TR-3.SBJ   DET   basket
        'She made the basket.' (non-applicative)
    b. *M-k̓úl-x-t-s*   *γ*   *núx̌ʷənx̌ʷ*   *tə*   *mim̓x.*
        PERF-make-APPL-TR-3.SBJ   DET woman   OBL basket
        'She made a basket for the woman.' (redirective applicative)

Unlike causatives, which show considerable uniformity regarding the semantics of the argument they introduce to the clause (see Section 2.1), applied objects can bear fairly disparate semantic roles, namely beneficiaries and maleficiaries, locations, instruments, and comitatives, among others.[45] Semantically unspecified applicatives are not uncommon; Indonesian *-kan*, for instance, derives both benefactive (b) and instrumental (d) applicatives:[46]

(112)   Standard Indonesian
    a. *Ibu*   *me-masak* *nasi* *goreng-nya* *untuk teman saya.*
        mother AV-cook rice   fried-DEF   for   friend 1SG
        'Mother cooked the fried rice for my friend.' (Sneddon 1996: 79)
    b. *Ibu*   *me-masak-kan*   *teman*   *saya nasi* *goreng-nya.*
        mother AV-cook-APPL friend   1SG   rice   fried-DEF
        'Mother cooked my friend the fried rice.' (Sneddon 1996: 79)
    c. *Dia*   *meng-ikat*   *anjing* *dengan* *tali.*
        3SG   AV-tie   dog   with   rope
        'He tied up the dog with a rope.' (Vamarasi 1999: 73)
    d. *Dia*   *meng-ikat-kan*   *tali*   *ke*   *anjing.*
        3SG   AV-tie-APPL   rope   to(wards) dog
        'He tied the rope to the dog.' (Vamarasi 1999: 73)

Another example of such general applicatives is found in Chaga (113), where the marker *-i* can be used in benefactive/malefactive (a), instrumental (b), locative (c), and circumstantial (d) applicative constructions:

(113)   Chaga (Bresnan & Moshi 1990: 148–149)
    a. *N-ǎ-í-lyì-í-à*   *mkà*   *kélyà.*
        FOC-I.SBJ-PRS-eat-APPL-ASP wife.I   food.VII
        'He is eating food for/on his wife.'

---

[44] See also Kittilä's (2002: 263–269) related distinction between "extended intransitives, benefactive/ malefactive constructions and cognate object constructions." Kittilä's main concern in his exposition is the effect of these three operations on the transitivity of events.

[45] See Austin (2001: 64f) for analogous phenomena in Balinese and the Ngeno-ngene variety of Sasak.

[46] In actual fact, Indonesian *-kan* is best seen as a general valency-increasing operator, since it also derives causativized verbs from monovalent bases.

b. *N-ã̀-ĩ́-lyì-í-à*   *màwòkő*   *kêlyâ.*
FOC-I.SBJ-PRS-eat-APPL-ASP   hand.VI   food.VII
'S/he is eating food with his/her hands.'

c. *N-ã̀-ĩ́-lyì-í-à*   *m̀rì-nyì*   *kélyà.*
FOC-I.SBJ-PRS-eat-APPL-ASP   homestead.III-LOC[47]   food.VII
'S/he is eating food at the homestead.'

d. *N-ã̀-ĩ́-lyì-í-à*   *njáá*   *kêlyâ.*
FOC-I.SBJ-PRS-eat-APPL-ASP   hunger.IX   food.VII
'S/he is eating the food because of hunger.'

Many languages, including some in the Bantu family, have specialized applicatives. Kinyarwanda, for instance, employs *-er, -iish,* and *-ho* as markers of the three cross-linguistically common applicative subtypes benefactive/malefactive, instrumental, and locative, respectively. The Tibeto-Burman language Hakha Lai (114) is also known for having morphologically distinct markers for its benefactive (a), instrumental (b), and comitative (c) applicatives:

(114)   Hakha Lai (Tibeto-Burman, Southeast Asia; Peterson 2007: 41)

a. *Tsewmaŋ=niʔ   door=ʔaʔ   ʔa-ka-kal-piak.*
T.=ERG   market=ALL/LOC   3SG.SBJ-1SG.OBJ-go-APPL:BEN
'Tsewmang went to the market for me.'

b. *Tiilooŋ   khaa   tivaa   kan-Ø-tan-naak.*
boat   TOP   river   1PL.SBJ-3SG.OBJ-cross-APPL:INS
'We used the boat to cross the river.'

c. *Ka-law   ʔan-ka-thloʔ-pii.*
1SG.PSR-field   3PL.SBJ-1SG.OBJ-weed-APPL:COM
'They weeded my field (together) with me.'

Furthermore, Hakha Lai shows some specialized applicatives that are cross-linguistically infrequent (115). There is an additional-benefactive applicative, which denotes that the agent-benefactor performs an action for his/her own benefit in addition to the benefit of another (a). There is a malefactive-allative applicative, which usually indicates "some kind of malice or harmful intent on the part of the subject towards the object it introduces" (Peterson 2007: 19) (b). With the prioritive applicative, the agent performs an action before the applied object (c). Lastly, with the relinquitive applicative, the subject leaves the applied object behind to perform an action (d):

(115)   Hakha Lai (Peterson 2007: 41,19)

a. *Thiŋ   ʔa-ka-laak-tseʔm.*
wood   3SG.SBJ-1SG.OBJ-carry-APPL:ADD.BEN
'He carried wood for me (in addition to carrying wood for himself).'

---

[47] Bresnan and Moshi (1990: 149) say that the Chaga locative suffix *-nyi* is to be understood not as an oblique case marker – which would question the object status, or at least the prototypical morphological marking, of the participant expressing location in such constructions – but as a "locative noun class" marker instead. In their analysis, the constituent *m̀rìnyì* is a bona fide applied object.

b. *Kheeŋ*   *ʔa-ka-hloʔn-hnoʔ.*
    dish   3SG.SBJ-1SG.OBJ-throw-APPL:MAL/ALL
    'She threw the dish at me.'

c. *Booy*   *ʔa-ka-toon-kaʔn.*
    chief   3SG.SBJ-1SG.OBJ-meet-APPL:PRIOR
    'He met the chief ahead of / before me.'

d. *ʔa-law*   *ʔa-ka-thloʔ-taak.*
    3SG.PSR-field   3SG.SBJ-1SG.OBJ-weed-APPL:RELINQ
    'He left me and weeded his field.'

In general, the roles borne by applied objects are usually more peripheral than those of base objects, but remember that some applicatives may also introduce patients – the Tolai example above (91) is a case in point – or, at least, involve some modulation of patientivity or affectedness. An example of the latter is the default German *be*-construction, which might be called COMPREHENSIVE APPLICATIVE following Haspelmath and Müller-Bardey (2004), because the applied object is more patient-like when compared to its semantic status before applicativization (the authors say that "the affectedness of the object participant is more important").[48] This is certainly the case with Examples (88) and (94) above, where *be-angeln* 'fish' and *be-laden* 'load' unmistakably imply that the object is affected in its near (relevant) entirety. Whereas one can *laden* 'load' a small or big amount of hay onto a wagon of any size, to *be-laden* 'load' a wagon means that the wagon is (almost) full after the process. The same happens in the following example, where the English translation attempts to capture this semantic effect; in (a) she could in principle throw only two eggs at him, while in (b) she either throws many more eggs, or 2–3 eggs that are so unusually large that he is covered in yolk and egg white nonetheless:

(116)   German (Haspelmath & Müller-Bardey 2004: 36)
        a. *Sie*   *schmeiß-t*   *Eier*   *auf*   *ihn.*
            she   throw-3SG   eggs   on   him
            'She throws eggs at him.' (non-applicative)
        b. *Sie*   *be-schmeiß-t* *ihn*   *mit*   *Eiern.*
            she   APPL-throw-3SG him   with   eggs
            'She bombards him with eggs.' (applicative)

2.3.4   Distribution of Applicatives

According to Polinsky (2013b), 45 percent of her 183-language sample have applicative constructions of some kind, but this figure probably

---

[48] We are glossing over two uses of German *be-* that deviate from this general pattern, namely its use with high frequency verbs (where it is often lexicalized and does not show the affectedness modulation, e.g., *schreiben* 'write' vs. *be-schreiben* 'describe') and its use with nominal elements (e.g., *Blume* 'flower' vs. *be-blumen* 'supply with flowers').

underestimates the real proportion (e.g., Yupik and Mapudungun appear as applicative-less languages in her study, but such a classification is problematic). Polinsky notes that applicatives are particularly common in some regions of the world (Africa, the western Pacific, and North and Meso-America) and some families (Bantu, Austronesian, Salishan, Uto-Aztecan, and Mayan). These constructions seem to be commonly found in languages with little or no case marking on NPs and with rather rich verb morphology – but Pama-Nyungan languages constitute an exception to this generalization, showing as they do rich case morphology. Polinsky also says that

> [t]he dearth of applicatives in Eurasia may thus be due to the widespread presence of rich nominal morphology in the languages of that area, and indeed, where applicatives are found is in languages like Abkhaz and Abaza (Northwest Caucasian; Georgia and Russia) [...].

Polinsky (2013b) further explores two sources of variation in her sample, namely the specificity related to valency mentioned at the beginning of Section 2.3.2 and the semantic specificity mentioned in Section 2.3.3.3. Even though her sample is relatively small (only 83 languages of her 183 have applicatives), the results are noteworthy (see Table 2.3 below). First, languages with applicatives formed exclusively from monovalent bases seem to be extremely rare; Polinsky's only instances are Wambaya (Mirndi, Australia) and Fijian (Oceanic, Fiji). (But Austin 2005 shows that many Pama-Nyungan languages have only applicatives from monovalent bases.) Second, applicatives that take bases of either valency appear to be much more common than restrictive ones. Third, even though benefactive applicatives are much more common than other semantically specialized ones, the most frequently found semantic type is the non-specialized one.

Peterson's (2007) work on a survey of 100 languages, 50 of which had applicatives, provides additional generalizations. While locus of marking and constituent order are not found to contribute to predicting whether languages have applicative constructions, a negative correlation with dominant accusative alignment appears to be robust. He also finds a positive correlation between benefactive and circumstantial applicatives and passives. Most remarkably, Peterson's findings clearly suggest the existence of an implicational hierarchy:

Table 2.3 *Polinsky's (2013b) two parameters of variation of applicatives*

	BEN only	BEN and other SRs	SRs other than BEN
Monovalent base only	—	—	2
Bivalent base only	4	2	1
Base of either valency	16	49	9

locative and circumstantial applicatives require the existence of other applicative constructions, whereas benefactive and instrumental/comitative applicatives do not.

2.4   Antiapplicatives

The term ANTIAPPLICATIVE has only seldom been used in descriptive, theoretical, or typological studies. If understood as a strict analogy to *antipassive*, it refers to an operation whose result is thought of as mirror image of the applicative in some way. Nevertheless, since the latter is often understood as a remapping, rather than as an installing, operation, *antiapplicative* largely overlaps with the P-demoting operation domain called *antipassive* – which perhaps explains the fact that nowadays most studies use the latter as an umbrella term and do not employ the term *antiapplicative* (see Section 2.4.1). If understood as an analogy to *anticausative*, by contrast, it refers to an operation that reverses the installing aspect of the applicative operation, that is, an operation deleting the P from the semantic argument structure. Such a voice is not well-attested, but the reports with which we are acquainted suggest that (i) it may actually exist and (ii) it may be much less frequent cross-linguistically than the anticausative (see Section 2.4.2).

2.4.1   P-Demotion or P-Suppression: Antipassives

According to Haspelmath and Müller-Bardey (2004), *antiapplicative* might be used for operations which do not delete the P from semantic argument structure but merely demote it in the morphosyntax, as in the following Hungarian example:

(117)   Hungarian (Uralic, Hungary; Károly 1982: 187)
    a. *Az   orvos   szán-ja   a   beteg-et.*
          DEF physician pity-3SG.DEF   DEF   patient-ACC
          'The physician pities the patient.'
    b. *Az   orvos   szán-akoz-ik   a   beteg-en.*
          DEF physician pity-ANTIP-3SG.INDEF DEF patient-SUPERESS
          'The physician feels pity for the patient.'

The subject remains unaltered in (b), but the object is demoted to adjunct (which appears here in the superessive case). The verb now takes the unproductive voice marker *-akoz* and changes its subject index from definite *-jA* (normally used with definite objects and subordinate clauses) to an indefinite conjugation index (normally used with indefinite objects, as well as with indefinite, interrogative, and relative pronouns). We call such operations lexically constrained antipassives in this book (see Section 3.2.2).

Haspelmath and Müller-Bardey see the term as equivalent to Geniušienė's "deaccusative" as applied to the *akoz*-construction in Hungarian. The latter author proposes a slightly different term ("deobjective") to cover a particular set of readings of the etymologic reflexive with some 70-odd verbs in Latvian and Lithuanian (Geniušienė 1987: 94). These verbs can be grouped into three classes according to the outcome of the derivation; consider the following example from the Class I:

(118)   Lithuanian (Balto-Slavic, Latvia and Lithuania; Geniušienė 1987: 94)
         a. *Petr-as*   *svaido*   *akmen-is.*
             P.-NOM.SG   throw.3SG   stone-ACC.PL
         b. *Petr-as*   *svaido-si*   *akmen-imis.*
             P.-NOM.SG   throw.3SG-ANTIP   stone-INS.PL
         Both: 'Peter is throwing stones.'

With verbs like 'throw', the effect of the operation is only to demote the direct object to adjunct: the subject remains unaltered. The syntactic demotion correlates with a semantic-pragmatic shift in prominence from the patient and the effect of the action towards the action itself, but the non-agentive argument is a patient in both constructions. Moreover, such derived verbs occur only in the imperfective aspect – base verbs have perfective and imperfective forms – typically with an iterative meaning.

   With Class II verbs like 'splash (in)', 'burrow (in)', and 'dig (in)', the direct object is also demoted to adjunct, but the case marking is different, suggesting that the semantic role has changed as well. According to Geniušienė, the patient of the base construction is a location in the derived one, which in turn no longer has a patient:

(119)   Lithuanian (Geniušienė 1987: 95)
         a. *Petr-as*   *kasa*   *duob-ę.*
             P.-NOM.SG   dig.3SG   pit-ACC.SG
             'Peter is digging a pit.'
         b. *Petr-as*   *kasa-si*   *duob-ėje.*
             P.-NOM.SG   dig.3SG-ANTIP   pit-LOC.SG
             'Peter is digging in the pit.'

   Lastly, with Class III verbs like 'get hold of', 'snatch (at)', and 'grasp', case marking is different as well, suggesting a semantic role of means or instrument rather than patient or location. In Geniušienė's account, instead of 'grasping something with the purpose of keeping it or use it' (a), the derived construction has a meaning of 'grasping at something that can serve as a support or instrument' (b):

(120)   Lithuanian (Geniušienė 1987: 96)
         a. *Petr-as*   *stvėrė*   *lazd-ą.*
             P.-NOM.SG   grasped.3   stick-ACC.SG
             'Peter grasped the stick.'
         b. *Petr-as*   *stvėrė-si*   *už*   *lazd-os.*
             P.-NOM.SG   grasped.3-ANTIP   at   stick-GEN.SG
             'Peter grasped at the stick.'

We also regard this Lithuanian operation as a non-prototypical antipassive (see Section 3.2.2), irrespective of the most adequate analysis of the semantic role modulation, because the P is arguably present in the semantic argument structure in all these cases. Haspelmath and Müller-Bardey (2004) further mention a slightly different group of examples, which they call "deobjectives" themselves. Marantz (1984) uses the term "indefinite object deletion" when noting that not all English verbs allow the alternation between a clause with and without a direct object (121). He surmises that the alternation "is limited to a restricted set of verbs cross-linguistically, and the [relevant] set in a given language seems to have some semantic coherence. [...] The core verbs [...] are the so-called ingestives, for example, 'eat,' 'drink,' and 'learn'" (1984: 193).

(121)   English (Marantz 1984: 179, 192)
    a.   *Elmer ate (mock porcupine pie) late last night.*
    b.   *Elmer locked *(the porcupine cage) late last night.*

Another example cited by Haspelmath and Müller-Bardey is what Shibatani calls "generalized object," which also targets verbs of ingestion:

(122)   Ainu (unclassified, Japan; Shibatani 1990: 46)
    a.   *Sake*   *a-ku.*   b.   *I-ku-an.*
          sake   1SG-drink   ANTIP-drink-1SG
          'I drink sake.'   'I drink.'
    c.   *Ya*   *a-ske.*   d.   *I-ske-an.*
          net   1SG-knit   ANTIP-knit-1SG
          'I knit a fishing net.'   'I do knitting.'

Lastly, note that Dayley's grammar (1989) calls the analogous *tU*-derivation in Panamint Shoshone "absolute antipassive," describes it as intransitivizing, and notes that indefinite and nonspecific objects are implied when the operation is used, as in (b/d) below:

(123)   Panamint Shoshone (Uto-Aztecan, USA; Dayley 1989: 38, 111)
    a.   *Wa'ippü*   *tukkuapi-tta* *saawa-nna.*
          woman[NOM]   meat-OBJ   boil-ASP
          'The woman is boiling the meat.'
    b.   *Nü*   *tü-saawa-ha.*
          1SG.NOM   ANTIP-boil-STAT
          'I am boiling (something).'
    c.   *Su-tü*   *pai*   *tühüya-nna*   *wasü-ppühantü.*
          that.NVIS-NOM three   deer-OBJ   kill.PL-PST.PFV
          'He killed three deer.'
    d.   *Sa-tü*   *tü-wasü-nnuwi.*
          that.VIS-NOM   ANTIP-kill.PL-walk.around
          'He is going around killing (things).'

Taking widespread current practice into account, which uses "antipassive" as a cover term for most P-demoting voice operations, we call the examples presented in (121)–(123) patientless antipassives in this study (see Section 3.2.2).

2.4.2   P-Removal: Antiapplicatives Proper

While anticausatives, that is, operations that remove an A from the argument structure, are not only well attested but also frequently found and often quite productive worldwide, antiapplicatives that actually remove a P are fairly rare.[49] Some examples come from Cariban languages; consider the following (hitherto apparently exhaustive) list:

(124)   Cariban languages (Gildea et al. forthcoming)
      a. Tiriyó   *ainka* 'grab P and run away' vs. *et-ainka* 'run away'
      b. Hixkaryana *owaxehto* 'stand up to P'   vs. *os-owaxehto* 'stand'
      c. Hixkaryana *ownohï* 'laugh at / mock P' vs. *os-ownohï* 'laugh'
      d. Akawaio *numï* 'leave P (in location X)' vs. *e'-numï* 'go away, leave'

The lexemes on the left-hand side are syntactically bivalent verbs; those on the right-hand side are syntactically monovalent verbs derived from them via affixation of a general detransitivizer, which in these instances arguably deletes the P from the semantics instead of merely demoting it in the syntax. The phenomenon seems to be fairly limited: examples (a–b) are found in the specified languages only, but (c) is found in Panare and Pemón as well, and (d) may exist in Ye'kuana.[50]

2.4.3   Envoi: An Unproductive Northern Sami Construction

Before concluding this section, it is in order to mention one recent, and somewhat perplexing, use of the term in the descriptive literature. Valijärvi and Kahn (2017: 255–257) employ the labels "applicative" and "anti-applicative" for two valency-modifying operations in their grammar of Northern Sami. The former is valency-increasing and specialized for base motion verbs, with an unmistakably causative flavor (and a marker that is "the same as" the causative, i.e., *-hi* ~ *-ahtti*); example pairs include *vázzit* 'walk' vs. *vácci-hi-t* 'walk/take (someone)', *vuodjit* 'drive' vs. *vuoji-hi-t* 'transport, give a ride', and *viehkat* 'run' vs. *viega-hi-t* 'run with (something) / after (someone)'. The "anti-applicative" is what we call a malefactive subjective undergoer nucleative in this book (see Section 2.5.2); it seems to be restricted to avalent meteorological and astronomical predicates. The few examples provided in the grammar include the following:

(125)   Northern Sami (Uralic, Scandinavia; Valijärvi & Kahn 2017: 256)
      a. *dálvat*   'become winter' *dálv-o-t*   'be caught unprepared for winter'
      b. *arvit*   'rain'   *arv-o-t*   'get soaked by rain'
      c. *sevnnjodit* 'get dark'   *sevnnjod-uvva-t* 'be caught by the darkness'

---

[49] See Section 6.2.2.4 for the same diathetical operation in uncoded alternations.
[50] We are indebted to Spike Gildea and Natalia Cáceres for an illuminating discussion of these verbs.

(126)   Northern Sami (Valijärvi & Kahn 2017: 257)
          Hánsa   *vikka-i*   *ceahkku-t*   *dan*   *stobu,*
          H.[NOM]   try-3SG.PST   build-INF   the.ACC   cabin.ACC
            muhto   *dálv-u-i.*
            but   become.winter-SUNUCL:MAL-3SG.PST
          'Hánsa tried to build the cabin, but he was caught unprepared by the winter.'

2.5   Subjective Undergoer Nucleatives

We saw in Section 2.3.2 above that sometimes a voice operation may introduce a non-agentive participant as a subject to the clause, which is like an applicative and a causative on the one hand, and quite unlike either on the other. In those cases, rather than the construction itself, it is the general syntactic organization of the language that leads to that outcome – more precisely, the existence of the patient voice, either as the only two-argument structure (e.g., in Dyirbal) or as one of two two-argument structures that obligatorily alternate under specific circumstances (e.g., in Mapudungun).

We now turn to another, more significant, kind of case in which a diathetical operation introduces a non-agentive participant as a subject to the clause, not as a corollary of the general syntax but as a hallmark of the operation itself. First, we address several kinds of operations that, when compared to the base clause type, can be said not only to install arguments different from (run-of-the-mill) agents and patients to the core of the clause, but also to grant them subject status (2.5.1). These subjective undergoer nucleatives play an important role in the description and the contextualization of a large number of Austronesian languages, and they occupy us further in Chapter 4. Second, we take a closer look at one particular (possibly twofold) kind of nucleative construction that seems to stand apart, or at least to be quite unlike those of Philippine languages, both structurally and semantically: the malefactive and possessive (2.5.2).

2.5.1   Philippine Undergoer Nucleatives Introduced

Consider the effect of applicativization and passivization in Mapudungun (127). The syntactically bivalent verb *palol-* 'make sound' in (a) can accommodate a further argument in the clause – here: a beneficiary – thanks to the *el*-applicative in (b). This new participant is introduced as primary object, but thanks to the *nge*-passive, it can be promoted to subject (c):

(127)   Mapudungun[51] (Salas 2006: 165)
          a. *Palol-i*   *wiño.*
              make.sound-IND   *chueca*.stick
              'S/he made a *chueca* stick sound.'

---

[51] Spanish *chueca* (Mapudungun *palin*) is the name of a series of games similar to hockey.

b. *Palol-el-ke-i-ngn*   *ñi*   *wiño.*
   make.sound-APPL-HAB-IND-3PL   3.PSR   *chueca*.stick
   'They make their *chueca* sticks sound for her.'

c. *Palol-el-nge-ke-i*
   make.sound-APPL-PASS-HAB-IND
   fentren   *wiño*   *ka*   *karoti.*
   many   *chueca*.stick   and   club
   'She has many *chueca* sticks and clubs made sound for her.'

Languages that have applicatives and passives, especially when the two operations are marked morphologically, normally allow a combination of both. What is special about some Austronesian languages, however, is that such a combined voice effect need not always be brought about by a two-stage operation: in so-called Philippine-type languages, several voice operations introduce peripheral arguments and promote them to subjecthood at the same time, often with a monomorphemic marker. In addition, clauses headed by such predicates are apparently used much more frequently, both in narratives and in everyday conversation, than their counterparts in North or South American languages similar to Mapudungun.

Consider in this context Ilocano as analyzed by Rubino (1997, 2005). In this language, any NP in the absolutive has to be identifiable by the addressee, is a core syntactic argument in all clause types (Rubino 1997: 448), and is "the most highly thematic argument of [the] clause" (Rubino 2005: 337). In the light of Rubino's morphological and syntactic characterization of this NP in his grammar, we will simply call this NP the subject for our present purposes, aware though we are of how problematic a simple interpretation of such a choice can be. This author describes the Patient Voice as a diathesis with two core arguments, one in the ergative and the other in the absolutive, and a verb marked with a dedicated affix (which shows an allomorphy that need not concern us here). By contrast, the Actor Voice is a one-argument clause with an NP in the absolutive, possibly other NPs in an oblique form, and a verb marked by one of several affixes – that is, an antipassive voice.[52] The following examples illustrate these clause types:

(128)   Ilocano (Austronesian, Philippines; Rubino 1997: 448–449)
   a. *Kaan-in=ko*   *dagiti*   *saba.*
      eat-ACT=1SG.ERG   PL[ABS]   banana
      'I ate the bananas.' (Patient Voice – patient voice)
   b. *Nang-kaan=ak*   *ka-dagiti*   *saba.*
      ANTIP-eat=1SG.ABS   OBL-PL   banana
      'I ate bananas.' (Actor Voice – antipassive voice)

[52] Note in passing that such voice oppositions show considerable variation within western Austronesian; see Section 4.1 for some discussion. In Balinese, for instance, both the Patient and the Actor Voice correspond to two-argument clauses, but verbs are morphologically unmarked with the former while they take a nasal prefix with the latter. In addition, there are two one-argument clauses (viz., the *ka-* and the *a-*passives); see Riesberg (2014b: 15–16) for details and references. In Northern Sasak, several nasal prefixes alternate on the Actor-Voice predicate, encoding the specificity of the P (Austin 2012).

In addition, Ilocano has other constructions that allow participants different from agents and patients to appear as subjects, namely Conveyance, Benefactive, and Directional Voices (plus the Comitative and Instrumental Voices, not illustrated here). These are precisely the clause types we call SUBJECTIVE UNDERGOER NUCLEATIVES from the perspective of grammatical voice: when compared to the base voice, they install an extra-thematic participant as core argument and grant it subject status. We keep Rubino's labels here for convenience (129); what he calls Conveyance is marked with a simple prefix *i-* and installs "a theme [. . .], i.e. an entity that is physically or psychologically conveyed" (2005: 337) (a); his Benefactive is marked by a circumfix *i-. . .-an* and installs a beneficiary (but is often lexicalized) (a–b); and his Directional is marked by a suffix *-an* and installs a source, a goal, or a partially affected patient (c):

(129)   Ilocano (Rubino 2005: 337, 446)
    a. *I-bagá=m*   *ta*
        SUNUCL:CONV-tell=2SG.ERG   CONJ
        i-dasar-án=ka=n.
        SUNUCL:BEN-set.table-SUNUCL:BEN=1SG→2SG=now
        'Tell me and I'll set the table for you (SG).'
    b. *I-gatáng-an=n=ak*
        SUNUCL:BEN-buy-SUNUCL:BEN=2/3SG=1SG.ABS
        man   *iti*   *bagás.*
        please OBL.SG rice
        'Please buy some rice for me.'
    c. *Panaw-an=da=ak=to.*
        leave-SUNUCL:DRCT=3PL.ERG=1SG.ABS=FUT
        'They will leave me.'

Such voices have played an important role in both linguistic theory and linguistic typology since the 1970s, and we address several important issues they raise in Chapter 4.

2.5.2   Malefactive and Possessive Subjective Nucleatives

The Philippine-type subjective undergoer nucleatives introduced in the preceding subsection typically cover extra-thematic notions like beneficiaries, goals, locations, and instruments. Those found in several other languages target maleficiaries and possessors instead.

First, note in (130) that Japanese has (among others) three similar constructions where the verbal clause head takes the suffix *-(r)are*, namely Direct Passive (a), an Indirect Passive (b), and a Possessive Passive (c) (the labels are the ones customarily used in Japanese studies):

(130)   Japanese (Oshima 2008: 145)
    a. *Zirō=ga* *Tarō=ni* *nagur-are-ta.*
        Z.=NOM T.=DAT hit-PASS-PST
        'Ziro was hit by Taro.'

    b. *Zirō=ga   Tarō=ni   Ken=o*   *nagur-are-ta.*
        Z.=NOM T.=DAT K.=ACC   hit-SUNUCL:MAL-PST
        'Taro hit Ken, adversely affecting Ziro.'

    c. *Zirō=ga   Tarō=ni   musuko=o*   *nagur-are-ta.*
        Z.=NOM T.=DAT son=ACC   hit-SUNUCL:POSS-PST
        'Ziro$_i$ had his$_i$ son hit by Taro.'

The clause in (a) is what we call a prototypical passive in this study (see Section 3.1.1); it does not introduce a new argument to the clause but reduces syntactic valency, promoting the P to subject status and demoting the A to adjunct status. The clause in (b), by contrast, introduces a new argument to the clause – a maleficiary that, despite not being an argument of the base verb *naguru* 'hit', is now the subject of the derived verb *nagur-are-* 'be adversely affected by (X) hitting (Y)'. Such so-called indirect passives are also possible with monovalent and even avalent verbs. We call this construction a MALEFACTIVE SUBJECTIVE UNDERGOER NUCLEATIVE. The clause in (c) above is similar to (b), but there is an uncoded possessive relationship between the patient (*musuko* 'son') and the affected participant (*Ziro*) in that case. Note that such POSSESSIVE SUBJECTIVE UNDERGOER NUCLEATIVES have, in principle, neutral semantics; both readings are possible in the following example:

(131)   Japanese (Oshima 2008: 148)
          Tarō=ga   *Hanako=ni*   *kodomo=o*   *home-rare-ta.*
          T.=NOM   H.=DAT   child=ACC   praise-SUNUCL-PST
          Malefactive: 'Hanako$_i$ praised her$_j$/the child, adversely affecting Taro.'
          Possessive: 'Hanako praised Taro's child.'

The following examples show that the malefactive differs from the possessive construction in two important respects. First, it does not appear to be semantically neutral, since even lexical elements suggesting a positive state of affairs, like those in (a), have to be construed as somehow contributing to the subject being negatively affected for the expression to be felicitous.[53] Second, it does not require a possessive involvement between the participants, since Taro may have heard a stranger called Hanako and her own piano at an airport, a concert hall, or anywhere else, for (b) to be felicitous:

(132)   Japanese (Tsuboi 2010: 419–420)
      a. *Tarō=wa   musuko=ni   shōshins-are-ta.*
          T.=TOP   son=DAT   get.a.promotion-SUNUCL:MAL-PST
          'Taro$_i$'s son got a promotion, much to his$_i$ chagrin.'

---

[53] More precisely, this undergoer nucleative actually seems to be neutral at its core, but a conversational implicature including negative effects of the state of affairs on the subject is one of its most salient, albeit still somewhat elusive, hallmarks. Factors that license the construction and/or trigger the implicature include lexical and grammatical features like sentience of the subject and high transitivity of the event, as well as pragmatic/contextual features like specific coreference relations between the participants and a general plausibility of the negative effect on the subject.

b. *Tarō=wa   Hanako=ni   piano=o   hik-are-ta.*
   T.=TOP   H.=DAT   piano=ACC   play-SUNUCL:MAL-PST
   'Taro was adversely affected by Hanako's playing the piano.'

Further note in (133) below that Japanese also has applicative(-like) peri-phrases with meanings and syntactic effects related to those of the malefactive nucleative. These operations are built with a converbal form of the lexical verb plus a finite form of an auxiliary, which can be a verb of receiving, like *morau* (b) or a verb of giving, like *yaru* 'give to 2/3' in (c):[54]

(133)   Japanese
      a. *Tarō=ga   Hanako=ni   kami=o   kir-are-ta.*
         T.=NOM   H.=DAT   hair=ACC   cut-SUNUCL-PST
      b. *Tarō=ga   Hanako=ni   kami-o   kitte   moratta.*
         T.=NOM   H.=DAT   hair=ACC   cut.CVB   receive.PST
      Both: 'Taro had his hair cut by Hanako.' (Oshima 2008: 148–149)
      c. *Boku=ga   Ken=ni   hon=o   yonde   yatta.*
         1SG=NOM   K.=DAT   book=ACC   read.CVB   give.to.2/3.PST
      'I read Ken a book.' (Shibatani 2003: 282)

The converbal constructions have clearly different semantics (i.e., 'do the favor of V-ing', 'V for the benefit of') and are more limited than the malefactive subjective nucleative regarding the possible valency of the lexical verb and a number of semantic and pragmatic factors. In fact, the malefactive subjective nucleative readily accommodates monovalent base predicates, which are basic-ally unavailable to the converbal constructions under normal circumstances:

(134)   Japanese (Tsujimura 1996: 278–279)
      a. *Tarō=wa   chichioya=ni   shin-are-ta.*
         T.=TOP   father=DAT   die-SUNUCL-PST
      'Taro's father died on him.'
      b. *Wareware=wa   kanjinna   toki=ni   shachō=ni*
         1PL=TOP   important   time=DAT   president=DAT
         taore-rare-ta.
         collapse-SUNUCL-PST
      'The president got ill when we needed him badly.'

Nevertheless, what is relevant here is that the *yaru*-construction has the expected outcome of an indirect applicative (i.e., the new participant, a beneficiary, is introduced as an indirect object to the clause), whereas the *morau*-construction does not (i.e., the introduced beneficiary is, like with malefactive nucleative, the new subject of the clause). We label the latter operation a BENEFACTIVE SUBJECTIVE UNDERGOER NUCLEATIVE.

---

[54] Japanese verbs of receiving and giving show honorificity distinctions. The common verbs of giving to a 2nd/3rd person are, in decreasing order of honorificity of the recipient, *sashiageru, ageru*, and *yaru*.

Before proceeding any further, note that the Japanese constructions we label subjective undergoer nucleatives here share several morphological and syntactic characteristics with prototypical passives: the demoted A appears in the dative and the verb is marked with *-(r)are*. They are not prototypical passives, however, in that the latter are both A-demotional and P-promotional, whereas the subjective undergoer nucleatives not only introduce an extra-thematic argument to the clause, but also grant it subject status.

Similar constructions have been found in other languages – some of them are areally (and culturally) close to Japanese, like Korean, but others cannot be said to be closely related. For instance, Even (135) shows the same *w*-marking on the verb, and the same marking of a (quasi-)A, in a passive (b), a possessive-malefactive subjective undergoer nucleative (c), and a malefactive subjective undergoer nucleative based on an avalent verb (d). (The passive in (b) is morphosyntactically prototypical but semantically restricted: it has to express states of affairs that affect the subject in a negative fashion.)

(135)   Even (Tungusic, Russia; Malchukov 1993: 21–23)
  a. *Nugde   etiken   gia-wa-n   maa-n.*
     bear[NOM]   old.man[NOM]   friend-ACC-3SG   kill-NFUT.3SG
     'The bear killed the old man's friend.' (active)
  b. *Etiken   nugde-du   maa-w-ra-n.*
     old.man[NOM]   bear-DAT   kill-PASS-NFUT-3SG
     'The old man was killed by the bear.'
  c. *Etiken   nugde-du   gia-j   maa-w-ra-n.*
     old.man[NOM]   bear-DAT   friend-REFL.POSS kill-SUNUCL-NFUT-3SG
     'The bear killed the old man's friend (the old man was negatively affected).'
  d. *Etiken   (imanra-du)   imana-w-ra-n.*
     old.man[NOM]   snow-DAT   snow-SUNUCL-NFUT-3SG
     'The old man is caught by the snowfall.'

Some constructions found in languages like Mapudungun and Yupik show an interesting complication. In the former language, the applicative suffix *-(ñ)ma* derives syntactically trivalent predicates from syntactically bivalent predicates, as in (136). In (a), with *ngilla-* 'buy', the perhaps older, purely separative, sense of the marker can be seen; in (b), the frequently derived malefactive reading can be seen with *leli-* 'look (at)'. (Actually, as will become apparent shortly, the original semantics of *-ñma* seems to have been neutral.)

(136)   Mapudungun (b–d: Salas 2006: 121–122)
  a. *Ngilla-n   chi   kawellu.*
     buy-1SG.IND   the   horse
     'I bought the horse.'
  b. *Ngilla-ñma-fi-n   Antonio   chi   kawellu.*
     buy-APPL-3.P-1SG.IND   A.   the   horse
     'I bought the/his horse from Antonio.'

  c. *Leli-fi-n*   *ñi*   *ñawe.*
    look.at-3.P-1SG.IND 3.PSR daughter.of.man
    'I looked at his daughter.'

  d. *Leli-ñma-fi-n*   *Kuan* *ñi* *ñawe.*
    look.at-APPL-3.P-1SG.IND   J.   3.PSR daughter.of.man
    'I looked at Juan's daughter to his detriment (e.g., with bad intentions).'

Now consider the morphosyntax of clauses with *-ñma* based on monovalent and avalent verbs, as illustrated in (137) below. With a syntactically monovalent verb like *lef-w-* 'escape' and an animate S, *-ma* simply applicativizes the predicate (a); the fact that the affected participant is the subject is related to the fact that the latter is 1SG – that is, this subject choice depends on the inversion system of the language (see Section 2.3.2) and is not related to the appearance of *-ñma*; the result would have been the same with an underived bivalent verb. With the syntactically monovalent verb *aku-* 'arrive here' and an inanimate S, however, only the verb's syntactic valency is increased (it can now take two arguments); its morphological valency is not altered (it is still inflected for one person only, unlike the bipersonal verb in (a), which indexes two arguments), and the new participant is the subject (b). Similarly, with the avalent verb *mawün-* 'rain', the verb inflects only for its new subject (1SG) (c):[55]

(137) Mapudungun (Smeets 2008: 302–303, Salas 2006: 125)

  a. *Lef-ma-w-e-n-mew.*
    run-APPL-REFL-INV-1SG.IND-3.A
    'S/he ran away / escaped from me.'

  b. *Iñche aku-ñma-n*   *kiñe küme dungu.*
    1SG   arrive.here-SUNUCL-1SG.IND one good message
    'I received a nice message.'

  c. *Mawün-ma-n.*
    rain-SUNUCL-1SG.IND
    'I got rained on.'

This is similar to what happens with monovalent predicates in Yupik; in (138), the syntactic valency of monovalent *tuqu-* 'die' increases via suffixation of *-(g)i*. Unlike in Mapudungun, the verb is morphologically bivalent; like in Mapudungun, however, it is not a 3SG→1SG form that is used (as the English translation and the behavior in bi- and trivalent clauses would suggest), but a 1SG→3SG verb form instead:

(138) Central Alaskan Yupik (Eskimo-Aleut, USA; Miyaoka 2012: 836)

  Tuqu-i-gaqa   *nulia-qa.*
  die-SUNUCL-IND.1SG→3SG wife-ABS.SG.1SG
  'My wife died on me.'

---

[55] Early sources (e.g., the first grammar and dictionary of the language, from 1606) mention optional passive morphology with such avalent predicates (e.g., *mawün-ma(-nge)-n* 'I got rained on'). This suggests that *-(ñ)ma* developed from simple applicative to applicative-cum-undergoer-nucleative rather recently.

2.5.3   Subjective Undergoer Nucleatives in a Nutshell

Like causatives and applicatives, some voice operations do not merely remap existing arguments onto grammatical relations but actually introduce new arguments to the syntactic core of the clause. Unlike causatives, however, some of these operations install non-agentive arguments (beneficiaries, maleficiaries, instruments, goals, or possessors); unlike applicatives, these operations install these arguments as subjects. The verbal morphology employed for these undergoer nucleatives is the same as passives use in some languages (Japanese, Even); in other languages, it is the same as applicatives use (Mapudungun, Yupik); in yet other languages, the morphology may have some connection with other voice operations, but is at least synchronically distinct (Philippine languages).

3   Changing Syntactic Valency: Passives, Antipassives, and Related Constructions

The voice operations addressed in this chapter modify the morphosyntactic structure of a clause without altering its semantic structure, at least regarding the number of semantic arguments and their broad type. The literature on grammatical voice labels such operations "meaning-preserving" (Kroeger 2005: Ch. 14), "derived," or "voice operations *sensu stricto*" (Kulikov 2011a). Table 3.1 (partly based on Croft 2001: Ch. 8) gives an overview of the voices covered here, all of which operate in a semantically bivalent space.

Table 3.1 *Selected semantically bivalent diatheses*

		P			
		SBJ	OBJ	ADJ	–
A	SBJ		agent voice	antipassive domain	
	OBJ	patient voice			
	ADJ	passive domain			
	–				

Studies of grammatical voice usually determine a base Active Voice or "transitive construction," namely a two-argument clause with a subject A and an object P; this is the AGENT VOICE in Table 3.1. Its mirror image, the PATIENT VOICE, features a subject P and an object A and has received varied treatment in the literature (some studies have proposed the term "ergative voice" or "ergative construction" for clauses that instantiate this diathesis, e.g., Shibatani 1988). It is either an alternative two-argument diathesis in languages that also show the agent voice or the only two-argument diathesis in languages that do not show the agent voice. In the present chapter, we acknowledge or assume the existence of one of these voices and address operations that create other voices. We deal with possible alternations between agent and patient voices in Chapter 4.

The present chapter concentrates on the PASSIVE and ANTIPASSIVE VOICE DOMAINS. The former includes voices that are one-argument clauses, which are usually seen as the result of a combination of A-demotion and P-promotion when compared to the agent voice. We present the voices of this domain as orbiting what most mainstream studies label PROTOTYPICAL PASSIVE (i.e., a voice with a subject P and an adjunct A). The latter domain includes voices that are also one-argument clauses, which are usually seen as the result of some kind of P-demotion, as well as – depending on how limited or broad the definition of antipassives is – A-promotion when compared to either the agent or patient voices. We present the voices of this domain as orbiting what most current mainstream studies label PROTOTYPICAL ANTIPASSIVE (i.e., a voice with a subject A and an adjunct P).

3.1   The Passive Domain

3.1.1   The Prototypical Passive

Passives have been known since antiquity; Dionysius Thrax's *Art of Grammar* (second century BCE) mentions the passive forms of Ancient Greek verbs (*Téchnē Grammatikḗ* 15). The PROTOTYPICAL PASSIVE is defined as follows, with the corresponding diathesis schematically represented in Figure 3.1 with an agent, "active," voice as vantage point:

(139)   Characteristics of the prototypical passive voice
   a.   Syntactic valency is one less than in the active diathesis (e.g., the verb is monovalent when its active counterpart is bivalent).
   b.   Its subject corresponds to the nonsubject P of the active voice.
   c.   Its peripheral, and optional, argument (typically marked by a non-core case or adposition) corresponds to the subject A of the active voice.
   d.   Passivization is formally coded on the predicate complex.

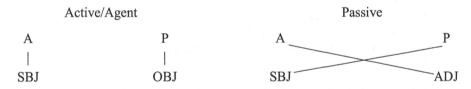

Figure 3.1 *Active/agent and passive diatheses*

Example (140) below illustrates the differences between the active/agent and the passive voices in Japanese:

(140)   Japanese (Tsujimura 1996: 274)
   a.   *Sensei=ga   Hanako=o sikat-ta.*
        teacher=NOM   H.=ACC   scold-PST
        'The teacher scolded Hanako.' (active)
   b.   *Hanako=ga   sensei=ni   sikar-are-ta.*
        H.=NOM   teacher=DAT   scold-PASS-PST
        'Hanako was scolded by the teacher.' (passive)

In the active construction (a), the A appears in the nominative case, the P occurs in the accusative case, and the verb has no voice marker. In the passive (b), by contrast, the A occurs in the dative, the P takes the nominative, and the verb takes the marker *-(r)are*. Moreover, the syntactic status of the arguments is different in both constructions: the A is the privileged argument in the active, as is the P in the passive, for the purposes of several grammatical processes (e.g., coreferential deletion in coordination and subject honorification).

The characterization of the passive prototype given above relegates to non-prototypical status constructions that exclude the overt expression of the A. The reason for this choice is simply that most contemporary studies of grammatical voice still see the passive in such terms (see, e.g., Kulikov 2011a). Alternative characterizations do exist in the literature, however: Shibatani (1985) and Keenan and Dryer (2007) suggest that the agentless passive should be regarded as the prototype instead.

3.1.2   Non-Prototypical Passives and Lookalikes

There are departures from the prototype introduced at the beginning of this section in several directions. First, and structurally closest to the proto-type, some P-promoting voices do not merely demote the A but actually suppress it, so that the latter argument cannot be expressed in the clause: such con-structions are frequent and are usually labeled AGENTLESS PASSIVES in the literature.[1] Figure 3.2 below graphically depicts this voice and Example (141) from Mapudungun illustrates their essential features:

(141)   Mapudungun
    a. *Chi wentru pe-fi-i-Ø*   *chi   domo.*
        ART man   see-3.P-IND-3 ART woman
        'The man saw the woman.'
    b. *Chi domo   pe-nge-i-Ø*   *(*chi wentru mew).*
        ART woman   see-PASS-IND-3 ART man   POSTP
        'The woman was seen.'

Chi domo 'the woman' is the primary object with the active voice (a) and the subject with the passive (b), but *chi wentru* 'the man' occurs only in the former, as the subject; with the passive construction, expression of the A argument is excluded. Such passives can be formed of bivalent or trivalent verbs only.

Second, some A-demoting voices do not promote the P argument completely, so the latter is not the subject of the derived voice. Such constructions seem to be somewhat less frequent than agentless passives and are called NON-PROMOTIONAL PASSIVES in the literature. Figure 3.3 below gives a graphic representation of (the simplest version of) this voice, and Example (142) from Polish below illustrates it:

---

[1] Lexical Functional Grammar assumes agentless passives to be prototypical in lexical mapping theory. Similarly, Keenan and Dryer (2007) regard passives that do not normally occur with an agent phrase (which can be syntactically allowed or excluded) as prototypical.

Figure 3.2 *Agentless passive diathesis*

Figure 3.3 *Non-promotional passive diathesis*

In the Polish *no/to*-construction, the verb/participle does not agree with any NP in the clause in (b) (it appears in the neuter singular instead), and the P retains the accusative marking it has in the active clause (a). The subject A (a) optionally appears as an adjunct in (b). Such a prototypical non-promotional passive does not have a subject and is therefore called IMPERSONAL PASSIVE.[2]

(142)   Polish (Slavic, Poland; Kulikov 2011a: 377)
      a. *Robotnicy*   *budują*   *szkołę.*
          worker(M).NOM.PL   build.PRS.3PL   school(F).ACC.SG
          'The workers build a school.' (active)
      b. *Zbudowan-o*   *szkołę*   *(robotnikami).*
          build.PTCP-N.SG   school(F).ACC.SG   worker(M).INS.PL
          'A school is built (by the workers).' (non-promotional / impersonal passive)

Example (143) from Ute as analyzed by Givón illustrates an instance of the non-promotional passive in which A-demotion is not complete in that construction. *Tʉkuavi* '(the) meat' is the nonsubject form in both (a) and (b) (the subject form is *tʉkuavi̱*, with a silent final vowel). Notably enough, even though the subject is suppressed in (b), it is still active: the verb could additionally take the plural subject marker *-qha̱* before the passive marker *-ta* if the meaning to be conveyed were that the meat was eaten by several people.

---

[2] IMPERSONALS are constructions that lack an (overt) subject. (A broader view sees them as constructions that lack a formally, semantically, and/or pragmatically prototypical subject.) Only some of these are directly relevant for the study of voice in general and of passives in particular, because several impersonals are simply instantiations of the active voice, and others do alter the morphosyntactic structure but are unmarked on the predicate. See Abraham (2006), Creissels (2007), and Malchukov and Siewierska (2011) for more details. See Blevins (2003) for a distinction between his "impersonals" on the one hand, which can be formed of either monovalent or bivalent verbs, and passives on the other, which can in turn be either "personal" (from bivalent verbs) or "subjectless" (from agentive monovalent verbs).

(143)   Ute (Uto-Aztecan, USA; Givón 2011: 249–250)

    a. *Tawachi*   *tukuavi*   *tuka-qha.*

        man.SBJ   meat.OBJ   eat-ANT

        'The man ate the meat.' (active)

    b. *Tukuavi*   *tuka-ta-qha.*

        meat.OBJ   eat-PASS-ANT

        'The meat was eaten.' (non-promotional passive)

Finnish presents a non-promotional passive in which A-demotion is complete but P-promotion is incomplete.[3] The P appears in the nominative when lexical (b) and accusative when pronominal (d),[4] but it is not indexed on the verb; the suffix *-tAAn* (PRS) ~ *-ttiin* (PST) is used irrespective of number and person of the P (b/d):

(144)   Finnish

    a. *Henkilö*   *rikko-i*   *maljako-n*   / *maljako-t.*

        person   break-PST[3SG]   vase-ACC.SG   vase-ACC.PL

        'A/the person broke the vase / the vases.' (active)

    b. *Maljakko*   / *maljako-t*   *riko-ttiin.*

        vase.NOM.SG   vase-NOM.PL   break-PASS.PST

        'The vase / the vases were broken.' (partially promotional passive)

    c. *Kalle*   *tappo-i*   *minut.*

        K.   kill-PST[3SG]   1SG.ACC

        'Kalle killed me.' (active)

    d. *Minut*   *tape-ttiin.*

        1SG.ACC   kill-PASS.PST

        'I was killed.' (non-promotional passive)

The examples from the three languages above can be summarized as in Table 3.2:

Table 3.2 *Selected non-promotional passives*

	P-promotion	A-demotion
Polish *-no/-to*	none	complete
Ute *-ta*	none	partial
Finnish *-tAAn ~ -ttiin*	partial	complete

The Polish construction exemplifies the prototype of the non-promotional passives. All examples except the Ute *ta*-construction are true impersonals

---

[3] Such forms are basically agentless, but some speakers, e.g., in sports commentaries, allow the expression of the A in an oblique phrase (e.g., *mieh-en toime-sta* [man-GEN task-ELAT] 'by the man' in (b)).

[4] The suffix *-t* on *maljako-t* covers both the nominative and the accusative in the plural.

that lack subjects. All examples except the Finnish *tAAn/ttiin*-construction are truly non-promotional constructions. All of them can be seen as non-prototypical passives that share at least some A-demotion as a unifying trait.[5]

Now consider the case of German, which has prototypical passivization of default bivalent clauses featuring a subject and a direct object (see (145) below) but also shows non-promotional passives.

(145)   German
    a. *Die   Gesetzgeber   berücksichtigten   die   Eltern   nicht.*
      ART   legislators   considered.3PL   ART   parents   NEG
      'The legislators did not consider the parents.' (active bivalent)
    b. *Die   Eltern   wurden   nicht   berücksichtigt.*
      ART   parents   became.3PL   NEG   consider.PTCP
      'The parents were not considered.' (prototypical passive)

In German, several kinds of verbs do not take a direct object in the accusative and occur in a form that morphologically resembles a passive (146). Syntactically monovalent verbs that do not take any kind of object (like *klatschen* 'clap' in (a–b)), but also verbs that take indirect objects (like *helfen* 'help' in (c–d)) or prepositional objects (like *warten* 'wait' in (e–f)), occur in this impersonal construction that features *werden* 'become' plus the participle. This is morphologically like the passive, but the syntax of the two constructions is different. The indirect object and the prepositional object retain their status in the impersonal construction, while the direct object in (a) becomes the subject of the passive in (b) in (145) above.

(146)   German
    a. *Das   Publikum   klatschte*
      ART   audience   clapped.3SG
      'The audience clapped.' (active monovalent, no OBJ)
    b. *Es   wurde   geklatscht.*
      it   became.3SG   clap.PTCP
      'People clapped.' (impersonal passive)
    c. *Die   Kinder   halfen   den   Eltern   im   Haushalt.*
      ART.NOM children   helped.3PL   ART.DAT parents   in.the   household
      'The children helped the parents with the domestic chores.' (active, IOBJ)
    d. *Den   Eltern   wurde   im   Haushalt   geholfen.*
      ART.DAT parents   became.3SG   in.the   household   help.PTCP
      'Someone helped the parents with the domestic chores.' (impersonal passive)
    e. *Der   Student   wartet   seit   Stunden   auf den   Professor.*
      ART.NOM student   wait.3SG   since   hours   on   ART.ACC professor
      'The student has been waiting for hours for the professor.' (active, PREPOBJ)

---

[5] A different kind of non-promotional passive is found in languages where it is the P, rather than the A, that is the subject in the base diathesis (see Chapter 4). In Balinese and Northern Sasak, for instance, the P is the subject in both the base and the passive diatheses, which differ only regarding the syntactic status of the A (Peter Austin, pers. comm.).

f. *Auf   den   Professor   wird   seit   Stunden   gewartet.*
on   ART.ACC professor   become.3SG since   hours   wait.PTCP
'People have been waiting for the professor for hours.' (impersonal passive)

What Kulikov (2011a) calls CONVERSIVE VOICE is similar to the non-promotional passive but represents a case of complete P-promotion together with incomplete A-demotion. In his analysis of the Russian example in (147), the conversive reverses the assignment of semantic roles to grammatical relations without turning the A into an optional adjunct (but into an "Indirect or Oblique Object of relatively high rank"; the A in Russian prototypical passives takes the instrumental, rather than the genitive):

(147)   Russian (Slavic, Russia; Kulikov 2011a: 380)
a. *Grom   ispuga-l   sobak-u.*
thunder(M)[NOM.SG] frighten-PST[M.SG]   dog(F)-ACC.SG
'The thunder frightened the dog.' (active)
b. *Sobak-a   ispuga-l-a-s'*   *grom-a.*
dog(F)-NOM.SG   frighten-PST-F.SG-CVRS   thunder(M)-GEN.SG
'The dog was frightened by the thunder.' (conversive)

A similar construction exists in Ibero-Romance, as illustrated in (148) with data from Spanish:

(148)   Spanish
a. *El   fantasma   asustó   a   los   niños.*
ART   ghost   scared.3SG to   ART   children
'The ghost scared the children.' (active)
b. *Los   niños   se   asustaron   {del   / con   el}   fantasma.*
ART   children CVRS   scared.3PL of.ART with ART   ghost
'The children got scared of the ghost.' (conversive)

Such constructions differ from anticausatives, despite their formal similarity, because they are arguably semantically bivalent: there is an A and a P in both the active and the conversive diatheses. Interestingly enough, however, both in Slavic and in Spanish the A is not a prototypical agent, and the P is not a prototypical patient, with such constructions. Rather than being productive, conversives are limited to verbs of perception and emotional states.

Let us finally turn to three passive lookalikes. The term PSEUDO-PASSIVE is employed in one sense to cover passivization of clauses headed by monovalent verbs – remember that prototypical passives apply to clauses headed by bivalent (or trivalent) verbs – like the following use of *thùuk* in Thai (*pay* 'go' could be used without specifying the goal):

(149)   Thai (Tai-Kadai, Thailand; Prasithrathsint 2003: 5)
Khǎw   thùuk   pay   prachum   thɛɛn   huanâa   lǎay   khráŋ.
3HUM   PASS   go   meeting   replace   boss   several time
'He has been made to attend meetings on behalf of his boss several times.'

Another sense of the term is more often found in the literature, however: it refers to the fact that, in some languages, prepositional objects can be promoted to subject as well, leaving the preposition stranded. (The literature, especially the most recent one, also uses the term PREPOSITIONAL PASSIVE.) Such constructions have attracted considerable attention, particularly in English studies, not least for their lexical restrictions (150); with some verbs, both the active and the pseudo-passive are available (a), but with others the latter construction is ruled out (b):

(150)   English
        a. *They can rely on William.*   vs.   *William can be relied on.*
        b. *They flew to Boston.*   vs.   **Boston was flown to.*

INVERSE constructions like the ones found in Algonquian languages, for example, have been mistaken for passives – among other reasons, because their translational equivalent in European languages was often given as a passive(-like) construction. Nevertheless, as detailed in Chapter 4, and irrespective of how different inverse clauses are best analyzed in syntactic terms, it is crucial to note that there is no evidence that supports a syntactically monovalent account of either direct (a) or inverse clauses (b) in examples like the following:

(151)   Ojibwa (Rhodes 1976: 202)
        a. *Aw*   *aniniw* *w-gii-waabam-aa-an*   *niw*   *kweew-an.*
            DEM.PROX   man   3.A-PST-see.TA-DIR-OBV   DEM.OBV   woman-OBV
            'The man (PROX) saw the woman (OBV).' (active, direct verb)
        b. *Aw*   *kweew* *w-gii-waabam-igw-an*   *niw*   *aniniw-an.*
            DEM.PROX   woman   3.A-PST-see.TA-INV-OBV   DEM.OBV   man-OBV
            'The man (OBV) saw the woman (PROX).' (active, inverse verb)

3.1.3   Functions of Passives

There are syntactic, semantic, and discourse-related motivations for choosing the passive voice instead of the active. In English, for instance, some particular constructions are available to a subset of participants (the "pivot"); coreferential NP-deletion is a case in point. Example (152) illustrates that this phenomenon patterns accusatively – put differently, only the subject (here: the S/A argument) is eligible for deletion. In order to delete, in the second clause, the NP coreferential with the P of a bivalent predicate like 'save' in the first clause, the verb has to be passivized, as in (c):

(152)   English
        a. *My friend$_i$ (S) arrived*   *and Ø$_i$ (S) laughed.*
        b. *My friend$_i$ (A) saved the boy$_j$ (P)*   *and Ø$_{i/*j}$ (S) laughed.*
        c. *The boy$_j$ (P) was saved by my friend$_i$ (A)*   *and Ø$_{*i/j}$ (S) laughed.*

Such restrictions on grammatical processes would suggest that P-promotion is the primary syntactic motivation, and that some kind of A-demotion is but a requisite of the syntax of natural languages (i.e., that a clause not have more than one subject, or at least that the two arguments highest in syntactic prominence not share all behavioral properties).[6] In fact, most syntax-centered accounts of the passive domain have taken P-promotion to be both its defining feature and its main function.

A possible semantic motivation for passives is the need to express a lower transitivity value, which is the combined effect of the reduction of syntactic valency and another semantic trait commonly associated with passives, namely stativization. Moreover, those passives that show some strong semantic (aspectual, modal, etc.) specificity beyond mere transitivity reduction have an even clearer semantic motivation (see Section 3.1.4.3).

Regarding discourse-related motivations, foregrounding the P may respond to particular communicative needs, especially in the case of highly individuated and topical Ps (see, e.g., Sansò 2006, but the idea can be traced back to Brugmann's writings from the early twentieth century). Many studies have noted that passives are used in different languages when the identity of the A is easily retrievable from the context, uncertain, unknown, potentially face-threatening, or irrelevant. Eliminating the explicit reference to the A via a passive construction may be more polite or generally more appropriate, which might be desirable when portraying interactions between specific persons (e.g., 1st and 2nd persons), thus leading to passive structures in the corresponding personal scenarios. This particular view, namely the primacy of the A-backgrounding function, is found in Shibatani (1985) and Comrie (1988), but also in earlier studies (Schiefer 1983).

Perhaps unsurprisingly, given that the two operations of P-foregrounding and A-backgrounding (Kazenin 2001a calls them "pragmatic demotion and promotion" of A and P, respectively) as possible motivations for the use of passives have been a much-discussed topic in the literature, some studies avoid privileging one over the other (e.g., Foley & Van Valin 1984). Work conducted by Givón and several other scholars in the early 1980s (e.g., Givón 1983 and references therein) see the effect of the combined operation as discourse-motivated ("agent-defocusing and patient-focusing"), especially in the sense of expressing particular relative topicality values of the involved arguments. This view sees passive structures as naturally correlating with topicality values of A and P that systematically differ from those these arguments have in active voice: the A is much less topical and the P is much more topical in the passive. Haspelmath (1990), however, notes that the etymologies of passive constructions invariably differ from strategies that express topicalization or focusing, and comes to the conclusion that, rather than solving the question of the main function of passives cross-linguistically, the study of the diachrony of such constructions leads to seeing their main origin in expressions of inactivization. Haspelmath (1990) sees this notion – roughly, the orientation of a linguistic

---

[6] For a case against considering either A-demotion or P-promotion in isolation the criterial trait for *defining* (rather than choosing to use) passives, see Kazenin (2001a).

expression towards an inactive (i.e., non-agentive) subject – as a prerequisite of A-backgrounding, which in turn would later lead to P-foregrounding.

3.1.4   Variation of Passives

3.1.4.1   Morphological Variation of Passives

The main strategies for distinguishing actives from passives are (i) a formally privative opposition between a zero-marked active and a nonzero-marked passive, and (ii) a formally equipollent opposition between the active and passive forms, which can be either (ii$_1$) the use of morphemes marking either voice, or (ii$_2$) the use of indexing sets specialized for voice in both voices.[7] Type (i) is cross-linguistically common and has already been illustrated by Japanese in (140), Mapudungun in (141), Ute in (143), German in (145)–(146), Russian in (147), Spanish in (148), Thai in (149), and English in (152). Type (ii$_1$) is comparatively rarer, though we have already seen examples from Finnish in (144). Additional examples come from Kafa, where active verbs reportedly take a suffix *-i* while passive verbs take *-e* (e.g., *qod-i-* 'divide' vs. *qod-e-* 'be divided', *čučč-i-* 'tie' vs. *čučč-e-* 'be tied'; Haspelmath 1990: 31), as well as from Sinhala, where passives make use of vowel fronting when compared to actives (e.g., *sōda-* 'wash' vs. *sēde-* 'be washed', *hūra-* 'scratch' vs. *hīre-* 'be scratched'; Haspelmath 1990: 31), and more in general from Semitic languages. Lastly, Type (ii$_2$) is possibly the least common of all three: it is found in Classical Sanskrit, Classical Greek, and Classical Latin, where specialized endings for the different person-number combinations distinguished an active form (e.g., *bhara-ti – phér-ei – fer-t* 's/he brings, bears') from a mediopassive form (e.g., *bhara-te – phér-etai – fer-tur* 's/he is brought, borne') in several tenses.

Passives mark this voice either SYNTHETICALLY (or morphologically), like Japanese in (140) above, or ANALYTICALLY (or syntactically), like English:

(153)   English
    a.   *Roger Bigod saw the castles.* (active)
    b.   *The castles were seen by Roger Bigod.* (passive)

In the passive, rather than a single morpheme expressing passive voice, a construction that differs from the active clause is used, namely an auxiliary (here: *be*) and a participle (*seen*). More in general, such analytic constructions have a structure like [V$_1$ V$_2$], where V$_1$ is typically a finite functional verb and V$_2$, which expresses the main lexical content of the predicate, typically occurs in

---

[7] See Haspelmath (1990) for two additional parameters of the exact morphological make-up of the passive, namely the position occupied by the passive affix in relation to the verb stem (i.e., suffix, prefix, infix, or circumfix) and the proximity of the affix to the stem (i.e., "additional stem affixes" like the passive markers illustrated here in the main body of text, which are adjacent to the verb stem, vs. "extra-inflectional affixes" like Danish *-s* and Icelandic *-st*, which follow all other derivational and inflectional material, in particular all person-number markers).

a nonfinite form. (In most serial verb constructions expressing passives, the finiteness asymmetry does not hold.)

Regarding the functional element V_1, the most common choices are either monovalent verbs (copulas, pseudo-copulas, and verbs of motion) or bivalent verbs (verbs of receiving and experiencer verbs) (Kazenin 2001a: 901 and Keenan & Dryer 2007: 336–339).[8] The English *be*-passive, the Latin *esse*-passive, the Italian *essere*-passive, and the Spanish *ser*- and *estar*-constructions, as well as the German *werden*-passive discussed below, are examples of the first monovalent type mentioned above: either a copula or a pseudo-copula like German *werden* 'become' are typically combined with a past passive participle to form the passive verb form. Verbs of motion occur in the Italian *venire*- and *andare*-passives. Auxiliaries originating in verbs of receiving are the English *get*-passive and the German *kriegen*-passive discussed below (which combine with a participle of the lexical verb), but also the Tzeltal passive with *-ich'* 'receive' and the Welsh passive with *cael* 'get, acquire' (154) (which combines with a nominalized form of the main lexical verb, like *ladd* 'kill, killing' below):

(154)   Welsh (Celtic, UK; Roberts 2005: 13)
         Cafodd   y   dyn   ei   ladd.
         got.3SG   ART man   his   kill(ing)
         'The man was killed.'

Auxiliaries originating in experiencer verbs are reportedly widespread in Southeast Asian languages, where the verbs used include 'suffer' and 'touch'. The following example from Thai illustrates the latter type (see also the Thai examples in (170) below):

(155)   Thai (Filbeck 1973: 33)
         Sùk   thùuk   rót   chon.
         S.   PASS   car   hit
         'Sook was hit by the car.'

Interestingly enough, sometimes different parts of the verbal paradigm use distinct passive morphology. Classical Latin, for example, shows a verbal suffix (mostly *-r*) in the non-perfect tenses of the indicative and the subjunctive, but a ['be' + PTCP]-construction in the perfect tenses of both moods. Ancient Greek, on the other hand, shows the *thē*-suffix in the future and aorist of all moods, but the mediopassive verb form in all other moods (characterized by portmanteau suffixes that contrast with those of the active voice).

Moreover, there is also variation within languages as to the frequency with which different constructions are used. While Written Spanish allows the participial passive in all tenses and moods, Colloquial Spanish favors the *se*-passive and 3PL constructions instead (e.g., *traen tarde los libros* 'the books are brought

---

[8] Both studies also mention the existence of a much less frequent choice of auxiliary, namely a verb of ingestion (e.g., 'eat'); see Shibatani (1998: 105) for examples.

late (lit. they bring the books late)'), especially in the present tense. But on occasion different markers are preferred on a lexical, rather than grammatical, basis. In Standard Italian, for instance, the AUX slot in the [AUX + PTCP]-passive is regularly occupied by *essere* 'be', but with some verbs *andare* 'go' is often used (e.g., *i documenti andarono smarriti* 'the documents were mislaid'); note, however, that *venire* 'come' is widely used in the modern language in the AUX slot, albeit only in the present tense (e.g., *il principio di sussidiarietà viene sempre lodato* 'the principle of subsidiarity is always being lauded').

A different source of morphological variation is the coding of the A when it is expressed. Some languages appear to have dedicated markers for passive As, like Hebrew *yedei* and Indonesian *oleh* (Keenan & Dryer 2007: 345). Most languages, however, employ markers that are also used in other constructions in the language. Japanese, for instance, employs the dative for passive As, which is also normally used in active clauses to mark recipients and some goals. German marks the adjunct A with either *von* 'of' or *durch* 'through' (156), which have a variety of other uses. Grammars often say that the former preposition is used with a human/animate A (a) while the latter is used with inanimates (b):

(156)   German
      a. *Das   Haus   wurde   vom   Eigentümer selbst gebaut.*
         ART   house   became[3SG] of.ART owner   self   build.PTCP
         'The house was built by the owner himself.'
      b. *Berlin wurde   durch eine Mauer geteilt.*
         B.   became[3SG] through a   wall   divide.PTCP
         'Berlin was divided by a wall.'

The *durch*-phrase can be understood as an instrument (i.e., as an additional participant) employed by a bona fide agent; for instance, a *von*-phrase could be added to (b) above to express that agent (e.g., *von den Behörden* 'by the authorities'). That there is more to it can be seen from the pair in (157), where the A is inanimate but can appear either in a *von*-phrase or a *durch*-phrase.

(157)   German
      a. *Das Haus wurde   von   einem Feuer zerstört.*
         the   house became[3SG] of   a   fire   destroy.PTCP
      b. *Das Haus wurde   durch ein Feuer zerstört.*
         the   house became[3SG] through a   fire   destroy.PTCP
      Both: 'The house was destroyed by a fire.'

German speakers typically describe such an opposition as involving different construals of *ein Feuer* 'a fire', namely either as somehow personified in (a) (i.e., with more characteristics of a prototypical agent) or as shorthand for a whole event, rather than merely a participant in it, in (b). An approximate rendition in English would make use of *by* in the former case and *by means of / with* in the latter.

It is possible to find similar oppositions in languages that are neither genealogically nor areally related to German, like Vangunu (158). Active clauses do not mark the difference between different kinds of subject As in this language, but passive clauses do; animate definite As take an agentive marker *teia* (a), while inanimate As appear unmarked (b); animate indefinite As like *kalakea tinoni* 'somebody' take a different agentive marker *pa* (c):

(158) Vangunu (Austronesian, Solomon Islands; Frank Lichtenberk, pers. comm.)
  a. *Ta-va-opo*   *teia*   *tinoni* *pia* *ia*   *mola.*
     PASS-CAUS-capsize AGT$_1$ man   this ART.SG canoe
     'The canoe was capsized by this man.'
  b. *Ta-va-opo*   *bolusu*   *ria*   *mola.*
     PASS-CAUS-capsize big.wave ART.PL canoe
     'The canoes were capsized by a/the big wave.'
  c. *Ta-va-lequ*   *pa*   *kalakea* *tinoni* *ia*   *bue pia.*
     PASS-CAUS-be.dead AGT$_2$ some   man   ART.SG pig this
     'This pig was killed by somebody.'

Keenan and Dryer (2007: 343–345) do not address the worldwide distribution of A-markers with passives, but they do propose a formal typology for them: (a) instrumental, (b) locative, (c) genitive, (d) zero, and (e) incorporated into V. Type (a) is illustrated by German *durch*-phrases, but also by the use of the preposition 'with' in Bantu languages. Type (b) is illustrated by English *by*-phrases and Spanish *por*-phrases, but also by the ablative-NP of Kayardild:

(159) Kayardild (Tangkic, Australia; Evans 1995: 350)
  Ngada   *ra-yii-ju*   *mun-da*   *balarr-ina* *maku-na.*
  1SG.NOM spear-PASS-POT buttock-NOM white-ABL woman-ABL
  'I will be injected in the buttocks by the white woman.'

Type (c) is illustrated by *von*-phrases in German and *de*-phrases in French. Type (d) consists of a zero-marked oblique A, which Keenan and Dryer suggest mirrors zero-marked (spatio-)temporal expressions in many languages.[9] Type (e) – if attested at all – would seem to be extremely rare.[10]

3.1.4.2 Syntactic Variation of Passives

In addition to the syntactic issues related to the very definition of the passive domain and its subtypes, which we mentioned in Section 3.1.2 above, the most important source of syntactic variation of (prototypical) passives is the nature of the object(s) in the active and passive voices. Passives promote to subject the object of the active voice that is most syntactically salient. If a language has indirective alignment, the direct object is the P in the bivalent clause and the T in the trivalent clause; consequently, the passive promotes the T,

---

[9] These authors provide examples from Vietnamese (the *bị-* and the *được*-constructions) and from Haya; analyzing the former two as prototypical passives is controversial, however (see Bruening & Tran 2015).
[10] Keenan & Dryer (2007: 345) mention the restricted occurrence of instances like *this project is State-controlled / government-regulated* in English and an incorporating construction allegedly found in Quechua.

and not the G (the indirect object), to subject. The following data from Spanish illustrate this situation:

(160)   Spanish
    a. *Jorge le   dio   el   libro   a   Marco.*
        J.   3SG.DAT   gave.3SG   ART   book   to   M.
        'Jorge gave the book to Marco.' (active trivalent)
    b. *El   libro   le   fue   dado   a   Marco.*
        ART   book   3SG.DAT   was.3SG   give.PTCP   to   M.
        'The book was given to Marco.' (passive bivalent)
    c. **Marco   fue   dado   el   libro.*
        M.   was.3SG   give.PTCP   ART   book
        (Intended: 'Marco was given the book.')

Other languages have secundative alignment instead, so the primary object is the P in the bivalent clause and the G in the trivalent clause; consequently, the passive promotes the G, and not the T (the secondary object), to subject. The following data from Yindjibarndi illustrate this situation:

(161)   Yindjibarndi (Pama-Nyungan, Australia; Keenan & Dryer 2007: 349)
    a. *Ngaara yungku-nha   ngayu   murla-yi.*
        man   give-PST   1SG.OBJ   meat-OBJ
        'A man gave me the meat.' (active trivalent)
    b. *Ngayi   yungku-nguli-nha   murla-yi   ngaarta-lu.*
        1SG   give-PASS-PST   meat-OBJ   man-INS
        'I was given the meat by a man.' (passive bivalent)
    c. **Murla   yungku-nguli-nha   ngayu   ngaarta-lu.*
        meat   give-PASS-PST   1SG.OBJ   man-INS
        (Intended: 'The meat was given to me by a man.')

Yet other languages allow both objects of the trivalent clause to be promoted to subject by the passive. The following data from Kinyarwanda illustrate this situation:

(162)   Kinyarwanda (Kimenyi 1980: 127)
    a. *Umugabo y-a-haa-ye   umugóre   igitabo.*
        man   he-PST-give-ASP   woman   book
        'The man gave the woman the book.' (active trivalent)
    b. *Umugóre y-a-haa-w-e   igitabo   n'-ûmugabo.*
        woman   she-PST-give-PASS-ASP   book   by-man
        'The woman was given the book by the man.' (passive bivalent 1)
    c. *Igitabo cy-a-haa-w-e   umugóre   n'-ûmugabo.*
        book   it-PST-give-PASS-ASP   woman   by-man
        'The book was given to the woman by the man.' (passive bivalent 2)

Lastly, languages like English have two active constructions with *give*, namely a clause with a primary object for the G and a secondary object for the T, similar to (a) from Yindjibarndi – (a) in (163) below – and a clause with a direct object for the T and a prepositional object for the G, equivalent to (a) from the Spanish in

(160) – (c) in (163) below. The former passivizes by promoting the primary object (the G) to subject, as in (b), and the latter does so by promoting the direct object (the T) to subject, as in (d):[11]

(163)   English
   a.   *Alan gave Beatrice the car.*
   b.   *Beatrice was given the car (by Alan).*
   c.   *Alan gave the car to Beatrice.*
   d.   *The car was given to Beatrice (by Alan).*

Now consider German prototypical passives, which consist of an [AUX + PTCP]-construction similar to the English passive. The default passive in (164) shows *werden* 'become' in the AUX slot and promotes to subject either the P of the bivalent active (*den Minister* 'the minister' in (a)) or the T of the trivalent active (*den Brief* 'the letter' in (c)), that is, invariably the direct object in the accusative. The indirect object in the dative (*dem Minister* '(to) the minister' in (c–d)) stays unaltered:

(164)   German
   a.   *Der*   *Schütze*   *beobachtet*   *den*   *Minister.*
        ART.NOM   shooter   observe.3SG   ART.ACC   minister
        'The shooter observes the minister.' (active, bivalent)
   b.   *Der*   *Minister*   *wird*   *vom*   *Schützen*
        ART.NOM   minister   become.3SG   of.ART.DAT   shooter.DAT
        beobachtet.
        observe.PTCP
        'The minister is observed by the shooter.' (passive, monovalent)
   c.   *Der*   *Schütze*   *gab*   *dem*   *Minister*
        ART.NOM   shooter   gave[3SG]   ART.DAT   minister
        den   *Brief.*
        ART.ACC   letter
        'The shooter gave the minister the letter.' (active, trivalent)
   d.   *Der*   *Brief*   *wurde*   *vom*   *Schützen*
        ART.NOM   letter   became[3SG]   of.ART.DAT   shooter.DAT
        dem   *Minister*   *gegeben.*
        ART.DAT   minister   give.PTCP
        'The letter was given by the shooter to the minister.' (passive, bivalent)

Another German passive (the *Rezipientenpassiv* 'recipient passive') has either *bekommen* 'receive' or *kriegen* 'get, catch' in the AUX slot (the former frequently in the written, the latter in the spoken, language). With trivalent active clauses, it is the G argument, rather than the T, that is promoted to subject in the passive:

---

[11] The literature on the dative shift and the passive in English often mentions the existence of variation in this respect. In colloquial registers of English as spoken in North West England, for example, *the car was given Beatrice* is acceptable, but this is not possible with all verbs (roughly, those verbs that allow the double object construction in the active voice, like *give*, allow such behavior in the passive more readily). See Biggs (2014) for details.

(165) German

  a. *Seine*   *Eltern*   *schenkten*   *ihm*   *einen*   *Wagen.*
      his   parents   gave.3PL   3SG.M.DAT   one.ACC   car
      'His parents gave him a car (as a gift).' (active, trivalent)

  b. *Er*   *kriegte*   *einen*   *Wagen*   *geschenkt.*
      3SG.M.NOM   got[3SG]   one.ACC   car   give.PTCP
      'He was given a car.' (passive, bivalent)

  c. **Ein*   *Wagen*   *kriegte*   *ihm*   *geschenkt.*
      one.NOM   car   got[3SG]   3SG.M.DAT   give.PTCP
      'A car was given to him.'

It is not only the recipients of verbs of giving that allow the construction, but addressee and beneficiary Gs are also possible:

(166) German

  a. *Sie*   *kriegte*   *den*   *Raum*   *gezeigt.*
      3SG.F.NOM   got[3SG]   ART.ACC   room   show.PTCP
      'She was shown the room.'

  b. *Sie*   *kriegte*   *den*   *Wagen*   *repariert.*
      3SG.F.NOM   got[3SG]   ART.ACC   room   repair.PTCP
      'She had the car repaired / the car was repaired for her.'

Bivalent active clauses with a subject and a direct object do not have such a passive counterpart; those with a subject and an indirect object, by contrast, have become variably possible (*er half ihr* 'he helped her' vs. $^?$*sie kriegte von ihm geholfen* 'she was helped by him').

Finally, the literature on passives also mentions the possibility of different adjuncts being promoted to subject in the undergoer voices of some Austronesian languages (e.g., Kazenin 2001a and Keenan & Dryer 2007). We will return to this issue in Chapter 4, but it will suffice to illustrate the situation with some data from Cebuano. This language shows four voices: Actor, Patient, Locative, and Conveyance. The privileged syntactic argument is the agent in (a), the patient in (b), the beneficiary or source in (c), and the means in (d):

(167) Cebuano (Austronesian, The Philippines: Wolff 1972: xv, 38, 361)

  a. *Akú=y*   *mu-palít*   *ug*   *isda?.*
      1SG=TOP   AV-buy   OBL   fish
      'I will buy some fish.'

  b. *Palit-ún*   *ku*   *ang*   *isda?.*
      buy-PV   1SG.GEN   NOM   fish
      'I will buy the fish.'

  c. *Palit-án*   *ku*   *siyá=g*   *kík.*
      buy-LV   1SG.GEN   3SG.NOM=OBL   cake
      'I will buy some cake for/from her.'

  d. *Wa?*   *ku=y*   *kwarta-ng*   *i-palít*   *ug*   *bugás.*
      NEG.exist   1SG.GEN=LNK   money-LNK   CV-buy   OBL   rice
      'I have no money to buy rice with.'

The main point for our present purposes is that there is not enough evidence to regard any of these Cebuano voices as a passive of any kind: none of these clauses is syntactically monovalent – not even the patient voice (b), which would be the obvious candidate for a passive analysis. Consequently, we end this section with a cautionary remark: unless a strong case can be made for a passive analysis of some undergoer voice (e.g., in an Austronesian language), passives can be said to target either direct/primary objects or indirect objects.

3.1.4.3   Semantic Variation of Passives

Several languages distinguish between passives along an aspectuality-related parameter. A common kind is a special case of the agentless passive, namely the PASSIVE OF RESULT, which has received varied treatment in the literature. For instance, even though the mainstream analysis of the German passive of result (e.g., *der Brief ist geöffnet* lit. 'the letter is opened') was, arguably during the whole second half of the twentieth century, in terms of a third voice (opposed to both the active and the passive of event), scholars have recently come to favor alternative analyses. One possibility consists in regarding such sentences as copular constructions (Maienborn 2007) while another consists in regarding them as resultatives (Nedjalkov 1988, Leiss 1992) – both of which are often regarded as preferable *alternatives* to the passive analysis. For instance, Haspelmath and Müller-Bardey (2004) follow Nedjalkov in placing the voice alternation (active in (a) and anticausative in (b) below) and the resultative construction (c) of Russian on different planes:

(168)   Russian (Haspelmath & Müller-Bardey 2004: 1134)

    a.   *Mira*   *zakryvaet*   *dver'.*
          M.(F).NOM   close.3SG   door(F)[NOM/ACC]
          'Mira is closing the door.'

    b.   *Dver'*   *zakryvaet-sja.*
          door(F)[NOM/ACC]   close.3SG-ANTIC
          'The door is closing.'

    c.   *Dver'*   *zakry-t-a.*
          door(F)[NOM/ACC]   close-PTCP-F.SG
          'The door is closed.'

Haspelmath and Müller-Bardey see the primary function of the resultative construction as expressing a state by means of an event word. They see the removal of the agent from the syntax and possibly also from the semantics – and therefore its similarity to a prototypical passive or an anticausative – as a secondary effect.

Nevertheless, in the view espoused in the present book, voices are not defined via primary vs. secondary functions, which can be difficult to determine unambiguously, but simply as morphological expressed diatheses, which can then be parameterized according to lexical restrictions, aspectual values, etc. To be sure, the passive of result is non-prototypical because it is restricted or specialized in scope, and because it is often lexically restricted. But note that prototypical passives can have some restrictions as well; in English, for example, some low-transitivity stative verbs like *have, belong,* and *suit* do not passivize, and other verbs like *weigh* show variable behavior: dynamic *he weighed the truck after loading the cargo* allows a passive counterpart, whereas stative *the truck weighed two tons* does not.[12] German passives of result appear to be even more heavily restricted: when based on atelic verbs, such constructions generally lead to fairly variable grammaticality judgements. The passive of result is also non-prototypical because it appears to be systematically ambiguous between a passive and an anticausative reading, like in the case of Russian *dver' zakryta* 'the door is closed' in (c) above. Consequently, we do not distinguish a resultative voice in its own right but propose to acknowledge that the resultative may, and usually does, correspond to A-backgrounding voices like some passives and/ or the anticausative.

Unlike English, where *the puppy is fed* can have either an interpretation focusing on the action or event (a habitual one, e.g., 'twice a day during our absence') or an interpretation focusing on the result of the action (e.g., 'so we can leave the house now'), other languages systematically distinguish the two – without any sociolinguistic correlates, unlike the English opposition between the *be*-passive and the *get*-passive (more on this below). Spanish, for example, uses a [*ser* 'be$_1$' + PTCP]-passive (or a *se*-passive) for the prototypical passive covering the event, and an [*estar* 'be$_2$' + PTCP]-construction for the passive of result. (Roughly, *ser* expresses more permanent states than *estar*.) The literature on German uses the terms *Vorgangspassiv* 'passive of process' and *Zustandspassiv* 'passive of state' for the same two types; this language employs a [*werden* 'become' + PTCP]-construction for the focus on the event and a [*sein* 'be' + PTCP]-construction for the focus on the result. This is summarized in Table 3.3 below, which also provides examples.[13]

Table 3.3 *Selected passives of event and result*

	Spanish			German		
Focus on event	*Clara* C.(F)	*es* is$_1$	*abandonada.* abandoned.F.SG	*Clara* C.(F)	*wird* becomes	*verlassen.* abandoned
			'Clara is (e.g., regularly) abandoned.'			
Focus on result	*Clara* C.(F)	*está* is$_2$	*abandonada.* abandoned.F.SG	*Clara* C.(F)	*ist* is	*verlassen.* abandoned
			'Clara is (now) abandoned (and we must help her).'			

[12] Note that the verbs 'cost', 'weigh', and possessive 'have' do not show such a restriction in Kinyarwanda (Kimenyi 1980).

[13] See also Section 2.2.2 for details on the similar resultative construction.

The existence of the *werden*-passive and the *sein*-passive in German leads us to the fact that English also shows two possible verbs in the AUX slot of the [AUX + PTCP]-construction: *be* and *get*. The alternation between these two passives is governed by several factors; one is a difference in agency features of their subject: the *be*-passive has a neutral P subject and the *get*-passive denotes some control, instigation, or responsibility on the part of the P subject. A simple minimal pair highlighting this difference follows:

(169)   English (Lakoff 1971:156)
   a.   *Mary was shot on purpose.*   (Someone purposely shot Mary.)
   b.   *Mary got shot on purpose.*   (Mary purposely got herself shot.)

Another difference between the two passives is that the *get*-passive is seldom found with an explicit mention of the oblique A in spontaneous speech, and it was originally used much more often to denote a negative effect of the action on the P (and therefore occurred more frequently with verbs that implicated or implied negative effects, like *stab* or *rob*). Lastly, the *get*-passive is more informal, and it is more widely used by American English speakers of lower education levels (Givón & Yang 1994, Downing 1996, Toyota 2008).

The adversative reading purportedly associated with the English *get*-passive in turn leads us to the question of the ADVERSATIVE PASSIVE. The term is used in two different ways in the literature. In one sense, it denotes constructions that are superficially similar to passives but cannot be characterized as bona fide instances of the passive voice, like the Japanese Indirect Passive; such valency-increasing constructions (nucleatives) are discussed in Section 2.5.2. The other sense in which adversative passive is understood in the literature refers to the fact that, in some languages, passive constructions may be limited to, or at least favored by, expressions conveying a misfortune or adversity. The idea is that the passive is only or more readily available with predicates that express adversity, or at least in contexts that are usually construed as such. This has been claimed to hold for a number of Southeast Asian languages, like Thai, Khmer, Vietnamese, and Malay (at least at some stage of the constructions' development, see Prasithrathsint 2004). The following examples illustrate the Thai marker *thùuk* (still used as a full verb with the meaning 'touch') in such a function, either with an explicit agent (a) or without it (b):

(170)   Thai (Smyth 2002: 74)
   a.   *Chán   thùuk   yuŋ   kàt.*
        1SG   PASS   mosquito   bite
        'I've been bitten by a mosquito.'
   b.   *Raw   thùuk   khamooy.*
        1PL   PASS   rob/steal
        'We were robbed.'

Finally, another special case of the agentless passive is the POTENTIAL PASSIVE. The meaning of such constructions typically includes an aspectual component of habituality and a modal component of potentiality, as in the following examples from Russian and Spanish. Adverbs like *well, easily, often,* etc. help disambiguate and/or identify such potential passives:

(171)   Russian (Kulikov 2011a: 376)

  a.   *Oni   otkryvajut   dver'.*
    3PL.NOM open.3PL.PRS door[NOM/ACC.SG]
    'They open the door.' (active)

  b.   *Dver'   otkryvajet-sja   legko.*
    door[NOM/ACC.SG] open.3SG.PRS-PASS easily
    'The door opens easily.' (potential passive)

(172)   Spanish

  a.   *(Ellos)   oyen la música.*
    3PL.M.NOM hear.3PL ART music
    'They hear the music.' (active)

  b.   *La música se   oye   claramente desde el vestíbulo.*
    ART music PASS hear.3SG clearly   from ART foyer
    'The music can be clearly heard from the foyer.' (potential passive)

3.1.5   Distribution of Passives

Some studies of the late twentieth century saw productive passives as a hallmark of languages with accusative alignment in their morphology (e.g., Dixon 1994: 152; Van de Visser 2006) and productive antipassives as a hallmark of languages with ergative morphological alignment (e.g., Silverstein 1976, Dixon 1979). Nevertheless, it is not difficult to find languages with morphological accusativity but without either a productive passive or a productive antipassive. Hungarian, for instance, has the three constructions illustrated in (173), but the prototypical passive present in older stages of the language is no longer in use:

(173)   Hungarian

  a.   *Meg-vizsgál-ják   a   gyerek-et.*
    COMPL-examine-PRES.3PL.DEF the child-ACC
    'They examined the child / the child was examined.' (3PL-impersonal)

  b.   *Az ajtó nyit-va   van.*
    the door open-PTCP is
    'The door is open.' (resultative)

  c.   *A ház fel-ép-ül-t.*
    the house up-build-MID-PST[3SG.INDF]
    'The house was/got built.' ("Middle" = agentless passive)

Basque exemplifies those languages that show morphological ergativity (further complicated by the existence of split intransitivity and differential object marking) but do not have productive passives or antipassives either (although it does have a heavily lexically restricted antipassive, see Zúñiga & Fernández forthcoming for details).

Conversely, both constructions are found in languages with morphological ergativity, like those of the Salishan, Eskimoan, Kartvelian, and Mayan families (Polinsky 2017: 329). For example, Eskimoan shows a rather simple ergative patterning of nominal case and has both antipassives and passives. Consider the following data:

(174)   Baffin Island Inuktitut (Eskimo-Aleut, Canada; Spreng 2005: 2–3)

    a. *Anguti-up*   *arna-q*   *kunik-vaa.*

        man-REL.SG   woman-ABS.SG   kiss-IND.3SG→3SG

        'The man kissed the woman.' (active)

    b. *Anguti*   *kunik-si-vuq*   *arna-mik.*

        man[ABS.SG]   kiss-ANTIP-IND.3SG   woman-INS.SG

        'The man is kissing a woman.' (antipassive)

    c. *Arna-q*   *kunik-tau-juq*   *(anguti-mut).*

        woman-ABS.SG   kiss-PASS-IND.3SG   man-ABL.SG

        'The woman was kissed (by the man).' (passive)

In a bivalent clause (a), the A appears in the ergative (called "relative" in Eskimoan studies), the P appears in the absolutive, and the verb takes bipersonal inflection. In the antipassive (b), the A occurs in the absolutive, the P occurs in the instrumental, and the verb takes an antipassive marker and monopersonal inflection. In the passive (c), the A also occurs in the absolutive, the P occurs in the ablative, and the verb takes a passive marker and monopersonal inflection. Both low-transitivity constructions are available in the language as counterparts of the high-transitivity active, independent of the case pattern. The correct generalization seems to be that (prototypical) passives are simply less common in languages with morphological ergativity (Nichols 1992: 158; Kazenin 2001a: 926; Polinsky 2017: 329).

Regarding the areal distribution of passives, 44 percent of the almost 380 languages surveyed by Siewierska (2013) have passive constructions. Passives seem to be extremely rare in Papua New Guinea and rather rare in Australia, but they occur somewhat more often in the Pacific and Southeast Asia. They are regularly found in the Americas, especially in (western) North America and the Amazon, and they are common in Africa (other than around the coast of West Africa)[14] and western Eurasia (other than in the Caucasus and in Tibetan languages).

3.2   The Antipassive Domain

3.2.1   The Prototypical Antipassive

Antipassive constructions have received considerable attention in the literature since Silverstein (1972: 395) suggested the term for a phenomenon he saw as a mirror image of the passive, and the core of the category is virtually

---

[14] Keenan and Dryer (2007: 329) note that Chadic languages are typically passive-less (except Hausa).

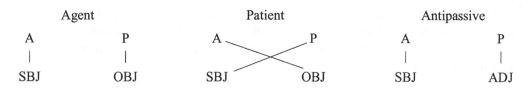

Figure 3.4 *Agent, patient, and antipassive diatheses*

uncontroversial.[15] We define the prototypical antipassive as follows (the diathesis is schematically represented in Figure 3.4):

(175)   Characteristics of the prototypical antipassive voice
    a. Its syntactic valency is one less than the one of the non-antipassive diathesis (e.g., it is monovalent when its counterpart is bivalent).
    b. Its subject corresponds to the A of the non-antipassive diathesis.
    c. Its peripheral, and optional, argument (typically marked by a non-core case or adposition) corresponds to the P subject of the non-antipassive voice.
    d. Antipassivization is formally coded on the predicate complex.

Example (176) below illustrates the opposition between patient and antipassive voices in Dyirbal:

(176)   Dyirbal (Dixon 1972: 65–66)
    a. *Balan   dyugumbil   baŋgul   yaṟa-ŋgu   balga-n.*
        ART.II.ABS woman(II)[ABS] ART.I.ERG man(I)-ERG   hit-NFUT
    b. *Bayi   yaṟa   bagun   dyugumbil-gu balgal-ŋa-nu.*
        ART.I.ABS   man(I)[ABS]   ART.II.DAT woman(II)-DAT hit-ANTIP-NFUT
        Both: 'Man is hitting woman.'

In the base construction (a) – which corresponds to the middle schema in Figure 3.4 – the A appears in the ergative, the P occurs in the absolutive, and the verb has no voice marker. In the antipassive (b), by contrast, the A occurs in the absolutive, the P takes the dative, and the verb takes the marker *-ŋa*. Moreover, according to most currently held views of Dyirbal syntax, the syntactic status of the arguments is different in both constructions: the P is the privileged argument (i.e., the subject) in the base voice, as is the A in the antipassive, for purposes of several grammatical processes (e.g., coreferential deletion in coordination and relativization).

Some recent studies of voice and voice-related phenomena work with a broader definition – interestingly enough, on both sides of the functionalist–formalist divide (see, e.g., Janic 2016 and Polinsky 2013a, 2017). According to

---

[15] According to Dixon, Silverstein coined the term in late 1968 specifically for "the *-ŋa-y* derivation in Dyirbal" (1994: 149). Jacobsen employed the notion cross-linguistically in a conference paper of 1969 (published in 1985) but used the label "agentive" instead.

such studies, the bivalent counterpart of the antipassive can be like the patient diathesis of Dyirbal, but it can also be like the agent diathesis of European languages. The following examples from Halkomelem illustrate the opposition with the latter clause type:

(177)   Halkomelem (Gerdts & Hukari 2000: 52)
  a. *Naʔət   qʷəs-t-əs*   *tθə*   *ƛeləm̓*   *sce:ɬtən.*
     AUX   go.in.water-CTRL-3.A   DET   salted   salmon
     'She put the salted fish in water.' (active)
  b. *Naʔət   qʷəs-els*   *ʔə*   *tθə*   *ƛeləm̓*   *sce:ɬtən.*
     AUX   go.in.water-ANTIP$_2$ OBL   DET   salted   salmon
     'She soaked the salted fish.' (antipassive)

Gerdts and Hukari (2000: 52–53) unmistakably say that the base diathesis of Halkomelem is of the agent type (subject A, object P) while the antipassive voice is its one-argument counterpart (with a subject S_A and an adjunct P).

Even though the mainstream literature on voice sees the antipassive as derived from the base voice in some way, and therefore the oblique P as a demoted version of the base P, some studies do not take such a view (e.g., Spreng 2010 and Aldridge 2012). Unlike the view that centers on infrequent cases like Dyirbal in (176), where antipassives are both P-demotional and A-promotional, but also unlike the broader view that uses the label for constructions like those found in Halkomelem as well, illustrated in (177), which are only P-demotional, antipassives are neither P-demotional nor A-demotional by definition in this third view.[16]

3.2.2   Non-Prototypical Antipassives and Lookalikes

Depending on whether the category is necessarily seen as A-promotional or not, the syntactic status of A in the base and antipassive clauses is either given by the definition – it is a nonsubject in the former and a subject in the latter – or a parameter of variation (i.e., some antipassives are promotional while others are not). Thus, the relatively infrequent A-promotional *ŋa*-operation of Dyirbal is always a (PROMOTIONAL) ANTIPASSIVE, but the relatively frequent *se*-constructions in Romance and their Slavic counterparts are antipassives only working with a definition that excludes A-promotion as a criterial trait. They therefore constitute instances of NON-PROMOTIONAL ANTIPASSIVES. With this caveat, both are prototypical.

---

[16] The idea of a non-demotional antipassive is not recent: based on his analysis of Eskimoan phenomena, Kalmár says that "[m]any, if not all, so-called ergative languages have at least two *transitive* clause types: the ergative and the antipassive" (1979: 118, emphasis added). Despite the differences in morphology between both construction types (i.e., case marking and inflection of the verb), this author explicitly maintains that the antipassive is not derived from the active (nor vice versa), and that both clause types are syntactically bivalent and have a subject and a direct object. Such a view of antipassive constructions is not found in mainstream studies of either Eskimoan languages in particular, or grammatical voice in general.

Regarding P-demotion, note that the argument in P function can be either demoted from the direct/primary status it has in the base voice to adjunct status, or it can be suppressed from the clause altogether. ADJUNCT-P ANTIPASSIVES correspond to the former type (i.e., the prototype): the Dyirbal and Halkomelem examples in (176)–(177) illustrate it. Note in passing that, on a superficial level, prototypical antipassives are seen in the literature as allowing, but not requiring, the overt expression of P, as in (a) below.[17] Nevertheless, antipassives that either require (b) or exclude (c) an overt expression of P also exist according to the current mainstream view:

(178)   a. Spanish
            Se   *confiesa*   *(de   sus   pecados).*
            ANTIP   confess.3SG   of   3.PSR.PL   sins
            'S/he confesses (his/her sins).'
        b. French (Janic 2016: 205)
            *Les   étudiants   s'-attaquent   *(aux   révisions)*
            the   students   ANTIP-start.3PL   to.the   revisions
            dès   le   mois   de   mars.
            from   the   month   of   March
            'The students start studying for the exam(s) (lit. tackle the revisions) in March.'
        c. Serbo-Croatian (Kučanda 1987: 79)
            Ivan   se   tuče.
            I.   ANTIP   beat.3SG
            'Ivan is beating somebody.'

In the PATIENTLESS or SUPPRESSING ANTIPASSIVE (e.g., (c) from Serbo-Croatian above), the P cannot appear in the clause. Other labels used in the literature for this type include "deobjective" (Haspelmath & Müller-Bardey 2004), "absolute transitive," "object suppressing" (Kulikov 2011a), and "absolute antipassive" (Janic 2016). The two antipassives of Comanche are further cases in point: one is typically used with human implicit Ps (marked by *ma* in (a)) and the other with nonhuman implicit Ps (marked by *ti-* in (b)):

(179)   Comanche (Uto-Aztecan, USA; Charney 1993: 128–129)
        a. *ma-tsaH-soʔi*
            ANTIP-by.hand-scratch
            'to scratch (someone)'
        b. *Ke   nii   ti-tsahani-wai-tɨ=.*
            NEG   1SG   ANTIP-drive-ASP-ASP
            'I'm not going to drive.'

---

[17] The study by Dixon and Aikhenvald (1997) is a case in point: "the underlying O argument [= the P] goes into a peripheral function, being marked by a non-core case, adposition, etc.; this argument can be omitted, although there is always the option of including it" (1997: 74).

Not only has this type been comparatively neglected in the typological literature, but there is also considerable disagreement among authors as to how descriptive work should label and treat such constructions – which in turn display an important degree of cross-linguistic variation. Charney's Comanche grammar, for instance, calls the relevant morphemes "indefinite object" (and most studies of Uto-Aztecan languages do something similar; cf. the "indefinite object prefixes" of Classical Nahuatl, for example).

A different kind of non-prototypical antipassive is found in Circassian languages – here, again, alongside a prototypical antipassive construction. In Besleney (180), for example, the suppressing antipassive may contrast with an active voice that has direct objects in the absolutive with *də* ~ *de* 'sew' (a–b) (i.e., prototypically), but also with a different kind of underived voice that has indirect objects in the dative with *pλ(ə)* ~ *pλe* 'look' (c). These two constructions can be called DIRECT and INDIRECT ANTIPASSIVE, respectively:

(180)   Besleney (Northwest Caucasian, Turkey; Letuchiy & Arkadiev forthcoming)
  a. *Pŝaŝe-m   žane   jə-də-n   xʷje.*
     girl-OBL   dress[ABS]   3SG.A-sew-POT   must
     'The girl must sew a dress.' (active)
  b. *Nataše   deʁʷwə   jəč'jə   daxwə   ma-de.*
     N.   well   and   beautifully   DYN-sew.ANTIP
     'Natasha sews well and nicely.' (direct antipassive)
  c. *ʁʷegʷəm   je-pλ-te-q̇əm   a-r   jə-ŝha*
     road-OBL   DAT-look-IPFV-NEG   DEM-ABS   POSS-head
     mədč'e   pλe-w   mədč'e   pλe-w
     there   look.ANTIP-ADV   there   look.ANTIP-ADV
     že-t   gʷəš'əʔe-r-wə.
     run-IPFV   talk-CVB-ADV
     'He did not look at the road; he would drive talking and looking here and there.' (active and indirect antipassive)

Some kinds of NOMINAL INCORPORATION are a special case of antipassivization. In some types of such constructions, the P is completely demoted from the clause like in the patientless antipassive, but there is still a lexical expression present, in the form of the incorporate (see 7.3 for details on other types). Consider the following example from Mapudungun (181). In (b), the status of A (*ñi chaw* 'my father') is the same as in the active (a)-clause but the P (*waka* 'cow(s)') has been demoted; the verb is now monovalent and *waka* is arguably no longer a primary object (which it was in the active construction):

(181)   Mapudungun (Salas 2006: 181)
  a. *Ñi   chaw   kintu-le-i*   *ta   chi   pu   waka.*
     1SG.PSR   father look.for-PROG-IND   PTCL   ART   PL   COW
     'My father is looking for the cows.'
  b. *Ñi   chaw   kintu-waka-le-i.*
     1SG.PSR   father look.for-cow-PROG-IND
     'My father is looking for (the) cows.'

Moving further away from the prototype, we can distinguish LEXICALLY CONSTRAINED ANTIPASSIVES like the following construction in Basque (see Zúñiga & Fernández forthcoming). This particular alternation between a two-argument (a) and a one-argument clause (b) exists in the language, but only with a dozen heterogeneous verbs; rather than an antipassive marker, the language employs an opposition between the "transitive" auxiliary *edun 'have' in (a) and the "intransitive" auxiliary izan 'be' in (b):[18, 19]

(182)   Basque (unclassified, Spain and France)
        a.   Ni-k   hura   gogoratu   dut.
             1SG-ERG   3SG.ABS   remember.PFV   have.1SG→3SG
        b.   Ni   gogoratu   naiz   hartaz.
             1SG[ABS]   remember.PFV be.1SG   3SG.INS
        Both: 'I remember him/her.'

A similar case is attested for Diyari, where only eight verbs can take the antipassive suffix -tharri (Austin 2005). Analogous phenomena are found in Romance – for instance, in Spanish, where the alternation shown in (183) with olvidar 'forget' is available only with a reduced number of verbs. Even with the semantically related verb recordar 'remember', the pair is not available in Standard Spanish (the corresponding syntactically monovalent verb is acordarse de, not *recordarse de);[20] with many verbs, se is a passive or impersonal marker (e.g., vender 'sell') or a telicizer (e.g., comerse 'eat up'), and with most suitable bivalent verbs se retains its original reflexive function (e.g., lavarse 'wash oneself').

(183)   Spanish
        a.   Olvidó   los   libros.
             forgot.3SG ART   books
        b.   Se   olvidó   de   los   libros.
             ANTIP   forgot.3SG of   ART   books
        Both: 'S/he forgot the books.'

Slavic languages show similar alternations and similar restrictions. The following pair from Ukrainian illustrates the active with a subject A in the nominative, an object P in the accusative, and an unmarked verb (a), and the antipassive with a subject A in the nominative, an adjunct P in a prepositional phrase headed by za 'at', and the verb marked by -sja (which is also used with reflexives) (b):

---

[18] Basque shows a similar, albeit much more productive, opposition with change-of-state verbs; see Example (29) in Section 2.1.3.1.

[19] Dixon's (1983) description of Nyawaygi (Pama-Nyungan, Australia) reports a similar opposition between base and antipassive verb forms that do not differ due to the presence/absence of an antipassive marker but thanks to distinct valency-specific conjugation classes.

[20] It is in order to note that several non-standard varieties of the language do have recordarse (de) for monovalent 'remember'; some non-standard varieties also retain an older meaning 'wake up' for monovalent recordarse.

(184)   Ukrainian (Slavic, Ukraine; Polinsky 2017: 308–309)
    a.   *Did*   *sxopyv*   *ripk-u.*
        grandfather(M)[NOM]   grab.PST.M   turnip-ACC
        'Grandfather grabbed the turnip.' (active)
    b.   *Did*   *sxopyv-sja*   *za*   *ripk-u.*
        grandfather(M)[NOM]   grab.PST.M-ANTIP   at   turnip-ACC
        'Grandfather grabbed at the turnip.' (antipassive)

By a similar token, some languages have LEXICALIZED ANTIPASSIVES. In addition to the prototypical antipassives we present later for Warungu (198), this language shows somewhat anomalous instances of the *kali*-construction with verbs of one particular class. Prototypically, the meaning of the predicate is the same in the active and antipassive voices. Nevertheless, several low-transitivity psych predicates consistently show somewhat expected but not entirely predictable meaning alternations in different contexts; for instance, *nyaka-* can mean 'see' and *tyaympa-* can mean 'find' in the active voice, but both can mean 'look for' in the antipassive:

(185)   Warungu (Pama-Nyungan, formerly spoken in Australia; Tsunoda 1988: 606)
    a.   *Nyula*   *nyaka-n*   *wurripa.*
        3SG.NOM   see-NFUT   bee[ABS]
        'He saw bees.'
    b.   *Ngaya*   *nyaka-kali*   *wurripa-wu*   *katyarra-wu.*
        1SG.NOM   see-ANTIP[NFUT]   bee-DAT   possum-DAT
        'I was looking for bees and possums.'
    c.   *Nyula*   *tyaympa-n*   *katyarra.*
        3SG.NOM   find-NFUT   possum[ABS]
        'He found possums.'
    d.   *Yinta*   *tyaympa-kali-ya*   *yampa-wu!*
        2SG.NOM   find-ANTIP-IMPER   camp-DAT
        'Look for the camp!'

In fact, the exact English translation also depends on other factors governing P-marking (i.e., referentiality/animacy and TAM form); accordingly, *ngawa-* can mean 'hear', but also 'listen' and 'understand'.

Morphologically, DIFFERENTIAL OBJECT MARKING (DOM) (Bossong 1991, 1998; Aissen 2003) may resemble antipassivization because there may be clauses in languages showing DOM in which different Ps appear marked with different affixes or adpositions. In Spanish, for instance, some objects obligatorily exclude flagging while others require the preposition *a* 'to' (otherwise used for recipients and goals of motion, i.e., indirect and prepositional objects). The following pair illustrates the clear-cut opposition between unmarked inanimates (a) and *a*-marked definite humans (b):

(186)   Spanish
    a.   *Vi*   *(*a)*   *la*   *revista.*
        I.saw   to   ART   magazine
        'I saw the magazine.'

b. *Vi   *(a)   la   actriz.*
   I.saw   to   ART   actress
   'I saw the actress.'

Syntactically, however, these two kinds of objects behave exactly alike, namely as bona fide direct objects. Moreover, Spreng (2010) and Polinsky (2017) argue that most of the semantic and pragmatic factors usually triggering DOM – animacy, person, definiteness, and specificity (Iemmolo 2011) – are different from those governing the use of antipassive clauses: specificity is the one factor where both phenomena can be seen as overlapping. In languages like Finnish (187), on the other hand, direct objects take either accusative or partitive case, essentially depending on transitivity, and the DOM pattern resembles the active–antipassive opposition even more closely than in Spanish. The accusative appears in high-transitivity clauses and the partitive in low-transitivity ones (e.g., in the contexts of negation, imperfectivity, some psych predicates and unbounded patients, like in the (b) sentence below). As in Spanish, however, this is neither an instance of an antipassive voice (the verb is unmarked) nor an antipassive diathesis (both the partitive-NP and the accusative-NP are direct objects):

(187)   Finnish
   a. *Silja   joi   maidon.*
      S.   drank[3SG]   milk.ACC
      'Silja drank the milk.'
   b. *Silja   joi   maitoa.*
      S.   drank[3SG]   milk.PTV
      'Silja drank (some) milk.'

The SPURIOUS ANTIPASSIVE (Halle & Hale 1997) of Chukchi deserves special mention here as well. In this language, 3SG→1SG and 2→1 interactions obligatorily occur in constructions like those in (c), which show characteristics of both the base (a) and the antipassive (b) voices:

(188)   Chukchi (Chukotko-Kamchatkan, Russia)
   a. *ɣəm-nan   ɣət   tə-ɬʔu-ɣət.*
      1SG-ERG   2SG[ABS]   1SG.SBJ-see-2SG.OBJ
      'I saw you (SG).' (Skorik 1977: 19) (base)
   b. *ʔaaček-ət   Ø-ine-nɬʔetet-ɣʔat   kimitʔ-e.*
      youth-ABS.PL   3PL.SBJ-ANTIP-carry-3PL.SBJ   load-INS
      'The youth carried a load.' (Kozinsky et al. 1988: 652) (antipassive)
   c. *ə-nan   ɣəm   Ø-ine-ɬʔu-ɣʔi.*
      3SG-ERG   1SG[ABS]   3SG.SBJ-INE-see-3SG.SBJ
      'He saw me.' (Skorik 1977: 44) (spurious antipassive)

Morphologically, the spurious antipassive is like the antipassive in that the verb takes monopersonal inflection and the antipassive marker *ine-* or *-tku* (depending on the person and number of the A and P), but it is like the base voice in that the argument NPs appear in the ergative and absolutive, respectively. Syntactically, however, the spurious antipassive appears to behave like the base voice (Bobaljik & Branigan 2006). Dunn's grammar (1999) treats such instances of *ine-* and *-tku* as person- and number-conditioned allomorphs of the inverse marker *ne-*. Even though the diachronic (and possibly synchronic) connection between *ine-* or *-tku* as voice markers and their index/inversion counterparts is interesting, spurious antipassives cannot be seen even as instances of antipassives.

Finally, consider the AGENT FOCUS CONSTRUCTIONS (AFCs) of Mayan languages (also called "agentive voice" and "focus antipassive" by Smith-Stark 1978 and Dayley 1981, respectively). They are used if the subject of a bivalent verb is to be focused, questioned, or relativized, but these constructions are morphologically and syntactically so heterogeneous that they cannot be lumped together. In some languages, the AFC is actually an antipassive voice. The Q'eqchi' example below illustrates such a construction: in (b), the verb is syntactically monovalent and the P takes a dative preposition instead of appearing in the unmarked form characteristic of the base voice (a):

(189)   Q'eqchi' (Mayan, Guatemala; Stiebels 2006: 505)
    a. *X-x-lop*   *li*   *cuink li*   *c'anti'*.
       REC.PST-3.A-bite DET man   DET snake
       'The snake bit the man.' (base)
    b. *Li*   *c'anti'*   *x-lop-o-c*   *re*   *li*   *cuink*.
       DET snake REC.PST-bite-ANTIP-ASP DAT.3 DET man
       'It was the snake that bit the man.' (AFC = antipassive)

In other Mayan languages, the AFC and the antipassive are different constructions. In Akatek, for instance, the verbal markers are different (*-on* for the AFC and *-wi* for the antipassive), indexing on the verb follows a different pattern (the 1SG A is expressed as an enclitic to the focal marker in (a) but the 2SG S is expressed as a proclitic to the verb in (b)), and flagging is different as well (the P is unmarked in (a) but obliquely marked in (b)):

(190)   Akatek (Mayan, Guatemala; Stiebels 2006: 554–555)
    a. *Ja'-in*   *ij-on-toj*   *naj*   *unin*.
       FOC-1SG carry.on.back-AF-DRCT CL   boy
       'It's I who carried the boy.' (AFC)
    b. *Ch-ach-tx'aa-wi*   *yiin*   *pitchile*.
       INCOMPL-2SG.S-wash-ANTIP LOC.3 clothes
       'You (SG) are washing the clothes.' (antipassive)

The point here is that not all Mayan AFCs can simply be regarded as examples of antipassives: each construction in the individual languages has to be examined separately.

3.2.3 Functions of Antipassives

Like with passives, there are syntactic, semantic, and discourse-related motivations for choosing the antipassive instead of the base voice. In Dyirbal and Chukchi, for instance, some particular constructions are available to a subset of participants (the "pivot"); coreferential NP-deletion in Dyirbal and relative clauses in Chukchi are cases in point. Example (191) illustrates that Chukchi relativization patterns ergatively; in order to relativize the A of a bivalent predicate like 'save', the verb has to be antipassivized, as in (e–f):

(191)   Chukchi (Polinsky 2013a)

   a.   *Ŋinqey*   *pəkir-ɣʔi.*
        boy[ABS]   arrive-3SG.S
        'The boy arrived.'

   b.   *pəkərə-lʔ-ən*   *ŋinqey*
        arrive-PTCP-ABS   boy[ABS]
        'the boy that arrived'

   c.   *Tumɣ-e*   *ŋinqey*   *rəyeɣtetew-nin.*
        friend-ERG   boy[ABS]   save-3SG→3SG
        'The friend saved the boy.' (base)

   d.   **ŋinqey*   *rəyaɣtala-lʔ-ən*   *tumɣətum*
        boy[ABS]   save-PTCP-ABS   friend.ABS
        (Intended: 'the friend that saved the boy')

   e.   *Tumɣətum*   *ŋinqey-ək*   *ine-nyeɣtele-ɣʔi.*
        friend.ABS   boy-LOC   ANTIP-save-3SG.S
        'The friend saved the boy.' (antipassive)

   f.   *ŋinqey-ək*   *ine-nyeɣtelewə-lʔ-ən*   *tumɣətum*
        boy-LOC   ANTIP-save-PTCP-ABS   friend.ABS
        'the friend that saved the boy'

Semantic motivations for the antipassive voice include the necessity to encode lower transitivity values than what a base voice normally expresses. More precisely, modality- or aspectuality-related factors (irreality, imperfectivity, durativity, habituality, or iterativity) can lead to the antipassive being preferred or even obligatory. In Bezhta, for instance, the antipassive has a general durative meaning; Example (192) shows the alternation between non-durative base (a) and durative antipassive (b):

(192)   Bezhta (Northeast Caucasian, Russia; Comrie et al. 2015: 553)

   a.   *Öždi*   *bäbä*   *m-üq-čä.*
        boy(I).OBL(ERG)   bread(III)[ABS]   III-eat-PRS
        'The boy eats the bread.'

   b.   *Öžö*   *bäbälä-d*   *Ø-üⁿq-dä-š.*
        boy(I)[ABS]   bread(III).OBL-INS   I-eat-ANTIP-PRS
        'The boy is busy eating the bread.'

Something similar is found in Eskimoan languages. Bittner (1987) mentions that the *llir*-antipassive "probably marks some kind of inceptive aspect." Example (a) shows an occurrence of the simple inceptive -*lir*, whereas (c) illustrates the use of the aspectually marked antipassive -*llir* as opposed to the base voice (b):

(193)   West Greenlandic (Eskimo-Aleut, Greenland; Bittner 1987: 200–201)
       a.   *Jaaku   maliq-lir-paa.*
           J.[ABS]   follow-INCEP-IND.3SG→3SG
           'He began to follow Jacob.'
       b.   *Atuagaq   taa-nna   atur-paa.*
           book[ABS.SG]   this-ABS.SG   use-IND.3SG→3SG
           'He used / is using this book.'
       c.   *Atuagaq-mik   taa-ssuminnga   atur-llir-puq.*
           book-INS.SG   this-INS.SG   use-ANTIP-IND.3SG
           'He's just now asking whether he can use this book.'

Note that this inceptive reading naturally correlates with a low affectedness of the P; the book is certainly less affected in examples like (c) above than in those like (b). In some languages, it can be exclusively the low affectedness of the P, without any aspectual correlate, that leads to choosing an antipassive construction, as in Chamorro:

(194)   Chamorro (Austronesian, Mariana Islands; Cooreman 1994: 59)
       a.   *Un-patek   i   ga'lago.*
           2SG.A-kick   the   dog
           'You (SG) kicked the dog.'
       b.   *Mamatek   hao   gi   ga'lago.*
           ANTIP.kick   2SG.ABS   LOC   dog
           'You (SG) kicked at the dog.'

Lastly, sometimes it is the low individuation of the P that drives the use of the antipassive. Polinsky (2013) reports an antipassive preference or requirement in case the P is plural (Bezhta; Kibrik 1981), indefinite (West Greenlandic; Seiler 1978), nonspecific (Archi; Kibrik et al. 1977), generic (Diyari; Austin 1981) or implicit (Mayan; Smith-Stark 1978, England 1988). The following example shows such an alternation with an indefinite P:[21]

(195)   West Greenlandic (Woodbury 1977: 323–324)
       a.   *Arna-p   niqi   niri-vaa.*
           woman-REL.SG   meat[ABS.SG]   eat-IND.3SG→3SG
           'The woman ate the meat.'
       b.   *Arna-q   niqi-mik   niri-nnig-puq.*
           woman-ABS.SG   meat-INS.SG   eat-ANTIP-IND.3SG
           'The woman ate (some) meat.'

As to discourse-related motivations for the use of the antipassive, the identity of the P participant may be unknown, uncertain, or irrelevant, so backgrounding

---

[21] Bittner (1987, 1994) makes a strong case in favor of analyzing the varied semantic effects of Inuit antipassivization – only some of which are interpretable in terms of definiteness – in terms of either wide or narrow scope (P in the base clause) vs. narrow scope only (P in the antipassive).

it may respond to particular communicative needs (Cooreman 1994). Eliminating the explicit reference to the P via an antipassive construction may be more polite or generally more appropriate, which might be desirable when portraying interactions between specific persons (e.g., 1st and 2nd persons; see Bickel & Gaenszle 2015).

3.2.4 Variation of Antipassives

Since we deal with most relevant aspects of syntactic variation of antipassives in Section 3.2.2 above, we outline the morphological and semantic variation of these constructions here.

3.2.4.1 Morphological Variation of Antipassives

Like passives, antipassives can in principle be distinguished from a base voice via (i) a formally privative opposition between a zero-marked active and a nonzero-marked antipassive, and (ii) a formally equipollent opposition between the base and antipassive forms, which can be either (ii$_1$) the use of morphemes marking either voice, or (ii$_2$) the use of indexing sets specialized for voice in both voices. We have not found clear examples of the latter situation, however. Type (i) is the most common cross-linguistically; most antipassives presented so far belong to this type. Type (ii$_1$) is attested as well, for instance, in Circassian (Letuchiy & Arkadiev forthcoming). The following examples from Dinka show an opposition between creaky vowels in the active and breathy vowels in the antipassive:[22]

(196)   Dinka (Nilotic, Sudan; Schröder 2015: 55)
         a. *Petero   a-pil*   *bël.*
             P.   3SG.INCOMPL-strip.ACT   cane
             'Peter is stripping the cane.' (active)
         b. *Petero   a-pïl.*
             P.   3SG.INCOMPL-strip.ANTIP
             'Peter is stripping.' (antipassive)

Again, like passives, antipassives mark this voice either SYNTHETICALLY (or morphologically), like in Dyirbal and the other examples outlined hitherto, or ANALYTICALLY (or syntactically), like in Mopan, where *uch* 'happen' is used as an auxiliary:

(197)   Mopan (Mayan, Guatemala and Belize; Hofling 2011: 14–15)
         a. *Walak-u-loch-ik-ech.*
             INCOMPL-3.I-bend-INCOMPL.TR-2SG.II
             'S/he bends you (SG).' (base)

---

[22] Note in passing that the passive is marked using similar means in this language, namely vowel lengthening: *bël a-piil Petero* (cane 3SG-strip.PASS P.) 'the cane is being stripped by Peter'. In addition, the creaky vs. breathy distinction of Dinka seems to correspond to a [+ATR] vs. [–ATR] opposition in other Nilotic languages (Schröder 2015: 55).

b.   *Uch-i*   *u-loch.*
happen-3SG.I[COMPL.ITR]   3.I-bend
'S/he bent (something).' (antipassive)

Unlike with passives, however, such periphrastic constructions seem to be rather rare (leaving aside those instances that simply contrast two different auxiliaries in the base and the antipassive voices). We do not know of any cross-linguistic studies that explore them.

Finally, the variation of the oblique marker that the P takes in prototypical antipassives has not been explored in as much detail as the variation of the A-marking in passives. A dedicated case marker for P does not appear to exist in antipassives. Instead, dative markers are found in Australian languages; the instrumental case is used in Eskimoan languages, Chukchi, and Basque; and possessive marking (*de* 'of') is used in Romance, but note that other spatial markers are also found in Romance and Slavic. In Warungu, the adjunct P appears in different cases, depending on several factors; while *kamu* 'water' is invariably in the unmarked absolutive in the base voice (a/c), it appears in the dative with the antipassive in (b) but in the instrumental with the antipassive in (d):[23]

(198)   Warungu (Tsunoda 1988: 598)
a.   *Pama-ngku   kamu   yangka-n.*
man-ERG   water[ABS]   search-NFUT
b.   *Pama   kamu-wu   yangka-kali-n.*
man[ABS]   water-DAT   search-ANTIP-NFUT
Both: 'A man looks/looked for water.'
c.   *Pama-ngku   kamu   pitya-n.*
man-ERG   water[ABS]   drink-NFUT
d.   *Pama   kamu-ngku   pitya-kali-n.*
man[ABS]   water-INS   drink-ANTIP-NFUT
Both: 'A man drinks/drank water.'

According to Tsunoda's (1988) analysis, the factors that determine the exact case marker taken by the P are referentiality/animacy, transitivity as lexicalized in the predicate, and P-affectedness as expressed in different TAM forms. Regarding the first factor, higher Ps tend to take the dative (personal pronouns obligatorily so) while lower Ps tend to take the instrumental. Regarding the second, predicates belong to four different classes (viz., "action" 'kill', 'eat', etc., "perception" 'see', 'hear', etc.; "pursuit" 'search', 'try in vain to get'; "three-place" 'give, 'tell', etc.); Ps of "action" verbs can take either the dative or the instrumental (see *pitya-* 'drink' in (c–d) above), but those of "pursuit" verbs (like *yangka-* 'search' in (a–b) above) can only take the dative. Lastly, P-affectedness as expressed in

---

[23] A similar phenomenon is found in Yidiny, where the variation is between locative and dative (Dixon 1977). Tsunoda (1988: 596) mentions that the ergative and the instrumental have similar, but not identical, forms in Warungu. The allomorphy of these case markers is immaterial to our present discussion.

different TAM forms with "action" predicates (purposive: rather dative; imperative: rather instrumental; nonfuture indicative: instrumental).[24] Something similar is attested in other Pama-Nyungan languages.

3.2.4.2   Semantic Variation of Antipassives

A special case of the suppressing antipassive is the POTENTIAL ANTIPASSIVE, which, like the potential passive (see Section 3.1.4.3), additionally conveys an aspectual meaning of habituality: unlike its passive counterpart, the modal component of this voice centers on the disposition of the A to perform the action expressed by the verb. Examples from Lithuanian and Udmurt follow:

(199)   Lithuanian (Geniušienė 1987: 83–84)
    a.   *Berniuk-as   muša   vaik-us.*
        boy-NOM.SG   beat[3SG]   child-ACC.PL
        'The boy beats children.' (active)
    b.   *Berniuk-as   muša-si.*
        boy-NOM.SG   beat[3SG]-ANTIP
        'The boy fights / is pugnacious.' (potential antipassive)

(200)   Udmurt (Uralic, Russia; Geniušienė 1987: 315)
    a.   *Puni̲   vańz-es   kurtči̲ļ-e.*
        dog[NOM]   all-ACC   bite-3SG
        'The dog bites everybody.' (active)
    b.   *Puni̲   kurtči̲ļ-iśk-e.*
        dog[NOM]   bite-ANTIP-3SG
        'The dog bites.' (potential antipassive)

In some languages, several antipassives contrast with each other. Innu, for example, has two patientless antipassive markers that are in complementary distribution; the *ue*-antipassive is used only with causativized bases:

(201)   Innu (Algonquian, Canada; Drapeau 2014: 240)
    a.   *Nipa-i-e-u.*
        die.AI-TA:CAUS-DIR-3
        'S/he kills him/her.'
    b.   *Eukuan   aueshish   nipa-i-ue-t.*
        it.is   animal   die.AI-TA:CAUS-AI:ANTIP-3
        'It is an animal that kills.'

---

[24] In some cases, the P takes genitive marking in the antipassive, apparently for "purely phonological" reasons (Tsunoda 1988: 603), while in others the P can appear in the unmarked absolutive case in the antipassive as well (Tsunoda's consultants accepted alternative versions with the dative or the instrumental in such cases).

The *tshe*-antipassive is used only with non-causativized bivalent bases:

(202)   Innu (Drapeau 2014: 238)
  a. *Puṅ   ashtu-ei-m-ᵘ   ishkuteṅu.*
      P.   put.off-TI-DIR.3–3   fire
      'Paul put off the fire.'
  b. *Puṅ   ashtu-ei-tshe-u.*
      P.   put.off-TI-AI:ANTIP-3
      'Paul puts off (things).'

In Halkomelem, there are actually two antipassives (marked by -*m* and -*els*, or some of their respective allomorphs) that, at first sight, appear to be structurally prototypical. (Recall Example (177) above, reproduced as (c–d) in (203) below.) Syntactically, both turn the verb from bivalent into monovalent by demoting the P; semantically, the P is usually 3rd person and animate, and can be either definite or indefinite but is often nonspecific:

(203)   Halkomelem (Gerdts & Hukari 2000: 51–52, 54–55)
  a. *Niʔ   q̓ʷəl-ət-əs   tᶿə   sce:ɬən.*
      AUX   bake-CTRL-3.A   DET   salmon
  b. *Niʔ   q̓ʷəl-əm   ʔə   tᶿə   sce:ɬən.*
      AUX   bake-ANTIP₁   OBL   DET   salmon
      Both: 'He cooked/barbecued the salmon.'
  c. *Naʔət   q̓ʷəs-t-əs   tᶿə   ƛ̓eləṁ   sce:ɬən.*
      aux   go.in.water-CTRL-3.A   DET   salted   salmon
  d. *Naʔət   q̓ʷəs-els   ʔə   tᶿə   ƛ̓eləṁ   sce:ɬən.*
      aux   go.in.water-ANTIP₂   OBL   DET   salted   salmon
      Both: 'She soaked the salted fish.'

The choice between both antipassivizers is largely lexically conditioned: 90 percent of the verbs in Gerdts and Hukari's sample take -*els*, 15 percent take -*m*, and a dozen of high-frequency verbs are antipassivized via a zero-operation. Nevertheless, there is more to it, as shown in (204). First, some verbs may take either suffix (*q̓ʷəs*- 'go in water' is one such verb) (a); second, some verbs may actually take both suffixes simultaneously (c):

(204)   Halkomelem (Gerdts & Hukari 2000: 55, 57)
  a. *Naʔət   q̓ʷəs-eʔəm   ʔə   tᶿə   ƛ̓eləṁ sce:ɬən.*
      AUX   go.in.water-ANTIP₁   OBL   DET   salted salmon
      'She soaked the salted fish.'
  b. *Niʔ   k̓ʷɬ-eʔəm   ʔə   k̓ʷ   ti   tᶿə   John.*
      AUX   pour-ANTIP₁   OBL   DET   tea   DET   J.
      'John poured some tea.'
  c. *Niʔ   k̓ʷɬ-eʔəm-els   ʔə   k̓ʷ   ti   tᶿə   John.*
      AUX   pour-ANTIP₁-ANTIP₂ OBL   DET   tea   DET   J.
      'John served some tea.'

While -*m* (actually, a middle marker; see Section 5.4) appears to have a default semantic effect, -*els* emphasizes the action in a particular way, namely by denoting that the activity is job-like, takes time and effort, and that the A is a delegated doer of some kind. Instead of being retrievable from the linguistic context, as is usually the case with antipassives, omitted Ps with the *els*-construction are understood from the *cultural* context of the activity in question (Gerdts & Hukari 2000: 55–56).

That the connection between antipassivization and aspectuality can be more complex than usually assumed is seen in Godoberi as analyzed by Tatevosov (2011). Examples like (205) suggest that antipassives in this language may be prototypical:

(205)   Godoberi (Tatevosov 2011: 138)
     a.   *ʕAli-di*   *q'iru*   *b-el-ata=da.*
         A.(M)-ERG   wheat(N)   N-thresh-IPFV.CVB=AUX
         'Ali is threshing wheat.'
     b.   *ʕAli*   *w-ol-a=da.*
         A.(M)[ABS]   M-thresh-ANTIP.CVB=AUX
         'Ali is threshing.'

There are several problems for a straightforward antipassive analysis of -*a*, however. First, less than half of the verbs that take this form are bivalent; more than half are monovalent (many of them agentive). Second, one particular class of bivalent verbs (Rappaport & Levin's 2008 "result verbs," e.g., 'open', 'break', 'tear') cannot take -*a*. Lastly, some verbs need to be reduplicated before taking the suffix. Tatevosov makes a strong case in favor of seeing the primary and general function of this -*a* as detelicization; not unlike with some passives of result (see Section 3.1.4.3 above), the antipassive voice is probably best seen as secondary here, in the sense that only with those bivalent bases that allow the marker does it denote diathetical change as a by-product of detelicization.

3.2.5   Distribution of Antipassives

Early work on antipassivization focused on languages that displayed some kind of ergativity, and some studies even suggested that the analysis of particular constructions as antipassives be restricted to such languages. Current mainstream studies, however, acknowledge that antipassives can be found in languages with varied morphosyntactic alignment patterns.

According to Polinsky (2013a), 75 percent of the almost 200 languages she surveyed are categorized as not having an antipassive construction. Other than in Caucasian languages, Basque, and some languages scattered in Southeast Asia, antipassives are rare in Eurasia and Africa. They occur somewhat more often in the Pacific and North America, but they are rather frequently found in Australia and Mesoamerica. Nevertheless, as mentioned by Polinsky, it is quite possible for antipassives to still be undetected, and some constructions similar to the "peripheral" ones mentioned at the beginning of this section might well be labeled and analyzed differently.

Among those antipassive voices already identified by the literature upon which Polinsky's study is based, roughly one third have an implicit P like the Comanche construction and two thirds have an explicit oblique-marked P like the Dyirbal one. By a related token, antipassives have been reported to apply only to a subset of bivalent predicates in some languages, thus giving rise to a classification in terms of productivity; according to Polinsky, roughly one third of antipassives are limited in this fashion and two thirds are fully productive. The latter further show some interesting genealogical and areal clustering: productive antipassives occur especially in Mayan, Salishan, Northeast Caucasian, Austronesian, and Pama-Nyungan languages.

3.3   Epilogue: Changing the Morphosyntactic Realization of Arguments

From a purely syntactic point of view, passivization and antipassivization can be seen as different manifestations of the same basic combined operation, namely the demotion of the argument that is syntactically most prominent and the promotion of its companion argument. As we have seen in this chapter, however, both domains are only approximately mirror images of each other. This is largely due to the bias towards dealing with the passive domain in a more principled, or at least more detailed, way found both in the Western descriptive tradition and in some theoretical traditions. But even after integrating more insights of the ever-growing body of descriptive literature than previous studies of grammatical voice, the passive domain seems to include a somewhat richer array of morphosyntactic phenomena than its antipassive counterpart. Furthermore, the factors governing the alternation between the base and the (anti-)passive voices are not only syntactic. The need to resort to a construction expressing low transitivity in the case of low referentiality of either the A or the P is indeed a similarity between both domains, but they differ regarding considerations of aspectuality: the passive domain is somewhat loosely related to perfectivity and stativization, whereas the antipassive domain is more closely related to imperfectivity and atelicity.

It is in order to note that there does not seem to exist a voice operation in its own right that suppresses both the A and the P at the same time – at any rate, not with a finite verbal predicate (i.e., not nominalizing it). We have found something close to it in Tugen, where it is possible to passivize an antipassive, as in (206) below. The effect is partly the expected one: the antipassive demotes the P, and the passive demotes the A; the combined result is not the promotion of any argument but the actual suppression of both:

(206)   Tugen (Nilotic, Kenya; Schröder 2015: 61)

    a.   *Kì-óm-ísy-éí*   *láákw-éé.*

        PST-eat-ANTIP-IPFV   child-DEF.SG

        'The child was eating.' (antipassive)

b. *Kì-kí-óm-ísy-éí.*
PST-PASS-eat-ANTIP-IPFV
'Eating was going on.' (passive + antipassive)

Kulikov (2011a) gives the following example from Welsh and analyzes it as an instance of what he labels the "absolute passive," which would correspond exactly to this A-demoting and P-demoting voice:

(207)   Welsh (Kulikov 2011a: 379)
          Nid   addol-ir   yn   y   capel.
          NEG worship-IMPRS.PRS   in   ART   chapel
          'There is no service in the chapel.'

Nevertheless, this analysis is not correct. These impersonal forms of the verb are attested in Insular Celtic languages in general; within Goidelic, Irish and Scottish Gaelic have them (Manx seems to have had only a couple of archaic vestiges of it when it was last spoken); within Brittonic, Breton and Literary Welsh have them (Cornish had them as well). In all Celtic languages that have a productive impersonal, monovalent and bivalent verbs occur in it; most languages, however, do allow the optional expression of the A (marked via an instrumental preposition 'with' in Goidelic and Welsh), with the notable exception of Breton:

(208)   Breton (Hewitt 2002: 17)
          *Prezeg   a   raffer   dissul   (*gant   an   Tad*
          preach.VN   PRED   do.IMPRS.FUT   Sunday   with   the   father
          Erwan Lagadeg).
          E. L.
          'One/somebody will preach on Sunday (*by Father Erwan Lagadeg).'

Still, the argument in P function can and usually does appear in the clause in all languages, and there is good evidence (compellingly so in Irish, see McCloskey 2007) to regard this NP as a bona fide object (209):

(209)   Welsh (Borsley et al. 2007: 283)
          a. *Torr-wyd   y   cupan   (gan   Megan).*
              break-IMPRS.PST   the   cup   with   M.
              'The cup was broken (by Megan).'
          b. *Fe='m   gwel-wyd   (i).*
              AFF=1SG   see-IMPRS.PST   1SG
              'I was seen.'

These Celtic constructions are therefore non-promotional impersonal passives, and the Breton construction is additionally agentless. Possibly, natural languages are simply not used in such a way that a specialized all-suppressing voice would arise. Within the semantically bivalent space of two arguments, the base, passive, and antipassive voices and their lookalikes seem to suffice.

4   In Search of Balance: Agent and Patient Voices

Several leading authors working on Austronesian languages postulate a typo-logical divide within that family that is partly based on the parameter of voice (e.g., Arka & Ross 2005 and Himmelmann 2005). In this view, some languages have ASYMMETRICAL VOICE ALTERNATIONS, that is, semantically and syntac-tically bivalent verbs regularly head either two-argument clauses (i.e., an active diathesis) or one-argument clauses (i.e., a passive diathesis). Example (210) from Maori illustrates such an alternation:

(210)   Maori (Austronesian, New Zealand; Chung 1977: 355)
    a. *Ka   hoko   te   matua i   ngā   tīkiti.*
       AOR buy   the.SG   parent ACC the.PL ticket
       'The parent buys the ticket.' (unmarked active)
    b. *Ka   hoko-na   ngā   tīkiti   e   te   matua.*
       AOR buy-PASS the.PL ticket   AGT the.SG   parent
       'The tickets were bought by the parent.' (*na*-passive)

According to these authors, other Austronesian languages show a SYMMET-RICAL VOICE ALTERNATION, where both clauses have a two-argument core and neither verb form can be said to be morphologically derived from the other. Consider the following example from Indonesian:

(211)   Indonesian (Sneddon 1996: 256–257)
    a. *Dia   men-jemput   saya.*
       3SG   AV-meet   1SG
    b. *Saya   di-jemput-nya.*
       1SG   PV-meet-3SG
    Both: 'He met me.'

The clause in (a) has an agent diathesis, with a subject A (*dia* '3SG') and an object P (*saya* '1SG'). Conversely, the clause in (b) has a patient diathesis, with a subject P (*saya*) and an object A (*-nya*). Both diatheses are morphologically marked as voices – the agent voice by *men-*, the patient voice by *di-*. These two voices were introduced in Chapter 3 and are schematically represented again in Figure 4.1 below.

At least some Austronesian languages indeed appear to have such voice alternations, which is significant not only for theories and typologies of voice, but also for theories of alignment and theories of syntax. Two issues raised here are particularly important. First, to what extent are diathetical

Figure 4.1 *Agent and patient diatheses*

oppositions in Austronesian languages as straightforward as the above account of the Maori and Indonesian examples suggests? The short answer is: it's complicated; we give a long answer in Section 4.1. Second, are there symmetrical voice alternations in languages that are neither areally nor genealogically related to Austronesian? The short answer is: yes, there are, *mutatis mutandis*: we elaborate on the noteworthy *mutanda* in Section 4.2. Section 4.3 summarizes what these discussions actually mean for an understanding of voice.

4.1   Symmetrical Voice in Western Austronesian

Both the existence and the exact nature of symmetrical voice oppositions have been the subject of debate for at least a century. We cannot possibly survey the discussion in detail here, nor can we provide answers to all the questions raised. We limit ourselves to outlining the essential points of the debate.

There are at least two reasons why the simple account of the Maori and Indonesian examples in (210)–(211) is not the whole story for Austronesian. The first reason is typological and historical: Austronesian languages show considerable variation as to voice alternations. Arka and Ross (2005) actually postulate four types, summarized in (212):[1]

(212)   Types of Austronesian languages according to voice (Arka & Ross 2005: 7)
       I: Philippine-type (Himmelmann 2002)
       II: Indonesian-type (Wolff 1996, Ross 2002)
       III: Flores-type
       IV: Eastern Austronesian type

The geographical designations are only approximate,[2] and "Flores-type" is our label (Arka & Ross 2005 say "certain isolating languages of Flores" but do not propose an impressionistic label). Type I consists of conservative languages that retain more

---

[1] See Himmelmann (2005: 113) for a somewhat different view.
[2] Type I includes languages spoken in the Philippines, but also in Taiwan, northern Borneo, northern Sulawesi, and Madagascar. Type II covers languages spoken in western Indonesia and Malaysia. Flores refers to the island of Flores in eastern Indonesia. Type IV languages are spoken in eastern Nusa Tenggara, New Guinea, Island Melanesia, Polynesia, and Micronesia.

than two voices, including the agent voice (called Actor Voice in Austronesian studies) and several voices with non-agentive subjects (called Undergoer Voices, which include a Patient Voice corresponding to the patient voice in Figure 4.1). In such languages, the Actor Voice may show lower transitivity, and even lower syntactic valency, than the Patient Voice. Type II languages retain only two of the original voices (supplemented by applicatives), the default voice being the Patient Voice. Languages belonging to Types III and IV are less well studied: the former appear to have lost a substantial part of their morphological potential and show uncoded diathetical alternations, and the latter may have applicatives and passives but do not have any kind of Actor–Patient Voice alternation.

The second reason that we need to survey western Austronesian in more detail is analytical: the clause types of some languages have been analyzed in crucially different ways. In what follows, we deal with multi-voice languages of Type I first, focusing on Tagalog, a Philippine language that has figured prominently in the whole debate (4.1.1). Then, we address purportedly two-voice languages of Type II, centering on Indonesian (4.1.2). Section 4.1.3 summarizes the findings and their significance for the study of Austronesian voice. We briefly mention Type III languages in Chapter 6, and Type IV languages need to be described in greater detail.

4.1.1   Tagalog

Tagalog belongs to the Central Philippine branch of the Malayo-Polynesian group of Austronesian. It has the largest speech community of the approximately 150 languages of the Philippines, with some 17 million first-language speakers and at least twice as many second- or third-language speakers (Riesberg 2014b: 6–7). Besides four regional varieties, there is a standard register, which is one of the two official languages of the Philippines (the other being English) and the variety addressed in what follows.

It is safe to regard the symmetrical-voice view (henceforth SVV) as the mainstream model of Tagalog voice in the current functional-typological literature. Many studies espouse it; suffice it to mention here Kroeger (1993), Shibatani (1988), Foley (2008), Riesberg (2014b), and Himmelmann (2005).[3]

4.1.1.1   The Symmetrical Account of Tagalog Voices

We start by noting the essential features of this view in two-argument clauses before complicating the picture by adding not only further clause types but also alternative analyses.[4] Consider the examples in (213):

---

[3] Not all of these studies use the term "symmetrical voice," which is a more recent coinage (Himmelmann 2005, Foley 2008). It is also in order to mention Guilfoyle et al. (1992) as an early study in the SVV spirit in the Chomskyan tradition.

[4] We have not included Klaiman's (1991) SVV treatment here, because it has not been influential. In her view, both clause types under scrutiny are two-argument clauses, but she tentatively sees them as instantiating the same diathesis: "it seems especially dubious to associate Philippine voices with strategies for moving nominals in and out of subject position" (1991: 258).

(213)   Tagalog (Aldridge 2012: 192–193; Foley 2008: 23)[5]
   a. *B<um>ili*   *ang*   *babae*   *ng*   *isda.*
       buy<AV>   NOM   woman   GEN   fish
       'The woman bought a fish.' (agent voice = Actor Voice)
   b. *Bibilh-in*   *ng*   *babae*   *ang*   *isda.*
       buy.IRR-PV   GEN   woman   NOM   fish
       'The woman will buy the fish.' (patient voice = Patient Voice)

Some features of these examples are uncontroversial. First, the predicate occurs clause-initially in neutral simple declarative clauses such as these and takes an affix (here: *<um>* and *-in*), which shows elaborate TAM-related and lexical allomorphy. Second, the constituents expressing the semantic arguments occur with proclitics (here: *ang* vs. *ng*, with common nouns; *si* and *ni* are used with proper nouns). Personal pronouns also show different forms, which correspond to the functions encoded by *ang/si* and *ng/ni*, respectively.[6] Lastly, the *ang*-phrase must be specific; the *ng*-phrase can have a specific or nonspecific reading.

Other features vary according to the particular analysis to which the data are subject. For instance, the affix on the predicate is presented as denoting either voice or syntactic valency. The proclitics usually receive case labels nowadays and are seen by some as marking subjects and objects, but there is still no consensus as to whether and how to apply these notions to the syntax of languages like Tagalog (Himmelmann 2005: Ch. 3.8).[7] We follow recent formulations of the SVV (e.g., Riesberg 2014b) here, according to which the affixes mark voices (either Actor Voice, via *<um>*, or Patient Voice, via *-in*) and the clitics mark grammatical relations in the clause (either subject or object); crucially, both (a) and (b) in (213) are analyzed as two-argument clauses.[8]

Let us now provide a more comprehensive picture of the Tagalog clause types. First, there are also one-argument clauses headed by monovalent predicates; the sole argument takes the nominative marker *ang*, and the verb can take either *<um>* or (less frequently) *mag-* in such clauses – as can bivalent predicates in two-argument clauses (sometimes lexically conditioned, sometimes making a semantic distinction; see Himmelmann 2006, 2008).

Notably, there are other clause types besides the ones given in (213); the array in (214), or some version of it, is often found in the literature on Tagalog voice.

---

[5] The glosses have been adapted to match Kroeger's (1993).

[6] We are simplifying matters here: common-noun nominative *ang*, genitive *ng*, and oblique *sa* (see (218); this is sometimes glossed as "dative") on the one hand and proper-noun nominative *si*, genitive *ni*, and oblique *kay* on the other are only superficially isomorphic. Roughly, *ng* covers a wider range of semantic roles than *ni*, and *sa* covers a narrower range of semantic roles than *kay*. Case marking on demonstratives and personal pronouns basically follows the common-noun and proper-noun patterns, respectively. See Himmelmann (2005) for details.

[7] Some scholars working on Austronesian voices have also used the term FOCUS for the voice markers and TOPIC for the non-English-like subject (e.g., McKaughan 1958). Other labels for the subject, typically understood as something *sui generis*, include TRIGGER and PIVOT.

[8] We are glossing over the thorny issue of noun-verb distinction here; see Himmelmann (2008) and Kaufman (2009, 2017) for details.

All clauses in (214) have a subject marked by *ang* and objects marked by *ng*, and the voice affix specifies the semantic role of the subject, namely agent (*<um>*), patient (unmarked here), location (*-an*), or goal (*i-*). Other arguments and some adjuncts take the oblique marker *sa* (plus some other element if needed, e.g., 'for the child' would be *para sa bata* in the non-Conveyance Voice counterpart of (d) below). An Instrumental Voice can be constructed adding *paN-* to the Conveyance Voice form, as in (e):

(214)   Tagalog (Kroeger 1993: 13–14)

    a. *B<um>ili   ang   lalake ng   isda sa   tindahan.*
       buy<AV>   NOM   man   GEN fish OBL store
       'The man bought fish at the store.' (Actor Voice)

    b. *B<in>ili   ng   lalake ang isda sa   tindahan.*
       buy<REAL>[PV]   GEN man   NOM fish OBL store
       'The man bought the fish at the store.' (Patient Voice)

    c. *B<in>ilh-an   ng   lalake ng   isda ang tindahan.*
       buy<REAL>-LV   GEN man   GEN fish NOM store
       'The man bought fish at the store.' (Locative Voice)

    d. *I-b<in>ili   ng   lalake ng   isda ang bata.*
       CV-buy<REAL>   GEN man   GEN fish NOM child
       'The man bought fish for the child.' (Conveyance Voice)

    e. *I-p<in>am-bili   ng   lalake ng   isda ang pera.*
       CV-IV<REAL>-buy GEN man   GEN fish NOM money
       'The man bought fish with the money.' (Instrumental Voice)

Table 4.1 gives some voice forms of *bili-* 'buy'; the voice affixes appear in boldface.[9]

Table 4.1 *Selected forms of Tagalog* bili *'buy'*

	Actor Voice	Undergoer Voices		
	Agent	Patient	Locative	Conveyance
Realis				
- PFV	*b<**um**>ilí*	*b<**in**>ilí*	*b<**in**>ilh-**án***	*i-b<**in**>ilí*
- IPFV	*b<**um**>ì~bilí*	*b<**in**>ì~bilí*	*b<**in**>ì~bilh-**án***	*i-b<**in**>ì~bilí*
Irrealis				
- PFV[10]	*b<**um**>ilí*	*bilh-**ín***	*bilh-**án***	*i-bilí*
- IPFV	*bì~bilí*	*bì~bilh-**ín***	*bì~bilh-**án***	*i-bì~bilí*

(Himmelmann 2008: 286)

Note in passing three morphological features of this paradigm. First, Patient Voice forms take the suffix *-in* in the irrealis but bear no segmental marking in the realis. Second, all Undergoer Voice forms take *<in>* in the realis. Third, imperfective forms feature a reduplicative affix.

---

[9] We are glossing over the prosodic structure of TAM forms here (i.e., the graphic accents in Table 4.1).

Syntactically, the two simpler clause types in (213), which correspond to (a) and (b) in (214), are two-argument clauses built on the predicate and its semantic arguments. The more complex clause types (i.e., (c–e) in (214)) are what we call SUBJECTIVE UNDERGOER NUCLEATIVES in Chapter 2; they install non-agentive subjects that are not semantic arguments of the base predicate. In principle, this operation is equivalent to applicativization (which introduces the new argument to the syntactic core) plus passivization (which promotes the non-agent to subject). The literature on Tagalog and other Philippine languages often emphasizes that here (i) a single morpheme does the job instead of an applicative-passive combination, and (ii) the system is not limited to few verbs (as some applicatives may be) but is productive: such voice alternations are pervasive in these languages.

Nevertheless, there are important caveats about how to understand these nucleatives. First, not all of those voices are equally frequent with all verbs – they resemble the distribution of real-world applicatives rather than that of prototypical passives. More importantly, the paradigm illustrated in (214) is misleading in that voice morphology shows non-negligible lexicalization. With verbs other than *bili* 'buy', *-an* and *i-* often target subjects with semantic roles different from locations and beneficiaries; similarly, *paN-* affixation can also target non-instrumental subjects. Lastly, and most significantly, it is not always clear how to determine whether a particular participant is a semantic argument of the base predicate. This methodological problem arises in all languages but is particularly recalcitrant in Tagalog, and possibly in other Philippine-type languages, not least because coreness tests (see the next subsection) are merely an imperfect proxy for semantic argumenthood.

Finally, proponents of the SVV for Tagalog also mention results from corpus studies based on actual discourse. Cooreman et al. (1984) is one of the much-cited articles arguing that the Undergoer Voices – not only the Patient Voice – are used frequently in texts; this study reports a 59 percent vs. 25 percent preference over Actor Voices in narrative texts.[11]

4.1.1.2   Asymmetrical Accounts of the Tagalog (and Philippine) Voices

In addition to the SVV account of the data in (213) above and their alleged equivalents in other Philippine languages, there are at least two asymmetrical-voice views (henceforth AVVs) in the literature. Early treatments

---

[10] This row contains the basic/unmarked forms with respect to TAM, which are used in the imperative, in control constructions, and as non-initial predicates in clause chains (Himmelmann 2008).

[11] Slightly higher figures hold for other Austronesian, even non-Philippine, languages; Norwood (2002) reports a 71 percent vs. 23 percent preference in Karo Batak, and Donohue (2002) reports a figure close to 70 percent for Undergoer Voices in Tukang Besi. Yet other Austronesian languages, however, show different distributions of Undergoer and Actor Voices in texts: Quick (2002) reports an almost equal distribution in Pendau, and Pastika (1999) reports a roughly equal distribution in spoken Balinese but a 30 percent vs. 70 percent distribution in written texts in that language. See Arka (2002) for more details.

see the Actor Voice as a two-argument agent clause and the Patient Voice as its one-argument passive counterpart (Bloomfield 1917, Blake 1925, Lopez 1937, 1965, Aspillera 1969, Bell 1983). Later treatments see the Patient Voice as a two-argument patient clause and the Actor Voice as its one-argument antipassive counterpart (Payne 1982; Cooreman et al. 1984; De Guzman 1988; Mithun 1994; Aldridge 2004, 2012; Liao 2004).

The passive analysis of the Patient Voice has been largely abandoned by now, but the debate it sparked led to a more principled discussion of the notion of subjecthood, both language-specifically and across languages. In particular, scholars have identified a number of diagnostics of syntactic prominence that are often used as tests for subject. The seven main tests employed to this day are: addressee of imperatives, control of reflexivization, coreferential omission in coordination, coreferential omission in subordination, the ability to launch floating quantifiers, relativization, and the ability to be questioned. Applying these tests to Kapampangan, for instance, Morris (1999) finds that the first four target the agent irrespective of its syntax while the last four target the subject irrespective of its semantics (note that there is an overlap with the fourth test).[12]

By contrast, the antipassive analysis of the Actor Voice is still debated. Specifically for Tagalog, for instance, Aldridge (2012) regards the affixes on the predicate as markers of syntactic valency (she uses the term "transitivity"): she glosses both <um> and mag- as 'INTRANSITIVE PERFECTIVE' (the latter allegedly restricted to agentive monovalent predicates, her "unergatives") on the one hand and <in> as 'TRANSITIVE PERFECTIVE' on the other. By defining antipassives not as demotional but as constructions that merely fail to promote the object (2012: 199), she interprets the purported one-argument clauses based on bivalent predicates in Tagalog as antipassives and finds functional parallels between them and antipassives in Mayan and Eskimoan. These parallels are the indefinite reading of the P, narrow scope, omissibility with predicates that "can be used unergatively" (like kain 'eat', 2012: 195), and an aspectual correlation between higher valency and telicity. The whole analytical move leads to distinguishing two homophonous instances of the proclitic ng, namely oblique in the intransitive and ergative in the transitive; ang is glossed as absolutive.

The fact that Aldridge sees realis <in> as a transitivity marker does not invalidate her general argument – nor does the fact that the opposition between <um>, mag- and the other voice affixes occurring on monovalent and bivalent predicates is more intricate than what Aldridge says. Aldridge herself addresses two objections made in the literature to an analysis of the Actor Voice as antipassive. First, regarding the results of one specific test for coreness adduced by Kroeger (1993), namely gap control in nonfinite embedded clauses, Aldridge says that her Minimalist account of the syntax of such constructions actually

---

[12] Applying these tests to Tagalog famously spawned a sizable volume of literature discussing those tests that identify the ang-phrase vis-à-vis those that identify the agent (see, e.g., Schachter 1977, 1996).

predicts the observed behavior despite considering the P an oblique instead of a core argument. Second, and less relevantly, Maclachlan (1996) argues that antipassives, being derived constructions, should be acquired later by children, but several studies show they are acquired in tandem with the Patient Voice; Aldridge replies that her antipassives are not derived but have "the same structural properties as a transitive clause" (Aldridge 2012: 201).

Other authors (e.g., Schachter & Reid 2009) present an "ergative account" of Tagalog syntax – i.e., a one-argument analysis of the Actor Voice – without engaging with alternative accounts directly. Yet other authors (e.g., Payne 1982) avoid some of the problems related to the antipassive analysis by postulating an opposition between underived one-argument and two-argument clauses (corresponding to the Actor and Patient Voices, respectively).

To our knowledge, an important objection to any analysis that sees the P in the Tagalog Actor Voice as an adjunct has not been addressed convincingly by proponents of an AVV, Aldridge included. Proponents of the SVV aptly emphasize the positive results of tests for adjunct in the language, which include participial adjunct constructions and the fronting of constituents for topicalization (Katagiri 2005). Kroeger (1993), Foley (2008), and Riesberg (2014b) mention the latter test at some length; the basic rule is seen operating in (215). Adjuncts can be fronted (a) while core arguments – either subjects (b) or objects (c) – cannot:[13]

(215)   Tagalog (Kroeger 1993: 44–45)
         a. [*Para kay   Pedro*]   *b<in>ili*   *ang laruan.*
            for   OBL   P.   buy<REAL>[PV]   NOM toy
            'For Pedro I bought this toy.'
         b. *[*Si   Pedro*] *ko*   *b<in>igay-an*   *ng   laruan.*
            NOM   P.   1SG.GEN give<REAL>-LV   GEN   toy
            (Intended: 'Pedro I gave this toy to.')
         c. *[*Ng   nanay*] *siya*   *p<in>alo.*
            GEN   mother   3SG.NOM   spank<REAL>[PV]
            (Intended: 'By mother he was spanked.')

The results of such a test suggest that both *ang/si* and *ng/ni* mark core arguments. Consequently, both the Actor and the Patient Voices are two-argument clauses, and the analysis in terms of agent and patient voices, respectively, seems warranted. For this empirical reason, but also on theoretical grounds, Aldridge's notion of a non-demotional antipassive is unlikely to be widely accepted in functional-typological studies in the near future.

4.1.2   Other Western Austronesian Languages

Numerous authors propose an SVV for western Austronesian languages. Shibatani's (1988) account of Cebuano and Tagalog and Clayre's

---

[13] Riesberg (2014b: 65f) also mentions that the behavior of floating quantifiers serves as coreness test in Indonesian, Balinese, and Totoli, but in Tagalog it is a subjecthood test only.

(2005) account of Lun Dayeh are cases in point. Riesberg (2014b) maintains that Totoli and Balinese voices, as well as some of the Indonesian voices, are also best described by the SVV. Nevertheless, other scholars working on Austronesian claim that some languages favor an analysis of the Actor Voice as one-argument clause. In what follows, we first sketch one such account (4.1.2.1) and then move on to Indonesian (4.1.2.2).

4.1.2.1   Ergative-Syntax Languages of the Philippines

As mentioned in the preceding subsection, so-called ergative accounts of the clausal syntax of Philippine languages are not rare. Several authors argue in favor of regarding the Actor Voice – often understood morphologically/historically rather than functionally – as some kind of one-argument clause; besides the studies dealing with Tagalog, Teng's (2005) account of Puyuma (southern Taiwan) is a case in point. To our knowledge, the strongest case for the existence of syntactic ergativity in Philippine languages made with published data involves a Northern Philippine language of central Luzon called Kapampangan.[14]

According to Mithun (1994), Kapampangan case marking – visible on enclitics that are always present in the clause (in addition to the nominal proclitics like those of Tagalog) – follows a run-of-the-mill ergative pattern (216). The one-argument clause in (a) features a 3rd-person absolute enclitic *ya* and the absolutive nominal proclitic *ing*, while the two-argument clause in (b) shows an enclitic *ne* encoding both the ergative and the absolutive 3sGs, as well as the nominal proclitics (absolutive *ing* and ergative *ning*):

(216)   Kapampangan (Mithun 1994: 254, 249)
  a. *Oneng   mapali=ya   ing   aldo.*
      but   hot=3SG.ABS   ABS   sun
      'But the sun was hot.'
  b. *Adakap=ne   ning   matying   ing   pau.*
      managed.to.catch=3SG→3SG   ERG   monkey   ABS   turtle
      'The monkey caught the turtle.'

Mithun (1994) further gives the examples below with *buklat* 'open', reminiscent of the voice array we saw for Tagalog in (214) above. Those in (217) are labeled "transitive" (Mithun says they are applicative derivations) while those in (218) are labeled "intransitive" (the labels in parentheses are hers):

(217)   Kapampangan (Mithun 1994: 257–258)
  a. *(I)buklat=ne.*
      open=3SG→3SG
      'He'll open it.'

---

[14] Mithun (1994) says it has one million speakers, and the 2000 census of the Philippines says over 2.3 million.

    b. *Buklatan=ne.*
       open.for=3SG→3SG
       'He'll open (it) for him.'
    c. *Pamuklat=ne.*
       open.with=3SG→3SG
       'He'll open (things) with it.'

(218)   Kapampangan (Mithun 1994: 258)
    a. *Mamuklat=ya.*
       open=3SG
       'He'll open up.' ("Antipassive")
    b. *Makabuklat=ya.*
       open=3SG
       'It is open / has been opened.' ("Passive")
    c. *Mibubuklat=ya.*
       open=3SG
       'It's opening.' ("Middle")

Even though Mithun does not segment the voice-encoding elements on the predicates, it is evident that the morphology is closely related to the make-up of Tagalog predicates we saw in Section 4.1.1. In (217) above, the affixes installing the beneficiary and the instrument seem to be *-an* (b) and *paN-* (c), respectively – but it is unclear from these examples whether they are applicatives (as suggested by the English translations) or nucleatives. In (218) above, the affixes seem to be *maN-* (a), *maka-* (b), and *mi-* (c), respectively – but with *maN-* it is clearer than with Tagalog that we are dealing with a one-argument clause. Consider:

(219)   Kapampangan (Mithun 1994: 271; Kitano 2006: 91)
    a. *Miglutu=ya(=ng   sagin).*
       cook=3SG=LNK   banana
       'She cooked (bananas).'
    b. *Linutu=no   reng   sagin.*
       cook=3SG→3PL   ABS.PL banana
       'She cooked bananas.'
    c. *Maglinis=ya(=ng   awang).*
       clean.AV=3SG=LNK window
       'He will clean up (windows).'
    d. *Linisan=no   reng   awang.*
       clean.PV=3SG→3PL ABS.PL window
       'He will clean the windows.'

These examples suggest that the Actor Voice is indeed a one-argument clause; the P does not need to be expressed, but if it is, it is neither case-marked (it is only licensed by a linker clitic *=ng*) nor indexed by the enclitic. It cannot be a prototypical antipassive, however, since the P is not oblique-flagged, and the Actor Voice does not distinguish between monovalent and bivalent predicates – which means this is not an antipassive at all. That there is more going on here can be seen from Mithun's last example of a different "Passive":

(220)   Kapampangan (Mithun 1994: 272)
       Me·lutu=no   reng   sagin.
       cooked=3SG→3PL   ABS.PL   banana
       'The bananas have been cooked.'

Mithun glosses *=no* as 'already/3PL.ABS' in this particular instance, but, as far as we can see, there is no good reason to do so. Mithun's consultants apparently gave her an impersonal 3SG form instead of a form parallel to *makabuklat=ya* 'it has been opened'.

4.1.2.2   Indonesian(-Type) Voices

According to Arka and Ross (2005), Indonesian-type voices appear as the simple opposition between an agent and a patient voice, without all the undergoer nucleatives that constitute both a semantic-syntactic and a morphological paradigm in languages like Tagalog. Indonesian-type languages may supplement this deficit, as it were, via applicative derivation. Such a description seems to apply to Madurese (Malayo-Sumbawan; Davies 2005) and to Sa'ban and at least some other Kelabitic languages (North Sarawakan; Clayre 2005).[15] Examples of the basic opposition in the former language follow:

(221)   Madurese (Davies 2005: 201)
       a. *Ali   N-baca   buku-na   Siti.*   (agent voice)
           A.   AV-read   book-DEF   S.
       b. *Buku-na   Siti   e-baca   Ali.*   (patient voice)
           book-DEF   S.   PV-read   A.
       Both: 'Ali read Siti's book.'

Madurese has a benefactive/instrumental applicative *-agi* and a directional/locative applicative *-e*, and the combined effect of such applicativization and the patient voice is equivalent to the undergoer nucleative, albeit as a two-step operation: the extra-thematic participant is installed in the clause and then promoted to subject.

Davies's account is quite succinct and does not deal with potential alternative analyses, but in absence of additional evidence we can give him the benefit of the doubt. We devote the rest of this subsection to showing why Indonesian, however, is not adequately described by the account Davies gives for Madurese.

Let us provide some background information on the language first. Malay belongs to the Malayic branch of the Malayo-Polynesian group within Austronesian. It is spoken by an uncertain but considerable number of people in

---

[15] Quick (2005) and Andersen and Andersen (2005) make the same claim for Pendau and Moronene, respectively, but since these studies center almost exclusively on morphology and discourse, it is not clear to us whether both the Actor and Patient Voices are two-argument clauses. For a Kelabitic language different from Madurese, see Kelabit (Hemmings 2015, 2016).

Southeast Asia – at least some 200 million, including first- and second-language speakers (Simons & Fennig 2017) – in Malaysia, Brunei, Singapore, and Indonesia, where it has official status. In the last country, the language is called Indonesian and has some 20–30 million first-language speakers (Simons & Fennig 2017). In addition to the standard ("formal") variety used in writing, education, government, and the media, there are numerous local ("colloquial") varieties, which are heavily influenced by some of the other 700–800 languages of Indonesia. We address the standard variety and occasionally comment on the colloquial varieties in what follows.

Our first stop regards the morphological make-up of clauses. *MeN-* (222), *di-* (223), and the unmarked form (224) are the semantically neutral options for bivalent predicates:[16]

(222)   Indonesian (Sneddon 1996: 255)
         Mereka   sudah   men-jemput   Tomo.
         3PL   PERF   ACT-meet   T.
         'They have met Tomo.'

(223)   Indonesian (Sneddon 1996: 257)
         a. *Tomo   sudah   di-jemput   (oleh)   mereka.*
             T.   PERF   DI-meet   AGT   3PL
             'Tomo has been met by them.'
         b. *Saya   di-jemput-nya.*
             1SG   DI-meet-3SG
             'He met me.'

(224)   Indonesian (Sneddon 1996: 249)
         a. *Dia   kami   jemput.*
             3SG   1PL   meet
             'We met him.'
         b. *Buku   ini   sudah   ku-baca.*
             book   this   PERF   1SG-read
             'I have read this book.'

Clauses headed by a *meN*-form in (222) have one form (with preverbal As and postverbal Ps). By contrast, clauses headed by an unmarked form in (224) can either show preverbal Ps and immediately preverbal As, as in (a), or have the element expressing the A bound to, and preceding, the predicate (the latter with 1SG *ku-* or 2SG *kau-*), as in (b). Also note that neither constituents like NPs/PPs nor grammatical markers like the negation or aspectual morphemes can occur between the pronominal A and the unmarked predicate. Lastly, clauses headed by a *di*-form can have the three forms illustrated in (223), namely with the P preceding, and the

---

[16] The reader is referred to Sneddon (1996: 117f) for details on the semantically more complex groups of clause types headed by either *ter-* or *ke-...-an*-verb forms. Briefly, the former are passives or low-agentivity forms, while the latter seem to cover possessive, malefactive, and other nucleative functions.

A following, the predicate, but with the A being either marked by *oleh* 'by' or unmarked (a), and with some As being bound to the predicate (*-nya*) (b).[17]

There is variation among speakers as to what determines the choice between *di*-forms and unmarked verbs. According to Sneddon (1996: 258–259), the person of the A plays a crucial role for most speakers: pronominal or lexical 3rd-person As trigger the use of a *di*-form, whereas pronominal As (i.e., 1st and 2nd persons, as well as "substitutes" like kinship terms used for SAPs) require an unmarked form. According to Chung (1976: 60f), however, a non-negligible number of speakers allow *di*-forms with SAPs as well. Some other aspects show little variation; for example, whether *oleh* is optional or not depends on the placement of the PP: immediately postverbal As allow its absence, while other positions do not.

As to the syntax of the clauses in (222)–(224), earlier accounts largely follow the morphology of the predicate and treat all *di*-forms as syntactically equivalent, namely as passives (e.g., Sneddon 1996), but some recent accounts apply tests for subject and tests for object and arrive at a differentiated view. We follow Arka and Manning (2008) and Riesberg (2014b: Ch. 2) in distinguishing the clause types detailed in Table 4.2 below.

Table 4.2 *Selected clause types in standard Indonesian*

	two-argument		one-argument
	agent diathesis	patient diathesis	passive diathesis
A: all persons	A *meN*-V P		
A: pronominal		P A(-)V	
A: 3rd person		P *di*-V-*nya*	P *di*-V (*oleh*) A

(based on Riesberg 2014b: 14)

Thus, from a syntactic viewpoint, Indonesian has two semantically neutral two-argument clause types: one with a subject A and an object P (the agent diathesis) and another with a subject P and an object A (the patient diathesis). Patient-diathesis clauses have a split morphosyntax; with pronominal As of any person, the verb is unmarked and the pronoun immediately precedes it (either as an independent form or as a bound element); with reduced 3SG As (marked by *-nya*), the verb appears in the *di*-form. Clauses headed by a *di*-form are split as well; in opposition to the patient voice with a reduced pronominal 3SG marker, those with full pronominal 3rd persons (either *dia* '3SG' or *mereka* '3PL') or lexical NPs are passives that can have their A marked via *oleh* 'by' or not.[18]

---

[17] Note that other western Austronesian languages show different formal oppositions; Balinese and Sasak, for instance, have verbs take a nasal prefix in the Actor Voice but unmarked verbs in the Patient Voice (Peter Austin, pers. comm.).

[18] Note that other modern accounts treat clauses headed by *di*-verbs uniformly (and as passives) but postulate the existence of a patient diathesis nonetheless (clauses headed by unmarked verb forms), not only for Standard Indonesian but also for other Malay varieties. See Cole et al. (2008) for details and references.

There are four lessons to be learned from such an account. First, Indonesian has a symmetrical diathetical opposition; there are two two-argument clauses, namely the agent and the patient diatheses. Second, it also has an asymmetrical diathetical opposition: there are passive clauses, namely those headed by some *di*-forms.[19] Third, the issue of voice symmetry (i.e., of verbal marking) in Indonesian is complicated: the passive is a voice, as are some patient-diathesis-constructions, but some other patient diatheses are uncoded – as is the agent diathesis in Colloquial Indonesian and parts of the agent-diathesis paradigm in Standard Indonesian. (In Colloquial Indonesian, *meN-* is frequently omitted in all environments. In Standard Indonesian, *meN-* is regularly omitted in certain imperatives and with a few common verbs; see Sneddon 2006: 72.) Fourth, even though the referential hierarchy [1/2 > 3PRO > 3NP] does not inform all diathetical choices, the system is not entirely independent from it: at least with subject Ps, the choice between different constructions is constrained by person, number, and pronominality of one of the arguments. In particular, a construction with a subject P and a lexical NP A has to be a one-argument clause.

There is a further asymmetry within Indonesian voice that we have not addressed so far. As shown by Arka (2009), once the tests for object are applied to the different phrases expressing the A with the subject P constructions, not only do reduced 3SG As (*-nya*) differ from the other 3rd-person As but the presence or absence of *oleh* 'by' also plays a role. Whereas the [*oleh* A] constituent does not pass any of the coreness tests and is a bona fide adjunct (hence the passive analysis), the [Ø A] constituent shows an intermediate behavior – arguably on the adjunct side, but less adjunct-like than the PP.[20]

4.1.3   Western Austronesian Variation

The current consensus among leading Austronesianists is that even languages of the Philippines show variation regarding voice oppositions; there is no consensus, however, as to how to best characterize that variation and its significance. The mainstream story (Blust 2002, 2003; Ross 2002; Himmelmann 2002) about erstwhile agent and patient voices plus several undergoer nucleatives – hallmarks of "the Philippine-type" – having been partially dismantled in several present-day languages is quite plausible. In this view, some languages – those of "the Indonesian-type" – gradually lost most undergoer

---

[19] At least some *ter*-forms are also passive; the syntax of several subtypes of clauses headed by *ke-...-an*-forms is not entirely clear to us.

[20] Riesberg (2014b) follows Aarts (2007) in postulating the gradience of syntactic categories like lexical categories and grammatical relations (but see Croft 2007 for a critique of Aarts's approach). Roughly, grammatical relations can be seen as central or peripheral but still distinct (i.e., as categories with a prototype structure but without fuzzy boundaries). It is well known that neither subjects nor objects are homogeneous in many languages, but how best to deal with this variation is a matter that lies beyond the scope of the present study. We limit ourselves to noting that research in this important area has already begun in the Austronesian context, especially with respect to grammatical voice.

nucleatives and developed ersatz constructions combining patient diathesis with applicatives. Other languages lost their voice morphology ("Flores"), or even diathetical oppositions altogether ("Eastern Austronesian").

Two additional parameters of variation are worthy of note from the perspective of the study of voice. The first has figured prominently in the literature and is still the matter of debate: how syntactically symmetrical are voice oppositions in western Austronesian in general and in Philippine languages in particular? The data and analyses available to us suggest that there is substantial fluidity, or perhaps rather gradience, to the exact syntactic status of the A and the P in several clause types. Pigeonholing these arguments as subjects, objects, and adjuncts based on diagnostics has proven to be feasible on the one hand but less than fruitful and illuminating on the other – which is probably the main reason that the issue of grammatical relations in general, and in western Austronesian in particular, is still largely unresolved. Traditional voice-analysis is possible for several of these languages: some have agent diatheses while others have antipassives instead. Nevertheless, the fact that the Actor Voice cannot be unequivocally classified in some languages plainly shows that the notion of voice was not developed based on western Austronesian phenomena. Even a notion as flexible as the one we espouse in the present book, which considerably abstracts from the morphological, syntactic, and semantic specifics observable in the classical languages, does not really do justice to Tagalog, Indonesian, and many other languages mentioned here. Despite the undeniable progress the linguistic profession has made since, say, the early 1970s or even the early 1990s, a model of clause alternations that is descriptively and explanatorily adequate for these languages is still work in progress.

The second parameter of variation has received somewhat less attention in the typological literature: what are the exact conditions determining the choice between diatheses? Most Austronesianist work aptly notes that specificity – one of the usual requisites of topic-worthiness – plays an important role in determining which argument can actually be the clause subject, thereby limiting the choice between competing constructions.[21] The affectedness of the P, naturally connected to TAM-related values, has been shown to play a role as well (Arka & Ross 2005). But we saw for Indonesian that at least some aspects of the choice between diatheses are not independent of the person of the arguments involved. To our knowledge, this angle should be explored more systematically from a comparative perspective, for reasons that will become apparent in the following section.

4.2   Symmetrical Voice in Non-Austronesian Languages

The present section shows that non-Austronesian languages can show voice phenomena that are both similar and different to those we have seen for

---

[21] We are indebted to Nikolaus Himmelmann for pointing out to us that earlier studies saw definiteness as the crucial feature.

Tagalog, Indonesian, and the other Austronesian languages mentioned in the preceding section. We first address some languages of South America (4.2.1) and then some languages of North America (4.2.2).

4.2.1 Selected South American Languages

This section sketches the voice oppositions found in three indigenous languages of South America that are neither areally nor genealogically related. Mapudungun is an unclassified language spoken by some 250,000 people in south-central Chile and Argentinian Patagonia; the interested reader is referred to Zúñiga (2006a, 2006b) for more facts, as well as analysis and references. Jarawara is an Arawan language spoken by some 150 people in the Brazilian Amazon; Dixon (2000a, 2004) provides additional information. Movima is an unclassified language spoken by some 500 people in the Bolivian Amazon; readers should consult Haude (2006, 2009, 2014) for details and references. For a study on symmetrical voice focusing on these and some other languages from the perspective of alignment typology, see Haude and Zúñiga (2016).

4.2.1.1 Mapudungun

Mapudungun regularly marks one or two arguments on verbs (some 3SG arguments are unmarked on some forms). In addition, predicates show voice morphology (more on this below) and a morphological opposition between direct and inverse forms. Consider the opposition depicted in (225):

(225)   Mapudungun[22]
    a. *Chi domo leli-fi-i*   *chi*   *wentru.* (direct, agent voice)
       the   woman   look.at-3.P-IND   the   man
    b. *Chi wentru leli-e-i-mew*   *chi domo.* (inverse, patient voice)
       the   man   look.at-INV-IND-3.A   the woman
    Both: 'The woman looked at the man.'

Even though the two 3rd-person NPs bear no morphological marking that might distinguish them (the language does not have case), they can be labeled proximate and obviative, respectively, on purely functional grounds.[23] Proximates are typically human/animate protagonists, and obviatives are secondary characters and can be either animate or inanimate.

There is no good reason to analyze either of the two clauses in (225) as syntactically monovalent; in particular, the inverse clause does not show any unequivocal signs of demotion of the A out of the syntactic core, and is therefore

---

[22] The Mapudungun examples give underlying forms; some elision, epenthesis, and resyllabification rules apply (e.g., *fi-i* > *fi, e-i-mew* > *eyew, e-n-mew* > *enew*). See Zúñiga (2006a) for details.

[23] See Section 4.2.2.3 for the usual characterization of these notions in Algonquian studies and Aissen (1997) for an interpretation of them abstracting from Algonquian specifics.

not a passive. Clauses headed by a direct form instantiate the agent voice, and clauses headed by an inverse form instantiate the patient voice. Nevertheless, the direct verb form (a) is morphologically simpler than the inverse form in the language (b). There is no direct segmental counterpart to the inverse marker *-e*, since the suffix *-fi* does not obligatorily appear on all direct forms (*leli-i* 's/he looked (at it)' is grammatical as well) and is merely a differential object marker, not a direct marker (Zúñiga 2010).

Semantics and pragmatics play a crucial role in the deployment of the two voices. (Henceforth, 1/2↔1/2 interactions will be called LOCAL, 3↔3 interactions NONLOCAL, and 1/2↔3 interactions MIXED.) In nonlocal scenarios, the choice between agent and patient voices is determined by animacy and topicality: patient voices are the marked option, to be used with animate and highly topical (proximate) Ps at selected junctures of narrative texts. To judge from text counts, roughly 66 percent of all expressions of 3↔3 interactions via verb forms that mark both syntactic arguments are instances of the agent voice (Zúñiga & Herdeg 2010). In mixed scenarios, Mapudungun also shows both voices, but their use is severely constrained: with a 1/2→3 interaction, only direct forms are possible (a); with a 3→1/2 interaction, only inverse forms are available (b):

(226)   Mapudungun
    a. *Leli-fi-n*   *chi   domo.*
        look.at-3.P-1SG.IND   the   woman
        'I looked at the woman.' (direct, AV)
    b. *Leli-e-n-mew*   *chi   domo.*
        look.at-INV-1SG.IND-3.A   the   woman
        'The woman looked at me.' (inverse, PV)

Mapudungun does not have antipassives, but it has an agentless passive, several causatives, and numerous applicatives. While the passive never takes inverse morphology, causatives and applicatives can occur in either direct or inverse clauses. The following examples illustrate these three groups of valency-changing operations:

(227)   Mapudungun
    a. *Leli-nge-i.*
        look.at-PASS-IND
        'Someone looked at him/her.' 'S/he was looked at.' (agentless passive)
    b. *Ngüma-l-fi-i.*
        weep-CAUS-3.P-IND
        'S/he made him/her weep.' (causative, direct)
    c. *Langüm-üñma-e-n-mew*   *kom   tañi*   *pu   pichi-ke*   *lamngen*
        kill-APPL-INV-1SG.IND-3.A all   1SG.PSR   PL   small-NSG   sister
        ta   *ngürü.*
        PART   fox
        'The fox killed all my little sisters on me.' (Salas 2006: 124) (applicative, inverse)

Notably, the alternation between either the agent or patient voice and the passive voice is asymmetrical: the latter construction reduces the syntactic valency of the non-passive clause by one. Even though causatives and applicatives interact with the direct–inverse opposition, they are strictly separate morphologically.

4.2.1.2   Jarawara

Consider the opposition depicted in (228) below. Dixon (2000a, 2004: 421–423) argues against both an antipassive analysis of (a) and a passive analysis of (b); both clauses are best analyzed as two-argument clauses:[24]

(228)   Jarawara (Dixon 2000a: 31)
      a. *Mioto*   *Watati*   *awa-ka.*   (agent voice)
          M.(M)   W.(F)   see-DECL.M
      b. *Watati*   *Mioto*   *hi-wa*   *hi-ke.*   (patient voice)
          W.(F)   M.(M)   PV-see   PV-DECL.F
      Both: 'Mioto saw Watati.'

Even though the syntax of these two Jarawara constructions may show symmetry, the morphology of the examples in (228) suggests that (b) might be derived from (a). When all possible person-number combinations of arguments in all TAMs are taken into account, however, a more complex picture emerges. Consider the following examples that express interactions between a 1SG and a 3PL:[25]

(229)   Jarawara (Dixon 2004: 421–422)
      a. *Mee*   *o-wa#katoma-ra*   *o-ke.*   (AV)
          3NSG   1SG.A-stare-TAM.F   1SG-DECL.F
      b. *Mee*   *o-wa#katoma-ra-ke.*   (PV)
          3NSG   1SG.A-stare-TAM.F-DECL.F
      Both: 'I stared at them.'
      c. *Owa*   *mee*   *ka#katoma-hara-ke.*   (AV)
          1SG   3NSG   stare-TAM.F-DECL.F
      d. *Owa*   *mee*   *ka#katoma-hara*   *o-ke.*   (PV)
          1SG   3NSG   stare-TAM.F   1SG-DECL.F
      Both: 'They stared at me.'

The Jarawara verbal complex is morphologically intricate, but suffice it to note here that the agent voice (a/c) is not always morphologically simpler than its patient counterpart (b/d), nor is the marker *hi* present in all person-number combinations (only the patient voice with 3↔3 interactions takes this marker).

Jarawara has neither passives nor antipassives, but it has causative and applicative derivations. These interact with the agent–patient voice alternation but are

---

[24] Dixon (2000a, 2004) calls these two clause types A-construction and O-construction, respectively.

[25] The feminine gender marker appears by default with 1st-person arguments (Dixon 2000a: 23) and bears no relation to the functional opposition between clause types.

morphologically and syntactically independent of it. The following examples illustrate these two operations:

(230)   Jarawara (Dixon 2004: 257)
  a. *Jara soni owa haahaa ni-hare   o-ke.*
     B.(M) fall.SUB 1SG laugh CAUS-TAM.EVID.M 1SG-DECL.F
     'The Branco's falling over made me laugh.' (causative – PV)
  b. *Mee haahaa o-ki-ne   o-ke.*
     3NSG laugh 1SG-APPL-TAM.F 1SG-DECL.F
     'I laugh at them.' (applicative – AV)

When considering two other aspects of the agent and patient voices, however, some asymmetries between them do emerge. First, even though the proportion of both voices as used in actual texts varies significantly, Dixon reports a clear preference – 70 percent vs. 30 percent – for the agent voice within his textual sample (2000a: 34).

Second, the deployment of both voices reflects communicative needs orbiting textual and thematic cohesion via topic continuity, but it is also sensitive to the category of person as instantiated by both arguments of bivalent clauses. Here we follow Dixon's outline of such distribution in four different languages of the Arawan family. In Jarawara, both voices are available with nonlocal and $1/2 \rightarrow 3$ interactions; $3 \rightarrow 1/2$ interactions are expressed in the agent voice and allow the patient voice under specific morphological conditions;[26] and local interactions allow only the agent voice. In Paumarí, both voices are also available with nonlocal and $1/2 \rightarrow 3$ interactions; by contrast, only the agent voice is available with $3 \rightarrow 1/2$ and local interactions.[27] Lastly, in Dení and Kulina both voices are available only with nonlocal interactions; all other interactions allow only one construction, which is formally like the patient voice with $1/2 \rightarrow 3$ interactions, like the agent voice with $3 \rightarrow 1/2$ interactions, and indeterminate with local interactions. This distribution is schematically summarized in Table 4.3.

Table 4.3 *Agent and patient voices in Arawan languages*

Interaction	Jarawara	Paumarí	Dení, Kulina
$3 \leftrightarrow 3$	AV + PV	AV + PV	AV + PV
$1/2 \rightarrow 3$	AV + PV	AV + PV	PV
$3 \rightarrow 1/2$	AV + PV*	AV	AV
$1/2 \leftrightarrow 1/2$	AV	AV	indeterminate

(based on Dixon 2000a: 54)

---

[26] These conditions are independent of person and number of the arguments, as well as of other transitivity-related factors that usually govern voice alternations in other languages; they are related to specific overt TAM markers and/or "secondary verbs" in the predicate complex (Dixon 2000a: 54).

[27] Paumarí also has an agentless passive construction, whose frequency in texts is low (Dixon 2000a: 34).

The Arawan agent voices often have a wider applicability range than the patient voices. Dixon (2004: 444) hypothesizes that Proto-Arawan had an agent voice for all interactions and a patient voice for interactions with 3rd-person Ps (like Paumarí). Dení and Kulina could have lost the agent voice with 1/2→3 interactions and the patient voice with 3→1/2 interactions (possibly motivated by a preference for having gender agreement with 3rd-person arguments). Jarawara could have extended the scope of the patient voice, subject to some morphological restrictions. Note that Jarawara does not look like Mapudungun at all regarding how the two voices are distributed with respect to personal scenarios; rather, the latter language resembles Dení and Kulina instead, with the important proviso that the distribution is exactly the opposite.

Thus, Arawan languages show two two-argument clause types: if Dixon's analysis is accurate, they are syntactically symmetrical. Their morphology is complicated, but none of the voices is systematically derived from, or even merely marked by less formal material than, the other; in this sense, they are morphologically symmetrical. They are asymmetrical, however, regarding their frequency in texts and their availability with different person scenarios: in Jarawara, the agent voice is more commonly used in texts, and in Jarawara and Paumarí, the agent voice is the only one available to the expression of all person interactions.

4.2.1.3   Movima

Movima distinguishes proximate from obviative arguments. The former are obligatorily overt, syntactically internal to the predicate phrase, and phonologically part of the predicate ("internal cliticization," symbolized by =). Obviative arguments, by contrast, are optional, syntactically external to the predicate phrase, and phonologically bound only if non-lexical ("external cliticization," symbolized by ≡). Two-argument clauses have verbs with either direct or inverse marking (-na and -kay, respectively, or some of their allomorphs), depending on whether the proximate-obviative hierarchy and the A-P hierarchy are aligned:

(231)   Movima (Haude 2006: 137, 519)

    a. *Ena'   kon-na='ne*   *is*   *empana:da.*
        TAM   drain-DIR=3SG.F.PRSNT   the.PL   empanada
        'She is taking out the empanadas (of the oil).' (direct, patient voice)

    b. *Ew-kaya='ne*   *os*   *alamre.*
        hold-INV=3SG.F.PRSNT   the.SG   wire
        'She got caught by the wire.' (inverse, agent voice)

Both proximates and obviatives can be either pronominal or lexical NPs, but the choice of person and number is constrained in two-argument clauses: 1st-person and 2SG arguments are obligatorily proximate, whereas 2PL and 3rd-person arguments can have either obviation status, and whenever SAPs interact with 3rd persons, the former are always proximate and the latter obviative:

(232)   Movima (Haude 2006: 276–277)
    a. *Inła*   *jema'*   *ew-na=Ø≡us.*
        1   also   grasp-DIR=1SG≡3SG.M.ABSNT
        'I held him, too.' (direct, PV)
    b. *Jema'*   *jul-pit-kay=Ø≡us.*
        also   hug-CL:half-INV=1SG≡3SG.M.ABSNT
        'He, too, hugged me around the waist.' (inverse, AV)

With nonlocal interactions, obviation status is determined by factors including topicality, animacy, and agentivity.

Like in Mapudungun and Jarawara, there are no good arguments in favor of analyzing either the clause headed by a direct verb form or the clause headed by an inverse form as one-argument clauses (Haude 2010). Notably, however, direct forms head patient-voice clauses and inverses head agent-voice clauses: it is the obviative, instead of the proximate, that is the subject (Haude & Zúñiga 2016) – precisely the opposite of the expected correspondence (i.e., proximate subjects and obviative objects), which is instantiated in Mapudungun and Jarawara.

Unlike Mapudungun and Jarawara, Movima has both antipassive and passive constructions (233). These clauses are headed by a direct form or an inverse form, respectively, and marked by the general detransitivizer *kwey* (b–c). Haude has been able to find passive examples in elicitation only (Haude 2010).

(233)   Movima (Haude 2006: 527–528)
    a. *Bay-a-cho=us*   *as*   *wa:so.*
        knock-DIR-inside=3SG.M.ABSNT the.SG glass
        'He broke a/the glass.' (direct, PV)
    b. *Usko*   *kwey* *bay-a:-cho*   *n-as*   *wa:so.*
        3SG.M.ABSNT DETR knock-DIR-inside OBL-the.SG glass
        'He was the one who broke a/the glass.' (direct, ANTIP)
    c. *Usko*   *kwey* *lap-kay* *n-os*   *mimi:di.*
        3SG.M.ABSNT DETR bite-INV OBL-the.SG snake
        'He was the one who was bitten by a snake.' (inverse, PASS)

In addition to the passive and the antipassive, Movima has a causative (234) and several applicatives (235). Causativization via *poj-* interacts with the agent–patient voice alternation as expected with semantically monovalent bases (a–b), whereas with bivalent bases an additional direct/inverse marker is needed (c–d) and the morpheme *-as* marks the inversion corresponding to the base predicate *leve-* 'chase off', rather than to the inversion corresponding to the functional predicate CAUSE in CAUSE [X, *chase.off* [Y, Z]]. Haude (2006) calls *-as* "causative inverse," but note that *-poj* and *-as* are not both causatives opposed along the direct/inverse parameter. Rather, while *-poj* denotes the CAUSE predicate and is unmarked for direct/inverse, *-as* denotes inversion, refers to the embedded predicate (here: *leve-* 'chase off'), and stands in opposition to an unmarked direct (c). Further note that the 1SG causer is the proximate argument in both (c) and (d), but the assignment of the arguments of 'chase off' in A ('[my] younger sister')

and P function ('the birds') to obviative-core and adjunct status is the opposite in
(c) and (d), respectively:

(234) Movima (Haude 2006: 392–393, 396–397)
   a. *Ela:-na=Ø≡'ne,*
       leave.behind-DIR=1SG≡3SG.F.PRSNT
          joro-poj-na=Ø≡'ne.
          sleep-CAUS-DIR=1SG≡3SG.F.PRSNT
       'I left her behind, I made her sleep.' (causative – PV)
   b. *Jayna   am-poj-kay=Ø≡is*   *n-os*
       then   enter-CAUS-INV=1SG≡3PL.ABSNT   OBL-the.SG
          tordeta.
          mosquito.net
       'Then they put me under the mosquito net.' (causative – AV)
   c. *Jayna   kino'*   *leve-na-poj-na=Ø*   *kinos*
       then   DEM.SG.F.ABSNT   chase.off-DIR-CAUS-DIR=1SG   the.SG
          a:na   *ni-kis*   *jo'me.*
          younger.sibling OBL-the.PL   bird
       'I have already made [my] younger sister chase away the birds [in the
       field].'
   d. *Jayna   kiro'*   *leve-na-poj-as-na=Ø*   *kis*
       then   DEM.PL.ABSNT   chase.off-DIR-CAUS-INV-DIR=1SG   the.PL
          jo'me   ni-kinos   a:na.
          bird   OBL-the.SG   younger.sibling
       'I already have the birds be chased away by [my] younger sister.'

The applicatives interact with the agent–patient voice opposition but are morphologically and syntactically independent from it. The following examples
illustrate the two most productive applicatives of Movima:

(235) Movima (Haude 2006: 402, 412)
   a. *Jayna   joy-a-łe=n   jayna   kis   pajwe:la.*
       then   go-DIR-APPL=2SG   then   the.PL match
       'You (SG) take your matches with you.' (direct, PV)
   b. *Inła   jempiteł   choñ   loj-'oj-eł-kay-a=n.*
       1SG   always   HAB   wash-clothes-APPL-INV-EPE=2SG
       'I wash for you (SG) all the time.' (inverse, AV)

   Finally, note that direct and inverse forms in Movima, and thus patient and
agent voices, are available for most semantically bivalent verbs (Haude 2006:
323–332) and have a predictable semantic effect.[28] Nevertheless, they are not
equally common in spontaneous discourse: with two-argument clauses and
nonlocal interactions, for instance, 90 percent of all clauses in Haude's 2006
textual sample correspond to the patient voice.

---

[28] The exceptions are *kay* 'eat' and *ya:lowe* 'drink', which only occur in the direct form.

4.2.1.4   Summary

Regarding the morphology of the three languages, the Mapudungun inverse marker *-e* can be regarded as a patient voice marker, as can the Jarawara "auxiliary" *hi-*. Jarawara also distinguishes the two voices morphologically via a complex interplay of indexation and TAM marking. Movima shows both an agent and a patient voice marker, namely the inverse marker *-kay* and the direct marker *-na*, respectively.

Regarding the syntactic make-up of the languages, they all have an opposition that appears to be best captured as symmetrical: two two-argument diatheses are available for semantically bivalent verbs. They differ as to how many asymmetrical oppositions they show: Jarawara does not seem to need either passives or antipassives, while Movima has both kinds of constructions and Mapudungun has only passives.

Regarding the conditions governing the choice between diatheses, the three languages differ significantly. Even though one of the voices is typically much less common than the other in actual narrative discourse in all languages, the relationship between voice and direction (i.e., the direct–inverse opposition), person, and obviation is not at all uniform. From the perspective of the discussion of morphosyntactic inversion in the 1990s, Mapudungun shows the expected pattern: proximates are preferred subjects and obviatives are preferred objects; proximate (obviative) As occur with direct (inverse) forms; SAPs align with proximates (Zúñiga 2006b). To the extent that Jarawara can be said to have proximates and obviatives as well, this language is similar to Mapudungun regarding the first two features, but not regarding the third: in Jarawara, SAPs do not align with proximates, and animacy does not seem to play a decisive role in obviation status and diathetical choice. Movima is like Mapudungun regarding the last two features, but not regarding the first: unexpectedly, obviatives are preferred subjects and proximates preferred objects.

These features of the voice oppositions discussed are summarized in Table 4.4:

Table 4.4 *Agent and patient voices in selected South American languages*

	Mapudungun	Jarawara	Movima
Verb morphology	Ø vs. *-e*	Intricate, but also Ø vs. *hi-*	*-kay* vs. *-na* (in CAUS: *-as* vs. Ø)
Clause syntax	AV VS. PV	AV VS. PV	AV VS. PV
Asymmetrical voices?	PASS	✗	ANTIP + PASS
Other voices?	CAUS + APPL	CAUS + APPL	CAUS + APPL
Frequency	66% vs. 33%	70% vs. 30%*	10% vs. 90%
Person sensitivity	SAP VS. 3rd	SAP VS. 3rd	1/2SG VS. 2PL VS. 3rd

* including all scenarios, i.e., 1/2↔1/2, 3↔3, and 1/2↔3 interactions

These South American languages and the Austronesian languages discussed in the preceding section show not only striking similarities but also important differences. Two syntactically bivalent clause types are not universal in western Austronesian or Philippine languages, but they are found in Mapudungun, Jarawara, and Movima. Topicality is an important conditioning factor of voice deployment in all languages that show voice symmetry, but person-sensitivity seems to be an indigenous American trait – even though it plays a non-negligible role in Indonesian, and it may simply have hitherto gone undetected in other Austronesian languages. The direct–inverse opposition, which we address in some more detail in the next section, is also an indigenous American, rather than an Austronesian, trait.[29] Most importantly, and despite the relatively rich array of applicatives of Mapudungun, none of the South American languages have anything directly comparable to the undergoer nucleative paradigm of Tagalog. With regard to voice, Mapudungun, Jarawara, and Movima more closely resemble the Indonesian-type languages than those belonging to the Philippine-type.

4.2.2   Selected North American Languages and "Inverse Voice"

The literature on grammatical voice since Klaiman (1991) has addressed some phenomena related to the direct–inverse opposition found in several indigenous languages of North America. The relevant data fall into three groups, namely those where a strong case can be made for the existence of an agent–patient voice opposition, those with an active–passive opposition conditioned by person-number values of the clausal arguments, and those where the direct–inverse opposition seems to be essentially orthogonal to diathetical oppositions. We deal with them in turn in what follows.

4.2.2.1   Conditioned Symmetrical Voice oppositions in North America

Descriptive studies suggest that agent–patient voice oppositions like those found in western Austronesian and in some South American languages are extremely rare in other languages, including those currently spoken in Native North America. What appears to be the clearest case is found in Arizona Tewa. The interested reader is referred to Kroskrity (1985), Klaiman (1991), and Zúñiga (2006b) for more details.

In this language, semantically bivalent verbs can head both agent- and patient-voice clauses. Agent-voice verbs take argument markers from Set II, whereas patient-voice verbs employ Set III markers. The examples in (236) illustrate some of these forms; (a–b) correspond to nonlocal scenarios, (c–d) to mixed scenarios, and (e–f) to local interactions:

---

[29] To be sure, similar direct–inverse oppositions are known from other areas (viz., the Himalayas, northeastern Siberia, and to some extent the Caucasus), but we are focusing on symmetrical voice oppositions here, which so far do not seem to be connected to morphosyntactic inversion outside the Americas.

(236)   Arizona Tewa (Kiowa-Tanoan, USA; Klaiman 1991: 204f; Kroskrity 1985: 309f)

    a. *Hẹ'i   sen   nɛ́'i   'enú   mán-k^{hw}ẹ́di.*
        that   man   this   boy   3SG.II-hit
        'That man (PROX) hit this boy (OBV).' (AV)

    b. *Nɛ́'i   'enú   hẹ'i   sen-di   'ó--k^{hw}ẹ́di.*
        this   boy   that   man-AGT   3SG.III-hit
        'That man (OBV) hit this boy (PROX).' (PV)

    c. *Nɛ́'i   k^{w}iyó   dó-tay.*
        this   woman   1SG.II-know
        'I know this woman.' (AV)

    d. *Hẹ'i   sen-di   'ų   wó--k^{h}ɛgen-'án.*
        that   man-AGT   2SG   2SG.III-help-COMPL
        'That man helped you (SG).' (PV)

    e. *'Ų   na·n-di   wí-tay.*
        2SG   1PL-AGT   1→2.III-know
        'We (PL) know you (SG).' (PV)

    f. *Na·   'ų-di   dí-k^{w}ek^{hw}ẹ́di.*
        1SG   2SG-AGT   2→1.III-shoot
        'You (SG) shot me.' (PV)

As in the South American languages surveyed in Section 4.2.1, the choice between the two voices is constrained by the person of the two arguments. When both are 3rd-person (a–b), both voices are available; topicality and animacy determine which argument has proximate, and therefore subject, status. When SAPs interact with 3rd persons (c–d), SAP→3 interactions are obligatorily expressed by the agent voice and 3→SAP clauses employ the patient voice. Lastly, if SAPs interact with each other (e–f), only patient-voice clauses are available.

Even though the argument in A function is marked with a semantically oblique-like suffix *-di* in the patient voice – it marks instruments and sources as well – , Kroskrity (1985) and Klaiman (1991) argue against considering such clauses passives. We have chosen to follow his analysis in the present study – among other things, in order to draw attention to the fact that, to our knowledge, rigorous subjecthood and objecthood tests have not been systematically applied to instances such as these. The available evidence is indirect in that, despite the morphology of patient-voice clauses, there do not seem to be any clear syntactic indications of the A having been demoted out of the clause core. Moreover, there is an agentless passive in the language, which predictably shows both specialized verbal marking (the detransitivizer *-tí·*) and the same Set-I prefixes used with semantically monovalent predicates:

(237)   Arizona Tewa (Kroskrity 1985: 309, 314)

    a. *'E·-p'up'í·le   na-'owídi-tí·.*
        child-newborn   3SG.I-bathed-DETR
        'The newborn child was bathed.' (agentless passive)

b. *Walabi-'í'í-di*   *na-mε.*
W.-there-from   3SG.I-go
'He went from Walpi.' (underived one-argument clause)

4.2.2.2 Conditioned Asymmetrical Voice Oppositions in North America

Coast Salishan languages have been noted in the literature for show-ing clear passive structures whose occurrence is conditioned by referential properties of the clausal arguments (Jelinek & Demers 1983, Aissen 1999). Table 4.5 below summarizes the patterns found in three such languages, namely Lushootseed, Lummi, and Squamish. While 3↔3 interactions allow both active and passive voices, others are restricted: mixed interactions either allow only the active voice (SAP→3) or show some variation (3→SAP), and local interactions allow only the active.

Table 4.5 *Voice alternations in selected Coast Salishan languages*

	Lushootseed			Lummi			Squamish	
	active	passive		active	passive		active	passive
3→3	✓	✓		✓	✓		✓	✓
1→3	✓	✗		✓	✗		✓	✗
2→3	✓	✗		✓	✗		✓	✗
3→1	✓	✓		✗	✓		✓	✓
3→2	✓	✓		✗	✓		✗	✓
1→2	✓	✗		✓	✗		✓	✗
2→1	✓	✗		✓	✗		✓	✗

(based on Aissen 1999: 690f and Jelinek & Demers 1983)

Something similar is found in varieties of Tiwa, a language closely related to Arizona Tewa. In both Picurís and Southern Tiwa, nonlocal interactions can be expressed by either active or passive clauses; clauses with mixed interactions are either active (SAP→3) or passive (3→SAP); unlike in Tewa, but like in Coast Salishan, clauses with local interactions are obligatorily active. The following examples from Southern Tiwa illustrate these patterns. Note that Tiwa languages have only two sets of personal prefixes:

(238)   Southern Tiwa (Klaiman 1991: 219–221, Rosen 1990: 698)
a. *Seuan-ide*   *mȝ-ban.*
man-SG   [3]see-PST
'S/he saw the man.' (active)
b. *Seuan-ide-ba*   *mȝ-che-ban.*
man-SG-OBL   [3]see-PASS-PST
'The man saw her.' (passive)
c. *Seuan-ide*   *ti-mȝ-ban.*
man-SG   1SG.II-see-PST
'I saw the man.' (active)

    d. *Seuan-ide-ba*   *te-mụ-che-ban.*
        man-SG-OBL   1SG.I-see-PASS-PST
        'The man saw me / I was seen by the man.' (passive)

    e. *I-mụ-ban.*   (*Na-ba   *a-mụ-che-ban.*)
        1→2SG-see-PST   1SG-OBL   2SG.I-see-PASS-PST
        'I saw you (SG).' (active)

    f. *Bey-mụ-ban.*   (*I-ba   *te-mụ-che-ban.*)
        2→1SG-see-PST   2SG-OBL   1SG.I-see-PASS-PST
        'You (SG) saw me.' (active)

4.2.2.3   The Search for "Inverse Voice"

    Let us start with some present-day reflexes of the Proto-Athabaskan verbal 3rd-person indices **ye-* and **we-*, namely *ye-* and *be-* in Koyukon (239) and *yi-* and *bi-* in Navajo (240), respectively (henceforth Y and B). For our purposes, the most important differences between these languages are: (i) Y and B are in complementary distribution with object NPs in Koyukon, whereas they appear in the clause irrespective of the presence of lexical NPs in Navajo, and (ii) the cognate morphemes express quite different meanings. Consider:

(239)   Koyukon (Thompson 1996: 87)
        a.   *John;*   *ye-neełaanh.*
            J.   Y-look.TAM
        b.   *John*   *be-neełaanh.*
            J.   B-look.TAM
        Both: 'John is looking at him/her.'

(240)   Navajo (Willie 2000: 364)
        a.   *Ashkii*   *łį́į́'*   *yi-ztał.*
            boy   horse   Y-kick.TAM
            'The boy kicked the horse.'
        b.   *Ashkii*   *łį́į́'*   *bi-ztał.*
            boy   horse   B-kick.TAM
            'The boy was kicked by the horse.' / 'The horse kicked the boy.'

    According to the mainstream Athabaskanist view (e.g., Rice 2000), Y and B are object markers that correspond to the argument in P function (sometimes called "direct" and "oblique," respectively), not only in these two languages but in Athabaskan in general. In this view, both the (a)-clauses and the (b)-clauses above instantiate the agent voice, with Y indexing a pragmatically less salient object than B (see also Thompson 1994, 1996).[30] We could therefore gloss Y as 'obviative object' and B as 'proximate object', respectively. In southern Athabaskan languages like Navajo, constituent order interacts with the Y–B

---

[30] We are glossing over the fact that the reflexes of **we-* are found with SAP subjects, that is, that the alternation between Y and B is restricted to nonlocal scenarios.

alternation and is constrained by a complex parameter including both lexical features of the arguments, related to animacy, and the ability of the agentive argument to be assigned some kind of superordinate A role of the event as a whole. This constraint is operative in (240) above, where *ashkii* 'boy' must precede *łį́į́'* 'horse' irrespective of the specific state of affairs in which they are involved (Hale 1972, 1973).

In an alternative view (e.g., Sandoval & Jelinek 1989 and Willie 1991, 2000), the (b)-clause in Navajo shows a reversal of grammatical relations, that is, it instantiates the patient voice – which is called "inverse voice" in this tradition. This view has not been compellingly presented in the literature so far, however: to the best of our knowledge, a rigorous and systematic application of subjecthood and objecthood tests to the Navajo data remains to be done.[31]

Furthermore, the term "inverse voice" has other meanings in the literature. Klaiman (1991) uses it to denote alternations between clauses headed by direct and indirect verb forms that are not exclusively governed by discourse factors, but in her view these alternations do not alter diathetical structure and are therefore not voices according to how we use the term in this book. Gildea (1994) uses the same term to denote alternations between clauses headed by direct and indirect verb forms when speakers have a choice (i.e., usually in nonlocal scenarios), as opposed to restricted assignments where speakers have to choose one form over the other depending on the exact interaction (i.e., usually in mixed scenarios), which he calls "inverse alignment." Givón (1994) calls these optional and the obligatory clause choices "pragmatic inverse" and "semantic inverse," respectively. While Givón leaves the question of syntactic structure open, Gildea is explicitly dealing with an agent voice only.

Moving on to Algonquian, note that all extant languages distinguish direct and inverse verb forms, with intricate morphological patterns that show remarkable consistency but also some variation. A verbal suffix that is reconstructed as 3P marker *-ā* for Proto-Algonquian developed into a direct marker, whereas the inverse *-ekw* is usually reconstructed with the same function its reflexes have in the present-day languages (Proulx 1985). Other so-called "theme" suffixes encoding patientive arguments (i.e., *-i* '1.P', *-eθe* '2.P') have either retained their erstwhile function or developed into portmanteaus that encode two arguments (e.g., in Plains Cree *-i* '2→1' and *-iti* '1→2'). In the nominal realm, all languages distinguish proximates from obviatives both functionally and formally, and some languages also distinguish a further obviative.

The person-sensitive distribution of direct and inverse forms should be familiar after seeing the indigenous American languages surveyed in the preceding sections. On the one hand, 1↔2 and 1/2↔3 interactions do not allow speakers to choose from different two-argument clauses: they are either specialized forms (1↔2) or obligatorily direct (1/2→3) or inverse (3→1/2). On the other hand,

---

[31] Willie (2000) reports some evidence regarding coreferential omission in coordination, but the data are compatible with both agent-voice and patient-voice interpretations.

3↔3 interactions can be direct (PROX→OBV) or inverse (OBV→PROX). The examples in (241) from Blackfoot illustrate these patterns with nonlocal (a–b) and mixed scenarios (c–d):

(241)   Blackfoot (Frantz 2009: 52, 56)[32]

    a. *Ikákomimm-ii-wa*   *n-ohkó-wa*   *k-itán-yi.*
        love-DIR$_1$–3SG.PROX   1-son-PROX   2-daughter-OBV
        'My son (PROX) loves your (SG) daughter (OBV).' (direct)

    b. *Ot-ikákomimm-ok-wa*   *n-ohkó-wa*   *k-itán-yi.*
        3-love-INV-3SG.PROX   1-son-PROX   2-daughter-OBV
        'Your (SG) daughter (OBV) loves my son (PROX).' (inverse)

    c. *Nit-ikákomimm-aa-wa*   *n-itán-wa.*
        1-love-DIR$_2$–3SG.PROX   1-daughter-PROX
        'I love your (SG) daughter (PROX).' (direct)

    d. *Nit-ikákomimm-ok-wa*   *n-itán-wa.*
        1-love-INV-3SG.PROX   1-daughter-PROX
        'Your (SG) daughter (PROX) loves me.' (inverse)

The syntax of such clauses presents the analyst with an inelegant picture. The usual assumption is that two-argument clauses have A subjects and P objects irrespective of the direct–inverse opposition. Based on the application of several morphosyntactic tests, Dahlstrom (1986: Ch. 3) arrives at precisely that conclusion for Plains Cree. The situation is somewhat less clear for Central Ojibwa: the tests applied in Rhodes (1994) give mixed results, with two phenomena following semantic roles (i.e., with an A pivot irrespective of direction marking or obviation), but at least one phenomenon following obviation (i.e., with a proximate pivot irrespective of semantic role). As far as we can tell, the behavior of phasal preverbs (e.g., 'start', 'stop'), floating quantifiers, and cross-clausal control in these languages, as well as in Blackfoot and possibly in Arapaho and Cheyenne, does not support a patient-voice analysis of clauses headed by inverse verb forms. Inverse clauses are certainly not passives, but they seem to simply instantiate the agent voice (cf. Zúñiga 2006b: Ch. III).

The same seems to hold for the inverse clauses of Kutenai (unclassified, Canada) and of Sahaptin (Sahaptian, USA), even though there the case against the existence of a symmetrical voice alternation, especially for the latter language, appears to be stronger (Zúñiga 2006b: Ch. IV and V). If "inverse voice" is understood as 'patient voice constrained by person and number of the arguments' – a phenomenon attested for some indigenous South American languages – it is not at all clear whether such a clause type is really found in indigenous North American languages outside Kiowa-Tanoan. The direct–inverse opposition in Algonquian and the Y–B alternation in Athabaskan are certainly prominent in those families, but an airtight case for a patient-voice

---

[32] The representation of the Blackfoot elements provides underlying forms, rather than surface forms; some morphophonemic rules apply (e.g., *ot-i* > *otsi*). The interlinear glosses omit the information regarding verb stem type (here: Transitive Animate). See Frantz (2009) for details.

analysis of the two-argument clauses with referentially, semantically, and/or pragmatically salient P arguments still has to be made.

4.2.3   Symmetrical Voices in the Americas and Beyond

Our brief survey of selected indigenous languages of the Americas showed that there is some evidence in favor of both the SVV and the AVV, not only across languages but also within individual languages. Both descriptive work in general and studies that deal with the issue of grammatical relations and voice alternations in particular suggest that some languages in South America (Jarawara, Movima, and Mapudungun) have agent and patient voices. In North America, this may hold in some individual cases (viz., varieties of Tewa) but does not appear to apply to cases treated in such terms by earlier literature (e.g., Klaiman 1991). Varieties of Tiwa and several Coast Salishan languages have agent and restricted passive voices instead, and Athabaskan and Algonquian languages show related phenomena but not really, or at least not clearly, symmetrical voice oppositions. Even in those languages that have two two-argument clauses with bivalent verbs, there are asymmetrical voice oppositions as well, at least in Movima and Mapudungun. And even these South American languages show some variation regarding morphological symmetry and especially a significant bias in terms of discourse frequency.

It is not clear how many languages elsewhere an SVV may apply to. Restricted passivization of the Coast Salishan type might be more widespread, and languages with something resembling the Algonquian direct–inverse opposition are obvious places to look systematically for patient voices.

4.3   Symmetrical Voice in a Nutshell

The main lesson to be learned from our survey of western Austronesian and non-Austronesian languages is that there are both similarities and differences between them with respect to voice alternations. The similarities include the existence of a symmetrical clausal syntax in several languages, the partly asymmetrical verb morphology and discourse use that characterize the alternating two-argument clauses, and – in a subset of western Austronesian languages – the fact that referential features of the arguments may play a role in determining which voices are available. Another, perhaps obvious, similarity is the fact that most languages with a symmetrical voice opposition pose some kind of difficulty to several theories of syntax with respect to the notions of core argument in general and subject in particular. Lastly, the asymmetries in discourse use show a heterogeneous picture in both Austronesian and non-Austronesian.

The differences between them, however, justify the separate treatment most studies have given western Austronesian and non-Austronesian voice systems.

Outside western Austronesian, subject undergoer nucleatives are rare, and where they exist they are not part of the same voice sub-paradigm as the agent and patient voices. In non-Austronesian, referential and semantic properties of the arguments play a much more prominent role than in western Austronesian. In Philippine-type languages, they do not seem to play a significant role in diathetical alternations.

5 The Affected Subject: Reflexives, Reciprocals, and Middles

5.1 Introduction

The literature on grammatical voice treats reflexives, reciprocals, and middles in disparate ways. Within the functional-typological tradition, some authors work with a narrow definition of voice and see reflexives, passives, and antipassives as voices, but reciprocals as something else (akin to causatives and applicatives), and middles as composite phenomena that show voice- and non-voice features (e.g., Mel'čuk 2006). A small number of authors see the middle as a fundamentally different kind of voice from the passive and antipassive, and see the reflexive and the reciprocal either as (non-core) meanings of the middle forms (Klaiman 1991) or as values that are on a par with, and in opposition to, them (Givón 2001). The current mainstream favors a view in which reflexives and reciprocals are a special kind of voice (see, e.g., Kulikov's 2011a "operational diatheses," i.e., "syntactic changes which preserve the inventory of semantic roles but impose certain operations on them") that is different from both passives and antipassives on the one hand and from causatives, anticausatives, and applicatives on the other. Other authors prefer not to integrate them too explicitly, or too rigidly, into a system of voices (e.g., Haspelmath & Müller-Bardey 2004).

Given the heterogeneity of the phenomena involved, such disparity is hardly surprising. Reflexives are relatively easy to define and show some variation; there are not many different semantic subtypes of reflexivity, and the morphosyntax of reflexives is moderately diverse (Faltz 1985, Lichtenberk 1994, Frajzyngier & Curl 2000a, König 2001, König & Gast 2008). Reciprocals, however, are quite varied regarding their semantics, their morphology, and their syntax, and pose interesting descriptive and typological challenges (Lichtenberk 1994, Frajzyngier & Curl 2000b, Nedjalkov 2007c, Evans 2008, Evans et al. 2011). Neither construction alters semantic valency when compared to their non-REFL/RECP counterparts, but both introduce an element of coreference to the picture. Their syntax is varied: some employ the agent or patient voice, and others use a different diathesis/voice that we call DUPLEX here. Lastly, middles are so heterogeneous that they represent a major terminological problem area, which we address in Section 5.4. The term is usually applied to multifunctional constructions that include reflexives, reciprocals, passives, antipassives, causatives, causative-reflexives, and/or autobenefactive (indirect) applicatives. Following

Kulikov (2011a), we suggest using the term "middle inflection" when covering cases like those found in Sanskrit, Greek, and Latin in cross-linguistic studies, and the term "middle cluster" for some of the extensive syncretisms observed. We suggest not using the term "middle voice" in typological studies, except when dealing with the classical languages, and then only with utmost caution.

In order to see what the main issue regarding reflexivity and reciprocity is, consider briefly the impersonal constructions in (242) below. All of them correspond to the usual definition – i.e., constructions that lack a formally, semantically, and/or pragmatically prototypical subject; see Section 3.1.2 – but from the point of view of voice they are heterogeneous. The Finnish construction in (a) is simply a special interpretation of a 3SG active form of the verb (called "zero person" in Finnish studies, see Laitinen 1995), analogous to the special interpretation of the 3PL form in many languages, including English. The German and Spanish constructions in (b) and (c) use the active voice as well, albeit featuring the (dedicated) impersonal pronoun *man* and the (syncretic) impersonal verbal marker *se*, respectively. Only the Finnish construction in (d) shows a voice different from the active, but it is not an "impersonal voice" in its own right; it is a non-prototypical passive with partial promotion:

(242)   Impersonal constructions
    a.   Finnish
       Sauna-ssa   *hikoile-e.*
       sauna-INESS   sweat-3SG.PRS
    b.   German
       In   der   Sauna schwitz-t   man.
       in   ART   sauna sweat-3SG.PRS IMPRS
    c.   Spanish
       En   el   sauna se   suda.
       in   ART   sauna IMPRS sweat.3SG.PRS
    d.   Finnish
       Sauna-ssa   *hikoil-laan.*
       sauna-INESS   sweat-PASS.PRS
    All four: 'One sweats in the sauna.'

The same happens with reflexives and reciprocals: some are a special interpretation of a form also used otherwise in a language, others have a special form but use an active (direct) diathesis, and yet others employ a diathesis different from the active. This diathesis – the DUPLEX – consists in a multiple, or at least double, assignment of semantic roles to grammatical relations, such that the subject is simultaneously the A and the P. This is schematically represented in Figure 5.1 below.

Many studies work with such an idea (e.g., Mel'čuk 2006 and Kulikov 2011a, but there are also numerous functional-typological studies working in different sub-traditions), and it corresponds closely to what lies behind the traditional label "Middle Voice." Suffice it to say here that our terminology does not refer to cases like Jackendoff's (1990) multi-tiered model of argument representation and

Figure 5.1 *Active and duplex diatheses*

realization, where English *John gave Mary the ball* assigns the subject the role of agent on the action tier and the role of source on the thematic tier, for example. Duplex diathesis refers to the fact that two roles on the same simple tier are assigned to one syntactic argument. Note that this notion of affected subject also differs from Næss's (2007) "affected agent," which corresponds to an agent that is necessarily affected by an event without being its primary target (the prototype is illustrated by the agent of 'eat').

Let us now introduce reflexives and reciprocals in more precise terms before dealing with them in Sections 5.2 and 5.3, respectively. Reflexivity and reciprocity denote departures from the default fashion in which arguments are mapped onto referents. With many semantically bivalent predicates – certainly so with high-transitivity predicates, like those with effected patients – the normal assumption is that the A and the P are assigned to different referents.[1] One possible departure therefrom consists in one referent corresponding to both the A and the P, like in English *Alan saw himself (in the mirror)*; this is what (direct) reflexivity denotes. Another possibility consists in several referents simultaneously corresponding to both the A and the P, like in English *Alan and Beatrix fought against each other*; this is the denotation of (strong) reciprocity. Note the difference between the reciprocal, where the two subevents correspond to 'Alan fought against Beatrix' and 'Beatrix fought against Alan', respectively. These reflexive and reciprocal meanings are schematically depicted in Figure 5.2, where R_1 and R_2 represent the referents named Alan and Beatrix, respectively, and solid and broken lines indicate the different seeing/fighting subevents. (Reciprocals can be more complex, especially when more participants are involved; see Figure 5.6.)

The meanings depicted in Figure 5.2 below are among those that are mapped onto grammatical relations in specific reflexive and reciprocal constructions. Supposing a duplex diathesis is used, then those diatheses can meaningfully be called reflexive and reciprocal subtypes of the duplex diatheses, respectively. Only if these diatheses are morphologically marked on the predicate complex do

---

[1] Traditional semantic analysis distinguishes between affected objects/patients, which change their state due to the state of affairs portrayed by the predicate (e.g., 'open the door'), and effected objects/patients, which come into being as a result (e.g., 'build the house').

Figure 5.2 *Selected reflexive and reciprocal meanings*

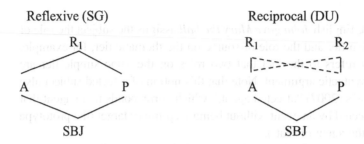

Figure 5.3 *Selected reflexive and reciprocal diatheses*

we obtain REFLEXIVE and RECIPROCAL (DUPLEX) VOICES like those depicted in Figure 5.3.

5.2   Reflexives and Voice

5.2.1   Two Prototypical Reflexives

There are two kinds of coded reflexives with respect to voice: (i) an agent/patient voice that denotes reflexivity via means unrelated to voice, and (ii) a duplex voice construction that has reflexivity as one of its possible readings or as its sole interpretation.[2] The examples in (243) illustrate the first two kinds for the direct reflexive with a singular participant:

(243)   Finnish
    a. *Lapsi   pes-i   itse-n-sä.*
       child[NOM] wash-3SG.PST self-ACC-3.PSR
    b. *Lapsi   pese-yty-i.*
       child[NOM] wash-REFL-3SG.PST
     Both: 'The child washed him/herself.'

In the active reflexive (a), the semantically bivalent predicate *pestä* 'wash' appears in a typical two-argument clause with a subject in the nominative and an

---

[2] Note in passing that, just as not all languages have passives or applicatives, reflexive constructions are not universal. See Section 6.5.1 for an example from Pirahã and a mention of Jiwarli, two languages without structural reflexives of any kind.

object in the accusative. What is special about it is that the object is a possessed form of *itse* 'self', an element that denotes coreference.[3] By contrast, in the duplex reflexive in (b), there can be no object NP in the clause, and the verb takes the reflexive suffix *-UtU*. These two reflexives differ not only regarding their morphological make-up (viz., nominal vs. verbal) but also regarding their syntactic structure: the syntactic valency of the predicate is two in the former and one in the latter. Moreover, the monovalent syntax is also a special diathesis because the subject is assigned two semantic roles.

Thus, we can define prototypical (singular) reflexives as follows:

(244)   Prototypical reflexive construction
    a.   The A and some other argument are coreferential. This is the P in the direct reflexive and the G/X° in the indirect reflexive.
    b.   If the predicate complex encodes the duplex diathesis formally, the construction is an instance of reflexive duplex voice.

5.2.2   Variation of Reflexives

5.2.2.1   Morphological Variation of Reflexives

Regarding their locus, reflexive markers can be argumental ("nominal") or verbal.[4] Nominal reflexives appear as/on NPs; the literature usually follows Faltz's (1985) seminal study in distinguishing four subtypes, illustrated in (245) below: the reflexive marker can be the noun-like NP head (a), an adjunct to a pronominal head (b), or a specialized reflexive pronoun, either a "true" one (c) or a "fused adjunct" (d):

(245)   Nominal reflexive markers
    a.   Japanese (Faltz 1985: 35)
          Tarō=wa   {Zirō=o / zibun=o}   mamotta.
          T.=TOP   Z.=ACC   REFL=ACC   defend.PST
          'Taro defended Ziro / himself.'
    b.   Irish (Celtic, Ireland; Faltz 1985: 40)
          Ghortaigh Seán   é   féin.
          hurt.PST   S.   3SG.M.DISJ REFL
          'Sean hurt himself.'
    c.   Polish (Frajzyngier 2000a: 133)
          W każdym razie nie będę   jej   podsuwał siebie.
          in any   case NEG be.FUT.1SG 3SG.F.DAT push   REFL.ACC
          'In any case I am not going to push my own person to her.'

---

[3] The P can appear in grammatical relations other than object in the active voice (e.g., as an adpositional object or as an adjunct). We are glossing over this possibility for ease of presentation only.
[4] A third, adjectival, type need not concern us further here; see Lichtenberk (1994) and Kazenin (2001b).

d. English
Barbara hit herself.

Verbal reflexives are typically affixes occurring on the verbal complex, as illustrated in (246). Some appear in the same templatic position that non-coreferential objects would take, like *ji-* in Swahili (a), while others appear in slots not occupied by subjects or objects, like (discontinuous) *á-di-* in Navajo (b) and *-w* in Mapudungun (c). The verbal reflexive found in the classical languages, illustrated here with Classical Greek (d), seems to be rare; rather than a separate morpheme, it consists of a separate set of indexes that also mark the Middle Voice:[5]

(246)   Verbal reflexive markers
a.   Swahili (Bantu, East Africa; Seidl & Dimitriadis 2003: 256)
    A-li-ji-on-a.
    1.SBJ-PST-REFL-see-ASP
    'He saw himself.'
b.   Navajo (Young 2000: 36)
    Á-di-nɨ-sh-'ɨ́.
    self-person-TH-1SG.SBJ-look.ASP
    'I am looking at myself.'
c.   Mapudungun
    Leli-w-n.
    look.at-REFL-1SG.IND
    'I looked at myself.'
d.   Classical Greek
    Loú-omai.   vs.   *Loú-ō.*
    wash-1SG.MID   wash-1SG.ACT
    'I wash myself.'   'I wash (something).'

There are three further parameters of variation for reflexive markers of either type, namely morphemic complexity, variability regarding person and number, and syncretism. As to the former, markers can be simple or complex – like we already saw for the verbal markers in (246) above: Swahili and Mapudungun have simple affixes while Navajo has a complex, polymorphemic, marker. Something similar happens with nominal markers, like those in Dutch (247): they can be "weak" *zich* (a) or "strong" *zichzelf* (b). (The choice between them depends on several syntactic, semantic, and pragmatic factors.)

(247)   Dutch (Germanic, Belgium and The Netherlands; Veraart 1996: 14–15)
a.   *Jan   schaamt   zich.*
    J.   be.ashamed.3SG   REFL$_1$.3
    'Jan is ashamed.'

---

[5] The 4th-person or reflexive conjugation in Eskimoan languages is somewhat similar in form, but its main function is to mark coreference of 3rd persons across clauses.

b. *Jan   bewondert   zichzelf.*
  J.   admire.3SG   REFL$_2$.3
  'Jan admires himself.'

Regarding inflectional potential, some markers are invariable, like Japanese *zibun*, Irish *féin*, and Swahili *ji-*, whereas others inflect for person and number. Compare the invariable marker *se-* of Sursilvan Romansh with the variable markers *me, nous, te, vous,* and *se* of French in Table 5.1:

Table 5.1 *Reflexives in two Romance languages ('wash', IND.PRS)*

	Sursilvan Romansh	French
1SG	*jeu selavel*	*je me lave*
1PL	*nus selavein*	*nous nous lavons*
2SG	*ti selavas*	*tu te laves*
2PL	*vus selaveis*	*vous vous lavez*
3SG	*el/ella selava*	*il/elle se lave*
3PL	*els/ellas/ei selavan*	*ils/elles se lavent*

(Liver 2014: 427–428)

Reflexive markers can also inflect for case: unlike French, which uses the same elements *me, te, se,* etc. listed in Table 5.1 above both with direct (e.g., *il se lave* 'he washes himself') and indirect reflexivity (e.g., *il se lave les mains* 'he washes his hands'), Latin distinguishes accusative *mē, tē, sē,* etc. from dative *mihi, tibi, sibi,* etc. Lastly, there are two different kinds of multifunctionality to consider regarding the issue of syncretism. The first concerns nominal markers: these are often syncretic with intensifiers (e.g., in *the president himself attended the ceremony*), as present in Uralic, Turkic, Semitic, Indo-Aryan, Mandarin, and English, and absent from Slavic, Romance, most of Germanic, and many Bantu languages (König 2001). The second kind of syncretism concerns verbal markers: these are often syncretic with valency-related operations like passives, antipassives, anticausatives, and recip-rocals. We deal with this topic in more detail in Section 8.2.2, but suffice it to note here that even though dedicated reflexive affixes are relatively uncommon, they do exist – see the Swahili and Navajo markers already illustrated in (246) above.[6]

5.2.2.2   Syntactic Variation of Reflexives

The literature on reflexives has paid special attention to the admissible grammatical relations of the antecedent and the possible domains of coreference ("binding domain"). As to the former, it appears that (i) nominal

---

[6] We are not aware of typological surveys that explore the distribution of nominal vs. verbal reflexives, or the distribution of agent/patient- vs. duplex-voice reflexives. König et al. (2013) survey 168 languages with respect to the formal identity of reflexive pronouns and intensifiers.

reflexives correlate with a wider range of GRs than verbal markers, (ii) the relevant implicational hierarchy is SBJ > DOBJ/POBJ > IOBJ/SOBJ > ADJ (i.e., if the reflexive strategy allows any given GR, it will also allow those to its left), and (iii) animacy and agentivity also play an important role in some languages. As to binding domains, languages like English require locally bound reflexives while other languages allow so-called long-distance reflexives. The following data from Mandarin illustrate some of these issues (248). The reflexive marker *zìjǐ* allows not only subjects but also other participants, like indirect objects, as antecedents – all of which must nonetheless be animate – (a); when occurring in an embedded clause, it can have its antecedent either within the same clause (*Lisi*) or in the matrix clause (*Zhangsan*) (b):

(248)   Mandarin Chinese (Huang & Tang 1991: 265)

    a. *Tā*   *gěi*   *wǒ*   *zìjǐ*   *de*   *shū.*
       3[SG]   give   1[SG]   REFL   ATTR   book
       'I gave him his own book.'

    b. *Zhāngsān*   *shuō*   *Lǐsì*   *cháng*   *pīpíng*   *zìjǐ.*
       Z.   say   L.   often   criticize   REFL
       'Zhangsan said that Lisi often criticized Lisi/Zhangsan.'

More important for our purposes, however, is the fact that there are different kinds of reflexives from the point of view of voice, as was noted in Section 5.1. On the one hand, there are active-voice reflexives like English *she saved herself* or the Tongan construction featuring the emphatic marker *pē* (249):

(249)   Tongan (Austronesian, Tonga; Otsuka 2006: 85)
    Na'e fakalangilangi'i 'e   Mele 'a   ia   pē.
    PST   praise   ERG M.   ABS 3SG EMPH
    'Mele praised herself.'

On the other hand, there are duplex-voice reflexives, like the one marked by *ine-* ~ *-tku* in Chukchi, which is syncretic with the antipassive (250), or the one marked by *-yii* ~ *-:* in Kayardild, which is syncretic with the passive (251).

(250)   Chukchi (Kurebito 2012: 184–185)
    a. *Tə-lpiw-ɣʔen*   *ottə-lɣən.*
       1SG.SBJ-cut-3SG.OBJ   wood-ABS
       'I cut the wood.'

    b. *Tə-lpiw-tku-ɣʔek.*
       1SG.SBJ-cut-REFL-1SG.SBJ
       'I cut myself.'

    c. *Qora-ŋə*   *tenti-tku-yʔi*   *rewəm-ək.*
       reindeer-ABS   tread-ANTIP-3SG.SBJ   stone-LOC
       'The reindeer trod on the stone.'

(251)   Kayardild (Tangkic, Australia; Evans 1995: 352, 2)
    a. *Dangka-a*   *raa-jarra*   *bijarrba-na*   *wumburu-nguni-na.*
       man-NOM   spear-PST   dugong-ABL   spear-INS-ABL
       'The man speared the dugong with a spear.'

b. *Ngada*   *bala-a-ja*   *karwa-wuru.*
    1SG.NOM   hit-MID-TAM   club-PROP
    'I was hit with a club.' / 'I hit myself with a club.'

c. *Bijarrba*   *ra-yii-ja*   *dangka-na.*
    dugong[NOM]   spear-PASS-TAM   man-ABL
    'The dugong is/was speared by the man.'

Note that the Kayardild marker leads to ambiguous readings, each of which has a different syntax, like in (b) above: the passive promotes the P, and the resulting voice is passive; the reflexive assigns A and P to the subject, and the resulting voice is duplex.

5.2.2.3   Semantic Variation of Reflexives

The most important parameter of semantic(-syntactic) variation consists of the distinction between direct and indirect reflexives. In the simplest case, the direct reflexive is based on a two-argument clause while the indirect reflexive is its three-argument counterpart. The latter can be built upon a trivalent predicate, like *dare* 'give' in Latin (252). The semantic arguments are an A (covert 'he' in (a) and overt *nemo* 'no one' in (b)) and a T (*pecūniam* 'money' in (a) and *beneficium* 'benefit' in (b)) in both cases, but the G and the A are coreferential only in the indirect-reflexive (b). This is schematically represented in Figure 5.4. The T is the direct object and the G is the indirect object in both (a) and (b) – both instances of the active voice.

(252)   Latin (Seneca, *On Benefits* 3.19, 5.9)

a. *Quia non potest crēditor   dominī   suī   fierī,*
    for   NEG can.3SG creditor[NOM] master.GEN his.GEN become.INF
    si   pecūniam illī   dederit.
    if   money.ACC 3SG.M.DAT   give.3SG.FUT.PERF
    'Because he cannot become his master's creditor if he gives him money.'

b. *Nemo   enim sibi   beneficium   dat.*
    no.one[NOM]   for   REFL.DAT.3   benefit[ACC] give.3SG
    'Because no one bestows a benefit upon himself (lit. gives a benefit to himself).'

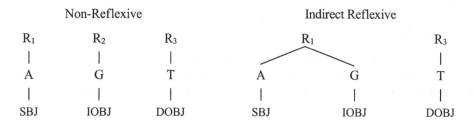

Figure 5.4 *Indirect reflexive diathesis*

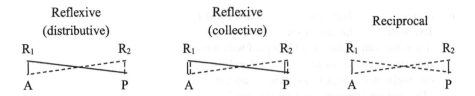

Figure 5.5 *Different reflexive and reciprocal meanings* (DU)

The specific diatheses found in some languages differ from the ones just outlined. One possible deviation consists in the particular language having primary and secondary objects instead of direct and indirect objects. Besides, the indirect reflexive may also employ the duplex, rather than the active, voice.[7] Most importantly, the third syntactic argument in such constructions is often not a base semantic argument of the predicate, like in the common case of external possession / benefaction (e.g., Spanish *se lavó (a sí misma)* 'she washed herself' vs. *se lavó las manos* 's/he washed her hands'); we then have a semantic argument structure of the type [A X° P] instead of [A G T]. (X° represents an extra-thematic or non-selected argument, e.g., one of Næss's 2007 "volitional undergoers" or Bosse et al.'s 2012 "non-selected arguments," i.e., external possessors, beneficiaries, attitude holders, or affected experiencers – a notion that has already been introduced in Chapter 2 for nucleatives.)

Another semantic variation of reflexives is related to the number of participants involved. The prototypical schema we gave in the introduction to this chapter corresponds to the simplest case, with a singular participant (e.g., in English *Alan saw himself*). With a nonsingular participant, however, the close connection between reflexivity and reciprocity becomes apparent. English *Alan and Beatrice saw themselves*, for instance, admits at least two extreme readings, namely distributive (each one saw each one, individually) and collective (both saw both, as a group). Mandarin is slightly different in that the bare reflexive marker admits only a distributive reading of the clause in (a), whereas the combined strategy [pronoun + reflexive] allows both readings in (b):

(253)   Mandarin Chinese (Huang 2002: 7–8)
a. *Zhāngsān hé Lǐsì zài pīpíng zìjǐ.*
   Z.   and L.   at   criticize REFL
b. *Zhāngsān hé Lǐsì zài pīpíng tā-men zìjǐ.*
   Z.   and L.   at   criticize 3-PL   REFL
Both: 'Zhangsan and Lisi are criticizing themselves.'

The collective and distributive readings of reflexivity, as well as strong reciprocity, are schematically represented for two referents in Figure 5.5 above. The solid and broken lines represent the subevents involved. In the distributive

---

[7] Note that the duplex voice is only available for direct reflexives in Finnish: indirect reflexives always use the pronominal construction.

reflexive, these subevents are 'Alan saw Alan' and 'Beatrice saw Beatrice'; in the reciprocal, the subevents are 'Alan saw Beatrice' and 'Beatrice saw Alan'; in one of the collective reflexives,[8] they are 'Alan saw Alan and Beatrice' and 'Beatrice saw Alan and Beatrice'.

5.3   Reciprocals and Voice

5.3.1   Two Prototypical Reciprocals

Leaving aside the uncoded reciprocals discussed in Chapter 6, there are two kinds of (monoclausal) reciprocals from the point of view of voice: (i) an agent/patient voice that denotes reflexivity resorting to means unrelated to voice, and (ii) a duplex-voice construction that has reflexivity as either one of its possible readings or as its sole interpretation.[9] The following examples from Tonga and Rotokas illustrate the first two kinds:

(254)   Tonga (Bantu, Zambia; Maslova 2008: 230)
Joni   *ba-la-yand-ana*   *amukaintu*   *wakwe.*
J.   3PL.SBJ-PRS-love-RECP   wife   his
'John and his wife love each other.' (lit. 'John mutually loves his wife')

(255)   Rotokas (Papuan, Papua New Guinea; Robinson 2011: 200–201)
a.   *Oira   kakae-ro   riako   kakae-ro   tario-pa-i-voi.*
     male   child-PL   female   child-PL   chase-CONT-3PL-PRS
     'The little boys are chasing the little girls.'
b.   *Oira   kakae-ro   ora   riako   kakae-ro*
     male   child-PL   and   female   child-PL
     ora-tario-pa-a-i.
     RECP-chase-CONT-3PL-PRS
     'The little boys and little girls are chasing each other.'

In the active reciprocal (254), the semantically bivalent predicate -*yand* 'love' appears in a two-argument clause with a subject and an object; what is special about it is that the verb takes the suffix -*ana*, an element that denotes coreference of the complex type we encounter with reciprocity. By contrast, (255) shows that the active in (a) differs from the duplex in (b). First, the verb in the former takes the suffixes -*i* and -*voi*, for 3PL subject and present, respectively, whereas the verb in the latter takes the suffixes -*a* and -*i* instead, which only occur on syntactically monovalent predicates, plus the (syncretic) reciprocal prefix *ora-*. Second, note that the boys and the girls appear as subject and object, respectively, in (a) but combined as subject in (b), a clause without an object. Even

---

[8] Collective includes object-collective (the reading chosen here), subject-collective, and all-collective.
[9] As with reflexives, the P can appear in grammatical relations other than object in the agent/patient voice (e.g., as an adpositional object or as an adjunct); we are glossing over this possibility for ease of presentation only.

though the reciprocals of Tonga and Rotokas share their (verbal) morphological make-up, they differ regarding their syntactic structure: the syntactic valency of the predicate is two in the latter and one in the former. Moreover, the monovalent syntax is also a special diathesis because the subject is assigned two semantic roles.

Thus, we can define the prototypical (strong) reciprocals as follows:

(256)   Prototypical reciprocal construction
   a. There are two simultaneous constitutive events: (i) Referent$_1$ is A while Referent$_2$ is P, and (ii) Referent$_1$ is P while Referent$_2$ is A.
   b. The A is the subject in the reciprocal and in the non-reciprocal counterpart.
   c. The P is not the subject in the non-reciprocal; in the reciprocal, it either bears the same grammatical relation (active) or it is the subject as well (duplex).
   d. If the predicate takes a formal marker in the duplex diathesis, the construction is an instance of reciprocal duplex voice.

5.3.2   Variation of Reciprocals

5.3.2.1   Morphological Variation of Reciprocals

Several taxonomies of reciprocal constructions have been proposed; in addition to the studies mentioned below, the reader is referred to Nedjalkov (2007c) and Evans (2008).

Monoclausal grammatical reciprocals consist of devices that mark either arguments or predicates – usually labeled as nominal and verbal, respectively. König and Kokutani (2006) give the examples in (257) and distinguish two kinds of nominal reciprocals ("pronominal" in (a) and "quantificational" in (b)), as well as two kinds of verbal reciprocals ("synthetic" in (c) and "compound" in (d)):

(257)   Grammatical reciprocals (a–c: König & Kokutani 2006: 276)
   a. German
      Seitdem   meiden   sich   die   beiden   Professoren.
      since.then   avoid.3PL   RECP   ART   both   professors
      'The two professors have avoided each other ever since.'
   b. English
      John and Pete hate each other.
   c. Swahili
      Ali   na   Fatuma   wa-na-pend-an-a.
      A.   and   F.   3PL.SBJ-PRS-love-RECP-ASP
      'Ali and Fatuma love each other.'
   d. Mandarin Chinese (Liu 2000b: 126)
      Tā-men   dǎ-lái-dǎ-qù.
      3-PL   fight-come-fight-go
      'They fought with each other.'

As with reflexives, the correlation between nominal vs. verbal expression of reciprocity on the one hand and the use of active vs. middle diathesis/voice on the other is only imperfect (Evans 2008: 44). More details follow in the next subsection.

5.3.2.2   Syntactic Variation of Reciprocals

Maslova (2008) proposes the following syntactic taxonomy of reciprocals. When compared with non-reciprocal constructions based on the same bivalent predicate, BINARY reciprocals have the same diathetical structure in that they also have two independent "morphosyntactic slots" for the two arguments, like an active-voice construction. This is perhaps naturally the case with biclausal constructions like the one shown in (258), but it can also be found with mono-clausal reciprocals like the one we have already seen for Tonga in (254).

(258)   Cantonese (Sino-Tibetan, China; Maslova 2008: 230)
         [*Ngóh béi-min kéuih*] [*kéuih béi-min ngóh*].
         1[SG] give-face 3[SG]   3[SG] give-face 1[SG]
         'He and I respect each other.'

With UNARY reciprocals, by contrast, this independence is dismantled (259). With argumental reciprocals (a), the syntactic object slot is often no longer occupied by a potentially variable object but by an invariable element, either simple, like in Bambara *ŋɔ́gɔn*, or complex, like English *each other*. With verbal reciprocals (b), moreover, there is often no syntactic object slot at all, and the duplex voice is deployed:

(259)   Unary reciprocals
         a. Bambara (Niger-Congo, Mali)
             Nzánga ní   à   mùsó`   bìla-là   ŋɔ́gɔn   ná.
             N.   and his wife.ART lean-PFV RECP   upon
             'Nzanga and his wife insulted each other.' (Maslova 2008: 229)
         b. Halkomelem
             Niʔ   ćawə-təl   kʷθə   John   ʔiʔ   Bob.
             AUX   help-RECP   DET   J.   and   B.
             'John and Bob helped each other.' (Gerdts 2000b: 140)

Although there is a tendency for verbal markers to be used more often than nominal markers with the duplex diathesis, there are exceptions. The example in (260) from Yélî Dnye shows the use of the nominal *numo* in a construction that is of reduced syntactic valency when compared to the two-argument clause in (a). In (b), the subject no longer takes ergative case, the nominal *numo* is incorporated in the default position of incorporated objects (i.e., between the TAM proclitic *wunê* and the verb *kp:anê*), and the clause-final clitic *mo* is the same that occurs with monovalent predicates:

(260)   Yélî Dnye (Papuan, Papua New Guinea; Levinson 2011: 180)
         a. *Kakan   ngê   Nganapwe wunê   kp:anê   Ø.*
            K.   ERG   N.[ABS] 3.TAM chasing 3SG.OBJ
            'Kakan habitually chases Nganapwe.'

    b. *Kakan   Nganapwe   wunê   numo   kp:anê mo.*
       K.[ABS] N.[ABS]   3.TAM RECP   chasing 3DU.SBJ
       'Kakan and Nganapwe habitually chase each other.'

Even more frequent than valency-reducing reciprocal strategies with nominals are valency-neutral or uncertain cases with verbal reciprocals. In Xârâgurè, the reciprocal affix *pu-* merely denotes coreference and does not alter the diathesis (261): the subject and object slots are the same in the non-reciprocal and in the reciprocal clauses (a). In Kuuk Thaayorre, even though some examples suggest that syntactic valency might have been reduced in the reciprocal, the use of the ergative in (b) is anomalous; in principle, it occurs only in bona fide two-argument clauses:

(261)   Verbal reciprocals
       a. Xârâgurè (Austronesian, New Caledonia; Evans 2008: 70)
         Nyärä   kêgai   nyärä. vs. *Nyärä   pu-kêgai   nyärä.*
         3PL   pinch   3PL   3PL   RECP-pinch   3PL
         'They pinch them.'   'They are pinching each other.'
       b. Kuuk Thaayorre (Pama-Nyungan, Australia)
         Ngal   nhaanhath-rr. vs. *Parr-n peln   ii   waarin-rr.*
         1DU.INCL watch.ASP-RECP   kid-ERG 3PL.ERG there chase-RECP
         'We (DU) are looking at each other.' 'All the kids are chasing each other.'
         (Gaby 2008: 260)   (Evans et al. 2007: 571)

Two of the three reciprocal constructions of Olutec differ as to syntactic valency (262). With the verb *kü?pa:t-* 'get married', it is possible to have a simple reciprocal construction marked with *ni-* and an inverse marker, which appears to be monovalent because of the S/P index and the allomorphy of the incompletive marker (not shown here) (a). It is also possible to have a marked strategy with a transitivized version thanks to the comitative applicative *mü-*, which syntactically resembles more closely its English translational equivalent (b):

(262)   Olutec (Mixe-Zoquean, Mexico; Zavala 2011: 268, 272)
       a. *Ta=ni-kü?pa:t-anüpa-:t   pek.*
         1.S/P=RECP-get.married-INV-PL.SAP real
         'It is true that we are going to get married.'
       b. *Tan=mü:-ni-kü?pa:t-anüpa=ja?.*
         1.A=APPL-RECP-get.married-INV=3
         'I am going to marry him.'

5.3.2.3 The Syntactic Status of Reflexives and Reciprocals

    Reflexives and reciprocals may be clear regarding their syntactic make-up, but sometimes they seem to occupy an intermediate, or unclear, position in terms of which clause type or diathesis they employ (Lichtenberk 1994, Mohanan & Mohanan 1998).

Evans et al. (2007) survey a number of Australian languages with clear and unclear, or default and intermediate, clause types. For example, several languages in their sample allow a subject in either the nominative (as in one-argument clauses) or the ergative (as in two-argument clauses) in reciprocal constructions. At least in Bunuba, which shows syncretic verbal marking for reflexives and reciprocals, nonsingular nominative subjects can have either reading, but nonsingular ergative subjects seem to require a reciprocal interpretation. Another form of hybrid morphosyntax consists in object suppression in tandem with the overt expression of a body part linked to a "phantom" object denoting the whole. In Dalabon (263), for instance, the reciprocal in (b) seems to be a one-argument clause in most respects, but the body-part noun *mim* 'eye' can be incorporated as though there were an object denoting the whole in the clausal syntax; (a) shows that the incorporate cannot be construed as instrument (i.e., as part of the subject) – it needs to be part of the object (*ngarrinj* 'hand' is part of the 1SG object in (a)), even though the object NP cannot appear in the clause in (b), and the verbal prefix *barra-* is the same as the one indexing a 3DU subject in a one-argument clause:

(263)   Dalabon (Evans et al. 2007: 575)
    a. *Ka-h-ngarrinj-yidjnja-n.*
        3SG→1SG-ASS-hand-hold/touch-PRS
        'S/he is holding my hand.'
        (Not: 'S/he is touching me with her/his hand.')
    b. *Barra-h-mim-na-rr-ûn.*
        3DU-ASS-eye-see/look-RECP-PRS
        'They (DU) are looking into each other's eyes (i.e., they are lovers).'
        (Not: 'They (DU) are looking at each other with their eyes.')

By a related token, reflexives and reciprocals may show structural discrepancies. In Yawuru, for instance, both constructions appear with the marker *-ndyi*, a single overt NP, and a monopersonal verb, but reflexives take the intransitive prefix *ma-*, used in one-argument clauses (a), while reciprocals (except in the 1INCL) take the transitive prefix *a-*, used in two-argument clauses (b):

(264)   Yawuru (Nyulnyulan, Australia; Evans et al. 2007: 578)
    a. *Ingarr-ma-bura-ndyi-n*   *kamba-rri.*
        3AUG.SBJ-INTR-see-REFL/RECP-IPFV   that-DU
        'They (DU) see themselves.'
    b. *Ingarr-a-bura-ndyi-n*   *kamba-rri.*
        3AUG.SBJ-TR-see-REFL/RECP-IPFV   that-DU
        'They (DU) see each other.'

In Chichewa, the reflexive and the reciprocal differ with respect to their morphology: (i) the verb takes the prefix *dzi-* with the former and the suffix *-an* with the latter, and (ii) the reflexive prefix appears in the object slot and is to be considered inflectional, while the reciprocal suffix derives a different verb stem. (The evidence in favor of this analysis is phonological, morphological, and syntactic.) The following pair illustrates the opposition between the two constructions:

(265)   Chichewa (Mchombo 2004: 102–103)
          a. *Mkángó   u-na-dzí-súpŭl-a.*
              lion.III   III.SBJ-PST-REFL-bruise-ASP
              'The lion bruised itself.'
          b. *Mikángó   i-ku-phwány-an-a.*
              lion.IV   IV.SBJ-PRS-smash-RECP-ASP
              'Lions are smashing one another.'

Crucially, their syntax is also different: the reflexive uses an active-voice construction and an object-coreference marker *dzi-*, without reducing syntactic valency, whereas the reciprocal uses a duplex-voice construction and reduces valency. There is also a semantic difference between the constructions, namely the admissible interpretations of clauses like those in (266). The reflexive only allows the so-called sloppy identity reading in (a); the reciprocal, by contrast, allows several interpretations (the last of which is the sloppy identity reading) (b):

(266)   Chichewa (Mchombo 2004: 106)
          a. *Alenje   á-ma-dzi-nyóz-á   ku-pósá   asodzi.*
              hunter.II   II.SBJ-HAB-REFL-despise-ASP   INF-exceed   fisherman.II
              'The hunters despise themselves more than the fishermen (despise themselves).'
          b. *Alenje   á-ma-nyoz-án-á   ku-pósá   asodzi.*
              hunter.II   II.SBJ-HAB-despise-RECP-ASP   INF-exceed   fisherman.II
              'The hunters despise each other more than the fishermen despise them.'
              'The hunters despise each other more than they despise the fishermen.'
              'The hunters despise themselves more than the fishermen despise themselves.'

Yukulta shows a different situation (267). In the active voice in a two-argument clause, the indicative has the form *-tha* and the 3PL subject is marked via the enclitic sequence *=l=ka* (a). In the reciprocal construction, the verb takes the same "transitive" indicative marker *-tha* but also the dedicated suffix *-nytyu ~ -nthu* and the 3PL subject marker *=li*, used in one-argument clauses (b). The reflexive construction does not have any reflexive morpheme, but the verb takes the "intransitive" indicative marker *-tya* and the 1SG subject marker *=ka*, used in one-argument clauses as well (c):

(267)   Yukulta (Tangkic, Australia; Laughren 2002: 3)
          a. *Pala-tha=l=ka=nta   ngawu-wa   thungal-urlu-ya.*
              hit-IND=3PL=TR=PST   dog-NOM   stick-INS-ERG
              'They hit the dog with a stick.'

    b. *Purlti-nytyu-tha=li=ngka*   *wangalk-urlu,*
         pelt-RECP-IND=3PL.ITR=PST   boomerang-INS
            laa-nthu-tha=li=ngka   *miyarl-urlu.*
           spear-RECP-IND=3PL.ITR=PST   spear-INS
         'They pelted one another with boomerangs and pierced one another with spears.'

    c. *Parrunthaya=ka=ti*   *mirliya-tya,*   *nayipi-urlu.*
         yesterday=1SG.ITR=PRS   cut-IND   knife-INS
         'Yesterday I cut myself with a knife.'

5.3.2.4   Semantic Variation of Reciprocals

Reciprocals display significant semantic variation. We limit ourselves here to mentioning what appear to be the six main subtypes of configurations (i.e., assignments of semantic roles with multiple referents) with English examples in (268) and schematic representations with referents R_{1-5} in Figure 5.6. The interested reader is referred to Evans et al. (2011) and Majid et al. (2011) for details.

(268)   Semantic configuration types of English reciprocals (Evans et al. 2011: 8)
        a. *The members of this family love one another.* (strong)
        b. *The people at the dinner party were married to one another.* (pair)
        c. *The graduating students followed one another up onto the stage.* (chain)
        d. *The drunks in the pub were punching one another.* (melee)
        e. *The teacher and her pupils intimidated one another.* (radial)
        f. *The children chased each other in a ring.* (ring)

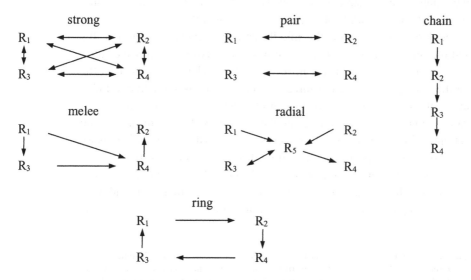

Figure 5.6 *Main reciprocal configuration types*

The examples above show that, as soon as more than two referents are involved, many possible assignments exist. In addition to the assignment of the roles A and P among referents – whether all or only some participate, and whether interactions are symmetrical or asymmetrical – another important parameter of variation is simultaneity vs. sequentiality.

5.4   Middles

5.4.1   Middle Voice as a Value of a Grammatical Category

In the original sense of the term, MIDDLE VOICE describes a particular form of the verb that denotes a meaning seen as intermediate between active and passive. The subject of such middle-form verbs is like the subject of active-form verbs in that it performs an action, and like the subject of passive-form verbs in that it is affected by that action. This terminological practice dates back to when the term *diáthesis* was introduced to denote that grammatical category of the verb in Ancient Greek. The author(s) of the *Téchnē Grammatikḗ* 'Art of Grammar' used *mesótēs diáthesis* 'middle diathesis' in the second century BCE; later grammarians used the same term (often as *mésē diáthesis*), as well as *medium verborum genus* 'middle genus/gender of verbs' and *vox media* 'middle voice'. (Several centuries before Dionysius, Pāṇini had used the analogous term *ātmanepada* 'word for oneself' for the partially analogous grammatical category in Sanskrit in his *Aṣṭādhyāyī* 'Eight Chapters'.)[10] Note that the middle is found in all attested stages of the language (i.e., Mycenaean, Archaic, Classical, Koine, Byzantine, and Modern Greek).

Table 5.2 below shows selected indicative forms for *lou-* 'wash' in Classical Greek. In the present tense, there are only active and middle forms; in the future, the active contrasts with a middle and a passive. Note that the active endings (*-ō*, *-eis*, etc.) regularly contrast with the middle endings (*-omai*, *-ei*, etc.) in the present and the future, and that passive morphology consists of a passive suffix *-thē* plus the middle endings. Forms in the imperfect behave like those in the present; in the aorist, there is also a three-way contrast between active, middle, and passive, but the neat compositionality of the future forms is absent.

Modern pedagogical grammars list a number of clearly distinct meanings and structures found with Greek middle-form verbs (e.g., Smyth 1974).[11] First, as we just saw, in those tense-aspect forms that do not have a specialized passive, the middle form covers that function as well (e.g., *loúomai* 'I am (being) washed'). Second, even though the anticausative function is not frequently found with middle forms, examples do exist (e.g., active *paúō* 'I make [X] cease' vs. middle

---

[10] The Latin Middle is roughly similar to its Greek counterpart, but the Sanskrit Middle is more complicated: there is evidence of a gradual takeover of the passive function by the *yá*-passives, as well as an obsolescence of the reflexive and reciprocal functions, in Vedic Sanskrit (Kulikov 2006).

[11] The reader is further referred to Kühner (1904) and Rijksbaron (1984: 126–158).

Table 5.2 *Selected indicative verb forms in Ancient Greek (lou- 'wash')*

	PRS.ACT	PRS.MID	FUT.ACT	FUT.MID	FUT.PASS
1SG	*loú-ō*	*loú-omai*	*loú-s-ō*	*loú-s-omai*	*lou-thḗ-s-omai*
2SG	*loú-eis*	*loú-ei*	*loú-s-eis*	*loú-s-ei*	*lou-thḗ-s-ei*
3SG	*loú-ei*	*loú-etai*	*loú-s-ei*	*loú-s-etai*	*lou-thḗ-s-etai*
2/3DU	*loú-eton*	*loú-esthon*	*loú-s-eton*	*loú-s-esthon*	*lou-thḗ-s-esthon*
1PL	*loú-omen*	*lou-ómetha*	*loú-s-omen*	*lou-s-ómetha*	*lou-thē-s-ómetha*
2PL	*loú-ete*	*loú-esthe*	*loú-s-ete*	*loú-s-esthe*	*lou-thḗ-s-esthe*
3PL	*loú-ousi(n)*	*loú-ontai*	*loú-s-ousi(n)*	*loú-s-ontai*	*lou-thḗ-s-ontai*

paúomai 'I cease'). Third, with nonsingular subjects the middle may express reciprocity (e.g., active *dianémō* 'I distribute' vs. middle *taûta dianemoûntai* 'they will divide this up among themselves') – but several of such cases do not alternate with active forms (e.g., middle *emáchonto* 'they fought with each other'; see below). Fourth, the middle form can express reflexivity, either direct (e.g., *loúomai* 'I wash myself'; see also (a) in (269) below) or indirect (e.g., *loúomai tà himátia* 'I wash the clothes for myself / my clothes'). Note in passing how, in cases like those illustrated in (269), the direct reflexive meaning can also be expressed by the active voice and a reflexive pronoun (b), or even, albeit rarely, with the middle voice and a reflexive pronoun for emphatic contrast or in the context of "difficult and unnatural actions" (Smyth 1974: 1724), as in (c):

(269)   Greek
a. *Phulássesthe*   *apò*   *pásēs*   *pleonexías.*
   guard.2PL.IMPER.PRS.MID from   all.GEN.SG   greed.GEN.SG
   'Be on your (PL) guard against all kinds of greed.' (Koine Greek, Luke
   12.15/*New International Version*)
b. *Teknía,*   *phuláxate*   *heautà*
   child(N).NOM.PL guard.2PL.IMPER.AOR.ACT   REFL.N.ACC.PL
   apò   *tôn*   *eidólōn.*
   from   ART.GEN.PL   idol.GEN.PL
   'Children, keep yourselves from idols.' (Koine Greek, 1 John 5.21/*NIV*)
c. *Ei*   *dé*   *ge*   *mēdamoû*   *heautòn*
   if   but   at.least   not.even.one.GEN.SG   REFL.M.ACC.SG
   apokrúptoito   *ho*   *poiētḗs...*
   hide.3SG.PRS.OPT.MID   ART.NOM.SG   poet.NOM.SG
   'But if the poet should conceal himself nowhere ...' (Classical Greek,
   Plato, *Republic* 393c)

The fifth function of Greek middle forms is the causative-reflexive. The first and second verb forms in (270) illustrate the direct ('be baptized!') and indirect subtypes ('wash your sins away!'), respectively:

(270)   Koine Greek
          ... *bápti-sai*   *kaì*   *apólou-sai*
          baptize-IMPER.AOR.MID.2SG   and   wash.away- IMPER.AOR.MID.2SG
          tàs   *hamartías sou* ...
          art   sins.ACC   2SG.PSR
          '[...] Be baptized and wash your sins away [...]!' (Acts 22:16/*NIV*)

In the argument structure of such constructions, the subject is simultaneously the
A of CAUSE (the causer) and the P (direct) or G (indirect) of the argumental
predicate (271) – both being kinds of the duplex diathesis. (See Figure 5.7 below:
the symbols *bA, bP, bT* and *bG* stand for the arguments of the base lexical
predicate.) The A of the lexical predicate (the causee) is left unexpressed in the
examples above.

(271)   Causative-reflexive: Argument structure
          a. Direct: CAUSE [A_i, P_j, *baptize* [A_k, P_j]]
          b. Indirect: CAUSE [A_i, P_j, *wash.away* [A_k, T_l, G_i]]

Direct CAUS-REFL (duplex$_3$)   Indirect CAUS-REFL (duplex$_4$)

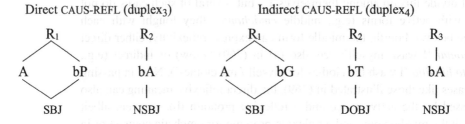

Figure 5.7 *Selected duplex reflexive diatheses*

   Sixth, in many cases where the middle contrasts with an existing active, the
former is said to "lay stress on the conscious activity, bodily or mental participation, of the agent" (Smyth 1974: 1728). Examples include pairs like active
bouleúō 'I plan, deliberate on' vs. middle *bouleúomai* 'I deliberate, resolve on'
and active *skopō* 'I look' vs. middle *skopoûmai* 'I consider'. They also include
the much-cited opposition between active *politeúō* 'I am a citizen' and middle
politeúomai 'I act as a citizen, perform my civic duties', as well as the pair active
presbeúō 'I am an elder/envoy' vs. middle *presbeúomai* 'I negotiate as an envoy
/ send envoys'. In pairs like these, there is a clear tendency regarding syntactic
valency: the verb in the active form is often bivalent while the verb in the middle
is often monovalent. Lastly, numerous DEPONENT VERBS appear only in one
voice: the so-called *media tantum* appear only in the middle. These verbs usually
belong to a small number of classes, namely verbs of bodily activity (e.g.,
orchéomai 'I dance' and *pétomai* 'I fly') and psych verbs (either cognitive, like
oíomai 'I forebode, conjecture', or affective, like *olophúromai* 'I lament, moan').
(Other verbs, like *akoúō* 'I hear', have all forms in some tenses and aspects but
regularly take only the middle form in the future.)
   These functions are summarized in Table 5.3 below. With regard to the
diatheses involved, the anticausatives (Section 2.2) and the active and passive

Table 5.3 *Main functions of the middle in Ancient Greek*

	Change in semantic argument structure	Change in syntactic valency	Diathesis
ANTIC	A-removal	decrease	ANTIC
CAUS.REFL:DIR	A-installment	decrease	$DUPLEX_3$
CAUS.REFL:INDIR	A-installment G-installment	increase	$DUPLEX_4$
RECP		decrease	$DUPLEX_{1/2}$
REFL:DIR		decrease	$DUPLEX_1$
REFL:INDIR	✗	decrease	$DUPLEX_2$
PASS		decrease	PASS
"participation"		(decrease)	ACT
media tantum	n/a	n/a	ACT(/DUPLEX)

(Section 3.1) do not need further explanation. The duplex diathesis falls into different subtypes depending on which companion argument shares subject status with the A, namely the P ($duplex_1$) or the G ($duplex_2$) with reflexives/ reciprocals (Section 5.2) and the base P (or T) ($duplex_3$) or the base G ($duplex_4$) with causative-reflexives (see above). Most of the *media tantum* seem to simply use an active diathesis, although some of the motion verbs might be construed as (etymologically) using a duplex structure.

5.4.2   The Middle as a Network of Meanings

Scholars working in the syntax-centered tradition tend to try to capture the essential aspects of this multifarious phenomenon by postulating the reduction of syntactic valency as central, and valency-neutral functions as peripheral, to the category (see Barber 1975 for an early study in this tradition). Nevertheless, scholars working in the function-centered tradition maintain that "it is almost impossible to discern any syntactic core of all the functions from the middle domain" (Kazenin 2001b: 923). In this second view, syntactic valency reduction is taken for granted with passives and anticausatives, but also with reflexives and reciprocals – something that is actually in need of discussion, as we have seen in the preceding sections of this chapter. But valency reduction is also seen as

> ... not obligatory in potential [passives], not unproblematic with logophoric
> middles [which signal coreference between matrix and embedded arguments
> in complementation with verba dicendi, FZ & SK] [...] and surely [not
> taking] place with deponents. This shows that in order to give an account for
> really all the functions from the middle domain, a semantic rather than
> structural explanation is called for.   (Kazenin 2001b: 923)

Semantic accounts of middles date back at least to Krüger (1846). Kuryłowicz (1964) simply postulates "lowered transitivity" as the general meaning of middles. In the English-language tradition, Lyons (1968) is generally credited with reinterpreting the original idea of an "action performed with special reference to the subject" for English phenomena, thereby partly dissociating the form from the meaning ("the 'action' or 'state' affects the subject of the verb or his interests," 1968: 373) and leading to quite a different sense of MIDDLE. In this new sense, the term refers to uncoded potential passives like English *bureaucrats bribe easily*, which do not have special verbal marking (i.e., they have an active form) but denote that the subject is affected by the event (i.e., they have a "passive meaning"), unlike constructions like *someone bribed the bureaucrats* (which have an active form and an "active meaning"). This gave rise to the term "middle verbs" for predicates that allow such alternations, in turn called "middle pairs," by Keyser and Roeper (1984); this terminology seems to have spread in Western linguistics chiefly via publications in the Chomskyan tradition.

Other early attempts at distilling a functional core or general meaning focus on the middles of semantically bivalent verbs and look for possible reasons for the widespread syncretic forms instantiating reflexives, reciprocals, passives, and anticausatives. Some studies see the reflexive (and the reciprocal) at the center and the other functions as extensions (e.g., Woodcock 1959, Geniušienė 1987, and Croft et al. 1987). Other studies see the passive at the center. For instance, Shibatani (1985) argues that the backgrounding ("defocusing") of the A is the common function of passives and anticausatives, as well as the core of the middle; he further sees European reflexives, reciprocals, and passives as showing "very strong correlations." Givón (1981) sees passives as simultaneously A-backgrounding, P-foregrounding ("topicalizing"), and event-stativizing, and sees the different middle readings as sharing one or more of these functions with the passive. Similarly, Givón's (2001) "[m]iddle-voice constructions are a cluster of variants on semantically-transitive verbs, most commonly involving a shift of the semantic focus away from the agent," which is achieved by focusing the patient's change, its potential state for such change, or its resulting state following the event (2001: II, 116). Givón's category includes potential passives, resultatives, and anticausatives but excludes reflexives and reciprocals.

By contrast, Kemmer's influential studies of the late 1980s and early 1990s do not address resultatives, include only a subset of reflexives and reciprocals, and see potential passives as "relatively distant" (1994) from her "middle situation types." She characterizes the latter as follows:

> (1) The middle is a semantic area comprising events in which (a) the Initiator is also an Endpoint, or affected entity and (b) the event is characterized by a low degree of elaboration. [...] The first property is a subaspect of the second. (2) Middle marking is in general a morphosyntactic strategy for expressing an alternative conceptualization of an event in which aspects of the internal structure of the event that are less important from the point of view of the speaker are not made reference to in the utterance.   (Kemmer 1993: 243)

This notion explicitly refers to a meaning that frequently finds an expression of a particular kind (her "middle marker"), rather than to a form or a consistent form-meaning pairing. Kemmer's (1994) ten middle situation types correspond to anti-causatives (e.g., 'vanish', 'recover'); natural autobenefactives (e.g., 'acquire', 'request') and natural reciprocals (e.g., 'embrace', 'converse'); three kinds of psych verbs ("emotion middles," e.g., 'be angry', 'be/become frightened', "emo-tive speech actions," e.g., 'complain', 'lament', and "cognition middles," e.g., 'believe', 'meditate');[12] and four bodily-action verbs (grooming or body care, e.g., 'wash', 'shave'; nontranslational motion, e.g., 'turn', 'bow', translational motion, e.g., 'climb up', 'fly', and change in body posture, e.g., 'sit down', 'rise').

Lastly, one of the hallmarks of Kemmer's view is the cline along what she labels "degree of distinguishability of participants" (1994: 209), which represents several situations according to their semantics. In Kemmer's view, two-participant events have both two semantic roles and two distinct referents associated to them; on the other end of the cline, one-participant events have one semantic role and one referent only. She sees the (direct) reflexive and the middle as having two separate semantic roles and only one referent, but "[t]he reflexive implies a conceptual differentiation of the referential entity into discrete subparts, whereas the middle is lacking in this differentiation," and the latter "lacks even the expectation of distinct participants" (Kemmer 1994: 208).

By a related token, Shibatani (2006: 234) defines his "active and middle action types" based on the "manner of the development of an action." With actives, "[t]he action extends beyond the agent's personal sphere and achieves its effect on a distinct patient." With middles, however, "[t]he development of an action is confined within the agent's personal sphere so that the action's effect accrues on the agent itself." He further divides the middle action types in three: "simple intransitive activities" (e.g., 'sit' and 'squat'), "reflexive situations" (e.g., 'hit oneself' and 'shave oneself'), and "body-care actions" (e.g., 'bathe', 'dress oneself', 'wash one's hands', 'comb one's hair').

Yet other studies focus on the middles of syntactically monovalent verbs, particularly on the *media tantum*. Klaiman (1991: 59), for instance, characterizes "deponency" as "action presupposing the logical subject's animacy and control, and relating either to physical state or attitude, or to mental disposition." She regards this as the semantic core not only of deponent verbs but also of the middle as a whole.[13]

Among recent studies of middles in this tradition, Kaufmann's (2007) study centering on Fula and including Ancient Greek, German, and Spanish data, merits special attention. She identifies the usual readings of middle forms as

---

[12] Kemmer says that, in the case of the psych verbs, "there is no distinguishability of participants" (1993: 141) and that more research is needed in order to adequately characterize that specific network of meanings.

[13] It is not at all clear how that informs her central notion of affectedness of the subject with the verbs that show both active and middle forms (Haspelmath 1994).

anticausative, direct and indirect reflexive, causative-reflexive, and facilitative ('be V-able'), but concentrates on the *media tantum*. Her semantic analysis is based on a concept of "control" elaborated on Klaiman's (1991) non-mainstream understanding of that term: "the inherent potentiality of an individual to control certain situations" (1991: 1689). Kaufmann claims that the middle voice "is not an operation on the argument structure of the active form, but basically a morphological device that serves to mark certain non-canonical semantic properties of the arguments of verbal stems" (Kaufmann 2007: 1678) – by which she means states of affairs in which the P or G (or no argument, as in her facilitative reading), rather than the A, is the controller. Lastly, note that Kaufmann's (2007: 1688) take on the *media tantum* differs markedly from Klaiman's:

> Historical data provide evidence that the *media tantum* develop after both the direct reflexive and the anticausative reading in languages that encode the middle function by reflexive verbs [...]. I therefore, [sic] assume that the existence of *media tantum* in middle marking languages is a consequence of a reinterpretation of the device which derives the differential readings [= those identified in verbs that appear in different voices, FZ & SK] [...], generalized to marking semantic verb classes with properties similar to that of the differential readings, i.e. verbs with inherently non-canonical control properties.

The diversity of functions of the classical middle (including the several diatheses they correspond to) and the multiplicity of accounts have led some modern commentators to regard the theoretical and typological applicability of the term MIDDLE VOICE as problematic (e.g., Dixon & Aikhenvald 1997 and Mel'čuk 2006). As surveyed in the present subsection, several studies argue that the "middle," often termed "middle voice," is best seen as either a general function or a network of specific functions, rather than as a form. But consider in this context the passives of Japanese and Mapudungun. In the former language, *-(r)are* covers several functions (272), namely the prototypical passive, the malefactive nucleative, a "potential," and an anticausative-like "spontaneous," and it also functions as subject-honorific marker:

(272)   Japanese (Shibatani 1985: 822–823; Shibatani 1998: 125)

a.   *Tarō=wa   sikar-are-ta.*
     T.=TOP   scold-PASS-PST
     'Taro was scolded.' (passive)

b.   *Tarō=wa   ame=ni   fur-are-ta.*
     T.=TOP   rain=DAT   fall-SUNUCL:MAL-PST
     'Taro was adversely affected by the rain's falling.' (undergoer nucleative)

c.   *Boku=wa   nemur-are-nakat-ta.*
     1SG=TOP   sleep-POT-NEG-PST
     'I could not sleep.' (potential)

d.   *Mukashi=ga   shinob-are-ru.*
     old.time=NOM   think.about-SPONT-PRS
     'An old time comes (spontaneously) to mind.' (spontaneous)

e. *Sensei=ga   waraw-are-ta.*
teacher=NOM   laugh-SBJ.HON-PST
'The teacher laughed.' (subject honorific)

In Mapudungun, *-nge* covers quite different functions (273). It is the agentless passive marker, the existential verb *nge-*, the NP verbalizer *-nge* (which some authors analyze as a copula), the permanent stativizer *-nge*, and the nowadays somewhat redundant suffix present in some cases of verbal reduplication:

(273)   Mapudungun
a. *Langüm-nge-i   chi   wentru.*
kill-PASS-IND   ART   man
'The man was killed.' (passive)

b. *Nge-la-i   chadi.*
exist-NEG-IND   salt
'There is no salt.' (existential verb)

c. *Weda-kona-nge-i-m-i.*
poor-strapping.lad-VBLZ-IND-2-SG
'You (SG) are a poor lad.' (verbalizer) (Salas 2006: 182)

d. *Kurü-nge-i   tami   sapatu.*
black(en)-STAT-IND   2SG.PSR   shoe(s)
'Your (SG) shoes are black.' (stativizer)

e. *Ngüma~ngüma-nge-i   chi   pichi-wentru.*
cry~ITER-be-IND   ART   little-man
'The child was crying and crying.' (iterative reduplication)

The multifunctionality of Japanese *-(r)are* is arguably semantically motivated (see Oshima 2008), but it is cross-linguistically much less frequent than the multifunctionality of Mapudungun *-nge*. Constructions with inactive auxiliaries like Mapudungun *nge-* 'be' are indeed a common source of passive constructions (see Chapter 8). It would not be useful, however, to label all uses of such elements as instances of a broad "passive voice" – either those uses that are highly language-specific, like the ones of Japanese, or those that are commonly found across areal and genealogical boundaries, like the ones of Mapudungun. There are two good reasons for this: such a usage would not employ the term "voice" in a principled way, and there is no need to blur formal lines while conducting a functional analysis in the first place. Unfortunately, that is exactly what the proposals by many of the studies mentioned in the preceding subsection do.

5.4.3   Middle Inflection, Voice, and Cluster

Following Kulikov (2011a), we use a more precise terminology in the present study. The term MIDDLE INFLECTION meaningfully refers to the formal phenomenon found in the classical languages and can be employed alongside the traditional term "Middle Voice." As outlined in Table 5.3 above for Greek, such forms can correspond to a number of different diatheses, namely active, passive, anticausative, and several subtypes of the duplex diathesis (viz., reflexive, causative-reflexive, and reciprocal). By contrast, the term MIDDLE CLUSTER refers to syncretisms based on the semantic connectedness of different event types, some of which can correspond to the duplex voice. The related term MEDIOPASSIVE is customarily used in descriptive studies, for instance, when the passive marker is syncretic with – in decreasing order of frequency – the reflexive, the reciprocal, the anticausative, and some marker occurring on monovalent motion or posture verbs.[14]

Similarly, the term MIDDLE MARKER can be aptly used for the suffix -*m* in Halkomelem (274), where it occurs on several syntactic monovalent verbs (a), but also with passive (b), antipassive (c), and ego-benefactive functions (d):[15]

(274)   Halkomelem (Gerdts & Hukari 2006: 44–45)

    a.   *təm̓š-ə́n̓ə-m*
        braid-ear-MID
        'braid one's hair'

    b.   *kʷən-ət-əm*
        take-TR-MID
        'be taken'

    c.   *qʷəl-əm*   *(ʔə*   *kʷ*   *sce:ɬtən)*
        cook-MID   OBL   DET   salmon
        'cook (some salmon)'

    d.   *ʔiləq-əɬc-əm*
        buy-APPL:BEN-MID
        'buy for speaker' (cf. -*θət* 'REFL', used with underived bivalent verbs)

Applying the term MIDDLE to the opposition between the subject markers of two sets in the Guaicuruan languages of central-eastern South America, however, is less straightforward. In Pilagá, for instance, the lexicon and grammar show split intransitivity (275). Numerous monovalent verbs take only Set I (mostly 'agentive') markers (a), some take only Set II (mostly 'affected') markers (b), and many allow markers from either set (c–d). Bivalent verbs take an object marker in addition to the subject marker (e–f):

(275)   Pilagá (Guaicuruan, Argentina; Vidal 2008: 415–416, 418, 427)

    a. *Se-taqa-tak.*   b. *ɲi-onayak.*
        1.SBJ.I-speak-PROG   1.SBJ.II-be.happy
        'I am speaking.'   'I am happy.'

    c. *S-ek-iseyem.*   d. *ɲ-ek-iseyem.*
        1.SBJ.I-go-up   1.SBJ.II-go-up
        'I go up.'   'I move like dancing/jumping in place.'

---

[14] Some studies employ this term more restrictively; for example, Alexiadou and Doron's (2012) theoretical syntactic study uses it to cover syntactically monovalent verbs "underdetermined for passive/anticausative."

[15] EGO-BENEFACTIVE means 'for the benefit of the speaker', which is crucially different from an AUTOBENEFACTIVE – consider *nem̓ č ʔiləq-əɬc-əm ʔə k̓w səplíl!* (go 2.SBJ buy-APPL:BEN-MID OBL DET bread) 'go buy some bread for me/*yourself!' (Gerdts & Hukari 2006: 61). Gerdts and Hukari label this function "logophoric reflexive."

e. *An-s-eʔet.*
2.OBJ-1.SBJ.I-fix
'I fix (= dress) you (SG).'

f. *An-ɲi-qotoʃon.*
2.OBJ-1.SBJ.II-wake.up
'I wake you (SG) up.'

Even though some verbs use the I–II alternation to signal reflexivity (e.g., *-yo* 'clean' in *si-yo* 'I clean (sthg./sbdy.)' vs. *ɲi-yo* 'I clean myself, get cleaned'), reciprocity actually requires the verbal reciprocal marker *-aʔt* (and reciprocal verbs usually take Set II subject markers, even though they can take Set I markers as well). Most importantly, verbs depicting actions that are not normally performed on oneself – i.e., neither grooming verbs nor a few others – also require the verbal reflexive marker *-(e)lʔat*, which invariably co-occurs with Set II subject markers.

(276)   Pilagá (Vidal 2008: 426)

a. *Ø-Y-alat.*
3.OBJ-3.SBJ.I-kill
'He killed him.'

b. *N-alat-elʔat.*
3.SBJ.II-kill-REFL
'He killed himself.'

Interestingly enough, neither Set II affixes nor the reflexive suffix appear systematically as anticausative markers (277); they do with some verbs (a–d), but with others, like *-ola* 'break', the job is apparently done by aspectual and directional morphology (e–g):

(277)   Pilagá (Vidal 2008: 422)

a. *S-ewat-eye.*
1.SBJ.I-open-forward
'I open it (e.g., the door).'

b. *N-ewat-tayi.*
3.SBJ.II-open-COMPL
'It (e.g., the door) is open.'

c. *Sa-ʧiya-lo.*
1.SBJ.I-tighten-PL.OBJ
'I tighten them.'

d. *N-ʧiya-lʔat.*
3.SBJ.II-tighten-REFL
'They shrank.'

e. *Ø-D-olat-iyi.*
3.OBJ-3.SBJ.I-break-down
'He breaks it.'

f. *D-ola-yi.*
3.SBJ.I-break-COMPL
'It broke.'

g. *D-ola.*
3.SBJ.I-break
'It is broken.'

In sum, the Set I–Set II opposition expresses subject affectedness in Pilagá (see Vidal's 2008 "viewpoint" and "affectedness" notions), but not in such a way that reflexivity, reciprocity, and anticausativity are systematically expressed by Set II forms – even though all reflexives and most reciprocals are expressed via a combination of Set II markers and dedicated affixes. Neither passives nor causative-reflexives are encoded by Set II markers, and the contrast between subject markers with bivalent verbs does not seem to be as productive and robust as in Ancient Greek. Consequently, labeling Set II "middle markers" would emphasize an important similarity in meaning but obscure significant discrepancies in distribution when compared to Halkomelem or the classical languages.

6   Covert Diatheses: Uncoded Alternations

6.1   Introduction

In line with most modern studies of voice, the preceding chapters have concentrated on diatheses that are explicitly coded on the predicate complex. The present chapter surveys diathetical alternations that may be present without a morphological coding on the verb or the auxiliary. We define such uncoded alternations here as follows:

(278)   Characteristics of uncoded diathetical alternations
   a.   There is a change in the number and/or syntactic status of semantic
         arguments.
   b.   The alternation is not formally coded on the predicate complex.

English examples include indefinite object deletion (a–b) and the causative alternation (c–d):

(279)   English
   a.   *Jill is eating a sandwich.*
   b.   *Jill is eating.*
   c.   *The sun melts the ice.*
   d.   *The ice melts.*

The number of syntactic arguments differs in each sentence pair – in the second pair, also the number of semantic arguments differs – and the diathetical effect is not coded on the verb.

The uncodedness of diatheses is intimately related to PREDICATE LABILITY: labile verbs allow two or more different manifestations of valency in the clause without this being encoded on them morphologically. Creissels (2014) typologizes lability based on three parameters. First, the central affected argument may be the A or the P; this is the usual distinction between A-LABILITY (= agent-preserving lability) and P-LABILITY (= patient-preserving lability) (Dixon 1994). Second, diathetical alternations may be ARGUMENT-STRUCTURE PRESERVING (i.e., the semantic roles do not change, but one of the arguments receives a non-specific interpretation, like the patient in uncoded antipassives) or ARGUMENT-STRUCTURE MODIFYING (where there are different, potentially varied, relations between the semantic roles of the arguments in the alternating clauses).

Creissels's third parameter, namely the distinction between WEAK and STRONG lability, merits special attention. The (a–b)-alternation in (279) above illustrates argument-structure preserving A-lability while the (c–d)-alternation illustrates argument-structure modifying P-lability. The former pair is an instance of weak lability, because the common argument (*Jill*) has identical coding in the alternating clauses, and the only difference lies in the presence/absence of an NP (*a sandwich*). The latter pair illustrates the first subtype of strong lability, in which the common argument (*the ice*) bears different formal coding in the alternating clauses; according to the syntactic make-up of English, the verb agrees with the argument only when it is the subject.

A different subtype of strong lability is found when the constructions show some other formal difference, beyond the omission of an NP, like the valency-related allomorphy of TAM markers in Jiwarli (280). The following example shows A-lability with *kampa-* 'cook':

(280)   Jiwarli (Pama-Nyungan, Australia; Peter Austin, pers. comm.)
          a. *Purrarti-lu   kampa-nha   pirru.*
             woman-ERG   cook-PRS$_1$ meat[NOM]
             'The woman is cooking some meat.'
          b. *Pirru   kampa-inha.*
             meat[NOM]   cook-PRS$_2$
             'The meat is cooking.'

The same phenomenon is found, although with more intricate paradigms, in Mandinka (281). Examples (a–b) show A-lability with *teyi* 'cross' (where the completive affirmative marker is either *ye* or *-ta*), and Examples (c–d) show P-lability with *dádáa* 'repair' (where the incompletive negative marker is either *te* or *tê*):

(281)   Mandinka (Mande, West Africa; Creissels 2015: 226–227)
          a. *Mŏo-lu   ye   báa   teyi.*
             person.DEF-PL   COMPL.AFF.TR   river.DEF   cross
             'The people crossed the river.'
          b. *Mŏo-lu   teyi-ta.*
             person.DEF-PL   cross-COMPL.AFF.INTR
             'The people crossed.'
          c. *Kew-ó   te   kúlúŋ-o   dádáa-la.*
             man-DEF   INCOMPL.NEG.TR   boat-DEF   repair-INF
             'The man will not repair the boat.'
          d. *Kúlúŋ-o   tê   dádáa-la.*
             boat-DEF   INCOMPL.NEG.INTR   repair-INF
             'The boat will not be repaired.'

A special kind of this second subtype of strong lability consists in verbs that index a different number of arguments in the alternating constructions. The examples from Nahuatl in (282), for instance, are like the English examples in (279) regarding the arguments targeted and the effect on argument structure:

(a–b) and (c–d) illustrate argument-structure preserving A-lability and argument-structure modifying P-lability, respectively. They differ, however, in that the Nahuatl verbs may index not only subjects (1SG in (a–b); 1SG in (c) and 3PL in (d)) but also objects (3SG in (a); 3PL in (c)):

(282)   Nahuatl (Uto-Aztecan, Mexico; Creissels 2014: 929)
    a. *Ni-c-tesi*   *in*   *tlaolli.*
        1SG-3-grind   DEF   maize
        'I am grinding the maize.'
    b. *Ni-tesi.*
        1SG-grind
        'I am making flour.' (lit. 'I am grinding.')
    c. *Ni-qu-in-tomāwa*   *in*   *pitsōmê.*
        1SG-3-PL-fatten   DEF   pig.PL
        'I am fattening the pigs.'
    d. *Tomāwâ*   *in*   *pitsōmê.*
        [3]fatten.PL   DEF   pig.PL
        'The pigs are fattening.'

By contrast, we regard alternations like the one in (283) from Basque as instances of (anti-)causative voice (see also Example (29) in Section 2.1.3.1):

(283)   Basque
    a. *(Ni-k)*   *leiho-a*   *apurtu*   *d-u-t.*
        1SG-ERG   window-DET[ABS]   break.PFV   [3.P]TAM-have-1SG.A
        'I have broken the window.'
    b. *Leiho-a*   *apurtu*   *d-a.*
        window-DET[ABS]   break.PFV   [3.S]-TAM
        'The window is/has broken.'

The alternating clauses use different auxiliaries (viz., *dut* in (a), a form of **edun* 'have' for "transitives," and *da* in (b), a highly irregular form of *izan* 'be' for "intransitives"), which in turn have bipersonal and monopersonal morphology, respectively. In our view, this auxiliary alternation counts as morphological coding on the predicate complex. We do not have anything to say about the question of directionality, particularly with respect to synchrony: both constructions are equally marked.

With respect to terminology, note that some scholars prefer to use the terms *causative* and *anticausative* for formal patterns and *causal* and *noncausal (verbs)* for semantic types (e.g., Haspelmath et al. 2014). (Nichols et al. 2004 use *induced* and *plain verbs*, respectively, for the latter.) In fact, the *causative-anticausative* pair was originally form-oriented and was extended to cover functional oppositions only relatively recently. The terminology we use in this book, however, distinguishes between (ANTI-)CAUSATIVE DIATHESIS, which may or may not be formally coded, and (ANTI-)CAUSATIVE VOICE, which, by definition, is formally coded. Consequently, we employ the term (ANTI-)CAUSATIVE ALTERNATION to denote all kinds of alternating constructions in this semantic field, in principle irrespective of coding specifics and further specifying (if necessary) whether the participating constructions show coding or not. In practice, we often use ALTERNATION like many other recent studies do, namely as a shorthand for 'uncoded alternation' – with all the diathetical alternations surveyed in this study.

The literature on uncoded alternations, especially regarding English phenomena, is vast; see Lehmann (2015b), Levin (1993, 2015), and the studies mentioned in the sections below for analysis and references. The definition in (278) above covers not only those alternations that are syntactic equivalents of coded alternations discussed in previous chapters but also other phenomena.[1] Section 6.2 addresses uncoded alternations that change semantic valency, while Section 6.3 addresses uncoded alternations that change syntactic valency only. Section 6.4 surveys valency-neutral uncoded alternations, Section 6.5 outlines uncoded reflexives and reciprocals, and Section 6.6 closes the chapter with some discussion.

6.2 Changing Semantic Valency via Uncoded Alternations

In this section, we discuss cases where the installment or removal of semantic arguments is not formally signaled on the predicate, namely uncoded (anti-)causatives (6.2.1) and uncoded (anti-)applicatives (6.2.2).

6.2.1 Uncoded (Anti-)Causatives: The Causative Alternation

The causative alternation already mentioned in 6.1 is a much-studied phenomenon, particularly with respect to English. Besides Levin (1993) and Haspelmath (1993b), interested readers should consult Schäfer (2008, 2009) and Alexiadou (2010) for data, analyses, and references.

Typical examples of predicates that allow this alternation are P-labile verbs denoting change of state (e.g., English *melt* and *break*) or of degree (e.g., English *thicken* and *widen*). Such verbs can be used either as bivalent verbs in two-argument clauses ("causative verbs," with an argument structure [A P]) or as patientive monovalent verbs in one-argument clauses ("anticausative/inchoative verbs," with an argument structure [S_P]), without any change in verb morphology to signal the shift. An English example of such a formally unmarked opposition is *he broke the vase* vs. *the vase broke*. Syntactically, it corresponds to the coded opposition between the unmarked base construction *quebró el florero* vs. its marked anticausative counterpart *el florero se quebró* in Spanish (which are translational equivalents of the English clauses above). Other predicates that allow the causative alternation are verbs of motion or change of location (e.g.,

---

[1] We have not included cases of variation in the marking of locations, sources, and goals. See Comrie (1986) for examples from Eastern Armenian and some discussion.

English *move, bounce, roll*), whose P argument is a theme rather than a patient, and some psych verbs (e.g., English *sadden, cheer, worry*), whose P argument is an experiencer.

This alternation is also found in Ait Seghrouchen Berber, where the verb agrees with the corresponding subject but there is otherwise no change in the morphology; both flagging and indexing follow a nominative-accusative pattern:[2]

(284)   Ait Seghrouchen Berber (Afro-Asiatic, North Africa; Guerssel 1986: 48)
    a.   *Y-rzem   wryaz   tawwurt.*
        3SG.M-open man(M).NOM door(F)
        'The man opened the door.'
    b.   *T-rzem   tewwurt.*
        3SG.F-open   door(F).NOM
        'The door opened / is open.'

An analogous situation is found in Abkhaz (285), but note that indexing follows an absolutive-ergative pattern in this language, so the common argument is marked alike on the verb:

(285)   Abkhaz (Northwest Caucasian, Abkhazia; Hewitt 1989: 168)
    a.   *Ye-pe-s-ee-yt'.*
        3.S/P-PVB-1SG.A-break-FIN
        'I broke it.' (causative)
    b.   *Ye-p-ee-yt'.*
        3.S/P-PVB-break-FIN
        'It broke.' (non-causative)

Such examples differ from those from Basque discussed in (283) and in Section 2.1.3.1 in that they consist of alternating clauses that may well show different formal make-up but no systematic opposition between predicate forms used in causative and non-causative constructions.

Occasionally, causative alternations have an additional semantic component. In Bezhta (286), for instance, several labile verbs can function both as patientive monovalent (a) and as bivalent predicates (b), but in the latter clause the A takes possessive (rather than ergative) case and its agentivity is portrayed as reduced:

(286)   Bezhta (Comrie et al. 2015: 550)
    a.   *Kid   y-uɣo-yo.*
        girl(II)[ABS] II-die/kill-PST
        'The girl died.'
    b.   *Öždi-qa   kid   y-uɣo-yo.*
        boy.OBL-POSS girl(II)[ABS] II-die/kill-PST
        'The boy could kill the girl.' / 'The boy accidentally killed the girl.'

---

[2] The differences between absolute and annexed/construct state are one of the debated issues in Berber studies. We follow here the traditional nominative-accusative account proposed, e.g., by Guerssel (1986), but we refer the interested reader to Mettouchi and Frajzyngier (2013) for a somewhat different analysis.

Note that a semantically related alternation is available in Bezhta with bivalent verbs like 'grind', 'break', and 'cut', but here neither the semantic argument structure nor the syntactic make-up of the clause changes. The following example illustrates this with *üč'*- 'cut':

(287) Bezhta (Comrie et al. 2015: 551)
    a. *Öždi*   *hini-s*   *zoλ'o*   *b-üč'-iyo.*
        boy.OBL(ERG)   self.OBL-GEN   finger(III)   III-cut-PST
        'The boy cut his finger.'
    b. *Öždi-qa*   *hini-s*   *zoλ'o*   *b-üč'-iyo.*
        boy.OBL-POSS   self.OBL-GEN   finger(III)   III-cut-PST
        'The boy could cut his finger.' / 'The boy accidentally cut his finger.'

6.2.2 Uncoded (Anti-)Applicatives

6.2.2.1 The Benefactive Alternation

The benefactive alternation is found with predicates that allow the expression of the beneficiary either as an adjunct or as an object in a double object construction (DOC) (e.g., in English *he baked a cake for me* vs. *he baked me a cake*).[3] This alternation increases semantic valency, because the beneficiary is not a semantic argument of the base predicate, in much the same way a benefactive applicative increases the semantic valency of the base predicate. In English and other languages that show the alternation, the DOCs are unproblematic with bivalent verbs of creation and obtaining, but their acceptance by speakers becomes heavily context-dependent with lower transitivity values, be it because of features of the arguments or due to their number (see, e.g., Green 1974, Oehrle 1976, Pinker 1989, and Shibatani 1996).

Further examples of this alternation are found in (288)–(289). Unlike in English, in Finnish and German the (optional) beneficiary cannot surface as a direct/primary object in the accusative in the DOC but bears other kinds of marking (here: allative and dative). Nevertheless, both the semantic and the syntactic valency of the resulting construction have increased by one.

(288) Finnish
    Vanhempi   *leipo-i*   *kaku-n*   *(lapse-lle).*
    parent[NOM]   bake-3SG.PST   cake-ACC   child-ALL
    'The parent baked a/the cake (for the child).'

(289) German
    Sie   *hat*   *(mir)*   *eine* *Suppe* *gekocht.*
    3SG.NOM.F   has   1SG.DAT   a   soup   cook.PTCP
    'She has made (me) a soup.'

---

[3] Occasionally, this is presented as a special case of the dative alternation (Larson 1988, Gropen et al. 1989, Emonds 1993).

The occurrence of the benefactive alternation is easily accounted for by the fact that most actions are performed for a reason, and most of them thus have some sort of beneficiary. This is the agent him/herself in many cases, as in *I just cooked food*, where the most plausible reading is that the agent has cooked food for him/herself. Especially in these cases, the beneficiary is often left implicit, but there is in principle always the option to include it. The uncoded nature of the alternation may follow from the fact that in languages that have a dedicated three-argument clause headed by trivalent predicates (typically: verbs of transfer), this construction can also be used as a benefactive, due to the obvious functional relatedness between transfer and benefaction. The only relevant difference between recipients and beneficiaries lies in the fact that many of the former are part of the base verbs' argument structure, while the latter are extra-thematic.

6.2.2.2   External Possession

External possession constructions (EPCs) split genitive phrases into their constitutive NPs, which denote the possessum and the possessor, respectively. This increases the semantic and syntactic valency of the clause by one: the possessum NP is a direct/primary object in both alternating clauses, but the possessor NP becomes an object and usually bears dative-like coding in the EPC (see, e.g., Payne & Barshi 1999, König 2001, Seržant 2016). Consequently, an EPC frequently resembles the default three-argument clause in the given language, in that both have an [A T G] argument structure.

Example (290) from German illustrates the alternation. The (a)-clause is a two-argument construction with an A subject (*Jutta*) and a P direct object (*die Hände des Kindes* 'the child's hands'). In the (b)-clause, the possessor has been externalized from the genitive phrase, takes dative coding, and is an indirect object. The verb bears no special marking in either case; the only difference between (a) and (b) lies in the coding of arguments. As noted above, formally (b) is a three-argument clause in that default G arguments – recipients of verbs of transfer – also bear dative coding in German:

(290)   German
      a. *Jutta hat* [*die*   *Hände* [*des*   *Kind-es*]] *gewaschen.*
          J.   has   the.ACC.PL   hands   the.GEN.SG   child-GEN   wash.PTCP
      b. *Jutta hat* [*dem*   *Kind*] [*die*   *Hände*] *gewaschen.*
          J.   has   the.DAT.SG   child   the.ACC.PL   hands   wash.PTCP
      Both: 'Jutta washed the child's hands.'

Similar alternations are found in Romance and Slavic languages, but also in non-Indo-European languages of Europe (Haspelmath 1999). Consider (291) from Finnish:

(291)   Finnish
      a. *Vanhempi*   *pes-i*   *lapse-n*   *käde-t.*
          parent[NOM]   wash-PST.3SG   child-GEN   hand-ACC.PL

b. *Vanhempi   pes-i   lapse-lta   käde-t.*
   parent[NOM]   wash-PST.3SG   child-ABL   hand-ACC.PL
   Both: 'A/the parent washed a/the child's hands.'

Clearly, and contrary to what is sometimes claimed in the literature (e.g., Payne & Barshi 1999), the external possessor does not have to take dative(-like) coding in EPCs. Unlike in Maltese, Hungarian, and Basque, it takes ablative coding in Finnish – which differs from the default three-argument clause in the language (where the G takes the allative).

There are further functional similarities between EPCs and default three-argument constructions: the former may be used to emphasize the beneficial or detrimental effect of the denoted event on the G argument. In this sense, EPCs resemble benefactive/malefactive applicative constructions, which in many languages are, regarding their syntax, default three-argument clauses. In contrast to default three-argument clauses, however, EPCs do not denote transfer but only benefaction (and also malefaction, under appropriate conditions). This difference is evident in Finnish, where constructions like the (b)-clause above denote benefaction/malefaction, but transfer is excluded due to the ablative coding of the external possessor; only allative may encode the recipient in Finnish.[4]

In languages that restrict this alternation, the crucial factor is nominal semantics of the possessum rather than predicate class. In most varieties of Spanish, for example, normal possessions allow the alternation with pragmatically appropriate predicates and usually trigger a benefactive/malefactive interpretation of the EPC (e.g., *rompí su computador* vs. *le rompí el computador* 'I broke his/her computer (on him/her)'). Kinship terms also allow the alternation, with a similar reading of the EPC, but such cases convey a particular affective/emotional nuance and are often disfavored in the formal registers (e.g., *insulté a su madre* vs. *le insulté a la madre* 'I insulted his/her mother (on him/her)'). By contrast, body parts and garments naturally occur in the EPC: a two-argument clause is possible but marked from a semantic-pragmatic viewpoint.

Consider in this context the data in (292) from Spanish below. The (a)-clause, an EPC, is the normal, neutral, way of expressing 'I cut his/her hair' in the language; the (b)-clause, a construction that marks the possessor twice (as external with *le* '3SG.DAT' and as internal with *su* '3.PSR'), is used to emphasize the possessor's affectedness. By contrast, the clauses in (c) and (d) do not have external possessors. The former is formally parallel to the English clause but functionally marked in Spanish: it would mean, for instance, that I cut his/her hair after it had been detached from his/her head. The unidiomatic (d)-clause could mean that I cut a random single hair that was lying on the floor:

---

[4] The allative would also be possible in (b), but the – highly marked – reading would be that the child did not have any hands prior to the washing event and comes to have hands as a result of it.

(292)   Spanish
    a. *Le   corté   el   cabello.*
       3SG.DAT   cut.1SG.PFV.PST   ART   hair
       'I cut his/her hair.' (marginally possible: 'I cut the hair for/on him/her.')
    b. *Le   corté   su   cabello.*
       3SG.DAT   cut.1SG.PFV.PST   3.PSR   hair
       'I cut his/her hair.' (emphatic)
    c. *Corté   su   cabello.*
       cut.1SG.PFV.PST   3.PSR   hair
       'I cut his/her hair.'
    d. *Corté   el   cabello.*
       cut.1SG.PFV.PST   ART   hair
       'I cut the hair.'

Finally, some EPCs have the possessum occur as a prepositional object rather than as a direct/primary object. The Yoruba construction with *ní* (which covers a wide range of semantic roles) is a case in point:

(293)   Yoruba (Niger-Congo, West Africa; Atoyebi 2015: 314)
    a. *Oníṣègùn   náà   pa   ọmọọ   Bọ́lá.*
       medicine.person DEF kill child.POSS B.
    b. *Oníṣègùn   náà   pa   Bọ́lá ní   ọmọ.*
       medicine.person DEF kill B.   PREP child
    Both: 'The medical practitioner killed Bola's child.'

The default two-argument clause in (a) has an object P, and the possessor is internal to the object NP. The EPC in (b) has the possessor as object and the P as *ní*-phrase. Such an alternation is possible with predicates like 'kill', 'break', 'peel', 'eat', 'cut', and 'steal' (Atoyebi 2015).

6.2.2.3   The Locative "Preposition Drop" Alternation

Another English alternation involves manner-of-motion verbs that take directional phrase complements (e.g., *climb, fly, jump, ride, row, run, swim, travel, walk*). The clause with the obliquely flagged argument expressing a goal, path, or source is seen as basic and the default two-argument clause as derived, as in English *she fled from the room* vs. *she fled the room*. To the extent that the location is adequately interpreted as an extra-thematic argument of the predicate (i.e., not as one of its base semantic arguments), such alternations are syntactically equivalent to prototypical applicativization, which increases semantic valency. Moreover, like comprehensive applicatives (see Section 2.3.3.3), these preposition-drop clauses show a "holistic interpretation" (Levin 1993); while in *Martha climbed up the mountain* the goal is not necessarily portrayed as attained, in *Martha climbed the mountain* it is.

6.2.2.4   P-removing/installing alternation

Section 2.4.2 argues that the P-removing antiapplicative voice is quite rare. This diathetical alternation might be more widespread with labile verbs, but we are not aware of any comparative studies on the topic. In Chintang (Tibeto-Burman, Nepal), for instance, many verbs can occur either with bipersonal morphology and

Table 6.1 *Selected labile verbs in Chintang*

cekt-	'speak, say'	*nad-*	'refuse, not eat'
hand-	'talk (about)'	*pes-*	'vomit'
hatt-*	'wait (for)'	*pokt-*	'leave'
haŋs-	'be hot (for)'	*ratt-**	'shout (at)'
khipt-, ŋed-	'read, study, count'[5]	*rett-**	'laugh (at)'
khoŋs-	'play (with)'	*yoŋs-*	'fast, abstain from'
kupt-*	'perch, hatch'		

(based on Schikowski 2013: 91)

two-argument syntax or monopersonal morphology and one-argument syntax. Consider the examples in Table 6.1 above, which constitute a subset of such verbs. All of these verbs can occur in the one-argument construction with a generic/nonspecific P, but those marked with an asterisk actually allow two interpretations with that morphosyntax (Schikowski 2013: 71–73). For instance, *kupt-* can be used either in clauses that feature fowl hatching eggs that are left unexpressed (P-demotion) or in clauses where the fowl are portrayed as simply perching (P-removal). This situation resembles the Russian *s'*-form where it is ambiguous between a passive (A-demoting) and an anticausative (A-removing) reading.

6.2.3   Uncoded Subject Undergoer (De-)Nucleatives

There are not many comparative studies on uncoded alternations that allow extra-thematic arguments to become subjects, but English alternations like *she opened the door with the key* vs. *the key opened the door* have received some attention (see Rissman 2013 and references therein). An interesting instance of such phenomena is found in the instrumental alternation of Japanese:

(294)   Japanese (Kishimoto et al. 2015: 788)
    a.   *Otoko=ga   zyū=de   mato=o   uti-nui-ta.*
        man=NOM   gun=INS   target=ACC   shoot-pierce-PST
        'The man shot the target with the gun.'
    b.   *Zyū=ga   mato=o   uti-nui-ta.*
        gun=NOM   target=ACC   shoot-pierce-PST
        'The gun shot the target.'

A small class of verbs like *uti-nuku* 'shoot through' and a small class of instruments like guns and bullets (but not knives) can occur in two types of clauses, as shown in (294). The default two-argument construction in (a) has a subject A, an object P, and an adjunct instrument. In the two-argument construction in (b), the object is unaltered, but the subject is an instrument-agent (i.e., it has to affect the P by

---

[5] The form *khipt-* comes from the Sambugaũ dialect and *ŋed-* from the Mulgaũ variety.

exerting its own force). In other words, this is much more semantically (and lexically) restricted than the English alternation mentioned above.

6.3   Changing Syntactic Valency via Uncoded Alternations

The passive and the antipassive uncoded alternations affect the syntactic valency of the predicate, and therefore the structural make-up of the clause, without altering its semantic valency. The dative alternation does something analogous, but via a contrast between two-argument and three-argument clauses. We discuss them in turn.

6.3.1   Passive Alternations

Some diathetical oppositions syntactically correspond to the English active–passive opposition without any formal coding on the predicate. This phenomenon is found in Eskimoan languages; the following example from Yupik illustrates the alternation with 'eat' between a two-argument clause (a) and an uncoded passive without an overt agent (b):

(295)   Central Alaskan Yupik (Miyaoka 2015: 1177, 1184)
    a.   *Angute-m*   *neqa*   *ner-aa.*
        man-REL.SG   fish[ABS.SG]   eat-IND.3SG→3SG
        'The man is eating the fish.'
    b.   *Neqa*   *ner'-uq*   *ak'a.*
        fish[ABS.SG]   eat-IND.3SG   already
        'The fish is / has been eaten.'

Examples of passives with overt agents can be found in Austronesian languages (of the "Flores-type" proposed by Arka & Ross 2005; see Section 4.1):

(296)   Manggarai (Arka & Kosmas 2005: 28)
    a.   *Aku*   *cero*   *latung=k.*
        1SG   corn   fry=1SG
        'I fry / am frying corn.' (active diathesis)
    b.   *Latung*   *hitu*   *cero*   *l=aku=i.*
        fry   that   corn   by=1SG=3SG
        'That corn is (being) fried by me.' (passive diathesis)

(297)   Palu'e (Donohue 2005: 60)
    a.   *Ia*   *cube*   *vavi*   *va'a.*
        3SG   shoot   pig   DEM
        'He shot the pig.' (active diathesis)
    b.   *Vavi*   *va'a*   *ia*   *cube.*
        pig   DEM   3SG   shoot
        'That pig was shot by him.' (passive diathesis)

The (a)-clauses illustrate default two-argument clauses in both languages. Their (b)-counterparts show one-argument constructions in which the base P object has been promoted to subject and the base A subject has been demoted to adjunct. This is achieved with some formal rearrangement in Manggarai (see the oblique marker *l=* and the 3SG marker *=i*, both absent from (a)) and solely via constituent order in Palu'e.

A much more exhaustively studied kind of alternation that corresponds to the opposition between active and passive voices is what the literature on English usually labels "middle alternation." Uncoded English alternations like the ones in (298) involve active and potential passive diatheses, corresponding as they do to the coded Spanish opposition in (299) between active and potential passive voices (see Section 3.1.4.3):

(298)   English
      a. *The chef cuts the meat.*
      b. *The meat cuts easily.*
      c. *The teacher reads the book.*
      d. *The book reads easily.*

(299)   Spanish
      a. *La   profesora lee   el   libro.*
          ART teacher.F read[3SG] ART book
          'The teacher reads the book.'
      b. *El   libro   se   lee   fácilmente.*
          ART book   PASS read[3SG] easily
          'The book reads easily.'

6.3.2   The Antipassive or Conative Alternation

In the conative alternation, a default two-argument clause contrasts with a clause that expresses lower transitivity ("attempted action") by coding the P as an oblique, like in English *Paula hit the fence* vs. *Paula hit at the fence*. The semantics of the verbs that allow this alternation in English seem to include features like contact and motion, but several verbs of cutting, pushing, and spraying, as well as some ingestion verbs (e.g., *drink, eat*), also participate in the alternation. Based on the history of such verbs in English, the two-argument clause is seen as basic and the one-argument clause as derived.

Such alternations are syntactically equivalent to antipassivization. The P loses its direct object status and becomes an adjunct flagged by an adposition. In languages with nominal case, the alternation does not alter the flagging of the A in the low-transitivity clause. The following examples from German (300) or Finnish (301) are cases in point:

(300)   German
      a. *Kirsten hat   ein   Haus gebaut.*
          K.   has   a.ACC.SG house build.PTCP
          'Kirsten built a house.'
      b. *Kirsten hat   an   einem   Haus gebaut.*
          K.   has   at   a.DAT.SG house build.PTCP
          'Kirsten was building a house.'

(301)   Finnish
    a. *Henkilö*   *maala-si*   *talo-t.*
       person[NOM]   paint-3SG.PST house-ACC.PL
       'A/the person painted the houses.'
    b. *Henkilö*   *maala-si*   *talo-j-a.*
       person[NOM]   paint-3SG.PST house-PL-PTV
       'A/the person painted some houses.'

Unsurprisingly, languages with absolutive-ergative case alignment show a different picture.[6] In Niuean (302), the A takes the ergative and the P takes the absolutive in the high-transitivity clause in (a) (a flagging pattern that is the default frame of two-argument clauses headed by semantically bivalent predicates). This contrasts with the low-transitivity clause in (b), where the A takes the absolutive and the P takes the oblique. According to the study available to us, (b) depicts the unmarked frame for the verb *fakalilifu* 'respect'; the P seems to be more salient in (a), but the semantic contrast is said to be minimal (Seiter 1980):

(302)   Niuean (Austronesian, Niue and Cook Islands; Seiter 1980: 336)
    a. *Fakalilifu e*   *ia* *e*   *tau momotua.*
       respect   ERG he ABS PL old.PL
    b. *Fakalilifu a*   *ia* *ke* *tau momotua.*
       respect   ABS he to   PL old.PL
    Both: 'He respects the old people.'

The same alternation is found in Eskimoan; consider the following example from Yupik:

(303)   Central Alaskan Yupik (Miyaoka 2015: 1177)
    a. *Angute-m*   *neqa*   *ner-aa.*
       man-REL.SG   fish[ABS.SG] eat-IND.3SG→3SG
       'The man is eating the fish.'
    b. *Angun*   *neq-mek*   *ner'-uq.*
       man[ABS.SG]   fish-ABL.SG eat-IND.3SG
       'The man is eating a fish.'

Another kind of antipassive alternation consists in indefinite object deletion – an instance of argument-preserving weak A-lability. Such constructions are frequently attested in languages with nominative-accusative case alignment, which allow the P to be omitted freely, as in English *John will be writing tomorrow* and *Jill is reading on the patio.* An analogous example from a language with absolutive-ergative case alignment is (304) from Tongan:

---

[6] See Simpson (1983: 158–165) for Warlpiri constructions where the P takes dative case to encode unachieved action ("conative or attempted action"), either as the only possibility with some few verbs (e.g., *warri-* 'seek') or productively alternating with clauses with Ps in the absolutive (e.g., *luwa-* 'shoot').

(304)   Tongan (Churchward 1953: 76)

     a. *Na'e inu   'a   e   kavá 'e   Sione.*
       PST   drink ABS the kava ERG J.
       'John drank the kava.'

     b. *Na'e inu   'a   Sione.*
       PST   drink ABS J.
       'John drank.'

The (a)-clause illustrates the default two-argument construction in the language, while in (b) the P has been demoted and omitted, and the A has been promoted to subject.[7]

Lastly, remember in this context the antipassive subtype of NOMINAL INCORPORATION (see Sections 3.2.2 and 7.3). With such constructions, there is usually no grammatical (i.e., non-lexical) marking on the predicate besides the incorporated nominal. Not only does the P lose its direct object status in such cases: it loses its morphosyntactic autonomy altogether and becomes incorporated into the verb. Such one-argument constructions typically express lower transitivity than their two-argument counterparts, like in the following Chukchi example:

(305)   Chukchi (Skorik 1948: 73)

     a. *Wala-t   mə-mne-rkənet!*
        knife-ABS.PL   1PL.SBJ.IMPER-sharpen-3PL.OBJ
        'Let us sharpen the knives!'

     b. *Mə-wala-mna-rkən!*
        1PL.SBJ.IMPER-knife-sharpen-1PL.SBJ
        'Let us sharpen knives!'

6.3.3   The Dative Alternation

The dative alternation, sometimes labeled "dative shift," comprises cases where an obliquely coded recipient, animate goal, or similar argument is promoted to direct/primary object (Pinker 1989, Rappaport Hovav & Levin 2008, and Croft 2012). This is often, yet not necessarily, accompanied by a change in word order that changes from TG to GT (Heine & König 2010). With such alternations, neither the number of semantic arguments nor the *number* of syntactic arguments changes – unlike with the benefactive alternation, which increases the semantic valency – but the *kinds* of nonsubject arguments change.

The shift leads to a DOC, like in English *Lisa gave a book to Phyllis* vs. *Lisa gave Phyllis a book*. The following example is from Dutch:

(306)   Dutch (Janssen 1997: 281)

     a. *Fred gaf   een   wandelstok   aan Tom.*
       F.   gave a   walking.stick to   T.
       'Fred gave a walking stick to Tom.'

---

[7] Tongan also allows the clause *na'e inu kava 'a Sione* (PST drink kava ABS J.) 'John drank kava', an instance of nominal incorporation (see Section 7.3).

b. *Fred gaf Tom een wandelstok.*
F.   gave T.   a   walking.stick
'Fred gave Tom a walking-stick.'

In English and Dutch DOCs, the argument in G function is promoted to primary object, which also results in a change in the order of T and G. Korean illustrates a different case: the flagging of G changes from dative to accusative, but constituent order does not change, and the two nonagentive NPs show different behavior in several syntactic tests (Lee 1997):

(307)   Korean (Jae Jung Song, pers. comm.)
a. *Kica-ka   enehakca-eykey   chayk-ul   ponay-ss-ta.*
    journalist-NOM   linguist-DAT   book-ACC   send-PST-IND
    'The journalist sent a/the book to the linguist.'
b. *Kica-ka   enehakca-lul   chayk-ul   ponay-ss-ta.*
    journalist-NOM   linguist-ACC   book-ACC   send-PST-IND
    'The journalist sent the linguist a book.' (DOC)

The predicates that allow the alternation clearly orbit those denoting transfer in a narrow sense – a semantic class that is often generalized to predicates denoting transfer in a broad sense. In English, the class also includes verbs that express ballistic motion (e.g., *throw*) and continuous deictic causation (e.g., *bring*), verbs that express transfer with satisfaction conditions (e.g., *promise*) or in the future (e.g., *grant*), and verbs of permission (e.g., *allow*);[8] see Croft (2012: 376) for details.

The reasons for using or avoiding the DOC may be semantic or pragmatic. In case of the former, the DOC emphasizes the permanence of transfer, as in Sochiapan Chinantec (see Foris 1998: 213), or the higher affectedness of the recipient, as in Dutch (Janssen 1997). A case of pragmatic motivation is when the definiteness of the non-agentive arguments favors one of the alternating clauses – as in English, where the DOC is dispreferred with SAPS in T function (e.g., *I will introduce him to you* vs. *??/*I will introduce him you*). Finally, the dative alternation may be optional or obligatory. It is basically optional in English with the predicates that allow it, even though it is subject to several soft constraints (Bresnan et al. 2007). In turn, it is obligatory in Drehu, where the animacy hierarchy determines which construction is used (see Moyse-Faurie 1983: 161–162, cited in Haspelmath 2007c: 86–87): pronouns and proper names surface as direct objects, while animate common nouns do not immediately follow the verb and are marked by a preposition. (See Haspelmath 2007c for more examples of animacy hierarchy effects on ditransitive coding.)

---

[8] Note that *promise* is like *allocate* and *grant* – and unlike many other Latinate verbs in English, like *donate* and *present* – in that it allows the dative alternation.

6.4   Valency-Neutral Uncoded Alternations

The locative alternation has received considerable attention in the literature. Another kind of valency-neutral alternation is found in some Austronesian languages that appear to have lost their voice morphology. We discuss them in turn.

6.4.1   The Locative Alternation

The locative alternation applies to sets of verbs that involve putting substances on surfaces or things in containers, or removing substances from surfaces or things from containers (Levin 1993: 50, Boas 2003, and Iwata 2008). Unlike with the benefactive and dative alternations, neither the number nor kind of syntactic or semantic arguments changes here – making this an instance of a symmetrical diathetical opposition.

Consider the following English examples:

(308)   English
　　　　a. *Bill loaded the hay on the truck.* vs. b. *Bill loaded the truck with hay.*
　　　　c. *Jane sprayed paint on the wall.* vs. d. *Jane sprayed the wall with paint.*

The effect on the referent of the direct object seems to be most communicatively salient, and affectedness appears to shift as well.[9] In (d), the wall is arguably viewed as being more directly, and more comprehensively, affected by the event than in (c).[10] Finnish provides a similar example with formally equipollent flagging of the non-agentive arguments (rather than the preposition-zero opposition shown above for English):

(309)   Finnish
　　　　a. *Henkilö*　　*lasta-si*　　*heinä-t*　　*rekka-an.*
　　　　　person[NOM]　load-PST.3SG　hay-ACC.PL　truck-ILL
　　　　　'A person loaded the hay onto the truck.'
　　　　b. *Henkilö*　　*lasta-si*　　*reka-n*　　*heinä-llä.*
　　　　　person[NOM]　load-PST.3SG　truck-ACC　hay-ADESS
　　　　　'A person loaded the truck with hay.'

A syntactically analogous (but semantically different) situation is found with the instrumental alternation in Bezhta:

(310)   Bezhta (Comrie et al. 2015: 550)
　　　　a. *Öždi*　　　*kid*　　　*k'obala-li-d*　　*y-äλ'el-ca.*
　　　　　boy.OBL(ERG)　girl(II)[ABS]　stick(III)-OBL-INS　II-hit-PRS

---

[9] Note that higher affectedness of the P is present with the comprehensive *be*-applicative of German (see 2.3.3.3) and with the locative *i*-applicative of Indonesian (e.g., *duduk* 'sit' vs. *duduk-i* 'occupy by sitting').
[10] Remember the semantic effect of comprehensive applicativization in German (Section 2.3.3.3).

b. *Ӧẓdi*   *kibba-l*   *k'obala*   *b-äλ'el-ca.*
boy.OBL(ERG)   girl(II).OBL-LAT   stick(III)[ABS]   III-hit-PRS
Both: 'The boy hits the girl with the stick.'

The A ('the boy') has the same flagging and the same syntactic status in both clauses, but the P ('the girl') and the instrument ('the stick') swap functions; note that the verb consistently agrees with the absolutive NP, namely the P in (a) and the instrument in (b).

6.4.2   Agent-Patient-Diathesis Alternations

Cross-linguistically, uncoded symmetrical voice alternations seem to be extremely rare. A clear example comes from Colloquial Indonesian, where the agent and at least some kinds of patient diathesis differ solely with respect to constituent order (311). The agent-diathesis (bivalent) verb is often unmarked, at least in the informal register; in the formal register, it tends to take the marked form it takes in Standard Indonesian (i.e., it takes the prefix *meN-*).[11] Patient-diathesis verbs with 1st- or 2nd-person As are unmarked. The agent diathesis shows an AVP order (a) and the patient diathesis a PAV order (b):

(311)   Colloquial Indonesian (Sneddon 2006: 97, 47)
a. *Gue   nggak   suka   cowok   pendek.*
   1SG   NEG   like   boy   short
   'I don't like short boys.' (agent diathesis)
b. *Cewek~cewek   di   Atma   gua   suka.*
   girl~PL   in   A.   1SG   like
   'I like the girls at Atma.' (patient diathesis)

Based on Arka and Ross's (2005) characterization of the Austronesian Flores-type languages, we assume that other such syntactically symmetrical uncoded alternations might be found there. As far as we know, more research is needed here.

Bantu languages show similar constructions, as illustrated in (312) below from Swahili. In (a), *watoto* 'the children' and *vyakula* 'the food' are the subject A and the object P of the agent/active clause, respectively; the former triggers subject agreement on the verb (*ya-*). In (b), the verb is passivized (*-w*), the A is an adpositionally marked adjunct (viz., with *na* 'with') and the P is the subject, triggering as it does subject agreement (*vi-*); in addition, the two arguments switch places with respect to the verb. In (c), it is also the fronted P that triggers subject agreement, and constituent order is like in (b), but the verb is unmarked for voice and the A does not have adpositional marking:

(312)   Swahili (Zwart 1997: 7–8)
a. *Wa-toto*   *wa-li-kul-a*   *vy-akula*
   II-child   II.SBJ-PST-eat-ASP   VIII-food
   'The children ate the food.' (active)

---

[11] There are several phonologically conditioned allomorphs of *meN-*; see Sneddon (2006: 20–22).

    b. *Vy-akula*   *vi-li-kul-w-a*   *(na   wa-toto)*.
        VIII-food   VIII.SBJ-PST-eat-PASS-ASP   with II.child
        'The food was eaten (by the children).' (passive)

    c. *Wy-akula*   *vi-li-kul-a*   *wa-toto*.
        VII-food   VIII.SBJ-PST-eat-ASP   II-child
        'The food was eaten by the children.' / 'The children ate the food.'

Note that the clause type in (c) is not a perfect mirror image of the agent/active-diathesis clause, because the latter allows object indexing on the verb under certain conditions (like in (a) below) while the former does not (like in (b)):

(313)   Swahili (Zwart 1997: 8)
      a. *Wa-nakijiji   wa-me-m-chek-a*   *Juma*.
         II-villager   II.SBJ-PERF-I.OBJ-laugh.at-ASP J.(I)
         'The villagers laughed at Juma.' (active)
      b. *Juma   a-me(*-wa)chek-a*   *wa-nakijiji*.
         J.(I)   I.SBJ-PERF-II.OBJ-laugh.at-ASP II-villager
         'The villagers laughed at Juma.'

Both the exact status and the homogeneity of these "quasi-passive" constructions in the individual Bantu languages are still unclear. Kimenyi (1980) calls such clauses instances of "object-subject reversal" in Kinyarwanda and analyzes them as something different from a voice operation, both morphologically and syntactically. By contrast, Ura (1996) calls them instances of an "inverse voice" (see Givón 1972 for a similar treatment) and regards them as restricted examples of two-argument clauses with a subject P and an object A. (The restrictions are related to semantic valency – trivalent predicates fail to allow a preverbal T as expected – and to semantic features of the arguments and the predicate. For example, if both A and P are equally animate, only semantically, or at least pragmatically, unequivocal verbs license the construction.) More research is needed here.

6.5 Covert Affected Subjects: Uncoded Reflexives and Reciprocals

      By making the definition of argument-structure preserving A-lability slightly broader – i.e., the semantic roles do not change between alternating constructions, but the P receives a *particular* (instead of *nonspecific*) interpretation – this phenomenon would have at least the following special cases: nonspecific P, reflexive-coreferential P, reciprocal-coreferential P.[12] Even without such a terminological treatment, however, uncoded reflexives and uncoded reciprocals are well attested and worth considering in a study of voice.

---

[12] See Malchukov (2017) for the same terminological suggestion.

6.5.1   Uncoded Reflexives

As discussed in Chapter 5, coded reflexives are basically formed in two different ways: either a reflexive (pro)nominal is used, or there is some kind of reflexive marking on the verb. With uncoded reflexives, reflexivity is not marked in any explicit way.

Typical examples of IMPLICIT REFLEXIVES include cases such as English *I just shaved*, which is a one-argument clause commonly interpreted as reflexive. Further examples are found in Finnish (314), where one-argument clauses are used. A reflexive pronoun could be added in (a–b), as in English *he shaved* (*himself*), which would not have any semantic consequences.

(314)   Finnish
    a. *Minä*   *pue-n*   *ensin.*
       1SG   dress-1SG   first
       'I will dress (myself) first.'
    b. *Aino* *meikka-si*   *ja*   *läht-i*   *ulos.*
       A.   make.up-3SG.PST and go-3SG.PST out
       'Aino put on makeup and went out.'

One of the reasons for omitting the pronoun with such grooming expressions is probably that they are more frequently performed on oneself than on others. An analogous optional omission of reflexive pronouns is not possible, for instance, with predicates like *tappaa* 'kill', *leikata* 'cut', and *puhdistaa* 'clean', which denote events whose patient is typically not the agent him/herself. Nevertheless, this phenomenon is language-specific – as can be seen in the following example from Leko, where cutting is something that can be performed on oneself without the use of any explicit marker or reflexivity (315). In fact, according to Van de Kerke (1998), such unmarked one-argument clauses are the only way to express reflexivity in the language:

(315)   Leko (unclassified, Bolivia; Van de Kerke 1998: 197)
    a. *Era* *cuchillu-ra* *ber-ki*   *de-wei-ate.*
       1SG knife-INS   one-ACC   3SG-cut-1SG.PST
       'I cut someone else with a knife.'
    b. *Era* *cuchillu-ra* *wei-ate.*
       1SG knife-INS   cut-1SG.PST
       'I cut myself with a knife.'

These implicit reflexives illustrate diathetical change without morphological marking and are therefore instances of a voice-like alternation.

A different kind of uncoded reflexive is found in Pirahã:

(316)   Pirahã (Mura, Brazil; Everett 1986: 216)
    a. *Ti* *hi* *xib-áobá-há.*
       1   3   hit-TAM-EVID
       'I hit him.'

b. *Ti   ti   xib-áobá-há.*
    1   1   hit-TAM-EVID
    'I hit myself.'

Example (a) illustrates the default two-argument construction of the language, while (b) illustrates the reflexive construction. Note that the latter has no overt marker of coreference in general or reflexivity in particular: the direct object is formally identical to any two-argument construction with a 1SG direct object.[13] The construction is thus explicit but NON-SPECIALIZED, and since there is neither distinguishing verb morphology nor apparent change of diathesis, it is not voice-like but merely voice-related.

6.5.2   Uncoded Reciprocals

The implicit expression of reciprocity is apparently not very common; it includes English clauses like *Hector and Achilles fought obsessively* and *Oscar and Pattie are in love*, which have both a reciprocal interpretation ('Hector and Achilles fought each other', 'Oscar and Pattie are in love with each other') and a non-reciprocal interpretation ('Hector and Achilles fought against Menelaus', 'Oscar is in love with Linda and Pattie with her work') (Haspelmath 2007a: 2089).

Reciprocity can also be expressed explicitly, either by non-specialized (biclausal) constructions like *Harry pinched Ingrid, and Ingrid pinched him back*, or by specialized (often monoclausal) reciprocal constructions. Such reciprocals can be either grammatical – some of which we addressed in Chapter 5 – or lexical, which are relevant in the present context. Such LEXICAL RECIPROCALS are clauses that do not show any grammatical marking but nonetheless express reciprocity, not as a special reading (like with the implicit reciprocals mentioned above), but as a rule. Such cases normally consist of clauses headed by underived predicate from a semantically restricted set – Haspelmath (2007a: 2104) calls them "allelic," from Ancient Greek *allēlo-* 'each other, mutual' – whose meanings commonly fall into three classes. These classes are social actions and relations (e.g., 'marry', 'be friends'), spatial relations (e.g., 'adjoin', 'be next to'), and (non-)identity relations (e.g., 'resemble', 'differ'). The first class can be further subdivided in those like 'marry' (joint action), those like 'quarrel' (competition), and those like 'be friends' (relationship). Social actions and spatial relations can be seen as including verbs like 'combine' and 'compare' (connection), as well as those like 'separate' and 'distinguish' (division).

Like uncoded reflexives, uncoded reciprocals typically resemble or are formally indistinguishable from default one-argument clauses of the language in which they occur. Unlike uncoded reflexives, however, some uncoded

---

[13] The same phenomenon is found in Jiwarli (Pama-Nyungan, Australia; Peter Austin, pers. comm.).

reciprocals cannot simply add a default specialized marker to emphasize reciprocity. Consider (317) from Finnish:

(317)   Finnish
    a. *Lapse-t   pes-i-vät   toisen-sa*   / **toisten-sa*   *kanssa*
       child-PL wash-PST-3PL RECP.ACC-3.PSR   RECP.GEN-3.PSR with
      / **keskenään*.
       among.themselves
      'The children washed each other.' (grammatical reciprocal)
    b. *Lapse-t   riitel-i-vät.*
       child-PL quarrel-PST-3PL
      'The children were quarrelling.' (implicit reciprocal)
    c. *Lapse-t   riitel-i-vät   keskenään*   / *toisten-sa*
       child-PL quarrel-PST-3PL among.themselves   RECP.GEN-3.PSR
      kanssa.   / **toisen-sa.*
      with   RECP.ACC-3.PSR
      'The children were quarrelling with each other.'

The clause in (a) illustrates the grammatical reciprocal of Finnish, which features a bivalent predicate and the reciprocal pronoun *toisensa*. The latter inflects for case and person and triggers the reciprocal reading. By contrast, (b) is an implicit reciprocal, to which a specialized marker can be added (c), but note that the latter differs from the one used with grammatical reciprocals, which is excluded in such cases. In turn, the specialized marker (either *keskenään* 'among themselves' or *toistensa kanssa* 'with each other') is ruled out with bivalent verbs that can also have a reciprocal reading.

6.6   Discussion

The use of covert diatheses may have functional motivations. Especially with reflexives and reciprocals, notions such as expectedness and naturalness appear to be relevant, which are in turn closely associated with frequency of use. As seen above, predicates of grooming ('shave', 'wash') and of social actions and relations ('marry', 'quarrel') can appear uncoded in some languages, possibly due to the fact that the events they portray are normally reflexive or reciprocal, respectively. In languages that allow such alternations with suitable predicates, explicit coding of reflexivity or reciprocity normally occurs when the intended reading cannot be retrieved otherwise. A similar explanation may apply to certain causative alternations. For example, even though it is possible to melt snow in a stove while camping in the mountains, most of the snow melts spontaneously in the spring, at least from a human perspective. This in turn might lead to expressions of agentless melting being more natural, and possibly more frequent, than the other way around, and to formally unmarked ways of expressing it.

One formal motivation for the existence and distribution of covert diatheses seems to be best captured by Malchukov's (2006) Primary Argument Immunity Principle (but see also Kittilä 2002 for similar remarks), which also resorts to the notions of expectedness and naturalness, albeit in a different sense. Unlike (anti-) passive-like alternations, (anti-)passive voices can be seen as mechanisms used to underline the unexpected semantic role borne by the promoted argument. Antipassive-like alternations are often attested in accusative-morphology languages, where the formally unmarked and marked arguments are typically A and P, respectively. Analogously, passive-like alternations are common in ergative-morphology languages, where the unmarked and marked arguments are typically P and A, respectively. Another way to describe this tendency is by saying that manipulation of the form of the unmarked argument (i.e., its flagging or presence) normally triggers a diathetic shift, which in turn may be expressed as a voice alternation. By contrast, manipulation of the form of the marked argument does not require such accommodating devices.

It is interesting to briefly consider alternations that never appear to be covert but, at least in the languages for which we have data, are always formally coded. Perhaps most prominently, uncoded causatives of bivalent predicates seem not to occur at all; we have not found robust alternations of the type *John built a house* vs. **I built a house by John* (where the latter represents the attempt to express 'I made John build a house'). Even though many languages show alternations that allow the non-signaled expression or omission of semantic arguments of predicates under adequate conditions, an external agent/causer in addition to the internal/base agent does not seem to be one of such arguments. As mentioned in Section 2.1, cross-linguistically, causativization is more restricted in general with bivalent predicates than with agentive monovalent verbs, which are in turn more restricted than with patientive monovalent verbs – thus suggesting a continuum of likelihood regarding base argument status for different participants, which seems to exclude external agents/causers.

7 The Fringes of Voice

The present chapter presents some phenomena that are neither instances of voice nor voice-like; we call them VOICE-RELATED based on their connection with voice proper. All of Hopper and Thompson's (1980) ten parameters appear to be relevant regarding alternations that show neither morphological marking on the predicate nor syntactic changes in the clause. We do not discuss parameters not directly related to argument structure here (viz., kinesis, aspectuality, and polarity), however, simply due to limitations of space. As seen in Chapters 2 and 3, for instance, aspectuality is often intimately connected to voice alternations and deserves an in-depth comparative study in its own right; many language-specific studies have addressed some of the issues that are relevant from the perspective of voice-related phenomena as well. Moreover, there is a non-negligible body of literature, usually also language- or family-specific (e.g., for Basque, Uralic, and Slavic), that deals with differential argument marking in connection with polarity.[1]

We focus here on selected phenomena related to argument structure – in particular, to semantic features of the arguments, like the agentivity of the A, the affectedness and individuation of the P, and the overall number of arguments, but we also mention some phenomena related to information structure. We first survey some constructions that signal transitivity modulation without any morpho-syntactic restructuring of the clause (other than constituent order and differential argument marking) (Section 7.1). Then, we mention a number of constructions that are rather unclear and may constitute a bridge between voice-like and voice-related phenomena (Section 7.2). We then present nominal incorporation and its voice-related variation (Section 7.3). Lastly, we survey some constructions that have received relatively little attention in the comparative and typological literature, namely clauses that lie formally and functionally between those expressing full intransitivity and full transitivity, respectively (Section 7.4).

7.1 Uncoded Syntax-Neutral Alternations

Some languages have straightforward mechanisms for achieving goals otherwise associated with voice(-like) alternations. For instance, the

---

[1] See, for instance, Miestamo (2014) for a cross-linguistic survey on the use of partitives with negation and Miestamo et al. (2015) for a collection of articles on negation in Uralic.

Swedish impersonal constructions in (318) rely on a special interpretation of a particular pronoun (a) or have a dedicated pronoun *man* 'one, people' (b) in order to signal a non-prototypical subject – rather than regarding its agentivity, with respect to its referentiality:

(318)   Swedish
      a. *De   säger   att   jag   inte   är   begåvad.*
         they say.PRS that 1SG   not   be.PRS talented
         'They say that I am not talented.'
      b. *Här äter   man gärna pizza och   pasta.*
         here eat.PRS man gladly pizza and   pasta
         'One likes to eat pizza and pasta here.'

Many languages resort to the manipulation of constituent order for pragmatic purposes, without any diathetical change. Consider (319) from German: the neutral V2 order with the postverbal direct object *es* 'it' of (a) can be replaced by a marked V2 order with the direct object *es* 'it' in clause-initial position, like in the second sentence in (b), to signal topic continuation. Passivization is therefore not necessary for P-topicalization (nor is it available with *haben* 'have'):

(319)   German
      a. *Sie   haben es nicht mehr.*
         you   have   it NEG   more
         'You (HON) don't have it anymore.'
      b. *Ihr Geld   ist nicht verloren. Es hat jetzt nur jemand   anderer.*
         your money is NEG   lost   it has now   only someone other
         'Your (HON) money is not lost. Just someone else has it now.'
         (Haider 2010: 140)

In Hungarian (320), a direct object (and other constituents) can appear in a preverbal position if in identificational focus (a) or in a postverbal position if in information focus (b), but diathetical structure is unaltered by such shifts.

(320)   Hungarian (Kiss 1998: 249; glosses are ours)
      a. *Mari   egy kalap-ot   nézett   ki   magának.*
         M.[NOM] one hat-ACC   picked[3SG] out REFL.3SG.DAT
         'It was a hat that Mary picked for herself.'
      b. *Mari   ki nézett   magának   egy kalap-ot.*
         M.[NOM] out picked[3SG] REFL.3SG.DAT one hat-ACC
         '(John and Mary are shopping.) Mary has picked herself a hat.'

Similarly, Japanese combines fronting with segmental topic marking (321). There is no diathetical change in such alternations, either; *Fred* is the subject and *mame* 'beans' the object in both clauses:

(321)   Japanese (Oshima 2005: 371)
      a. *Fred=wa   mame=o   tabe-ta.*
         F.=TOP   beans=ACC eat-PST

    b. *Mame=wa*   *Fred=ga*   *tabe-ta.*
       beans=TOP   F.=NOM   eat-PST
    Both: 'Fred ate beans.'

Finnish can employ constituent order not only to topicalize a nonsubject but also to additionally modulate transitivity (322). The A is not a prototypical agent in the default two-argument clause in (a) simply because of the verb semantics, but the degree of the A's agency, especially in intentionality and volitionality, is further reduced when the order of the NPs is reversed, like in (b):

(322)   Finnish (from Hiirikoski 2002; glosses are ours)
    a. *Häne-n*   *vaimo-nsa*   *loukka-si*   *minu-a.*
       3SG-GEN   wife-3SG.PSR   offend-3SG.PST   1SG-PTV
       'His wife offended me.'
    b. *Minu-a*   *loukka-si*   *häne-n*   *vaimo-nsa.*
       1SG-PTV   offend-3SG.PST   3SG-GEN   wife-3SG.PSR
       'I was offended by his wife / his wife offended me.'

The differential treatment of objects for transitivity modulation is a well-documented phenomenon (see Section 3.2.2). Consider (323) from Malayalam, for instance, where the animate object in (b) triggers accusative marking on the NP:

(323)   Malayalam (Dravidian, India; Asher & Kumari 1997: 151, 203)
    a. *Avan*   *kaar̠ə*   *vaŋŋi.*
       3SG.M   car   buy.PST
       'He bought a car.'
    b. *Avan*   *oru*   *paʃuvine*   *vaŋŋi.*
       3SG.M   a   cow.ACC   buy.PST
       'I bought a cow.'

In Hebrew, it is definiteness of the object that triggers accusative marking:

(324)   Hebrew (Afro-Asiatic, Israel; Aissen 2003: 453)
    a. *Ha-seret*   *her'a*   **('et-)ha-milxama.*
       DET-movie   showed   ACC-DET-war
       'The movie showed the war.'
    b. *Ha-seret*   *her'a*   *(*'et-)milxama.*
       DET-movie   showed   ACC-war
       'The movie showed a war.'

Crucially, the P is invariably the primary object in such clauses irrespective of its flagging.

7.2   Uncoded Unclear-Syntax Alternations

    With many alternations between constructions that bear no morphological marking on the predicate and express some kind of transitivity modulation, the exact syntactic import of such alternations is not entirely clear. First, some involuntary agent constructions (see Section 2.2.2) do not show any verbal marking, but the descriptions suggest that these are instances of a diathetical operation, that is, not a voice-related but a voice-like phenomenon. Rather than related to specific verb classes, like many of the alternations presented in Chapter 6, these voice-like alternations denote lower transitivity values based on low agentivity on the part of the A. The following examples from Lezgian, Samoan, and Folopa are cases in point:

(325)   Lezgian (Haspelmath 1993a: 292)
        a. *Zamiradi   get'e   xa-na.*
           Z.ERG   pot   break-AOR
           'Zamira broke the pot.'
        b. *Zamiradi-waj   get'e   xa-na.*
           Z.OBL-ADEL   pot   break-AOR
           'Zamira broke the pot accidentally.'

(326)   Samoan (Austronesian, Samoan Islands; Mosel & Hovdhaugen 1992: 423, 731)
        a. *Na   va'ai   e   le   fafine   le   pule=ā'oga   i*
           PST   see   ERG   the   woman   the rule=school LD
           l=o=na   ofisa.
           the=POSS=3SG   office
           'The woman saw the principal at her office.'
        b. *Na   va'ai   le   fafine   i   le   pule= ā'oga i   le   maketi.*
           PST   see   the   woman   LD   the   rule=school LD   the   market
           'The woman saw the principal at the market (accidentally).'

(327)   Folopa (Teberan, Papua New Guinea; Anderson & Wade 1988: 7)
        a. *No-ó   kale naaọ   o   make   ẹ   di-ale-pó.*
           brother-VOC DEF 2SG.PSR sago young   1SG.ERG   cut-PST-IND
           'Brother, I (intentionally) cut down your (SG) sago tree.'
        b. *No-ó   kale naaọ   o   make   yọlo   di-ale-pó.*
           brother-VOC DEF 2SG.PSR sago young   1SG.ABS   cut-PST-IND
           'Brother, I (mistakenly) cut down your (SG) sago tree.'

In all of these languages, ergative coding – a case suffix in Lezgian, a particle in Samoan, and a suppletive pronoun in Folopa – appears whenever the action by the agent is viewed as volitional (and, more in general, the agent displays a high degree of agency), like in the (a)-clauses. In the (b)-clauses, the coding changes from ergative to adelative, locative, or absolutive marking, depending on the language. (See Kittilä 2005 and Fauconnier 2012 for a discussion of this phenomenon across languages.)

Other cases are less clear. In (328) below from Nêlêmwa, it is the animacy of the A that triggers the alternating construction. The action is performed by a volitional human agent, the A NP takes the expected ergative coding, and the subject pronoun *i* is obligatory in (a). In (b), in turn, the agent is inanimate, which triggers a special ergative coding and makes the subject pronoun optional. (According to Bril 1997: 379, the pronoun is expressed only under specific circumstances.) Semantically, these examples are similar to anticausatives in that, as noted in Section 2.2.3, even spontaneous events are caused, but the cause(r) is not salient. In (328) however, there is no marking on the predicate. There are both an allomorphy of the ergative and different subject marking, but the syntactic status of the A in (b) is not entirely clear:

(328)   Nêlêmwa (Austronesian, New Caledonia; Bril 1997: 379)
    a. *I   tûûlî   pwaxi   eli   a   Kaavo.*
       3SG dry   child   that   ERG₁   K.
       'Kaavo is drying the child.'
    b. *(I)   thâlî   daan   ru   ciiy-ena.*
       3SG   block   road   ERG₂   tree-this
       'This tree has blocked the road.'

Moreover, the only difference between the alternating constructions is in the allomorph ergative suffix (i.e., not in the syntactic status of the A) in Tsakhur:

(329)   Tsakhur (Northeast Caucasian, Azerbaijan and Russia; Schulze 1997: 58)
    a. *Adam-e   jizr^z*   *alebt'e.*
       man-ERG₁   bridge(III)[ABS]   III.destroy.PST
       'The man destroyed the bridge.'
    b. *Dama-n   jizr^z*   *alebt'e.*
       river-ERG₂   bridge(III)[ABS]   III.destroy.PST
       'The river destroyed the bridge.'

While such differential A coding is obligatory in Nêlêmwa and Tsakhur, it is optional in other languages. Archi (330) and Samoan (331) have absolutive-ergative case alignment, and prototypical A NPs take ergative marking, which is also possible for inanimate causers, alternating with oblique marking (i.e., sub-ablative case in Archi and a locative adposition in Samoan).[2]

(330)   Archi (Northeast Caucasian, Russia; Schulze 1997: 58)
    a. *Q'ˤt'i-li*   *lo*   *eˤwq'ni.*
       thunder-ERG   boy(III)[ABS]   III.frighten.AOR
       'The thunder frightened the boy.'
    b. *Q'uˤt'i-li-tɬt:'iʃ*   *lo*   *eˤwq'ni.*
       thunder-SAF-SUB.ABL   boy(III)[ABS]   III.frighten.AOR
       'The boy was afraid of the thunder.'

(331)   Samoan (Mosel & Hovdhaugen 1992: 423–424)
    a. *Na   tapuni   e   le   matagi   le   faitoto'a.*
       PST   close   ERG   the   wind   the   door
    b. *Na   tapuni   i   le   matagi   le   faitoto'a.*
       PST   close   LOC   the   wind   the   door
       Both: 'The wind closed the door.'

The descriptions available to us suggest that the oblique marking correlates with adjunct status in these languages – which means that these optional alternations are voice-like rather than voice-related.

---

[2] In the Archi examples, default case marking denotes a specific event and oblique case marking denotes a general disposition or habit (Wolfgang Schulze, pers. comm.).

Finally, in many languages it is the opposition between main and dependent clauses that triggers a construction alternation. In Quechuan languages, for instance, the P of some dependent clauses appears in the unmarked form instead of the accusative (which is the default in main clauses); verb morphology and some syntactic tests, however, suggest that such unmarked Ps are simply objects (see Lefebvre & Muysken 1988 for Cuzco Quechua). Something superficially similar occurs in some Australian languages. In Jiwarli (332), for instance, the P shows different forms in different kinds of dependent clauses; instead of the matrix-default nominative or accusative, it takes the allative in purpose clauses (a) and the dative in "imperfective dependent clauses" (b):

(332)   Jiwarli (Peter Austin, pers. comm.)
         a. *Ngatha   puna   pirru-rla   thika-ru.*
            1SG.NOM   go.PRS   meat-ALL   eat-SS.PURP
            'I am going (in order) to eat meat.'
         b. *Ngatha   ngunha   nhanya-nha   pirru-wu   thika-iniya.*
            1SG.NOM   DEM.ACC   see-PRS   meat-DAT   eat-DS.IPFV
            'I see the one eating meat.'

Crucially, however, such Ps seem not to be objects (or, more generally, core arguments) of the dependent verb.

7.3   Nominal Incorporation Constructions (NICs)

At least since Sapir's (1911) seminal article on the subject, most studies use the term "noun incorporation" for the array of interrelated phenomena that occupies us here. The earlier literature focuses on cases where a nominal root or stem forms a tight formal and functional unit with a verbal predicate, but a more recent strand draws attention to the existence of more complex ("phrasal") incorporates in some languages – special cases occasionally called "pseudo noun incorporation" (Massam 2009). To our knowledge, however, any restrictions to structural complexity of possible incorporates and related wordhood issues are orthogonal to the semantic role the corresponding argument may bear, and to the syntactic valency of the resulting complex predicate.[3] We use the term NOMINAL INCORPORATION to cover all cases where nominal and verbal elements are integrated into words or word-like units.[4]

---

[3] See Bickel and Zúñiga (2017) for a discussion of wordhood issues related to polysynthesis, and Zúñiga (2017) and Massam (2001) for accounts of such "phrasal" incorporates in Mapudungun and Niuean, respectively.

[4] The literature from the 1980s and 1990s tends to center on a lexical vs. syntactic debate ("where are incorporated structures generated?"), while early 21st-century studies concentrate more on semantic and pragmatic issues. The reader is referred to Mithun (1984), Rosen (1989), Sadock (1986), Baker (1988), and Massam (2009) for data, analyses, and references.

From the perspective of diathetical structure, there are three main types of nominal incorporation: antipassive, applicative, and syntactically neutral. The former corresponds to Mithun's (1984) Type I ("lexical compounding") and involves the demotion of the P to non-argument or to some (often unclear) low-prominence grammatical relation. Consider Example (333) from Niuean; in the default two-argument clause in (a), A and P take ergative and absolutive marking, respectively, while in the NIC in (b), the A is in the absolutive and the P occurs as a nominal incorporate. The NIC is the favored option when the P is indefinite and nonspecific:

(333)   Niuean (Massam 2001: 157)
    a. *Takafaga tūmau   nī   e   ia   a   tau ika.*
       hunt   always EMPH ERG he   ABS PL fish
    b. *Takafaga ika   tūmau nī   a   ia.*
       hunt   fish   always EMPH ABS he
    Both: 'He is always fishing.'

Mithun (1984) calls such NICs "composition by juxtaposition" and contrasts them with those analogous to the NIC of Mapudungun (334), which she calls "morphological compounds"; the distinction is phonological-morphological, not syntactic:

(334)   Mapudungun
    a. *Tachi pu trewa ina-le-i   (chi pu) mara.*
       ART   PL dog   chase-PROG-IND ART PL   hare
       'The dogs are chasing (the) hares.'
    b. *Ina-mara-le-i   tachi   pu   trewa.*
       chase-hare-PROG-IND   ART   PL   dog
       'The dogs are chasing hares.' (Salas 2006: 181; our glosses)

This type of nominal incorporation is cross-linguistically common: besides Oceanic (see next section), it is often found in languages of (poly)synthetic morphology in the Americas, Eurasia, and Australia.

The second type corresponds to Mithun's Type II ("manipulation of case") and is similar to a prototypical applicative in that the incorporate corresponds to the base object, which allows the incorporating verb to take a new object. In (335) from Paraguayan Guaraní, the first NIC is of the antipassive-like type; the P *mba'e* 'thing' is incorporated into the verb *-jogua* 'buy', turning the complex predicate syntactically monovalent (a–b). In the second NIC, by contrast, the incorporate is the body-part noun *po* 'hand' and the complex predicate built on *-pete* 'slap' is still syntactically bivalent (see also the external possessor constructions discussed in Section 6.2.2.2) (c):

(335)   Guaraní (Tupí-Guaraní, Paraguay)
    a. *A-joguá-ta   petei   mba'e.*
       1SG.A-buy-FUT   one   thing
       'I'll buy something.' (Velázquez-Castillo 1996: 107)

b. *A-mba'e-joguá-ta*   *ko-ka'aru.*
   1SG.A-thing-buy-FUT   this-afternoon
   'I'll go shopping this afternoon.' (Velázquez-Castillo 1996: 107)

c. *Ai-po-pete*   *la*   *mitã.*
   1SG.A-hand-slap   DEF   child
   'I slapped the child in the hand.' (Velázquez-Castillo 2002: 157)

Analogous examples come from Mohawk (336). In (a), the verb *-óhare* 'wash' incorporates the body-part noun *hsin* 'leg' and can still take a subject and an object (the latter being the possessor of the patient); in (b), the verb incorporates a noun that is not a body part:

(336)   Mohawk (Iroquoian, USA and Canada)
   a. *Wa'-khe-hsin-óhare-'.*
      TAM-1SG→3SG.F-leg-wash-TAM
      'I washed her leg.' (Baker 1999: 294)
   b. *Wa-hi-'sereht-anv́hsko.*
      TAM-3SG.M→1SG-car-steal
      'He stole my car.' (Mithun 1984: 868)

Such applicative NICs seem to be less widespread than antipassive-like NICs but appear to be a relatively stable family-specific feature.

Syntactically neutral NICs come in at least two subtypes. One corresponds to Mithun's Type IV ("classificatory incorporation") and involves generic nouns as incorporates, whose reference can be specified by external object NPs. The following examples from Apurinã show instances of *pe* 'pulp' and *xiti* 'earth' as examples of such generic nouns; their incorporation into semantically bivalent verbs (*usonãka-...-ka* 'dry' and *yotika-...-ta* 'burn', respectively) does not alter the object status of the P (which can be overt, like *komuru* 'manioc' in (a), or anaphorically expressed, like *kiko* 'field' in (b)):

(337)   Apurinã (Arawakan, Brazil; Aikhenvald 2017: 299)
   a. *Ata*   *komuru(-pe)*   *usonãka-pe-ta-ka.*
      1PL   manioc-pulp   dry-pulp-VBLZ-CAUS
      'We put manioc pulp to dry.'
   b. *Ata*   *yotika-xiti-ta*   *tha-ru.*
      1PL   burn-earth-VBLZ   AUX-3SG.M.OBJ
      '(First, we prepare the field_i by cutting down the trees. Then,) we set it_i on fire.'

This subtype is attested in Iroquoian, Australian, and Amazonian languages.

Example (338) from Yanomami as analyzed by Aikhenvald and Dixon (1999) illustrates the second subtype of valency-neutral NICs, which is much less well documented. In both (a) and (b), the A NP takes ergative case, and the description says *sipara* 'axe' has core argument status. The process merely serves to background "a topically continuous participant which is not in focus" (1999: 350) and is therefore akin to Mithun's Type III ("manipulation of discourse structure") – with the important proviso that the latter notion refers to the use, rather than to the structure, of NICs (and can therefore also cover Types I and II from a structural perspective).

(338)   Yanomami (Yanomamic, Brazil; Aikhenvald & Dixon 1999: 350)
    a. *(Kamijə-nɨ)   sipara   ja-puhi-i.*
        1SG-ERG   axe   1SG-want-DYN
        'I want an/the axe.'
    b. *(Kamijə-nɨ)   ja-sipara-puhi-i.*
        1SG-ERG   1SG-axe-want-DYN
        'I want (it), the axe.'

7.4   Transitivity Discord Constructions (TDCs)

Transitivity discord constructions (Margetts 2008), also called "semitransitive constructions" (Sugita 1973, Dryer 2007, Zúñiga 2016), are clauses that share features of one-argument and two-argument clauses – usually coding properties of the arguments involved, that is, flagging, indexing, and constituent order patterns.[5] They seem to be used for comparable purposes in languages related neither areally nor genealogically, but their formal and functional specifics are remarkably similar within language families. Like nominal incorporation constructions, TDCs show variation from the perspective of diathesis and voice: some are lexically restricted antipassives (7.4.1), others are lexically unrestricted but have no diathetical effects (7.4.2), and yet others seem to have some diathetical effects but are severely restricted from a lexical perspective (7.4.3). We present this variation in what follows.

7.4.1   Transitivity Modulation with Voice Alternation: Algonquian

Before addressing selected TDCs of Algonquian, we need to mention some essential characteristics of the structure of these languages. Algonquian verb stems come in at least four guises with respect to their morphology, syntax, and semantics. So-called final suffixes derive stems that are then used in clauses either without any objects ("Intransitives") or have primary objects ("Transitives"). These stem-deriving suffixes also specify the grammatical gender of the subject, if there is no object, or of the primary object, if there is one ("Animate" vs. "Inanimate"). The four basic stem types are, accordingly, Inanimate Intransitive (II), Animate Intransitive (AI), Transitive Inanimate (TI), and Transitive Animate (TA). Typically, II and AI stems are inflected for their subject only, whereas TI and TA stems are inflected for their subject and at least their primary object.[6]

---

[5]   Kleinschmidt (1851) uses the term *halbtransitiv* "semitransitive" for the Eskimoan antipassive. Benton (1967) labels the semitransitive verb class in Trukese "nontransitive" instead.
[6]   We do not address default three-argument clauses here, which are headed by a TA verb and have a subject A, a primary object G, and a secondary object T.

The following Blackfoot examples illustrate a one-argument clause headed by the AI verb *soká'pssi-* 'be good' with a subject (a), as well as the default two-argument clauses with the equivalent of English 'borrow' (TI *waahkomá't-atoo-* in (b) and TA *waahkomá't-at-* in (c), for inanimate and animate primary objects, respectively), which have a subject and a primary object:

(339)   Blackfoot (Russell et al. 2012)
      a. *Soká'pssi-wa.*
         [3]be.good.AI-3SG.PROX
         'S/he / it (ANIM) is good.'
      b. *Waahkomá't-atoo-m-wa*   *ni-asóka'siM-yi.*
         [3]borrow-TI-INAN.TH-3SG.PROX   1-jacket-INAN.SG
         'S/he borrowed my jacket (INAN).'
      c. *Waahkomá't-at-ii-wa*   *n-otá's-yi.*
         [3]borrow-TA-DIR-3SG.PROX   1-horse-OBV
         'S/he borrowed my horse (ANIM).'

Blackfoot allows a third stem for 'borrow' (AI *waahkomá't-aa-*), which can be used with a secondary object:

(340)   Blackfoot (Russell et al. 2012)
      Waahkomá't-aa-wa   *isspiksísoka'siM-i.*
      [3]borrow-AI-3SG.PROX   coat-NSPEC
      'S/he borrowed a coat.' (TDC)

The AI verb form *waahkomá'taawa* can also be used without an overt argument in P function, in which case the interpretation is 's/he borrowed (something)' or 's/he borrowed (whatever is adequate according to the context)'. Thus, there is a systematically potential mismatch between the morphological valency of the predicate (one) and the syntactic valency of the clause (one or two) with many, perhaps most, semantically bivalent AI stems. As far as transitivity is concerned, Blackfoot uses such clauses for the expression of states of affairs of reduced transitivity; the typical triggering factor is a nonspecific P.[7]

Innu shows a slightly more complicated picture. There is one, rather numerous, class of AI stems that can and frequently do occur in clauses with inanimate objects and are paired to TA stems (e.g., TA *aia-u* vs. AI[TD1] *aia-* 'buy', TA *uni-* vs. AI[TD1] *uni-ta* 'lose'). A second, relatively small, class consists of AI stems that can also occur in clauses with 3rd-person objects, but more often occur in clauses without them. They may be paired to TA stems (e.g., TA *amatshue-tutam-* vs. AI[TD2a] *amtashue-tuate-* 'climb a slope with (a load) on one's back'), in which case they take an inanimate object, or not have a TA counterpart (e.g., AI[TD2b]

---

[7] Algonquian studies call TDCs like the one in (340), and/or verbs that head them, "pseudo-transitive" (Bloomfield 1957: 33–34 for Eastern Ojibwa), "intransitive verbs with an implied object" (Bloomfield 1962: 46–47 for Menominee), "semi-transitive" (Cowell & Moss 2008: 125 for Arapaho), and "paratransitive" (Frantz 2009: 41 for Blackfoot). Some descriptions postulate a separate stem class for such verbs, alongside the traditional TI and TA classes, usually called AIO or AI+O (Rhodes 1985, Dahlstrom 2009).

tshimuti- 'steal'), in which case their object can be either animate or inanimate. The last, also rather small, class consists of AI stems that may be paired to TA stems or not, with the same patterning of animacy and objecthood as the second class (e.g., AI^{TD3b} *tshishi-patua-* 'start off running carrying').

Transitivity discord in Algonquian does not only occur with AI verbs. In Innu, for instance, there are two kinds of TI stems, namely typical (those actually taking objects) and atypical (those inflecting like TIs but not taking objects of any kind). Semantically, the latter consist of psych verbs on the one hand ('be happy', 'reflect', 'be bored') and motion verbs that express displacement by means of boat or foot on the other; they do not seem to be numerous.[8] The following example illustrates default AI *nikamu-* 'sing' (a) and TI^{TD} *apashenitam-* 'come to' (b), both of which take the causativizer for monovalent verbs -*i* – unlike default TI *kutam-* 'swallow', which takes the causativizer for bivalent/trivalent verbs -*uni* (c):

(341)   Innu (Drapeau 2014: 222–223)

    a. *Kakashtekupeshkueu nikamu-i-e-u*   *auass-a.*
        nun   sing.AI-TA:CAUS-DIR-3   child-OBV
        'The nun makes the child(ren) sing.'

    b. *Natukunnish apashenitam-i-e-u*   *nit-akushiunnim-inan-a.*
        physician   come.to.TI^{TD}-TA:CAUS-DIR-3   1-sick-1PL-OBV
        'The physician makes our sick person come to.'

    c. *Kakashtekupeshkueu kutam-uni-e-u*   *auass-a*
        nun   swallow.TI-TA:CAUS-DIR-3   child-OBV
        natukun-nu.
        medicine-OBV
        'The nun makes the child swallow a medicine.'

There appear to be two syntactically different kinds of TDCs in these languages: two-argument clauses with morphologically monovalent verbs and one-argument clauses with morphologically bivalent verbs. The latter kind might be closer to the intransitive pole than the former – if semantics and syntax are seen as more central indicators of transitivity than merely verb morphology. Moreover, some languages have a P-suppressing antipassive (e.g., Innu, Ojibwa, and Meskwaki). This construction is morphologically and syntactically distinct from the TDC, appears not to be a fully productive operation either, and seems to fall in between the two different TDCs regarding transitivity.[9] In terms of

---

[8] Bloomfield finds an analogous situation in Menominee and Ojibwa: there are morphologically (quasi-)AI verbs that can take objects (either animate or inanimate), and there are morphologically (quasi-)TI verbs that do not take objects. For Menominee, he says that atypical AI verbs take "implied objects," and atypical TI verbs have "purely formal objects" (1962: 46–47). For Ojibwa, he uses a somewhat different terminology for what is essentially the same phenomenon: atypical AI verbs are "pseudo-transitive" and take "pseudo-objects," and atypical TI verbs are "pseudo-intransitive" and take "purely formal objects" (1957: 33–34).

[9] We have found neither P-suppressing antipassives in Blackfoot nor prototypical demotional antipassives elsewhere in Algonquian. See also Zúñiga (2016).

grammatical voice, the AI-TDC is a lexically somewhat restricted antipassive that demotes the P from primary to secondary object, while the TI-TDC seems to be merely a one-argument clause showing a (synchronically) anomalous verb morphology. This is summarized in Table 7.1.

Table 7.1 *Selected TDCs in Algonquian languages*

	Derivation	Inflection	Syntax
Transitive	default TA/TI	bipersonal	A=SBJ, P=POBJ
Intermediate	AI-TDC	monopersonal	A=SBJ, P=SOBJ
	AI:ANTIP	monopersonal	A=SBJ, P suppressed
	TI-TDC	bipersonal	S=SBJ
Intransitive	default AI/II	monopersonal	S=SBJ

7.4.2   Transitivity Modulation without Diathetical Alternation ▬▬▬

In some languages, TDCs have a function similar to the Algonquian AI-TDCs when compared to default two-argument clauses, but do not involve a diathetical shift. This is the case in several eastern Kiranti languages. We follow Schikowski's (2013) in-depth study on one such language, Chintang, in what follows.

The default one-argument and two-argument clauses of Chintang are illustrated in (342) below.[10] Subject NPs are either unmarked (a) or take the ergative (b),[11] and object NPs are always unmarked (b). Verbs agree with their subject only (a) or with both subject and object (b); note that one-argument subjects and two-argument subjects usually trigger different indexing patterns on verbs:

(342)   Chintang (adapted from Schikowski 2013: 28)
  a. *Nunu   hap-no.*
     baby   cry-IND.NPST[3SG.SBJ]
     'The baby is crying.'
  b. *Dhami-ce-ŋa   dokha u-loĩs-o-ko.*
     shaman-NSG-ERG   illness 3[PL].SBJ-bring.out-3[SG].OBJ-IND.NPST
     'The shamans remove the illness.'

There are two clause types that fall in between.[12] First, some clauses omit the A and simply alter verbal indexing (Schikowski 2013: 34), as shown in (343).

---

[10] We are disregarding special constructions with psych verbs here.
[11] The ergative is optional with most SAP pronouns (Schikowski 2013: 33).
[12] Schikowski labels the operations that create the deviant patterns "S/O detransitivization" and "S/ A detransitivization," respectively.

This is possible with roughly 20 percent of all semantically bivalent predicates, can correspond to an anticausative (b) or an agentless passive diathesis (d), and is therefore an instance of strong P-lability:

(343)   Chintang (Schikowski 2013: 34)
    a. *Rame-ŋa*   *u-tec-ce*   *kosi-beʔ*
       R.-ERG   3SG.PSR-clothes-NSG   river-LOC
       lums-u-c-e.
       sink-3.OBJ-NSG-IND.NPST[3SG.SBJ]
       'Ram dumped his clothes into the river.' (two-argument clause)
    b. *Kosi-beʔ*   *maʔmi*   *lums-e.*
       river-LOC person   sink-IND.NPST[3SG.SBJ]
       'Someone sank in the river.' (one-argument clause)
    c. *Sa-ŋa*   *u-lett-o=kha*   *phuŋ?*
       who-ERG   3[PL].SBJ-plant-3[SG].OBJ[SUBJ]=NMLZ   flower
       'Who planted the flower?' (two-argument clause)
    d. *Makkai-ce*   *u-lett-a-ŋs-e.*
       maize-NSG   3[PL].SBJ-plant-PST-PERF-IND.PST
       'The maize plants have been planted.' (one-argument clause)

In the second deviant pattern, A and P NPs are normally present in the clause,[13] but both case marking and verbal indexing change, as illustrated in (344). In this TDC, both subject and object are unmarked, and the verb indexes the subject only:

(344)   Chintang (Schikowski 2013: 39)
    a. *Debi-ŋa* seu   *kond-o-ko.*
       D.-ERG   apple look.for-3[SG].OBJ-IND.NPST[3SG.SBJ]
       'Debi is looking for the/an apple.' (two-argument clause)
    b. *Debi* *seu* *kon-no.*
       D.   apple look.for-IND.NPST[3SG.SBJ]
       'Debi is looking for apples.' (TDC)

The TDC is available with all semantically bivalent predicates, but two-argument clauses occur much more frequently in texts (72 percent of the time; see Schikowski 2013: 39–40 for details).

Three further features of the Chintang TDC are significant here. First, several argumenthood tests show that the P is not demoted in such constructions and must be considered a core object (Schikowski 2013: 111). Second, the factor that triggers the use of the TDC is the unquantifiability of the P. (Its quantifiability is a prerequisite for its specificity.) Third, the phenomenon is not limited to Chintang; other Kiranti languages of Nepal – Athpare, Bantawa, Belhare, Chiling, Limbu, Puma, and Yakkha – show it as well (Schikowski 2013: 111–119).

---

[13] The P NP can be omitted for pragmatic reasons, which is much more frequently the case with otherwise default two-argument clauses (Schikowski 2013: 47–49).

The syntactic status of the P in TDCs appears to be analogous in Belhare and Puma (but rather uncertain in other languages). Specificity is at the core of the alternation's functionality (albeit, predictably, with some language-specific modulation). Lastly, the phenomenon is largely unrestricted from a lexical perspective, at least in those languages that have been explored in detail in this respect: all verbs allow it in Yakkha, most/many verbs allow it in Bantawa and Limbu, and its productivity is uncertain in others.

A similar phenomenon is found in the Sahaptian languages of North America. A TDC in Nez Perce, for instance, seems to occur with all bivalent verbs (345).[14] This construction (b) resembles a one-argument clause (c) in that the A NP is unmarked (it takes the ergative in the two-argument clause) and the verb indexes the subject only. It resembles a two-argument clause (a) in that there are two non-oblique NPs in the clause – even though the P NP is always unmarked in the TDC:

(345)   Nez Perce (Sahaptian, USA; Rude 1988: 552, 547)
    a. *Háama-nm*   *pé-exn-e*   *miya'ás-na.*   (two-argument clause)
        man-ERG   3→3SG-see-PST   child-OBJ
    b. *Háama*   *hi-héxn-e*   *miyá'c.*   (TDC)
        man   3.SBJ-see-PST   child
    Both: 'The man saw the child.'
    c. *Háama*   *hi-páayn-a.*   (one-argument clause)
        man   3.SBJ-come-PST
    'The man came.'

The TDC is less than half as frequently found as two-argument clauses in narrative texts (Rude 1988, 1997a) and is mostly used with indefinite and/or inanimate Ps. When it occurs with definite and animate Ps, like in (b) above, it denotes coreference of the A and the possessor of the P (i.e., 'the man saw his child', which is arguably a case of low transitivity, like indirect reflexives). Even though the descriptive literature has not explored the syntactic status of the P in these TDCs in detail, the construction does not seem to be demotional. The cognate construction in Sahaptin is both more complicated and less well explored than in Nez Perce (Rigsby & Rude 1996, Rude 1997b), but it seems to work alike.

7.4.3   Lexically Restricted Transitivity Modulation: Oceanic and Beyond

In some languages, TDCs turn out to be lexically restricted. For instance, they are possible only with a number of low-transitivity predicates in Koyraboro Senni, including several psych verbs, as well as *hima*

---

[14] Noel Rude labels this construction "antipassive" in his work on Sahaptian.

'resemble', *man* 'approach', and *hiija* 'marry'. The pair in (346) below illustrates the formal opposition between default two-argument clauses (a) and one-argument ones (b) in this language. The former have a transitivity marker *na* and an APV order, whereas the latter have no transitivity marker and an SV(X) order (where X represents an adjunct, or at least a nonobject, marked with a postposition):

(346)   Koyraboro Senni (Songhay, Mali; Heath 1999: 165)
 a. *A   na   ham   ŋaa.*
     3SG   TR   meat   eat
     'He ate meat.' (two-argument clause)
 b. *A   koy   koyr-aa   ra.*
     3SG   go   town-DEF   LOC
     'He went to the city.' (one-argument clause)

Semantically bivalent verbs like *hambur ~ humbur* 'fear' and *dii ~ di* 'see', however, routinely occur in clauses that occupy an intermediate zone, as shown in (347). There is no transitivity marker in such clauses, and the P NP is postverbal (like adjuncts) but unmarked (like objects):

(347)   Koyraboro Senni (Prost 1956: 124, 87)
 a. *Ay   ga   humbur   hans-o.*
     1SG   INCOMPL   fear   dog-DEF
     'I am afraid of the dog.'
 b. *Ay   di   né   wand-o.*
     1SG   see   2SG   wife-DEF
     'I saw your (SG) wife.'

While these clauses do not alternate with default two-argument clauses for the same verbs, their P does not appear to be syntactically less prominent than the default object P counterparts. The verbs that occur in the TDC do not seem to appear in the valency-reducing *a*-form (either an anticausative or a suppressing antipassive), but they can occur with the agentless passive *-andi*, with a potential reading: *duu* 'get' vs. *duwandi* 'be obtainable', *dii* 'see' vs. *diyandi* 'be seen/visible' (Heath 1999: 166–168). Although the transitivity marker *na* occurs in non-imperative clauses between the A and P NPs (either pronominal or lexical), it does not mark the predicate complex and can therefore not be considered a voice marker. Thus, the Koyraboro Senni TDC appears to be merely a clause type that signals lowered transitivity values in lexically specified instances without altering either predicate morphology or diathetical structure.[15]

The TDCs found in several Western Oceanic languages are lexically restricted as well, but they regularly alternate with default two-argument

---

[15] See Austin (1982) for a similar phenomenon in Diyari, where cognate-object constructions (e.g., 'dance') have the A marked as the S despite having a P in the clause.

clauses for those predicates that occur with them. Consider (348) below, which illustrates the formal opposition between default two-argument and one-argument clauses in Manam. The former have a transitive marker *-á'* on the verb, which indexes both arguments (a–b); the latter lacks the transitive marker and indexes only one argument (c):

(348)   Manam (Margetts 2008: 34; Lichtenberk 1983: 28)
   a. *Bóro   e   u-rere-t-á'-di.*
      pig   this   1SG.SBJ.REAL-like-TH-TR-3PL.OBJ
      'I like these pigs.'
   b. *Áine   patú   i-tabé'a-r-á'-i.*
      woman   stone   3SG.SBJ.REAL-defecate-TH-TR-3SG.OBJ
      'The woman excreted the stone.'
   c. *U-táŋ.*
      1SG.SBJ.REAL-cry
      'I cried.'

Some semantically bivalent verbs can also occur in a construction that resembles not only a two-argument clause (because there is an object) but also a one-argument clause (because there is no transitive marker and no object indexation), like those in (349). These low-transitivity predicates include psych verbs, like *rere* 'like' (a), and verbs of excretion and secretion, like *tabé'a* 'defecate' (b):

(349)   Manam (Margetts 2008: 34)
   a. *Deparóbu   u-rerére.*
      rice   1SG.SBJ.REAL-like
      'I like rice (in general).'
   b. *Áine   tá'e   i-tabé'a.*
      woman   feces   3SG.SBJ.REAL-defecate
      'The woman defecated.'

The crucial features that inform the speakers' choice regarding which clause type to use are specificity and animacy (distinguishing humans or certain domestic animals from all other referents). TDCs are excluded with Ps that rank high on both grounds, obligatory with Ps that rank low on both grounds, and optional if the P ranks high with respect to only one of the features (Lichtenberk 1983: 271).[16] Unlike their Koyraboro Senni counterparts, Manam TDCs do show a morphological asymmetry in the form of the predicate, but it is unclear whether they are syntactically bivalent (Margetts 2008: 41–42).

Saliba constitutes an interesting case in that it has both TDCs and NICs. The examples in (350) show default two-argument clauses, which are headed by

---

[16] In (b), however, the P is a specific cognate object rather than simply a nonspecific one.

verbs indexing both arguments (a–b), and a one-argument clause, headed by a verb indexing only one:[17]

(350)   Saliba (Margetts 2008: 34–36, Margetts 1999: 75)[18]
a.   *Ya-numa-ya-ko.*
     1SG.SBJ-drink-3SG.OBJ-PERF
     'I drank it already.'
b.   *Niu*   *se-pulisi-di.*
     coconut   3PL.SBJ-husk-3PL.OBJ
     'They husked the coconuts.'
c.   *Ya-lage.*
     1SG.SBJ-arrive
     'I arrived.'

The examples in (351) show counterparts that look like one-argument clauses in that they do not appear with an object NP and the verbs index only one argument. They differ among each other, however, in that in one case we have a TDC (a) and in the other an NIC, with the nominal element within the complex predicate (b):

(351)   Saliba (Margetts 2008: 34–36)
a.   *Ya-numa-ko.*
     1SG.SBJ-drink-PERF
     'I drank already.' (TDC)
b.   *Se-niu-pulisi.*
     3PL.SBJ-coconut-husk
     'They husked coconuts.' (NIC)

Note that *numa* 'drink' above belongs to Class I, one of the four morphological verb classes that allow TDCs. (This class of A-labile verbs includes *kai* 'eat', *huwa* 'plant₁', and *daibi* 'clean'.) The other three classes consist of non-labile monovalent-bivalent paired verbs. Class IIa consists of verbs like *kuma* 'plant₂', *tano* 'collect', or *bahe* 'carry', which take the applicative *-i* in order to derive their syntactically bivalent counterpart:

(352)   Saliba (Margetts 2008: 36)
a.   *Ka-na   labiya ye-bahe-i.*
     CL-3SG.PSR sago   3SG.SBJ-carry-APPL[3SG.OBJ]
     'He brought her sago.'
b.   *Hita   hinage puwaka ta-bahe   ta-lao.*
     1PL.INCL   also   pig   1PL.INCL.SBJ-carry 1PL.INCL.SBJ-go
     'We (INCL) also carry pigs and go.' (TDC)

---

[17] The potential structural ambiguity of forms with a zero-marked 3SG object is resolved when the object index is followed by another suffix, in which case 3SG.OBJ is marked via *-ya* rather than zero. See Example (350).

[18] Saliba orthography regularly writes subject prefixes separately; we chose to deviate from this convention in order to show wordhood regularities (particularly NICs) more clearly.

Class IIb verbs, like *biteli* 'hit', *keli* 'dig', or *deuli* 'wash', take the antipassive *kai-* in order to derive the syntactically monovalent predicate:

(353)   Saliba (Margetts 2008: 35)
          a. *Kaleko   ka-deuli-di.*
              clothes   1PL.EXCL.SBJ-wash-3PL.OBJ
              'We (EXCL) washed the clothes.'
          b. *Kaleko   ka-kai-deuli.*
              clothes   1PL.EXCL.SBJ-ANTIP-wash
              'We (EXCL) washed clothes / did the laundry.' (TDC)

Lastly, Class IIc verbs are some (non-productive) compounds like *lao-liga* [go-cook] 'cook' or *kabi-henaku* [touch/hold-chase] 'chase':

(354)   Saliba (Margetts 2008: 37)
          a. *Waw   crew   boy   wa   se-henaku-di.*
              now   crew   boy   ANA   3PL.SBJ-chase-3PL.OBJ
              'They chased away the crew boys.'
          b. *Rascolo   ye-kabi-henaku.*
              rascal   3SG.SBJ-touch-chase
              'He chased rascals.' (TDC)

In Saliba, Ps are most individuated when expressed by objects in default two-argument clauses. TDCs express less transitive interactions – usually habitual activities – and the P can be either specific or nonspecific but frequently refers to the kind of entity involved. In such constructions, the P NP may even take the determiner *ne* or the anaphoric marker *wa* (as in (354) above), which denotes that the referent has already been introduced in the discourse, or that the P NP be the head of a relative clause; most frequently, however, it is (directly or indirectly) possessed:

(355)   Saliba (Margetts 2008: 38)
          Natu-di-yao   se-bahe   se-lu   se-lao   nukua   ne.
          child-3PL.PSR-PL 3PL.SBJ-carry 3PL.SBJ-go.in 3PL.SBJ-go bush   DET
          'They would carry their children and go into the bush.'

NICs also express interactions low in transitivity, possibly often with nonspecific Ps, but Margetts (2008) says that the precise semantic difference between TCDs and NICs is hard to determine – even for those cases where the same verb allows both constructions. Clearly, however, many NICs are additionally restricted in terms of the particular incorporates they allow, and several are lexicalized (e.g., 'carry the wood' > TDC 'carry wood' and NIC "wood-carry" 'have a wedding feast', cf. Margetts 2008: 41).

It seems clearer than in the case of Manam that Ps in Saliba TDCs are syntactically restricted in several respects (Margetts 1999: 181–188).

Consequently, from the viewpoint of grammatical voice, we have four syntactic possibilities of these lexically constrained alternations, which correspond to the morphological types detailed above: strong A-lability (Class I verbs), two valency-increasing derivations (viz., non-prototypical applicativization with Class IIa verbs and verb compounding with Class IIc verbs), and one valency-decreasing derivation (viz., non-prototypical antipassivization with Class IIb verbs).

In sum, the Oceanic TDCs surveyed alternate with default two-argument clauses. Several constructions also show formal marking on the predicate that distinguishes them from default two-argument clauses in addition to argument indexing; the exceptions are the TDC in Manam and the TDC with labile verbs in Saliba. Lastly, even though more research is needed in this respect, there does not seem to be a diathetical shift in Manam, while there do seem to be diathetical shifts in Saliba.[19] This is summarized in Table 7.2 below.

Table 7.2 *Selected TDCs in Oceanic languages*

	Alternation	Coding Morphology	Diathetical Shift
Manam	✓	✓	(✗)
Saliba lability	✓	✗	(✓)
Saliba -*i*	✓	✓	(✓)
Saliba *kai-*	✓	✓	(✓)
Saliba compounds	✓	✓*	(✓)

7.4.4   Variation and Unity of TDCs

From the perspective of voice, the TDCs surveyed in this section are heterogeneous. Some are non-prototypical voices in that they are lexically restricted – some severely so. The TDC with A-labile verbs in Saliba is voice-like in that there apparently is a diathetical effect without predicate morphology (i.e., there is an uncoded alternation comparable to the ones surveyed in Chapter 6; as we have seen, this is lexically restricted as well). Three TDCs are

---

[19] Sugita's (1973) brief article addresses four Micronesian Oceanic languages: Marshallese and Trukese (which show TDCs), and Kosraean and Pohnpeian (which show NICs). As to the TDCs, Sugita is explicit regarding the default syntactic nature of their objects, but it is unclear which lexical restrictions apply to them.

merely voice-related in that there is no diathetical shift between the alternating constructions. Lastly, the TDC with TI verbs in Innu is, synchronically at least, a mere anomaly, since there is no alternation between constructions with those verbs (like in Manam, where the TDCs seem to express lower transitivity). This is summarized in Table 7.3 below.

Table 7.3 *Selected TDCs (summary)*

w/Saliba -*i*	lexically restricted APPL	voice
Blackfoot AI-TDC	lexically restricted demotional ANTIP	
Innu AI-TDC		
w/Saliba -*kai*		
w/Saliba compounds		
Saliba lability	A-lability	voice-like
Chintang	lexically restricted low-transitivity two-argument clause type	voice-related
Nez Perce		
Koyraboro Senni		
Innu TI-TDC	anomalous morphology in some two-argument clauses	–

8   Diachronic Aspects of Voice

The diachronic sources of voices and voice operations range from well-known in the case of languages whose history is profusely documented, or at least partially reconstructed, to completely unknown in many other cases. For instance, the development of the syntactically symmetrical voices discussed in Chapter 4 is not well understood yet, especially in the case of indigenous languages of the Americas. (In the case of western Austronesian, many diachronic issues are even more controversial than synchronic questions; see Kaufman 2017.) Much less is known about the origins of particular diatheses and voices than their cross-linguistic distribution and their synchrony (see Haspelmath & Müller-Bardey 2004 for a similar remark).

This chapter presents the essential features of what we know about the diachrony of voice. (We leave out uncoded alternations in what follows.) We start by examining the development of individual voices and then discuss voice syncretisms, that is, which multifunctionality patterns are attested. Since such syncretisms usually have a functional motivation (see Givón 2001: 94), this exploration provides us with important insights into the semantics of voice and diathesis.

8.1   Source Morphology

8.1.1   Sources of Causatives

Complex predicates are the main attested source of causative constructions. The causative markers typically originate in verbs with clear causative semantics, like 'make', 'do', 'cause', and 'let', but *verba dicendi* are also attested. Such sources are still visible in many periphrastic causatives, as in English *I made him build a house* or *the general let the soldiers attack the enemy*. These lexical verbs may retain that function even after they have become causative markers and may later develop into morphological markers of causativization as they lose their phonological and morphosyntactic independence. For instance, the Diyari denominal causative suffix -*nganka* originated in the verb *ngank-* 'make, do, cause' (e.g., *nhari* 'dead' > *nhari-nganka-* 'kill'), which is still in use (Austin 2011: 171), and the Avar verbal causative suffix *-ẓabi* (e.g., *t'eha-ẓabi* 'make blossom', from *t'eha-* 'blossom') derives from a peri- phrastic construction with the infinitive in *-ze* plus the verb *habi* 'make' (e.g., *t'eha-ze habi* > *t'eha-ẓ-abi*) (Haspelmath & Müller-Bardey 2004: 12). Another frequent etymon of causative markers is 'give', especially in South and Southeast Asian languages, which can be used in purposive constructions at an earlier stage of development (Song 1996, Jenny 2010):

(356)   Thai (Song 1996: 86–87, cited from Vichit-Vadakan 1976)
   a. *Khǎw   khiǎn   còtmǎay   hǎy   khun   tòop.*
      he   write   letter   give   you   answer
      'He wrote a letter so that you would answer.' (purposive)
   b. *Sǎakhǎa   hǎy   dèk   wîŋ.*
      S.   give   child run
      'Saka had a child run.' (causative)

The origin of many morphological causatives is uncertain, however. Occasion- ally, their multifunctionality may suggest a possible etymology – but directionality is seldom clear in such cases, like in Southern Agaw, where the exact origin of causative *-s* is opaque (Hetzron 1969: 21), and in Ijo (357), where *-mó* is both a directional and a causative marker:

(357)   Ijo (Niger-Congo, Southern Nigeria; Song 1996: 87–88, cited from William- son 1965: 35)
   a. *Ṭ ọbọu   wẹnị-mọ́!*
      child   walk-DIR
      'Walk towards the child!'
   b. *Wónì   uru   akị́-nị̀   u-bọu-mọ́-mí.*
      we   wine   take-ASP him-drink-CAUS-ASP
      'We made him drink wine.'

Wolfenden (1929: 46f, 199f) is more confident about the Tibetan and Burmese causatives having originated in a "general directive element" that originally expressed "a direction into the condition or state denoted by the verb" or an action towards or for an entity and was later "metaphorically extended" to the causative (Song 1996: 76).

Song (1996: Ch. 3) proposes a more comprehensive hypothesis regarding possible sources of causatives. In his view, in addition to the complex predicates involving verbs of doing or giving mentioned above, certain biclausal strategies (e.g., purposive constructions) can be recruited to express causation and may end up evolving into monoclausal constructions, with the erstwhile subordinator turning into a causative affix instead of the functional verb. More research is needed in order to ascertain how robustly attested, and how widespread, such a development path really is.

8.1.2   Sources of Applicatives

The main attested sources of applicative constructions are complex predicates and adverbs/adpositions (Haspelmath & Müller-Bardey 2004 and Peterson 2007: 124–125).[1]

As to the former, particular verbs may develop, via serial or converbal constructions, into auxiliaries and possibly further into affixes. The benefactive applicative often originates in a verb of giving (see Foley 1986: 141f for Papuan languages, Radetzky & Smith 2010 for, e.g., Japanese, Korean, and Telugu, as well as Creissels 2010 for a typological survey of periphrastic benefactives with an emphasis on African languages). The following examples from Crow illustrate how the verb *kuú* 'give' can be used as an applicative in (a) and both lexically and as an applicative in (b):

(358)   Crow (Siouan, USA; Graczyk 2007: 311–312)
    a. *Hinne*   *káalee-sh*   *isbaapíte*   *baláxxii-kaashi-m-nak*
        this   old.woman-DET her.grandchild now-real-DET-and
        alúut-kaas-uu-m-nak   *día(-a)-kuu-ak* ...
        arrow-real-PL-DET-and   make-CONT-APPL:BEN-SS
        'This old woman made a bow and some arrows for her grandchild ...'
    b. *Bilaxpáakee-m dí-ss-baa-kaan-nak*   *kuu-a-kuú-k!*
        person-DET   2P-DAT-INDF-ask.for-COND give-CONT-APPL:BEN-IMPER
        'If a person asks for something from you (SG), give it to him!'

The directive applicative goes back to 'see' in the Papuan language Dani (Bromley 1981: 107–109). The instrumental applicative comes from 'take' in Chickasaw (Muskogean; Munro 1983); the verb *ish-* 'get, take' first appears as a subordinate form in the converbal construction (a) and then as the grammaticalized instrumental applicative *isht-* in (b):

(359)   Chickasaw (Muskogean, USA; Munro 1983: 234)
    a. *Tali'* *ish-li-t*   *isso-li-tok.*
        rock   take-1SG.A-CVB hit-1SG.A-PST
        'Taking a rock, I hit him.'
    b. *Tali'* *isht-isso-li-tok.*
        rock   APPL-hit-1SG.A-PST
        'I hit him with a rock.'

The second common source of applicative markers is adverbs or adpositions. Haspelmath and Müller-Bardey mention the dynamic local adverb 'at' as the source of their "directive applicative" (which promotes goals of motion to objecthood), like German *be-* and the Oceanic markers (Pawley 1973). The

---

[1] There are occasional mentions of possible nominal sources in the literature (e.g., Craig & Hale 1988 for Warlpiri), but we have not found any unequivocal cases of such a direct development path; nouns seem to become adverbs or adpositions before turning into applicatives. See Peterson (2007: 140–141) for a similarly cautious remark regarding the possible connection between a Halkomelem applicative and the noun 'face'.

adpositional origin of the applicative is illustrated in (360) below from
Nadëb. The element expressing 'on top of' can occur as the postposition *yó*
(a), with a clause-initial subject, the verb, and a clause-final PP. It can also
occur as an applicative marker (b), either phonologically integrated into
the verb (the prefix *ya-*) or not (preverbal *yó*), with a clause-initial object,
the subject, and the clause-final verb (the default constituent order of Nadëb
is OSV).

(360)   Nadëb (Nadahup, Brazil; Weir 1986: 299–300)
         a. *Kalapéé a-sooh   bxaah yó.*
            child   PFX-be.sitting   tree   on.top.of
         b. *Bxaah kalapéé ya-sooh   / yó   sooh.*
            tree   child   APPL-be.sitting   APPL   be.sitting
         Both: 'The child is sitting on the tree.'

Similarly, in (361) from San Andrés Yaá Zapotec, the adposition *neen* 'with'
(a) has been incorporated into the verb in (b):

(361)   San Andrés Yaá Zapotec (Galant 2015: 229–230)
         a. *Yell=a'   tweegh   dzh-eegh=be' La' neen Kwann=a'.*
            M.=DEM   sometimes   HAB-go=3INF   O.   with J.=DEM
            'Miguel sometimes goes to Oaxaca with Juan.'
         b. *Yell=a'   dzh-eegh-neem=be'   Kwann=a' La' tweegh.*
            M.=DEM   HAB-go-with=3INF   J.=DEM   O.   sometimes
            'Miguel sometimes goes to Oaxaca with Juan.'

8.1.3   Sources of Passives

Since passives are common and prominent in many well studied
Indo-European languages, it is unsurprising that their diachrony has been studied
in considerable detail. We follow Haspelmath (1990) in postulating four major
sources of passives, namely auxiliaries plus a nonfinite verb form, indefinite
subject constructions, reflexives, and causatives.[2]

8.1.3.1   Auxiliary plus nonfinite verb form

It is rather easy to find cases where passives are formed by an
auxiliary and a (passive) participle of the verb. Illustrative examples come from
familiar Indo-European languages, such as English *the door was painted*. The
development of this kind of passive is easily accounted for: the participles (which
often also function as adjectives) denote a state resulting from an action, and the
auxiliary added makes the given construction dynamic in nature. This type of
passive is often polysemous: constructions such as *the door is painted* allow both
a passive and an adjectival reading.

---

[2] Haspelmath also mentions the (less frequent) possibility of lexical expansion of initially idiosyncratic derivational elements, like Ancient Greek *-thē ~ -ē*.

The auxiliary displays some variation, not only across languages but also within individual languages. Auxiliaries attested in these kinds of passive include, for instance, 'be' (English, Hungarian), 'become' (German, Swedish), 'go' (Ecuadorian Quechua), 'come' (Finnish), 'fall' (Tamil), 'eat' (Sinhalese), 'receive, get' (German, English), 'suffer' (Vietnamese), and 'touch' (Thai, Burmese) (see Haspelmath 1990: 38ff for data and references). It is not uncommon for the auxiliaries to further develop into affixes. For example, in Mapudungun, *nge-* 'be, exist' that has turned into an affix as a passive marker: *nge-la-i chadi* (exist-NEG-IND salt) 'there is no salt', *langüm-nge-i chi wentru* (kill-PASS-IND the man) 'the man was killed'.

There is also some variation in the participles employed in this type of passive – typically between adjectival participles and resultative participles. According to Haspelmath (1994: 167) passive participles come from adjectival ones (that can also form verbal adjectives, such as German *-lich*) via analogy. By a related token, Gildea (2015) suggests that passives may grammaticalize from nonfinite forms different from participles, namely from patient nominalizations. The examples from Panare in (362) below illustrate this plausible claim. In Stage I, the patient nominalization refers to an entity that results from an action (a). In Stage II, the patient nominalization is used as a predicate in a predicate-nominal construction (b). Lastly, the patient nominalization predicate is reinterpreted as referring to an event in Stage III (c):

(362)   Panare (Cariban, Venezuela; Gildea 2015: 9–10)

    a. *Tina   upa-sa'   karoma-ñe   paka.*
        water dry-NMLZ   drink-TAM   cow
        'The cows drink stagnant (i.e. 'dried up') water.'

    b. *Tina   mën   upa-sa'.*
        water 3.INAN.COP   dry-NMLZ
        'The water is dried up.'

    c. *Y-amaika-sa'   məən   y-uya.*
        3-keep-PASS   sit   1-DAT
        'It is kept by me.' (lit. 'it is a kept thing by me')

8.1.3.2 Indefinite Subject Constructions

Passives can originate in indefinite subject constructions (ISCs) like the following:[3]

(363)   Modern Greek (Haspelmath 1990: 49)
    Su   tilefoni-s-an.
    2SG.DAT   phone-AOR-3PL
    'Someone called you (SG).'

The subject of these ISCs is pronominal and has an arbitrary ('anyone'), indefinite ('someone'), or generic ('people in general') reference. Typically, a 3PL

---

[3] Haspelmath (1990) labels it "generalized-subject construction."

pronoun is used, but also a dedicated impersonal pronoun, such as *man* of German and Swedish, may be used.

Functionally, the use of such elements in a passive function is easily accounted for, because their use backgrounds the agent. In some languages, these are best seen as uncoded passives, because the only attested change concerns the form of the subject; there is no special voice marking on the verb. In other languages, however, these may develop into bona fide passives, like in Kimbundu:

(364)   Kimbundu (Bantu, Angola; Givón 1994: 26)
    a. *Nzua {aana / Ø}   a-mu-mono.*
       N.   children   3PL.SUBJ-3SG.OBJ-see
       'Nzua, the children / they saw him.'
    b. *Nzua a-mu-mono*   (*kwa   meme*).
       N.   PASS-3SG.SUBJ-see   by   me
       'Nzua was seen (by me).'

The (a)-clause illustrates a typical ISC, where reference of the 3PL marker *a-* is open; it could be referential (e.g., anaphoric) or nonreferential ('people'). In (b), it has lost its status as a genuine person marker and has been reanalyzed as a passive marker – note also the oblique marking of the optional A.

8.1.3.3   Reflexives

Passives that originate in reflexives are a process robustly attested for many Indo-European languages, especially for Romance, Balto-Slavic, and Scandinavian Germanic. In these cases, the element that grammaticalizes into a passive marker comes from the PIE reflexive pronoun **s(w)e* (e.g., French *se*, Polish *się*, Russian *-sja/-s'*, and Swedish *-s*). This process is rather infrequent outside Europe, however (Haspelmath 1990: 43). We address this development path in more detail in Section 8.2.2.

Reflexives may acquire passive-like readings under favorable circumstances in languages that have separate constructions for both functions. Consider the following example from German, where normal passives take the form [*werden* 'become' + PTCP] but reflexive *sich* can encode potential passives in colloquial expressions (formal Standard German still favors expressions like *lassen sich schreiben* [let.3PL REFL write.INF] or *können geschrieben werden* [can.3PL write.PTCP become.INF]):

(365)   German (online blog source)[4]
    Kleine   Kurznachricht-en   schreib-en   sich   einfach
    small.PL   text.message-PL   write-3PL   PASS   easily/just
        schneller   als   E-Mails...
        quicker   than   email
    'Short text messages can just be written more quickly than emails...'

---

[4] Available at http://www.daniel-net.de/index.php/gedankenablage-blog/it-technik/7-spark-und-openfire-die-interne-kommunikationsloesung.

It would be interesting to see whether a similar stage is attested also in languages where the process has been completed.

8.1.3.4 Causatives

The close connection between causatives and passives and the development of passives from causatives has been known at least since Gabelentz (1861). Passives that originated in causatives are attested in Tungusic languages (Haspelmath 1990: 48, Knott 1995) and West Greenlandic (Fortescue 1984: 265), as well as in Japanese (Washio 1992) and, more in general, in languages of East and Southeast Asia (Yap & Iwasaki 2007). The following example is from Korean:

(366)   Korean (Soon Mi Hong-Schunka, pers. comm.)
    a. *Ku   saram-i   na-rul   po-ass-ta.*
       DET person-NOM 1SG-ACC   see/look-PST-DECL
       'The man saw me.'
    b. *Ku   saram-i   po-i-ess-ta.*
       DET man-NOM   see/look-PASS-PST-DECL
       'The man was seen.'
    c. *Ku   saram-i   na-eykey   kurim-ul   po-i-ess-ta.*
       DET man-NOM   1SG-DAT   picture-ACC see/look-CAUS-PST-DECL
       'The man showed me the picture.'

Upon closer inspection, the relation between valency-increasing causatives and valency-decreasing passives turns out to be rather intimate.[5] Consider causative-reflexives like English *I had the barber shave me / I had myself shaved by the barber*, and German *er lässt sich fotografieren* 'he has his picture taken', where *lassen* creates a causative and *sich* a passive reading. In such constructions, the subject allows itself to be targeted by an action, but the relevance of the A is backgrounded: it performs the denoted action but is not the primary instigator of the event. In a similar vein, the relevance of the A is backgrounded in passives. Consequently, a passive reading can evolve when the requirement of agency is lost. Lastly, passives and causatives have in common that they center on the affectedness of the P, rather than on the agency of the (base) A (see Haspelmath 1990: 45).

8.1.4 Sources of Antipassives

The grammaticalization of antipassives is seldom clear: Sansò's (2017) specialized study states that most antipassives in his sample (55 percent)

---

[5] Note in this context that causatives have detransitivizing functions in some languages (see Section 2.1), which may also be seen as relevant to the development of passives (Kittilä 2013).

do not have a transparent source. Those that are traceable appear to have three major sources: (i) nominalizations, (ii) generic/indefinite object constructions, and (iii) reflexives (Jacques 2014 forthcoming; Sansò 2017). We conclude this subsection by pointing out a possible connection with aspectual markers.

8.1.4.1 Nominalizations

This source falls into two subtypes, namely agentive and action nominalization. An example of the former is the antipassive *-nan* of Misantla Totonac:

(367)   Misantla Totonac (Totonacan, Mexico; MacKay 1999: 321, 322)
    a. *Ut   šqaa.*
        3SG   harvest
        'She harvests (obj.).'
    b. *Ut   šqaa-nan.*
        3SG   harvest-ANTIP
        'She does some harvesting.'
    c. *hun-tii-nV$^{\textup{ʔ}}$*
        DET-dance-NMLZ
        'dancer'

According to Sansò, MacKay (1999: 382) traces the antipassive *-nan* back to a suffix *-nV$^{\textup{ʔ}}$* that derives agent nominalizations. The development of the antipassive is easily accounted for by the functional and syntactic features the two constructions share. Agent nominalizations refer to a person habitually involved in the action described by the nominalized predicate: a dancer usually dances and a painter usually paints. Expressing habitual actions is one of the functions of antipassives, which makes the link between agent nominalizations and antipassives direct.

The second subtype consists in antipassives originating in action/result nominalizations, like in Japhug Gyalrong:

(368)   Japhug Gyalrong (Sino-Tibetan, China; Jacques 2014: 11–12, 15–16)
    a. *Ku-sɤ-sat   jo-ɕe.*
        SBJ.NMLZ-ANTIP.HUM-kill   EVID-go
        'He went to kill [people].'
    b. *Tɤ-rʑaβ   nɯ   pjɤ-rɤ-ɕpʰɤt.*
        INDF.PSR-wife   top   EVID.IPFV-ANTIP.NHUM-mend
        'The wife was mending (clothes).'
    c. *rɤ-ŋgɯm* 'lay an egg' < *ŋgɯm* 'egg'
    d. *sɤ-rmi* 'give a name' < *(tɤ)-rmi* 'name'

Japhug Gyalrong has two antipassive prefixes, *sɤ-* and *rɤ-*, which demote a human and a non-human object, respectively. These affixes also function as productive denominal verbalizers, as shown in (c) and (d).

8.1.4.2   Indefinite Object Constructions

Antipassives may originate in indefinite object constructions, and/or an incorporation of generic/indefinite elements in the object slot. The source of the Ixcatec antipassive $-mi^2$ is Proto-Popolocan $*hmi$ 'person' (see mi^2-nda^2wa^2 'man' and $t\int a^2h$-mi^2 'people'):

(369)   Ixcatec (Otomanguean, Mexico; Adamou 2014: 383, as cited in Sansò 2017: 182)
$\phi i^2ka^2hu^2$-mi^2 $Di^2ni^2sjo^2$-ri^2.
bring-ANTIP   D.-HON
'Mr. Dionisio brought (us).'

The previous stage of such a development can be seen in Beng, where the generic nouns zá 'matter', p̄ɔ 'thing', and sɔ̀ŋ 'person' are used in the object slot when the P is semantically underspecified or irrelevant:

(370)   Beng (Mande, Ivory Coast; Paperno 2014: 71–72)
    a.   Ó   zá   pè.
            3SG.PST   matter   say.LT
            'He said (sthg.).'
    b.   Ŋ́ó   pɔ̄a   blē.
            1SG.AFF.STAT   thing   eat.LT
            'I will eat (things).'
    c.   Ŋ̀ò   sɔ̀ŋ   dὲ.
            3PL.HAB   person   kill.LT
            'They kill.' (i.e., they are killers)

8.1.4.3   Reflexives

Finally, reflexives may be the source of antipassives as well. (They are the most frequent source in Sansò's 2017 study.) In Polish (371), for instance, the reflexive marker się was in time recruited to antipassivize verbs, as shown in (b). The marker occupies the object slot (see dzieci 'children' in (a)), thus excluding the expression of an object. Functionally, this makes the patient indefinite:

(371)   Polish (Janic 2016: 133, as cited in Sansò 2017: 193)
    a.   Wasz   syn   bije   dzieci.
            2SG.HON.NOM.SG.M   son   hit.PRS.3SG   child.PL.ACC
            'Your (HON) son is beating children.'
    b.   Wasz   syn   bije   się.
            2SG.HON.NOM.SG.M   son   hit.PRS.3SG   ANTIP
            'Your (HON) son fights / is used to beating up (people).'

Similarly, the Tirmaga reciprocal affix -ínɛn, shown in (372) below, excludes the overt expression of an object (evidenced by the ungrammaticality of (c)) and was recruited as antipassive marker (b):

(372)   Tirmaga (Surmic, Sudan; Bryant 1999: 92–94, as cited in Sansò 2017: 194)
    a.   *Ka-ɗak-ínɛn-ó-tɔ.*
        1.SBJ-hit-RECP-PL-IPFV
        'We (EXCL) are hitting each other.'
    b.   *Kɔ́-kɔ́h-inɛ́n-Ø-tɔ.*
        1.SBJ-weed.IPFV-ANTIP-SG-IPFV
        'I am weeding.'
    c.   **Kɔ́-kɔ́h-inɛ́n-Ø*   *gu.*
        1.SBJ-weed.IPFV-RECP-SG   garden[SG]
        (Intended: 'I am weeding a garden.')

The functional link between antipassives and reflexives/reciprocals is not founded in habituality but in the non-prototypicality of the P. In antipassives, the P is demoted because it is indefinite; in reflexives and reciprocals, the P is the A itself. Consequently, in both cases the events denoted deviate from prototypical, high-transitivity events. Remember from Chapter 5 that it is not uncommon for reflexives and reciprocals to demote or suppress Ps syntactically, which probably also contributes to their use as antipassive markers.

8.1.4.4   Aspectual Markers

The literature on antipassives commonly reports syncretisms with aspectual markers. With respect to Bezhta, Comrie et al. (2015) say that the morphemes *la/lā*, *da/dā*, and *ya*, which are found in bona fide antipassive constructions in the language, also appear on monovalent predicates, with an iterative meaning (373). In such cases, these markers do not modify the absolutive case taken by the subject when found with patientive monovalent verbs (b); even though they do change the ergative case taken by the subject to absolutive with agentive monovalent verbs (d), they do not appear to alter the syntactic structure (and therefore the diathesis) of such clauses:

(373)   Bezhta (Comrie et al. 2015: 552)
    a.   *Öždää*   *b-ogi<ba>c'-iyo.*
        boy.PL[ABS]   HUM.PL-jump<PL>-PST
        'The boys jumped (once).'
    b.   *Öždää*   *b-ogi<ya-ba>c-ca.*
        boy.PL[ABS]   HUM.PL-jump<ITER-PL>-PRS
        'The boys jump many times.'
    c.   *Öždi*   *öhλö-yö.*
        boy.OBL(ERG)   cough-PST
        'The boy coughed (once).'
    d.   *Öžö*   *öhdä-yö.*
        boy[ABS]   cough.ITER-PST
        'The boy was coughing.'

Consequently, and unlike in Eskimoan languages, such uses of the morphology in question are not instances of antipassivization but of multifunctionality: the same elements are used in constructions that denote a voice different from the active and in those that do not. This might well indicate that the morphemes *la/lā*, *da/dā*, and *ya* originated in iterative markers and were later syntactified (i.e., they signaled a diathetical shift in the antipassive constructions), but the question of change directionality is difficult to answer in cases like this.

8.1.5   Sources of Reflexives

Even though some reflexives have unknown etymologies, those that are traceable originate in nouns, pronouns, verbs, and adverbs/adpositions (Schladt 2000, Heine 2000, Heine & Miyashita 2008). We address them in turn in what follows – but bear in mind that (pro)nominal reflexives are not commonly used with the duplex diathesis, so the sources presented here are not frequent sources of a "reflexive voice" but merely of some reflexive markers.

8.1.5.1   Nouns

Nouns are by far the most common source of reflexive markers. Most frequently, especially for nominal reflexives, the nouns recruited are body-part expressions. The attested instances include the items for 'head' in Mordvinian (Geniušienė 1987: 303) and Cape Verdean Creole (Morais-Barbosa 1967: 22), 'soul' in (Modern) Arabic (Schladt 2000: 114), and 'body' in Bura (Hoffmann 1963: 157). Other nouns recruited for the expression of reflexivity include the element meaning 'self', like Finnish *itse* (< 'shadow', see Kok 2016; Schladt 2000 gives 'reflection' as the original meaning) and Paumarí *abono* (Chapman & Derbyshire 1991: 178), as well as items meaning 'person' and 'owner'. Both nominal sources of reflexives are easily accounted for: not only names of body parts, but also expressions referring to the A's constitution naturally develop into building blocks of constructions denoting actions that the A acts on itself.

8.1.5.2   Pronouns

Pronouns are attested as sources of reflexive markers. They can be "emphatic pronouns," that is, pronominal elements reinforced by intensifiers, like in Irish:

(374)   Irish (Heine & Miyashita 2008: 175)
    Ghortaigh   *Seán é.*   vs. *Ghortaigh*   *Seán é*   *féin.*
    hurt.PST   S.   3SG.M   hurt.PST   S.   3SG.M self
    'Sean hurt him.'   'Sean hurt himself.'

Pronouns can also simply be 1st- or 2nd-person object pronouns, like in German (375). The object pronoun *mich* can be used in the active clause (a) and in the reflexive construction (b):

(375)   German
    a. *Du*   *hast*   *mich*   *verletzt.*
        2SG.NOM   have.2SG   1SG.ACC   hurt.PTCP
        'You (SG) (have) hurt me.'

b. *Ich   habe   mich   verletzt.*
   1SG.NOM   have.1SG   1SG.ACC   hurt.PTCP
   'I (have) hurt myself.' (Heine & Miyashita 2008: 174)

An intensifier *selbst ~ selber* can be optionally added in German, but the pronouns suffice to denote reflexivity.

8.1.5.3   Verbs

Verbs are infrequent as sources of reflexives, but the literature occasionally mentions some of such instances. The "reflexive serial verb" *dibon* in Namakir (Sperlich 1993) and *ko-* 'return' in Sanumá are examples of such verbs:

(376)   Sanumá (Yanomamic, Venezuela and Brazil; Borgman 1991: 43)
         Atakusa a-nö   kama nia   sapa   ko-pa-so-ma.
         gun   3SG-INS 3SG shoot DRCT:reverse return-SAF-FOC-COMPLS
         'He shot himself with a gun.'

Since, in reflexives, an action can be naturally construed as "returning" to the A instead of proceeding to a P (thus leaving the A's sphere), it is perhaps surprising that this development path is not found more often.

8.1.5.4   Adverbs/adpositions

Adverbial and adpositional are apparently quite rare as sources of reflexive markers, but they are mentioned in the literature. The elements *nanǫǫs* 'alone' and *nomo* 'only' are used in Ute and Bislama, respectively (optionally in the latter case, to disambiguate):

(377)   a. Ute (Burch 1980: 149)
            Ta'wáci   'u   nanǫǫs   nȕká-y.
            man.SBJ   he   alone/REFL hear-TAM
            'The man himself/alone heard (sthg.).' / 'The man heard himself.'
         b. Bislama (English-based Creole, Vanuatu; Crowley 1990: 311)
            Tufala gel ia   i   sakem paoda   long   tufala (nomo).
            two   girl the   PART   tip   powder   LOC   two   only/REFL
            'The two girls tipped powder over themselves.'

Similarly, Schladt (2000) mentions the locative preposition *tì* 'on' as the etymon in Zande:

(378)   Zande (Niger-Congo, Central Africa; Tucker and Bryan 1966: 150)
         Mí-ȉȉmí   tì-rȅ.
         I-kill   on-me
         'I kill myself.'

While adverbs like 'alone' are plausible sources of reflexives, prepositions like 'on' seem much less natural and probably have an idiosyncratic history.

8.1.6   Sources of Reciprocals

Reflexives and reciprocals are coded alike in many Indo-European languages, as well as in Mansi and in Tamil (see Nedjalkov 2007b: 260 for more examples and references). Reciprocity is conceptually different from reflexivity (see Chapter 5), however, and it should come as no surprise that the respective markers can evolve independently. In fact, Maslova and Nedjalkov (2013) survey 175 languages and find the following proportions with respect to the formal identity of reciprocal markers and reflexive markers: 25 percent show only syncretic markers, 9 percent are languages that have both dedicated and syncretic reciprocal markers, and 56 percent have distinct markers (and 9 percent only have iconic constructions, i.e., those constructions that have two occurrences of the main verb). Dedicated markers predominate in Eurasia, whereas the rest of the world has no predominant type, which may reflect the diachronic instability of the reciprocal-marking types. Having both dedicated and syncretic markers is particularly common in Europe.

The same disclaimer as with reflexives applies here: only some reciprocal markers are used with the duplex diathesis. We follow Heine and Miyashita (2008: 178f) in distinguishing the following known sources of reciprocals (in addition to reflexives): nouns that express interpersonal relationships, bipartite NPs, adverbs, expressions of repetition, and others. The first are nouns whose meaning implies reciprocity, like 'comrade', 'mate', 'companion', 'friend', etc. The following example from Koromfe illustrates the use of grammaticalized *dombʌ*, the plural of 'comrade':

(379)   Koromfe (Niger-Congo, Western Africa; Rennison 1996: 112)
   Ʊ dáĩ hĩ̃ jellʌʌ dombʌ.
   1PL house.PL two see.PROG RECP
   'Our two houses see one another.'

Bipartite NPs include the familiar ones from English (i.e., *each other, one another*); see König and Vezzosi (2002) for some grammaticalization scenarios in western European languages. Perhaps unsurprisingly, the conceptual affinity between plurality and reciprocity has led to plural markers, either nominal or verbal, being recruited in some Turkic languages (Nedjalkov & Nedjalkov 2007: 1155f). In Tuvan, nouns such as 'group of people' serve as the source for reciprocals, and similar cases are attested also in Yukaghir, Mundari, Tagalog, Kabardian, and Toqabaqita (Nedjalkov & Nedjalkov 2007: 1156).

Adverbs include elements that can denote reciprocity with a plural subject and a suitable predicate, as *siak* 'together' in Mupun *mo tu siak* (3PL kill RECP) 'they killed each other' (Frajzyngier 1993: 279). Expressions of repetition include verbal reduplication, as in Godié *wa wà~wà* (3PL love~RECP) 'they love each other' (Heine & Miyashita 2008: 183), but also (pro)nominal iteration, as in Yagaria:

(380)   Yagaria (Trans-New Guinea, Papua New Guinea; Renck 1975: 148)
        Lapagae-tipi   lapagae-tipi   game'   a-si-io!
        2PL-yourselves   2PL-yourselves   fight   NEG-do-IMPER.PL
        'Do (PL) not fight against each other!'

8.1.7   Sources of Anticausatives

Anticausatives have two major known sources: reflexives and passives. The former development is found, for instance, with Finnish *-UtU*, German *sich*, and Spanish *se*. With respect to the latter development, Kulikov (2011b) argues that anticausatives emerged from passives via impersonalization in Vedic Sanskrit and other Indo-European languages. He presents the following path for this development: 'Y is V-ed by somebody' > 'Y is V-ed [by somebody]' > 'Y is V-ed [by generic passive A]' > 'Y is V-able' (2011b: 229). In the last stage where the impersonalization has been completed, and the agent is omitted altogether semantically, the construction has become an anticausative.

8.2   Voice Syncretisms

Dedicated (productive) voice markers exist: examples include the causative *-chi* in Quechuan, the passive *-thē* in Ancient Greek, and the reflexive *-ohsi* and the reciprocal *-(o)tsiiyi* in Blackfoot. Fairly often, however, even in cases where the etymology of the voice markers is not entirely clear, it is evident that they are multifunctional. Examples are easy to find and include German *sich*, Romance *si/se*, Quechuan *-ku*, and Indonesian *-kan*. The literature usually refers to such multifunctionality patterns via the terms "voice syncretism," "voice isomorphism," "voice correlation," or "voice ambivalence," but also via the terms "cluster" or "family" for the voices that systematically share a formal expression (Shibatani 2004, Kulikov 2011b). The present section surveys the main cases of this phenomenon and explains how and why such clusters may arise.

A note on the term "syncretism" is in order before proceeding. The notion traditionally, and most precisely, refers to cases of homonymy in inflectional paradigms. An example is the Latin nominal suffix *-ō*, which covers both the dative and the ablative singular of the second declension (e.g., in *domin-ō* 'to/from the master'). This raises two issues. First, formal identity may be the result of phonological or morphological change; it seems that the vast majority of multifunctional voice markers are instances of the latter.[6] In other words, one

---

[6] A possible exception is the neutralization of the benefactive applicatives *-pa*, *-pu*, etc. in Quechuan languages.

form becomes obsolescent and eventually ceases being used altogether, while another form takes over, which, if the forms are functionally related, is an instance of polysemy rather than homonymy.[7] Homonymy and polysemy are not always easy to distinguish, however, so we have opted for the neutral term "multifunctionality" here, but we concentrate on the prominent cases where a connection can be meaningfully postulated between erstwhile functions of a syncretic marker and its later extensions. The second issue is related to the problematic inflection–derivation distinction still frequently made in theories of morphology. Suffice it to say here that, even though most studies of morphology not centered on voice mention voice (usually in passing) as one of the inflectional grammatical categories, there is no consensus in the literature as to how to treat voice markers in this respect. Some voice markers are more inflection-like than others, both across and within languages. Consequently, we use *syncretic* in a broad sense in what follows, simply to refer to the multifunctional nature of selected voice markers.

8.2.1   The Transitivizing Cluster (= CAUS-APPL Isomorphism)

The literature has repeatedly noted that causatives and applicatives are marked alike in some languages (Nedjalkov & Sil'nickij 1973; Austin 1997; Shibatani 2000; Malchukov 2016, 2017). The following examples from Tauya illustrate the basic pattern; the marker *fe-* can work either as a causative (b) or as an applicative (d):[8]

(381)   Tauya (Trans-New-Guinea, Papua New Guinea; MacDonald 1990: 196)
   a. *Zumu-a-za.*
       die-3SG.SBJ-IND
       'He died.'
   b. *Zumu   fei-fe-a-za.*
       die   3SG.OBJ-CAUS-3SG.SBJ-IND
       'He killed him.'
   c. *Wate   ezi-i-za.*
       house   make-3PL.SBJ-IND
       'They built a house.'
   d. *Wate   ezi   ya-fe-i-za.*
       house   make   1SG.OBJ-APPL-3PL.SBJ-IND
       'They built a house for me.'

---

[7] An example of this comes from Greek. Second-declension masculine nouns, like many proper names, traditionally distinguish, in the singular, between a nominative ending in *-os*, an accusative ending in *-on*, and a vocative ending in *-e*. In Colloquial Modern Greek, however, those nouns only distinguish between nominative *-os* and accusative-cum-vocative *-o*, that is, the accusative is taking over because the *e*-vocative is considered too formal or archaic.

[8] Peterson (2007: 64–66) notes that the syncretism is better known, and possibly more frequent, with such benefactive applicatives than with either comitative or instrumental applicatives.

Analogously, the following examples from Hualapai show three occurrences of the suffix *-o/-wo/-yo*; it is an applicative in (a–b) and a causative in (c):

(382)   Hualapai (Yuman, USA; Ichihashi-Nakayama 1996: 228, 230)
    a.   *Tom-ch gwèviyám nyi-wi-·h   Mary gwa·m-ò-k-wi.*
          T.-SBJ car   REL-own-DEIC M.   drive-APPL-3-AUX
          'Tom is driving his pickup for Mary.'
    b.   *Jean-ch ba   ma-swa·d-o-y-k-i.*
          J.-SBJ PL.OBJ 3→2-sing-APPL-FUT-3-AUX
          'Jean will sing for you all.'
    c.   *Bos nya   nyi-háḏa-ch wà-nyi-miye·-wo-k-wi.*
          cat 1SG.PSR REL-pet-SBJ STEM-3→1-be.mad-CAUS-3-AUX
          'My cat makes me mad.'

These Hualapai clauses illustrate not only the phenomenon but also its cross-linguistically common distribution: it is with bivalent bases (a) and agentive monovalent bases (b) that *-o* or some of its allomorphs functions as applicative, and with patientive monovalent bases (c) it functions as causative. This distribution is parallel to the widespread restrictions on causatives and applicatives that are not syncretic: bivalent bases are the least (most) restrictive, and patientive monovalent bases are the most (least) restrictive, for applicatives (causatives).

Note in passing that the particular system of Hualapai shows some fluidity; consider the examples in (383), where the same verb 'cry' may be construed as either agentive (a) or patientive (b):

(383)   Hualapai (Ichihashi-Nakayama 1996: 236)
    a.   *Ma·-ch mi-i'-m   nyi-mi-·wo-'-i.*
          2SG-SBJ 2-say-DS 1→2-cry-APPL-1-AUX
          'You (SG) told [me to] and I cried for you (SG).'
    b.   *Ma·-ch nya   mi-mi·-wò-ng-wi-ny.*
          2SG-SBJ 1SG   2→1-cry-CAUS-2-AUX-PST
          'You (SG) made me cry.'

Causative-applicatives are documented for other indigenous languages of the Americas, but also for Austronesian and Australian languages. According to Austin (1997, 2005), in addition to Central/Eastern Australian languages that behave like Tauya and Hualapai, there are others that have dedicated causatives and/or applicatives, and yet others that draw the familiar line between agentive and patientive monovalent bases but exclude bivalent predicates from both causativization and applicativization.[9]

---

[9] A potential counterexample to the apparent generalization from the Hualapai and Australian data – "a strong tendency [...] to avoid the morphological causativization of active verbs, and to assign an applicative function to the causative morphemes found with active verbs" (Shibatani & Pardeshi 2002: 118) – comes from Mapudungun. In this language, *-m* and *-(e)l* causativize monovalent bases (albeit along a control, rather than agentivity, parameter; see Golluscio 2007), and the most widely used applicatives (especially with bivalent bases) are separative *-(ñ)ma* 'V away from' and appropinquative *-(l)(e)l* 'V towards'. Crucially, the control causative *-(e)l* and the appropinquative applicative *-(l)(e)l* seem to be historically related – but the details are complicated (Zúñiga 2014).

It seems that some of such multifunctional markers originate as causatives that extend their function (see Shibatani & Artawa 2015 for Balinese) – possibly most, or at least many, of them (Shibatani & Pardeshi 2002). Others, however, develop in the opposite direction. A case in point is Yucatec as analyzed in Lehmann (2015a); while the applicative -*t* (a) and the causative -*ans* (b) are in principle distinct, the former is occasionally found encroaching upon the latter's territory (c):

(384)   Yucatec Maya (Maya, Mexico and Belize; Lehmann 2015a: 1457)
      a. *Le   tsíimin-o'   t-u   y-áalkab-t-ah   le   beh-o'.*
          DEM   horse-DEIC PFV-3.SBJ EPE-run-APPL-COMPL   DEM   way-DEIC
          'That horse ran the path.' (applicative)
      b. *T-in   w-áalkab-ans-ah   le   tsíimin-o'.*
          PFV-1SG.SBJ   EPE-run-CAUS-COMPL   DEM   horse-DEIC
          'I raced that horse.' (causative)
      c. *Le   peek'-o'b-o'   k-u   y-áalkab-t-ik-o'b*
          DEM   dog-PL-DEIC   IPFV-3.SBJ   EPE-run-APPL/CAUS-INCOMPL-3PL
          le   k'éek'en-o'b-o'.
          DEM   pig-PL-DEIC
          'The dogs run behind the pigs / make the pigs run.'

That the border between causativization and applicativization is porous is something we briefly mention in Sections 2.1 and 2.2. In fact, Austin (1997, 2005) suggests treating both operations as special cases of a general process of predicate composition involving a functional predicate AFFECT that takes two arguments A and P and a base predicate with its own argument structure. The Yucatec Maya development illustrated in (384) would consist of the (a)-structure being reanalyzed as the (b)-structure in (385) below. With regard to the functional predicate AFFECT (with its two versions APPLY and CAUSE), the dogs and the pigs are always the A and the P, respectively; the reanalysis simply affects who is seen as the (main) runner. (The symbol *bX* represents an argument X of the base predicate.)

(385)   Argument structure reanalysis in predicate composition: APPL (bS) > CAUS (bS)
      a.   APPLY [dogs, pigs, *run* [dogs]]
          'the dogs run behind the pigs'
      b.   CAUSE [dogs, pigs, *run* [pigs]]
          'the dogs make the pigs run'

Analogously, instrumental applicatives provide a natural bridge between the two operations with bivalent base predicates, but in the opposite direction (386). The (a)-structure can easily be reanalyzed as the (b)-structure by merely changing the A of the base predicate: the reanalysis affects who is seen as the main cutter. As in (385), the A and P of the functional predicate remain unaltered:

(386)   Argument structure reanalysis in predicate composition: CAUS (bA bP) >
           APPL (bA bP)
    a.   CAUSE [I, knife, *cut* [knife, bread]]
         'I make the knife cut the bread'
    b.   APPLY [I, knife, *cut* [I, bread]]
         'I use the knife to cut the bread'

In other words, predicate composition of these kinds would always involve an
A and a P, but extending the applicative to cover the causative, as in (385), would
allow the functional P to become the S of the base predicate. Conversely,
extending the causative to cover the applicative, as in (386), would allow the
functional A to become the A of the base predicate.[10]

Malchukov (2017) briefly and tentatively suggests precisely the developments detailed above within the transitivizing cluster (see Figure 8.1 below,
adapted from Malchukov 2017: 24). This is an attractive, but still underdevel-
oped, proposal in the light of our current state of knowledge. More research is
needed here, especially on change directionality.

Figure 8.1 *The transitivizing cluster*

8.2.2   The Detransitivizing Cluster (= MID Cluster)

As discussed in Section 5.4, there are, in some languages, several
functions related to voice that may share a particular means of formal
expression. They can include passives and antipassives, direct reflexives and
reciprocals, and anticausatives; they can also include indirect reflexives,
autobenefactives, and causative-reflexives. This is most of the coverage of
the Greek middle inflection, for example; Spanish *se* and Russian *-sja/-s'* cover
a similar range. Such multifunctional markers may be the product of development paths leading to passives either from reflexives or from causatives. We
deal with these in turn.

8.2.2.1   The Path from REFL

The first way in which such clusters may arise consists in a reflexive
marker extending its functional range to encode passives and antipassives.
Consider in this context Example (387) from Spanish, which uses *se* in the
(direct) reflexive-reciprocal (a), like Latin. In addition to the participial passive

---

[10] With regard to the benefactive applicatives in (384)–(386), the bridge between the operations
   may be related to a reanalysis of an indirect and perhaps unintentional causer as a beneficiary.

inherited from the latter language (b), however, Spanish developed a *se*-passive (c) and a *se*-antipassive (d):[11]

(387)   Spanish

    a. *Se*   *vieron*   *en*   *el*   *espejo.*
       REFL/RECP see.3PL.PFV.PST in ART   mirror
       'They saw themselves / each other in the mirror.' (reflexive/reciprocal)

    b. *Las*   *pirámides*   *fueron* *construidas*   *por obreros*
       ART.F.PL pyramid(F).PL were build.PTCP.F.PL by workers
       hábiles.
       skilled
       'The pyramids were built by skilled workers.' (participial passive)

    c. *Las*   *pirámides*   *se*   *construyeron*   *en* *ese*
       ART.F.PL pyramid(F).PL PASS build.3PL.PFV.PST in that
       período.
       period
       'The pyramids were built in that period.' (*se*-passive)

    d. *Se*   *olvidó*   *de* *los* *libros.*
       ANTIP forgot.3SG of ART books
       'S/he forgot the books.' (*se*-antipassive)

The *se*-reflexive-reciprocal (a) is available for bivalent and trivalent predicates of suitable semantics and the verb agrees with its A-P subject (covert here: *ellos/ellas* 'they'). Speakers can disambiguate if needed by making the object explicit (*a sí mismos* 'themselves') to force a reflexive reading, or by adding a reciprocal sign of some sort (e.g., *unos a otros* 'each other / one another' or *mutuamente* 'reciprocally') to force a reciprocal interpretation. The *se*-passive (c) is available for 3rd-person Ps with syntactically bivalent and trivalent predicates, and the verb then agrees with its P subject (*las pirámides* 'the pyramids'); some speakers allow an overt A as an adjunct, but for many speakers the *se*-passive is agentless. It is more widely used than the participial passive in colloquial registers, especially in some tenses (e.g., the present), and shows some sensitivity to the formality of the lexical material present in the clause as well. The *se*-antipassive (d) is lexically restricted – only a limited number of bivalent verbs occur in the construction – and the verb then agrees with its A subject (covert here: *él/ella* 's/he'). With the appropriate verbs, however, the construction is widely used; in some varieties, the etymological active voice *olvidó los libros* 's/he forgot the books' is seldom used at all, being replaced by either (d) or the related construction of similar meaning *se le olvidaron los libros* (which relieves the A of responsibility even more strongly than (d)).

    There are usually intermediate stages between the reflexive and passive functions, however. The first extension of the reflexive on its way to the prototypical passive is to encroach upon the territory occupied by implicit

---

[11] We are glossing over the fact that Spanish *se* also occurs in an impersonal construction and in a range of other contexts (see Maldonado 2000).

reflexives and lexical reciprocals in some languages and, more in general, other predicates of the grooming and bodily action classes.[12] Examples of this are easy to find, especially in Slavic and Romance; suffice it to mention here the following instances of marking with the original reflexive *-sja/-s'* (we have glossed them REFL* for convenience here):

(388)   Russian (Haspelmath 2003: 224)
   a.   *Batseba   umyla-s'.*
        B.   washed.F.SG-REFL*
        'Bathsheba washed.'
   b.   *Učitel'   poversnul-sja.*
        teacher   turned.M.SG-REFL*
        'The teacher turned around.'
   c.   *Elizaveta   i   Marija   vstretili-s'.*
        E.   and   M.   met.PL-REFL*
        'Elizabeth and Mary met.'

Reflexive markers can later also extend their functional range to express anticausativity. This happened with Spanish *se* (e.g., *la puerta se abrió* 'the door opened') and with Russian *-sja/-s'* (e.g., *dver' otkryla-s'* 'the door opened'), but also with Finnish *-UtU* and German *sich*.[13] The following examples illustrate the same kind of extension of the Amharic reflexive/reciprocal *t(ə)-*:

(389)   Amharic (Amberber 2000: 315–316)
   a.   *Bər-u   (bə-t'inik'k'ak'e)   tə-kəffətə.*
        door-DEF   with-care/attention   ANTIC/PASS-open.PERF.3M
        'The door opened / was opened (with care)'. (anticausative/passive)
   b.   *T'ərmus-u   bə-lij-u   tə-səbbərə.*
        bottle-DEF   by-boy-DEF   PASS-break.PERF.3M
        'The bottle was broken by the boy.' (passive)

In this language, the prefix *t(ə)-* may nowadays either passivize or anticausativize a semantically bivalent predicate: the semantics of the verb in question (plus semantic content of other lexical elements in the clause, like adverbials such as 'with care') determines which function is instantiated, as shown in (390). In (a), 'open' allows a total omission of the agent, which in turn makes the anticausative reading possible. In (b), by contrast, 'cut' implies the use of an instrument by an agent, which excludes the anticausative reading, leaving only the passive interpretation:

(390)   Amharic (Amberber 2000: 314–315)
   a.   *Bər-u   tə-kəffətə.*
        door-DEF   ANTIC/PASS-open.PERF.3M
        'The door (was) opened.'

---

[12] Haspelmath (1987) labels some of these diathetical/argumental configurations "endoreflexive."
[13] See also Haspelmath (1987: 24–25) for more examples and Koivisto (1995) for a thorough discussion of Finnic.

b. *Gəməd-u*   *(bə-Aster)*   *tə-k'orrət'ə.*
   rope-DEF   by-A.   PASS-cut.PERF.3M
   'The rope was cut (by Aster).'

The third and last extension of the reflexive on its way to the prototypical passive is to encode the potential passive. The German reflexive marker *sich*, for instance, was extended to encode all but the last function:

(391)   German
          a. *Der*   *Mann*   *drehte*   *sich*   *um.*
             ART   man   turned[3SG]   REFL*   around
             'The man turned around.'
          b. *Die*   *Tür*   *öffnete*   *sich.*
             ART   door   opened[3SG]   ANTIC
             'The door opened.'
          c. *Das*   *Buch*   *liest*   *sich*   *leicht.*
             the   book   read.3SG   POT.PASS   eas(il)y
             'The book reads easily.'

The development from reflexive via anticausative to passive is best understood as an instance of semantic bleaching. First, agentivity is no longer required and the marker is made available to a subclass of monovalent predicates. Second, it is made available to a wider range of bivalent predicates as well, by re-installing an A, for instance with inanimate Ps, and later with all bivalent predicates (Haspelmath 1990, Gildea 2015). This development path is schematically summarized in Figure 8.2 below.

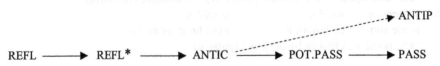

Figure 8.2 *The middle cluster I (path from REFL)*

The reflexive-antipassive polysemy is attested in a number of language families (most of which are related neither areally nor genealogically), including Slavic, Romance, Kartvelian, Chukotko-Kamchatkan, Manding, Cariban, Tacanan, and Pama-Nyungan (Janic 2010: 159f).[14] The following example from a language belonging to the latter group illustrates the polysemy:

(392)   Diyari (Austin 2011: 157, 159)
          a. *Nganhi*   *murruwa-tharri-yi.*
             1SG.NOM   scratch-REFL-PRS
             'I scratch myself.'

---

[14] Similarly, Diyari *-tharri* encodes reflexives, passives, and antipassives; it can also express continuous or continuative aspect without affecting syntactic valency (Austin 2011: Ch. 4.7). Dyirbal shows a reflexive-antipassive polysemy, with a "false reflexive" expressing unachieved or durative actions (Dixon 1972: 90–91).

b. *Nganhi   karlka-tharri-yi   nhangkangu   wilha-nhi.*
1SG.NOM   wait.for-ANTIP-PRS   3SG.F.LOC   woman-LOC
'I wait for the woman.'

Nevertheless, the path leading from the reflexive to the antipassive is not well understood yet; we have tentatively placed a dashed line in Figure 8.2 (itself adapted from Haspelmath 1987: 35, 1990: 54, and 2003: 225) leading directly to the antipassive, based on our impression of how old the antipassive extensions seem to be in Slavic and Romance, but this requires more research. One thing that antipassives and reflexives have in common is P-backgrounding. In antipassives, the backgrounded P is demoted because its referent is indefinite or generic: in reflexives, especially in the duplex-reflexives, the P is backgrounded and demoted because it is coreferential with the A.

Finally, note that the passive-antipassive syncretism of the "asymmetric" Slavic/Romance type seems to be more widespread than markers which passivize or antipassivize verbs equally productively.[15] General detransitivizers like Movima *kwey* (Section 4.2.1.3) and Paumarí *-a* (393) are rather difficult to find. (Observe that neither in Movima nor in Arawan is such a transitivizer identical to either the reflexive or reciprocal. The Movima REFL/RECP is *-chel*, and Jarawara and Paumarí use a different, non-verbal-marking construction to express reflexivity and reciprocity.)

(393)   Paumarí (Arawan, Brazil and Peru, Chapman & Derbyshire 1991: 298)
a. *Mamai-a   bi-soko-ki   hida   makari.*
mother-ERG   3SG-wash-NTH   DEM   clothes
'Mother is washing clothes.'
b. *Soko-a-ki   hida   mamai.*
wash-ANTIP-NTH   DEM   mother
'Mother is washing.' (antipassive)
c. *Soko-a-ki   hida   makari.*
wash-PASS-NTH   DEM   clothes
'The clothes are being washed.' (passive)

8.2.2.2   The Path from CAUS

The second major path relevant in the present context consists in causatives becoming passives (via causative-reflexives, as suggested, but not shown, by Keenan 1985 and Haspelmath 1990). In several 'give'-causatives found in several languages of Eurasia, moreover, a permissive reading of the causative seems to play a central role in this development.

Consider the multifunctionality of Cantonese *béi* 'give' as illustrated in (394) below. The *béi*-causative can have a coercive reading ('make X V'), but in the first development stage the subject loses part of its agency ('let X V') (a).

---

[15] See the Epilogue of Chapter 3 for more on passivization and antipassivization as imperfect mirror opposites.

The second stage, the causative-reflexive, consists of coreference between the causer and the base P to allow a passive interpretation while the P retains some agency (b). The last stage consists in removing the agency requirement altogether while simplifying the argument structure, thereby leading to a passive clause (c):[16]

(394)   Cantonese (Yap & Iwasaki 2007: 199–200)
          a. *Léih   dimgaai   mh   béi   ngóh   zou   zau   ne?*
             you   why   NEG CAUS me   early leave Q
             'Why won't you (SG) let me leave early?' (permissive causative)
          b. *(Léih)   chinkei   mhou   béi   yàhn   ganjung (léih) aa!*
             you   make.sure   don't   CAUS/PASS people follow   you   PART
             'Make sure you (SG) don't let anyone follow you!' (permissive causative-reflexive) /
             'Make sure you (SG) are not followed!' (passive)
          c. *Kéuih   chamjat   yauh béi   yàhn   laau.*
             s/he   yesterday again PASS people scold
             'S/he got scolded again yesterday.' (passive)

This development path, schematically represented in Figure 8.3 below, explains the rise of 'give'-passives not only in several Sinitic languages but also in a number of East and Southeast Asian languages with varying degrees of closeness to the core of the Sinosphere. In Evenki, for instance, the erstwhile causative -*v* has incorporated several other valency-increasing and valency-decreasing functions, including the passive and some fossilized uses, so that speakers created a new, productive, causative (-*vkAn*) (Knott 1995: 57).[17]

CAUS ─────────▶ CAUS-REFL ─────────▶ PASS

Figure 8.3 *The middle cluster II (path from CAUS)*

It is important to observe that there is no evidence that the causative-reflexive and autobenefactive functions of the classical Middle arose via this development path (which would suggest that the set of Middle inflections ultimately derive from a verb of giving that also marked reflexivity, or something similar). To judge from later developments within Indo-European, these particular functions are best seen as extensions of the Middle cluster originating in the reflexive (Section 8.2.2.1).

---

[16] The surface A *yàhn* '(by) people' when there is no specific A can later be removed, as in some Colloquial Mandarin constructions like *fángzi geĭ shāo-le* (house PASS burn-ASP) 'the house was burned down'; see Yap and Iwasaki (2007: 202).

[17] See Section 8.2.3 for one of the other valency-increasing functions, namely subject undergoer nucleativization, also in other languages (see also Malchukov 1993).

8.2.3   Other Syncretisms

The antipassive-applicative syncretism seems to be rare. For instance, the Central Alaskan Yupik marker *-(g)i* can occur on monovalent predicates like *kit'-* 'sink' (a–b) or bivalent predicates like *ner-* 'eat' (c–d), in which cases it is an applicative or a subjective undergoer nucleative with a malefactive reading; it promotes a negatively affected participant to core argument – to object in (d) and even to subject in (b).

(395)   Central Alaskan Yupik (Miyaoka 2012: 1080, 1100)
    a.   *Kicaq*   *kit'-uq.*
        anchor.ABS.SG   sink-IND.3SG
        'The anchor sank.' (monovalent active)
    b.   *Kic-i-aqa*   *kicaq.*
        sink-SUNUCL:MAL-IND.1SG→3SG   anchor.ABS.SG
        'I had the anchor sunk (me negatively affected).' (bivalent nucleative)
    c.   *Neqe-m*   *neqcaq*   *ner-aa.*
        fish-REL.SG   bait.ABS.SG   eat-IND.3SG→3SG
        'The fish ate the bait.' (bivalent active)
    d.   *Ner-i-anga*   *neqe-m*   *neqca-mnek.*
        eat-SUNUCL:MAL-IND.3SG→1SG   fish-REL.SG   bait-ABL.1SG.SG
        'The fish ate my bait (on me).' (trivalent undergoer nucleative)

With *allg-* 'tear' in (396), however, it is an antipassive. Note that the two distinct markers can co-occur on a verb (c):

(396)   Central Alaskan Yupik (Miyaoka 2012: 915, 1099)
    a.   *Angute-m*   *kuvya-ni*   *allg-aa.*
        man-REL.SG   net-ABS.SG.3SG.PSR   tear-IND.3SG→3SG
        'The man tears/tore his (own) net.' (bivalent active)
    b.   *Angun*   *kuvya-minek*   *allg-i-uq.*
        man.ABS.SG   net-ABL.SG.3SG.PSR   tear-ANTIP-IND.3SG
        'The man tore his (own) net.' (antipassive)
    c.   *Ini-i-gi-anga*   *neqerrlug-nek.*
        hang-ANTIP-SUNUCL-IND.3SG→1SG   dried.fish-ABL.PL
        'She is hanging out dried fish on/for me.' (bivalent undergoer nucleative)

Something similar happens in Inuktitut and West Greenlandic (397). The suffixes *-a* and *-si* are two of the antipassives of Greenlandic; the former works as a subjective undergoer nucleative in (a) while the latter is an impersonal marker in (b). (Note in passing the flagging – instrumental instead of absolutive for the S – and the indexing – 3SG instead of 3PL – in this latter, non-promotional, construction.)

(397)   West Greenlandic
    a.   *Hansi-p*   *natsi-q*   *anna-a-vaa.*
        H.-REL.SG   ringed.seal-ABS.SG   get.away-SUNUCL-IND.3SG→3SG
        'The ringed seal got away from Hansi.' (Fortescue 1984: 269)

b. *Qilalukka-nik   pui-si-vuq.*
whale-INS.PL   come.to.surface-IMPRS-IND.3SG
'There appeared whales on the surface [of the sea].' (Bok-Bennema
1991: 264)

Malchukov (2017) analyzes the Yupik data, particularly the *ut*-antipassive (for which Mithun 2000 proposes a slightly different explanation), as well as the *ine-/ena*-applicative in Chukchi (Mel'čuk 2006) and the Sliammon multifunctional suffix *-ʔəm* (Watanabe 2015). This author suggests that the development is to be understood in the light of the syntactic restrictions imposed by the syntaxes of the respective languages on the number of objects. In a first stage, the applicative promotes a non-patient to object, but the base patient must be demoted. In a second stage, the operation is purely demotional, not promoting any other argument to object, which is tantamount to antiapplicativization.

Passives do not seem to share a formal expression with applicatives, but they can be syncretic with, and possibly the source of, subjective undergoer nucleatives – which is unsurprising given the grammatical relations involved in both kinds of constructions. The Japanese so-called Direct and Indirect Passives are a case in point:

(398)   Japanese (Nobufumi Inaba, pers. comm.)

a. *Onna=ga   otoko=o   korosita*
woman=NOM   man=ACC   kill.PST
'The woman killed the man.'

b. *Otoko=ga   (onna=ni)   koros-are-ta*
man=NOM   woman=DAT   kill-PASS-PST
'The man was killed (by the woman).' (Direct Passive = prototypical passive)

c. *Otoko=ga   sinda.*
man=NOM   die.PST
'The man died.'

d. *Onna=ga   otoko=ni   sin-are-ta*
woman=NOM   man=DAT   die-SUNUCL:MAL-PST
'The man died on the woman.'
(Indirect Passive = malefactive subjective undergoer nucleative)

The causative-anticausative syncretism is especially striking, given the semantic and syntactic disparity of the two effects, and we have found only one clear case of it in the literature. In Ainu (399), the marker *-ke* may either remove an A, as in (b), or install one, as in (d). Note that semantically and syntactically bivalent *mak-* 'open' is explicitly marked in (a), while there is no marker for the monovalent variant of *ray-* 'die/kill'. (This may aid the speakers in keeping the two functions of this polysemous marker apart.)

(399)   Ainu (Tamura 2000: 211–212)

a. *mak-a*   c. *ray*
open-TR   die
'to open (TR)'   'to die'

b. *mak-ke*   d. *ray-ke*
open-ANTIC   die-CAUS
'to open (INTR)'   'to kill'

8.2.4   Summary

Even though different voices differ from each other in their origin, the attested syncretisms are not random. Some syncretisms are infrequent or perhaps even inexistent, probably for good reasons. Since prototypical causatives have little in common with either reflexives or antipassives – their etymology, their semantics, and their syntax are too disparate – such syncretisms do not seem to be attested. Several voices have their typical origin outside the voice domain, like reflexive and reciprocal markers (whether they occur in agent/patient- or duplex-diathesis constructions), while others, most notably the anticausative, always seem to evolve from other voices. Valency-increasing categories, like the causative and the applicative, predictably originate in elements that are capable of introducing an argument to the base structure because they have semantic and syntactic valency of their own, like verbs and adpositions. Valency-reducing categories, like the passive and the antipassive, may evolve from constructions that are structurally expedient because they already demote (pragmatically, morphologically, or syntactically) the argument that is to be backgrounded, like clauses built upon nominalized structures, or indefinite subject/object constructions. Such developments lead to constructions that show some multifunctionality, although speakers of several languages apparently tend to disambiguate ISCs/IOCs from their (anti-)passive product, which in turn often leads to distinct constructions in the end. Passives and antipassives may also evolve from constructions that are semantically expedient because they denote reduced transitivity while backgrounding the appropriate argument, like reflexives or some later development thereof. Such developments seem to lead to extensive and stable multifunctionality.

9   Revisiting Voice Theory

Klaiman's (1991) typological study drew linguists' attention to the important fact that many operations that manipulate clause structure are not mere variations on the theme of (anti-)passivization. One aspect of the book was particularly appealing at the time, and still is: the attempt to integrate apparently quite disparate phenomena, like the Greek Middle, the English Passive, the Cree Inverse, and the Tagalog Patient Voice, into an overarching theory. In Klaiman's proposal, voice is a formally coded form-meaning correspondence, which is what all these phenomena have in common. Her forms are modeled as a hierarchy of grammatical relations, which at the time were assumed to be constant or at least directly comparable across languages. Her meanings are what distinguishes the above phenomena: is the relevant parameter related to predicate semantics (i.e., the arguments' semantic roles), argument semantics (i.e., the arguments' animacy and speech-act role), and/or discourse function (i.e., the arguments' topicality)? Later studies found the specifics of Klaiman's control-and-affectedness analysis of predicate and clause semantics less useful than originally thought.[1] In particular, her proposal regarding the classical Middle did not directly contribute to a better understanding of that challenging phenomenon. Similarly, even though argument semantics and discourse functions undoubtedly play a role in shaping grammatical structures and patterns of use, later studies explored alternative ways in which they could be taken into account when dealing with grammatical voice and related phenomena.[2]

From a present-day perspective, another problem with Klaiman's book is its firm anchor in late-twentieth-century holistic typology. The study postulated not only specific analyses of morphosyntactic operations but also kinds of oppositions in which they stood in individual languages (so-called "voice systems") and even kinds of correlations between grammatical and lexical structure. In line with mainstream views of linguistic diversity prevalent at the time, Klaiman saw

---

[1] See, for instance, Croft (1994) for not only a critical answer to the widespread focus on (how to define and operationalize) the notions of control and affectedness but also an early formulation of an alternative that takes all relevant details of the causal chain seriously. Croft (2012) is the author's comprehensively articulated counterproposal in the same vein, which features an explicit modeling of the close connection between (causal-chain) argument structure and (aspecto-) temporal structure.

[2] Here we refer to the work conducted since the 1970s by the Leningrad / St. Petersburg Typology Group, as well as by Max-Planck-Institutes-orbiting scholars (including those that were Leipzig-based).

her structural types – basic voice, derived voice, and two subtypes of pragmatic voice – as bundles of organizational principles at work in the lexicon, the morphology, and the syntax of languages. Unlike much work on alignment and voice conducted in the 1980s, Klaiman's book and later articles aptly paid more than mere lip service to acknowledging how complex and varied those bundles can be. Nevertheless, most leading scholars working on linguistic diversity in the early twenty-first century have moved away from holistic typology and towards a different understanding of crucial notions like "system" and "language." By reframing the Greenbergian study of language universals as the exploration of the distribution of phenomena formulated as typological variables (many of which are increasingly seen as emergent), present-day typologists perform detailed analyses of patterns of language structure and language use that try not to assume correlations between different subdomains of a linguistic "system." Rather, the current emphasis is on a non-aprioristic and atomistic understanding of the individual elements and patterns found in natural languages of different areas and genealogical units, as well as on a cautious and principled exploration of connections between those elements and patterns.

Accordingly, voice theories like the one proposed in Klaiman (1991) are no longer as attractive as they admittedly were twenty-five years ago. Just as principled studies of morphology and syntax nowadays avoid using imprecise impressionistic labels like "ergative languages" as technical terms, it is no longer apposite to describe, say, varieties of Cree as instances of "inverse languages" – at least not if by the latter one understands languages that show fundamentally different voice oppositions when compared to Greek, English, and Tagalog. Like other Algonquian languages, Cree has causatives and applicatives; it has a passive and an antipassive (both of them non-prototypical), as well as a transitivity discord construction; and its direct–inverse opposition does not seem to mirror a Philippine-type agent–patient voice opposition (regarding either its conditioning factors or its syntactic consequences). From a descriptive perspective, the task is to characterize the diathetical operations of Cree in as much detail as possible, including their frequency and conditions of use in all the surviving registers of the language. From a typological perspective, there are a number of interesting voice-related questions. Given that Cree has a particular kind of causative, for instance, what else do we know about the language's structure, both within and outside the realm of voice? How do the Cree applicatives differ from similar constructions, like the applicatives found in Eskimoan, Bantu, or Pama-Nyungan, as well as from related phenomena, like the English dative alternation? How has the current division of labor of antipassives and transitivity discord constructions in Algonquian languages come about? The present book provides analysts with a theory and a survey that help them tackle precisely these tasks; a thorough investigation of voice typology lies beyond the scope of the present study, however.

Critical readers may question the adequacy of the theory advanced in this book, especially against the background of wanting to eschew aprioristic methodologies and views. Are our voices and related operations justifiable vantage points from which to explore these structural and functional domains, that is, are they bottom-up enough? More generally, is the notion of voice as used in this book useful for language description, linguistic typology, and linguistic theory?

We would like to claim that both questions receive a positive answer. As to how adequate our prototype voices and operations are, it is true that, from a structural viewpoint, diathetical operations may be simple (i.e., they involve a change that affects only one argument) or complex (i.e., they involve a change involving two or more arguments). For instance, German applicativization as shown in (400) is simple; it merely consists of promoting *dieses Haus* 'this house' from prepositional object in (a) to direct object in (b):

(400)   German
    a. *Sie*   *wohn-en*   *in*   *diesem*   *Haus.*
        3PL.NOM dwell-3PL in   this.DAT.SG house
        'They dwell in this house.'
    b. *Sie*   *be-wohn-en*   *dieses*   *Haus.*
        3PL.NOM APPL-dwell-3PL this.ACC.SG house
        'They inhabit this house.'

German applicativization as shown in (401), however, is a complex operation; in order to turn (a) into (b), *das Gelände* 'the area' is promoted from prepositional adjunct to direct object and *Häuser* 'houses' is demoted from direct object to prepositional adjunct at the same time:

(401)   German
    a. *Er*   *bau-te*   *Häuser*   *(auf dem*   *Gelände).*
        3SG.M.NOM build-PST[3SG] houses[ACC] on ART.DAT area
        'He built houses (in the area).'
    b. *Er*   *be-bau-te*   *das Gelände (mit Häuser-n).*
        3SG.M.NOM APPL-build-PST[3SG] ART area with houses-DAT
        'He covered the area with buildings.'

Antipassivization as sometimes understood (e.g., in Janic 2016), several duplex-voice operations, and some instances of non-prototypical passivization consist of single syntactic operations, like the applicativization shown in (400). Several other instances of prototypical (anti-)passivization, prototypical (anti-)causativization, nucleativization, and the agent–patient voice alternation consist of two syntactic operations, like the applicativization shown in (401). Uncoded alternations also fall into single-operation and multiple-operation subtypes.

There are probably different reasons why some voice operations are simple while others are complex. Since no new subject or object is introduced in duplex-diathesis reflexives and reciprocals, for example, they can be simple operations. By contrast, most complex operations can be explained via restrictions to the number and kind of arguments permitted in a clause. For instance, either introducing a new argument as a subject or promoting another argument to subject will virtually always lead to the demotion of the base subject, because languages do not normally allow two-subject clauses. Something similar usually happens regarding direct/primary objects and indirect/secondary objects, which in many languages are at most one per clause. (This is the case in German, where clauses with two direct objects are severely restricted, which therefore leads to instances of applicativization like the one illustrated in (401) being complex.)[3]

In order to cover the semantic and structural space, we work not only with prototypical operations, most of which have been identified and analyzed in the linguistic literature, but also almost exclusively with traditional labels. Our presentation of the theory, then, does include a typology, claiming as it does that some operations and some operation combinations are common (e.g., proto-typical and agentless passives) while others are less frequent (e.g., some non-prototypical causatives and undergoer nucleatives) and yet others unattested (e.g., operations that install an agentive object). In other words, to judge from the extant literature, most of our prototypes are reasonably well documented within their semantic-structural domain, even though they noticeably differ as to their relative frequency. Bearing in mind that much systematic typologizing of voice alternations is still work in progress, adaptations of the current version of the theory in terms of what the best prototypes are would be easy to implement and would not invalidate the general approach espoused here.

The main operations discussed in the book are summarized in Tables 9.1 (involving A and P) and 9.2 (involving G) below. (The symbol X means that the status of that argument is not altered when compared with its status in some vantage point, e.g., an agent diathesis. The symbol → means that the result of the operation is a particular diathesis.) Remember from Chapters 2 to 7 that the labels for many diathetical operations cover more than one possible combination of A-, P-, and G-related operations. The tables do not include non-prototypical operations that are syntactically neutral (e.g., agentive causativization), but they do include uncoded operations. (For PASS, for instance, read both 'passivization' and 'passive-like alternation'. (Anti-)applicativization also covers the bene-factive alternation and the locative "preposition drop" alternation.)

Operations that alter argument structure appear as peripheral in Table 9.1, involving as they do the installment and/or the removal of arguments. Causati-vization installs an A, prototypically without affecting the P (if any), and the causer is the new subject in languages of the familiar European type; anticausativization removes the A, promoting the P from object to subject in languages with a default two-argument clause instantiating an agent diathesis.

---

[3] A handful of German verbs allow two objects in the accusative (e.g., *abfragen* 'prompt, test', *angehen* 'concern', *lehren* 'teach', *unterrichten* 'instruct, tutor', *kosten* 'cost', and *nennen* 'call (sbdy. sthg.)'), and with such verbs it is possible to find clauses with two direct objects (although not all of them passivize regularly). Note, however, that in some colloquial varieties of the language some of them (e.g., *lehren* and *kosten*) may take an indirect object in the dative for the animate non-agentive argument.

Table 9.1 *Diathetical operations involving A and P (simplified)*

Effect on A \ Effect on P	Installment (×)	Promotion (⇨C ⇧C)	Demotion (C⇨ ⇩C)	Removal (⇩C)
Installment (⇨C)	CAUS →	APPL →		
Promotion (⇨C ⇧C) ×			ANTIP →	
Demotion (C⇨ ⇩C)	REFL/RECP* TD →	PASS →	NI (boxed) / TD (boxed)	AV →
Removal (⇩C)		PV →	ANTIC →	ANTIA →

⇨C: promotion into core
⇧C: promotion within core
C⇨: demotion from core
⇩C: demotion within core

Applicativization is more diverse: it either installs or promotes a P as object in languages of the familiar European type, prototypically without affecting the A; the infrequent and ill-understood antiapplicativization *sensu stricto* removes a P from semantic argument structure.

Operations that alter syntactic structure alone appear as more central in Table 9.1; they involve only the promotion and/or demotion of arguments. Passivization demotes the A out of the core and is prototypically P-promotional (but non-promotional passivization appears as well in the table). Antipassivization demotes the P out of the core and either promotes the A from object to subject or leaves it unaltered. The operations leading from agent diathesis to patient diathesis and vice versa simply promote and demote the A and the P within the clause core.

Other operations in the central area of the table are less straightforward. From a purely syntactic perspective, some well-known instances of nominal incorporation (NI) are special cases of antipassivization *sensu latiore*, since they cause the demotion of the P out of the core. (Remember from Section 7.3 that other instances are applicatives and yet others are valency-neutral.) All Transitivity Discord Constructions target the P, but they do so with diverse syntactic consequences: some do not affect its status and belong to the very center of the table, whereas others demote the P more or less extremely and appear a little to the right. Lastly, reflexivization and reciprocalization can leave valency unaltered and are therefore depicted in the table center, but to the extent that some of such constructions are not valency-neutral (viz., those that instantiate some version of the duplex diathesis), they may encroach upon the neighboring (anti-)passive territory.

We addressed some operations involving a recipient- or goal-like argument rather tangentially, but they are by no means marginal (see Malchukov et al. 2010 and Malchukov & Comrie 2015a, 2015b). We mentioned some of them in Chapter 2 in the context of applicativization, others in Chapter 4, where the Philippine-type alternations can promote or demote Gs, and yet others in Chapters 6 and 7, in the context of external possessor constructions and nominal incorporation constructions, respectively. The dative alternation (DA) and the locative alternation (LA) are located at the center of Table 9.2., since they remap the arguments in T and G functions to grammatical relations without installing or removing any of them from the semantic argument structure.

Table 9.2 *Diathetical operations involving G (simplified)*

	G-installment	G-promotion	✗	G-demotion	G-removal
A-pro-/ de-motion	→GV/PASS			→AV	
✗	EP		DA/LA		
P-pro-/ de-motion		→APPL/NI		→PV	

As to how adequate our notion of voice is in the first place, let us zoom in on five salient hallmarks of the theory presented here. First, voice is not a Eurocentric, or Hellenocentric, grammatical category. (If it were, the classical Middle would most likely not pose many problems, either terminological or analytical.) By taking particular features of the active–passive opposition as the point of departure and abstracting away not only from the morphological but also from several semantic and syntactic specifics of the old European voices, it is possible to identify significantly similar and interestingly different voices in many languages related neither areally nor genealogically to Indo-European. Second, we distinguish between prototypical and non-prototypical diathetical operations. This is, as mentioned above, largely a terminological choice. Rather than working without prototypes altogether, we think that future refinements and developments of a functional-typological theory of voice are likely to merely propose prototypes that differ from ours slightly or markedly. Third, we distinguish between coded and uncoded operations. This is essentially a terminological choice – one we made in the present study in order not to break unnecessarily with Western linguistic tradition. Crucially, we capture comparable syntactic phenomena in languages of different morphologies, as well as related phenomena in the same languages, whether there is morphological marking on the predicate or not. Fourth, we distinguish between diatheses and voices on the one hand and diathetical and voice operations on the other. This is less inconsequential than it may seem: by focusing too strongly on (anti-)passivization, many studies neglected not only other operations but also constructions that are significant for the study of voice despite not showing alternations with the same predicates (including clauses headed by *activa*, *passiva*, and *media tantum*, either monovalent or bivalent). Changing semantic argument structure, changing syntactic clause structure, and not changing either but simply showing a different argument realization pattern are all relevant phenomena on a multidimensional continuum, and our theory does not a priori favor some of these over the others – even though we do devote ample space to many coded alternations and their variation in the book. Fifth, this theory allows us both to exclude phenomena like the syntax-neutral direct–inverse opposition of verb forms (unlike Klaiman 1991) and to integrate phenomena like causatives and applicatives (unlike Mel'čuk 2006). Consequently, grammatical voice emerges as a category that is simultaneously coherent and broad enough. Including operations that do not alter syntactic clause structure as representing a different kind of voice operation is not useful if the category is to be conceptually simple yet analytically powerful. Jettisoning operations that alter semantic argument structure is not consistent if they also alter syntactic clause structure, and the diachrony of several operations suggests that all diathetical operations are best studied together.

Finally, it is in order to mention two obvious inadequacies of the theory presented here, which are not exclusive of the functional-typological study of grammatical voice. We define voice as a morphologically marked semantic-syntactic correspondence but model both semantics and syntax in a rather loose way.

With respect to semantics, recent studies have aptly pointed out that a simple semantic-role-based model of argument realization is inadequate on several grounds (e.g., Levin & Rappaport Hovav 2005, Croft 2012, Kittilä & Zúñiga 2014). A more sophisticated modeling of the causal chain and the exact semantic relations between the predicate and its arguments, perhaps also integrating the domain of aspectuality, would constitute an important refinement that would lead to a more appropriate formulation of semantic argument structure; our version thereof is to be regarded as a simplified approximation of what is necessary. With respect to syntax, the problem of how to handle grammatical relations, both within and across languages, is still recalcitrant from a functional-typological perspective (see, e.g., Polinsky 2012). Since diathesis is defined as a semantics-syntax correspondence, there is no way around the issue of how clause structure is modeled. We have not tried to solve the fundamental problem here but have merely worked with familiar labels (e.g., subject, object, adjunct) to denote notions whose exact definitions and status have to be articulated by theories of syntax and theories of grammar. Our version of syntactic structure here is to be regarded as a simplified approximation of what is currently possible.

References

Aarts, B. (2007). *Syntactic Gradience: The Nature of Grammatical Indeterminacy.* Oxford: Oxford University Press.

Abraham, W. (2006). Passivization and typology: Form vs. function. A confined survey into the research status quo. In: Abraham, W. & Leisiö, L., eds., *Passivization and Typology: Form and Function.* Amsterdam: John Benjamins, pp. 1–29.

Adamou, E. (2014). L'antipassif en ixcatèque. *Bulletin de la Société de Linguistique de Paris* 109.1: 373–396.

Aikhenvald, A. (2000). Transitivity in Tariana. In: Dixon, R. M. W. & Aikhenvald, A., eds., *Changing Valency: Case Studies in Transitivity.* Cambridge: Cambridge University Press, pp. 145–172.

(2017). Polysynthetic structures of Lowland Amazonia. In: Fortescue, M.; Mithun, M. & Evans, N., eds., *The Oxford Handbook of Polysynthesis.* Oxford: Oxford University Press, pp. 284–311.

Aikhenvald, A. & Dixon, R. M. W. (1999). Other small families and isolates. In: Dixon, R. M. W. & Aikhenvald, A., eds., *The Amazonian Languages.* Cambridge: Cambridge University Press, pp. 341–384.

Aissen, J. (1997). On the syntax of obviation. *Language* 73.4: 705–750.

(1999). Markedness and subject choice in Optimality Theory. *Natural Language & Linguistic Theory* 17.4: 673–711.

(2003). Differential object marking: Iconicity vs. economy. *Natural Language & Linguistic Theory* 21.3: 435–483.

Aldridge, E. (2004). Ergativity and word order in Austronesian languages. Ph.D. dissertation, Cornell University.

(2012). Antipassive and ergativity in Tagalog. *Lingua* 122: 192–203.

Alexiadou, A. (2010). On the morpho-syntax of (anti-)causative verbs. In: Rappaport Hovav, M., Doron, E. & Sichel, I., eds., *Syntax, Lexical Semantics and Event Structure.* Oxford: Oxford University Press, pp. 177–203.

Alexiadou, A. & Doron, E. (2012). The syntactic construction of two non-active voices: Passive and middle. *Journal of Linguistics* 48: 1–34.

Alsina, À. (1992). On the argument structure of causatives. *Linguistic Inquiry* 23.4: 517–555.

Alsina, À. & Mchombo, S. (1993). Object asymmetries and the Chicheŵa applicative construction. In: Mchombo, S., ed., *Theoretical Aspects of Bantu Grammar 1.* Stanford: CSLI Publications, pp. 17–45.

Amberber, M. (2000). Valency-changing and valency-encoding devices in Amharic. In: Dixon, R. M. W. & Aikhenvald, A., eds., *Changing Valency: Case Studies in Transitivity.* Cambridge: Cambridge University Press, pp. 312–332.

(2002). *Verb Classes and Transitivity in Amharic.* Munich: Lincom Europa.

Andersen, S. & Andersen, T. D. (2005). Semantic analysis of the Moronene verbal prefix *moN-*. In: Arka, I. W. & Ross, M., eds., *The Many Faces of Austronesian Voice Systems: Some New Empirical Studies*. Canberra: Pacific Linguistics, pp. 243–278.

Anderson, N. & Wade, M. (1988). Ergativity and control in Folopa. *Language and Linguistics in Melanesia* 19.1–2: 1–16.

Arka, I. W. (2000). Voice and being core: Evidence from (Eastern) Indonesian languages. Paper read at Austronesian Formal Linguistics Association 7 in Amsterdam, May.

(2002). Voice systems in the Austronesian languages of Nusantara: Typology, symmetricality and undergoer orientation. Paper read at the 10th National Symposium of the Indonesian Linguistics Society, Bali, July.

(2009). The core-oblique distinction and core index in some Austronesian languages of Indonesia. Keynote paper presented at the International Association of Linguistic Typology VI conference, Padang, Indonesia, 21–25 July 2005.

Arka, I. W. & Kosmas, J. (2005). Passive without passive morphology? Evidence from Manggarai. In: Arka, I. W. & Ross, M., eds., *The Many Faces of Austronesian Voice Systems: Some New Empirical Studies*. Canberra: Pacific Linguistics, pp. 87–117.

Arka, I. W. & Manning, C. (1998). Voice and grammatical relations in Indonesian: A new perspective. In: Butt, M. & King, T. H., eds., *Proceedings of the LFG98 Conference*. Stanford: CSLI Publications, pp. 45–69.

(2008). Voice and grammatical relations in Indonesian: A new perspective. In: Austin, P. & Musgrave, S., eds., *Voice and Grammatical Relations in Austronesian Languages*. Stanford: CSLI Publications, pp. 45–69.

Arka, I. W. & Ross, M. (2005). Introduction. In: Arka, I. W. & Ross, M., eds., *The Many Faces of Austronesian Voice Systems: Some New Empirical Studies*. Canberra: Pacific Linguistics, pp. 1–17.

Arka, I. W. & Wouk, F. (2014). Voice-related constructions in the Austronesian languages of Flores. In: Arka, I. W. & Indrawati, N. L. K. M., eds., *Argument Realisations and Related Constructions in Austronesian Languages*. Canberra: Asia-Pacific Linguistics, pp. 313–333.

Arkadiev, P. & Letuchiy, A. (2009). The syntax and semantics of event structure and Adyghe causatives. Ms., Russian Academy of Sciences.

Arnott, D. W. (1970). *The Nominal and Verbal Systems of Fula*. London: Oxford University Press.

Asher, R. E. & Kumari, T. C. (1997). *Malayalam*. London: Routledge.

Aspillera, P. (1969). *Basic Tagalog for Foreigners and Non-Tagalogs*. Rutland, VT: Tuttle.

Atoyebi, J. D. (2015). Valency classes in Yorùbá. In: Malchukov, A. & Comrie, B., eds., *Valency Classes in the World's Languages, Vol. 1: Introducing the Framework, and Case Studies from Africa and Eurasia*. Berlin: Mouton de Gruyter, pp. 299–325.

Austin, P. (1981). *A Grammar of Diyari, South Australia*. Cambridge: Cambridge University Press.

(1982). Transitivity and cognate objects in Australian languages. In: Thompson, S. & Hopper, P., eds., *Syntax and Semantics, Vol. 15: Studies in Transitivity*. New York: Academic Press, pp. 37–47.

(1997). Causatives and applicatives in Australian Aboriginal languages. In: Matsumura, K. and Hayashi, T., eds., *The Dative and Related Phenomena.* Tokyo: Hitsuji Shobo, pp. 165–225.

(2001). Verbs, valence and voice in Balinese, Sasak and Sumbawan. *La Trobe Working Papers in Linguistics* 11.3: 47–71.

(2005). Causative and applicative constructions in Australian Aboriginal languages. Ms., University of London. Available online at hrelp.org/aboutus/staff/peter_austin/AustinCausatives.pdf.

(2011). A grammar of Diyari, South Australia. Ms., University of London. Available online at academia.edu/2491078/A_Grammar_of_Diyari_South_Australia.

(2012). Too many nasal verbs: Dialectal variation in the voice system of Sasak. *NUSA: Linguistic Studies of Languages in and around Indonesia* 54: 29–46. Available online at http://repository.tufs.ac.jp/bitstream/10108/71804/2/nusa5403.pdf.

Baker, M. (1988). *Incorporation: A Theory of Grammatical Function Changing.* Chicago: The University of Chicago Press.

(1999). Body parts, incorporation, and argument structure. In: Payne, D. & Barshi, I., eds., *External Possession.* Amsterdam: John Benjamins, pp. 293–324.

Barber, E. (1975). Voice – Beyond the passive. In: Cogen, C., Thompson, H., Thurgood, G., Whistler, K. & Wright, J., eds., *Proceedings of the First Annual Meeting of the Berkeley Linguistics Society.* Berkeley: University of California Press, pp. 16–24.

Beck, D. (2009). A taxonomy and typology of Lushootseed valency-increasing suffixes. *International Journal of American Linguistics* 75.4: 533–569.

Bell, S. (1983). Advancements and ascensions in Cebuano. In: Perlmutter, D., ed., *Studies in Relational Grammar.* Chicago: University of Chicago Press, pp. 143–218.

Benton, R. (1967). *An Introduction to the Trukese Language for Speakers of English.* Honolulu: Pacific and Asian Linguistics Institute, University of Hawaii.

Bickel, B. (2011). Grammatical relations typology. In: Song, J. J., ed., *The Oxford Handbook of Linguistic Typology.* Oxford: Oxford University Press, pp. 399–444.

Bickel, B. & Gaenszle, M. (2015). First person objects, antipassives, and the political history of the Southern Kirant. *Journal of South Asian Languages and Linguistics* 2.1: 63–86.

Bickel, B. & Zúñiga, F. (2017). The 'word' in polysynthetic languages: phonological and syntactic challenges. In: Fortescue, M., Mithun, M. & Evans, N., eds., *The Oxford Handbook of Polysynthesis.* Oxford: Oxford University Press, pp. 158–185.

Biggs, A. (2014). Passive variation in the dialects of Northwest British English. Ms., University of Cambridge.

Bittner, M. (1987). On the semantics of the Greenlandic antipassive and related constructions. *International Journal of American Linguistics* 53.2: 194–231.

(1994). *Case, Scope, and Binding.* Dordrecht: Kluwer.

Blake, F. R. (1925). *A Grammar of the Tagalog Language, the Chief Native Idiom of the Philippine Islands*. New Haven, CT: The American Oriental Society.

Blevins, J. P. (2003). Passives and impersonals. *Journal of Linguistics* 39.3: 473–520.

Bloomfield, L. (1917). *Tagalog Texts with Grammatical Analysis*. Urbana, IL: University of Illinois.

(1957). *Eastern Ojibwa. Grammatical Sketch, Texts and Word List*. Ann Arbor: The University of Michigan Press.

(1962). *The Menomini Language*. New Haven, CT: Yale University Press.

Blust, R. (2002). Notes on the history of 'focus' in Austronesian languages. In: Wouk, F. & Ross, M., eds., *The History and Typology of Western Austronesian Voice Systems*. Canberra: Pacific Linguistics, pp. 63–78.

(2003). Three notes on early Austronesian morphology. *Oceanic Linguistics* 42.2: 438–478.

Boas, H. (2003). Towards a lexical-constructional account of the locative alternation. Available online at sites.la.utexas.edu/hcb/files/2011/02/Boas2003a_Locative_Alternation.pdf.

Bobaljik, J. D. & Branigan, P. (2006). Eccentric agreement and multiple case-checking. In: Johns, A., Massam, D. & Ndayiragije, J., eds., *Ergativity: Emerging Issues*. Dordrecht: Springer, pp. 47–77.

Bok-Bennema, R. (1991). *Case and Agreement in Inuit*. Berlin: Foris.

Borgman, D. (1991). *Dicionário Sanumá*. Boa Vista: Missão Evangélica da Amazônia.

Borsley, R., Tallerman, M. & Willis, D. (2007). *The Syntax of Welsh*. Cambridge: Cambridge University Press.

Bosse, S., Bruening, B. & Yamada, M. (2012). Affected experiencers. *Natural Language & Linguistic Theory* 30.4: 1185–1230.

Bossong, G. (1985). *Empirische Universalienforschung: differentielle Objektmarkierung in den neuiranischen Sprachen*. Tübingen: Narr.

(1991). Differential object marking in Romance and beyond. In: Wanner, D. & Kibbee, D., eds., *New Analyses in Romance Linguistics*. Amsterdam: John Benjamins, pp. 143–170.

(1998). Le marquage différentiel de l'objet dans les langues d'Europe. In: Feuillet, J., ed., *Actance et valence*. Berlin: Mouton de Gruyter, 193–258.

Bowden, J. (2001). *Taba: Description of a South Halmahera language*. Canberra: Pacific Linguistics.

Bresnan, J. & Moshi, L. (1990). Object asymmetries in comparative Bantu syntax. *Linguistic Inquiry* 21.2: 147–185.

Bresnan, J., Cueni, A., Nikitina, T. & Baayen, R. H. (2007). Predicting the dative alternation. In: Boume, G., Kraemer, I. & Zwarts, J., eds., *Cognitive Foundations of Interpretation*. Amsterdam: Royal Netherlands Academy of Science, pp. 69–94.

Bril, I. (1997). Split ergativity in the Nêlêmwa language. In: Van der Hulst, H., Klamer, M., Odé, C. & Stokhof, W., eds., *Proceedings of the Seventh International Conference of Austronesian Linguistics*. Amsterdam: Rodopi, 377–394.

Bromley, M. (1981). *A Grammar of Lower Grand Valley Dani*. Canberra: Australian National University.

Brown, D., Chumakina, M. & Corbett, G., eds. (2013). *Canonical Morphology and Syntax*. Oxford: Oxford University Press.

Bruce, L. (1984). *The Alambak Language of Papua New Guinea (East Sepik)*. Canberra: Pacific Linguistics.

Bruening, B. & Tran, T. (2015). The nature of the passive, with an analysis of Vietnamese. *Lingua* 165.A: 133–172.

Bryant, M. G. (1999). Aspects of Tirmaga grammar. Ph.D. dissertation, University of Texas.

Bugenhagen, R. D. (1995). *A Grammar of Mangap-Mbula: An Austronesian Language of Papua New Guinea*. Canberra: Pacific Linguistics.

Burch, L. (1980). *Ute Reference Grammar*. Ignacio, CO: Ute Press.

Chandralal, D. (2010). *Sinhala*. Amsterdam: John Benjamins.

Chapman, S. & Derbyshire, D. C. (1991). Paumari. In: Derbyshire, D. & Pullum, G., eds., *Handbook of Amazonian Languages, Vol. 3*. Berlin: Mouton de Gruyter, pp. 161–352.

Charney, J. O. (1993). *A Grammar of Comanche*. Lincoln: University of Nebraska Press.

Chomsky, N. (1965). *Aspects of the Theory of Syntax*. Cambridge, MA: The MIT Press.

Chung, S. (1976). On the subject of two passives in Indonesian. In: Li, C., ed., *Subject and Topic*. New York: Academic Press, pp. 57–98.

(1977). Maori as an accusative language. *The Journal of the Polynesian Society* 86.3: 355–370.

Churchward, C. M. (1953). *Tongan Grammar*. New York: Academic Press.

Clayre, B. (2005). Kelabitic languages and the fate of 'focus': Evidence from the Kerayan. In: Arka, I. W. & Ross, M., eds., *The Many Faces of Austronesian Voice Systems: Some New Empirical Studies*. Canberra: Pacific Linguistics, pp. 17–57.

Cole, P., Hermon, G. & Yanti (2008). Voice in Malay/Indonesian. *Lingua* 118.10: 1500–1553.

Comrie, B. (1973). The ergative: Variations on a theme. *Lingua* 32.2: 239–253.

(1975). Causatives and universal grammar. *Transactions of the Philological Society* 1974: 1–32.

(1976). The syntax of causative constructions. In: Shibatani, M., ed., *Syntax and Semantics, Vol. 6: The Grammar of Causative Constructions*. New York: Academic Press, pp. 261–312.

(1981). *Language Universals and Linguistic Typology*. Oxford: Blackwell.

(1985). Causative verb formation and other verb-deriving morphology. In: Shopen, T., ed., *Language Typology and Syntactic Description, Vol. III: Grammatical Categories and the Lexicon*. Cambridge: Cambridge University Press, pp. 309–348.

(1986). Markedness, grammar, people, and the world. In: Eckman, F., Moravcsik, E. & Wirth, J., eds., *Markedness*. New York: Plenum Press, pp. 85–106.

(1988). Passive and voice. In: Shibatani, M. ed., *Passive and Voice*. Amsterdam: John Benjamins, pp. 9–23.

(2000). Valency-changing derivations in Tsez. In: Dixon, R. M. W. & Aikhenvald, A., eds., *Changing Valency: Case Studies in Transitivity*. Cambridge: Cambridge University Press, pp. 360–374.

Comrie, B. & Polinsky, M., eds., (1993). *Causatives and Transitivity*. Amsterdam: John Benjamins.

Comrie, B., Khalilov, M. & Khalilova, Z. (2015). Valency and valency classes in Bezhta. In: Malchukov, A. & Comrie, B., eds., *Valency Classes in the World's Languages, Vol. 1*. Berlin: Mouton de Gruyter, pp. 541–570.

Cooreman, A. (1994). A functional typology of antipassives. In: Fox, B. & Hopper, P., eds., *Voice: Form and Function*. Amsterdam: John Benjamins, pp. 49–88.

Cooreman, A., Fox, B. & Givón, T. (1984). The discourse definition of ergativity. *Studies in Language* 8.1: 1–34.

Cowell, A. & Moss, A. (2008). *The Arapaho Language*. Boulder: The University Press of Colorado.

Craig, C. & Hale, K. (1988). Relational preverbs in some languages of the Americas: Typological and historical perspectives. *Language* 64.2: 312–344.

Cranmer, D. (1976). *Derived Intransitivity*. Tübingen: Niemeyer.

Creissels, D. (2007). Impersonal and anti-impersonal constructions: a typological approach. Ms., University of Lyon.

(2010). Benefactive applicative periphrases: A typological approach. In: Zúñiga, F. & Kittilä, S., eds., *Benefactives and Malefactives: Typological Perspectives and Case Studies*. Amsterdam: John Benjamins, pp. 29–69.

(2014). P-lability and radical P-alignment. *Linguistics* 52.4: 911–944.

(2015). Valency properties of Mandinka verbs. In: Malchukov, A. & Comrie, B., eds., *Valency Classes in the World's Languages, Vol. 1: Introducing the Framework, and Case Studies from Africa and Eurasia*. Berlin: Mouton de Gruyter, pp. 221–260.

Creissels, D. & Nouguier-Voisin S. (2008). Valency-changing operations in Wolof and the notion of co-participation. In: König, E. & Gast, V., eds., *Reciprocal and Reflexives: Theoretical and Typological Explanations*. Berlin: Mouton de Gruyter, pp. 289–305.

Croft, W. (1994). Voice: Beyond control and affectedness. In: Fox, B. & Hopper, P., eds., *Voice: Form and Function*. Amsterdam: John Benjamins, pp. 89–117.

(2001). *Radical Construction Grammar: Syntactic Theory in Typological Perspective*. Oxford: Oxford University Press.

(2007). Beyond Aristotle and gradience: A reply to Aarts. *Studies in Language* 31.2: 409–430.

(2012). *Verbs: Aspect and Causal Structure*. Oxford: Oxford University Press.

Croft, W., Shyldkrot, H. B.-Z. & Kemmer, S. (1987). Diachronic semantic processes in the middle voice. In: Giacalone Ramat, A., Carruba, O. & Bernini, G., eds. *Papers from the 7th International Conference on Historical Linguistics*. Amsterdam: John Benjamins, pp. 179–192.

Crowley, T. (1990). *Beach-la-Mar to Bislama: The Emergence of a National Language in Vanuatu*. Oxford: Clarendon Press.

Curnow, T. J. (1997). A grammar of Awa Pit (Cuaiquer). An indigenous language of South-Western Colombia. Ph.D. thesis, Australian National University.

Dahlstrom, A. (1986). Plains Cree morphosyntax. Ph.D. dissertation, University of California at Berkeley.

(2009). OBJ$_\Theta$ without OBJ: a typology of Meskwaki objects. In Butt, M. & King, T. H., eds., *Proceedings of the LFG09 Conference*. Stanford: CSLI Publications, pp. 222–239.

Daniel, M. Maisak, T. & Merdanova, S. (2012). Causatives in Agul. In: Suihkonen, P., Comrie, B. & Solovyev, V., eds., *Argument Structure and Grammatical Relations: A Crosslinguistic Typology*. Amsterdam: John Benjamins, pp. 55–114.

Davies, W. (2005). The richness of Madurese voice. In: Arka, I. W. & Ross, M., eds., *The Many Faces of Austronesian Voice Systems: Some New Empirical Studies*. Canberra: Pacific Linguistics, pp. 197–220.

Dayley, J. (1981). Voice and ergativity in Mayan languages. *Journal of Mayan Linguistics* 2: 3–82.

(1989). *Tümpisa (Panamint) Shoshone Grammar*. Berkeley: University of California Press.

De Guzman, V. P. (1988). Ergative analysis for Philippine languages: An analysis. In: McGinn, R., ed., *Studies in Austronesian Linguistics*. Athens, OH: Ohio University Center for International Studies, pp. 323–345.

Derbyshire, D. (1985). *Hixkaryana and Linguistic Typology*. Arlington: SIL.

Dixon, R. M. W. (1972). *The Dyirbal Language of North Queensland*. Cambridge: Cambridge University Press.

(1977). *A Grammar of Yidiɲ*. Cambridge: Cambridge University Press.

(1979). Ergativity. *Language* 55.1: 59–138.

(1983). Nyawaygi. In: Dixon, R. M. W. & Blake, B., eds., *Handbook of Australian Languages 3*. Amsterdam: John Benjamins, pp. 430–531.

(1994). *Ergativity*. Cambridge: Cambridge University Press.

(2000a). A-constructions and O-constructions in Jarawara. *International Journal of American Linguistics* 66.1: 22–56.

(2000b). A typology of causatives: Form, syntax and meaning. In: Dixon, R. M. W. & Aikhenvald, A., eds., *Changing Valency: Case Studies in Transitivity*. Cambridge: Cambridge University Press, pp. 30–83.

(2004). *The Jarawara Language of Southern Amazonia*. Oxford: Oxford University Press.

Dixon, R. M. W. & Aikhenvald, A. (1997). A typology of argument-determined constructions. In: Bybee, J., Haiman, J. & Thompson, S., eds., *Essays on Language Function and Language Type. Dedicated to T. Givón*. Amsterdam: John Benjamins, pp. 71–113.

(2000). Introduction. In: Dixon, R. M. W. & Aikhenvald, A., eds., *Changing Valency: Case Studies in Transitivity*. Cambridge: Cambridge University Press, pp. 1–29.

Donohue, M. (1999). *Tukang Besi*. Berlin: Mouton de Gruyter.

(2002). Voice in Tukang Besi and the Austronesian focus system. In: Wouk, F. & Ross, M., eds., *The History and Typology of Western Austronesian Voice Systems*. Canberra: Pacific Linguistics, pp. 81–99.

(2003). Morphological templates, headedness, and applicatives in Barupu. *Oceanic Linguistics* 42.1: 111–143.

(2005). The Palu'e passive: From pragmatic construction to grammatical device. In: Arka, I. W. & Ross, M., eds., *The Many Faces of Austronesian Voice Systems: Some New Empirical Studies*. Canberra: Pacific Linguistics, pp. 59–85.

Downing, A. (1996). The semantics of get-passives. In: Hasan, R., Cloran, C. & Butt, D., eds., *Functional Descriptions: Theory in Practice*. Amsterdam: John Benjamins, pp. 179–206.

Dowty, D. (1991). Thematic proto-roles and argument selection. *Language* 67.3: 547–619.

Drapeau, L. (2014). *Grammaire de la langue innue*. Québec: Presses de l'Université du Québec.

Dryer, M. (2007). Clause types. In: Shopen, T., ed., *Language Typology and Syntactic Description, Vol. I: Clause Structure*. Cambridge: Cambridge University Press, pp. 224–275.

Dunn, M. J. (1999). A grammar of Chukchi. Ph.D. dissertation, Australian National University.

Duranti, A. & Ochs, E. (1990). Genitive constructions and agency in Samoan discourse. *Studies in Language* 14: 1–23.

Emonds, J. (1993). Projecting indirect objects. *The Linguistic Review* 10: 211–263.

Enfield, N. (2007). *A Grammar of Lao*. Berlin: Mouton de Gruyter.

England, N. (1988). Mam voice. In: Shibatani, M., ed., *Passive and Voice*. Amsterdam: John Benjamins, pp. 525–545.

Eriksen, P., Kittilä, S. & Kolehmainen, L. (2010). Linguistics of weather: cross-linguistic patterns of meteorological expression. *Studies in Language* 34.3: 565–601.

Evans, N. (1995). *A Grammar of Kayardild: With Historical-Comparative Notes on Tangkic*. Berlin: Walter de Gruyter.

(2008). Reciprocal constructions: Towards a structural typology. In: König, E. & Gast, V., eds., *Reciprocals and Reflexives: Theoretical and Typological Explorations*. Berlin: Mouton de Gruyter, pp. 33–103.

Evans, N., Gaby, A. & Nordlinger, R. (2007). Valency mismatches and the coding of reciprocity in Australian languages. *Linguistic Typology* 11.3: 541–597.

Evans, N., Levinson, S., Gaby, A. & Majid, A. (2011). Introduction: Reciprocals and semantic typology. In: Evans, N., Gaby, A., Levinson, S. & Majid, A., eds., *Reciprocals and Semantic Typology*. Amsterdam: John Benjamins, pp. 1–28.

eds., (2011). *Reciprocals and Semantic Typology*. Amsterdam: John Benjamins.

Everaert, M. (1986). *The Syntax of Reflexivization*. Dordrecht: Foris.

Everett, D. (1986). Pirahã. In: Derbyshire, D. & Pullum, G., eds., *Handbook of Amazonian Languages, Vol 1*. Berlin: Mouton de Gruyter, pp. 200–325.

Faltz, L. (1985). *Reflexivization: A Study in Universal Syntax*. New York: Garland.

Fauconnier, S. (2012). Constructional effects of involuntary and inanimate agents: a cross-linguistics study. Ph.D. thesis, University of Leuven.

Filbeck, D. (1973). The passive in Thai. *Anthropological Linguistics* 15.1: 33–41.

Fleck, D. (2002). Causation in Matses (Panoan, Amazonian Peru). In: Shibatani, M. ed., *The Grammar of Causation and Interpersonal Manipulation*. Amsterdam: John Benjamins, pp. 373–415.

Foley, W. (1986). *The Papuan Languages of New Guinea*. Cambridge: Cambridge University Press.

(1991). *The Yimas Language of New Guinea*. Stanford, CA: Stanford University Press.

(2008). The place of Philippine languages in a typology of voice systems. In: Austin, P. & Musgrave, S., eds., *Voice and Grammatical Relations in Austronesian languages*. Stanford, CA: CSLI Publications, pp. 22–44.

Foley, W. & Van Valin, R. (1984). *Functional Syntax and Universal Grammar*. Cambridge: Cambridge University Press.

Foris, D. (1998). Sochiapan Chinantec GIVE: a window into clause structure. In: Newman, J., ed., *The Linguistics of Giving*. Amsterdam: John Benjamins, pp. 209–248.

Fortescue, M. (1984). *West Greenlandic*. London: Croom Helm.

Frajzyngier, Z. (1993). *A Grammar of Mupun*. Berlin: Dietrich Reimer.

    (2000). Domains of point of view and coreferentiality: System interaction approach to the study of reflexives. In: Frajzyngier, Z. & Curl, T., eds., *Reflexives: Forms and Functions*. Amsterdam: John Benjamins, pp. 125–152.

Frajzyngier, Z. & Curl, T., eds., (2000a). *Reflexives: Forms and Functions*. Amsterdam: John Benjamins.

    (2000b). *Reciprocals: Forms and Functions*. Amsterdam: John Benjamins.

Franjieh, M. J. (2012). Possessive classifiers in North Ambrym, a language of Vanuatu: explorations in semantic classification. Ph.D. thesis, SOAS, University of London.

Frantz, D. (2009). *Blackfoot Grammar*. 2nd edition. Toronto: University of Toronto Press.

Frawley, W. (1992). *Linguistic Semantics*. Hillsdale, NJ: Lawrence Erlbaum.

Gabelentz, H. C. von der. (1861). Über das Passivum. Eine sprachvergleichende Abhandlung. *Abhandlungen der Königlich-Sächsischen Gesellschaft der Wissenschaften* 8: 450–546.

Gaby, A. (2008). Distinguishing reciprocals from reflexives in Kuuk Thaayorre. In: König, E. & Gast, V., eds., *Reciprocals and Reflexives: Theoretical and Typological Explorations*. Berlin: Mouton de Gruyter, pp. 259–288.

Gair, J. W. (1970). *Colloquial Sinhalese Clause Structures*. The Hague: Mouton de Gruyter.

    (1990). Subjects, cases and INFL in Sinhala. In: Verma, M. K. & Mohanan, K. P., eds., *Experiencer Subjects in South Asian Languages*. Stanford, CA: CSLI Publications, pp. 13–41.

Galant, M. (2015). Changes in valence in San Andrés Yaá Zapotec. In: Operstein, N. & Sonnenschein, A., eds., *Valency Changes in Zapotec. Synchrony, Diachrony, Typology*. Amsterdam: John Benjamins, pp. 213–236.

Geniušienė, E. (1987). *The Typology of Reflexives*. Berlin: Mouton de Gruyter.

Gerdts, D. (1984). A relational analysis of Halkomelem causals. In: Cook, E. D. & Gerdts, D., eds., *The Syntax of Native American Languages. Syntax and Semantics 16*. New York: Academic Press, pp. 169–204.

    (2000). Combinatory restrictions on Halkomelem reflexives and reciprocals. In: Frajzyngier, Z. & Curl, T., eds., *Reciprocals: Forms and Functions*. Amsterdam: John Benjamins, pp. 133–160.

    (2004). Halkomelem directional applicatives. In: Brown, J. C. & Peterson, T., eds., *39th International Conference on Salish and Neighboring Languages*. Vancouver: University of British Columbia, pp. 189–199.

Gerdts, D. & Hukari, T. (2000). Multiple antipassives in Halkomelem Salish. *Annual Meeting of the Berkeley Linguistics Society* 26.2: 51–62.

    (2006). The Halkomelem middle: A complex network of constructions. *Anthropological Linguistics* 48: 44–81.

Gerstner-Link, C. (1998). How transitive are habituals? *Sprachtypologie und Universalienforschung* 51.4: 327–534.

Gildea, S. (1994). Semantic and pragmatic inverse: 'Inverse alignment' and 'inverse voice' in Carib of Surinam. In: Givón, T., ed., *Voice and Inversion*. Amsterdam: John Benjamins, pp. 187–230.

(2015). Diachronic typology of passive in the Cariban family. Paper read at the Workshop on Voice Systems in Diachrony: A Comparative Perspective, Università degli Studi di Pavia, September 2014. Available online from academia.edu as of 2017–08–01.

Gildea, S., Cáceres, N., Sapién, R. & Meira, S. (forthcoming). Antipassive and semantic classes of verbs in the Cariban family. In: Janic, K., Witzlack-Makarevich, A. & Creissels, D., eds., *The Multifaceted Aspects of the Antipassive*. Amsterdam: John Benjamins.

Givón, T. (1972). Review of some problems in transitivity in Swahili. *African Studies* 31: 273–277.

(1979). *On Understanding Grammar*. New York: Academic Press.

(1981). Typology and functional domains. *Studies in Language* 5.2: 163–193.

(1983). *Topic Continuity in Discourse*. Amsterdam: John Benjamins.

(1994). Introduction. The pragmatics of de-transitive voice: Functional and typological aspects of inversion. In: Givón, T., ed., *Voice and Inversion*. Amsterdam: John Benjamins, pp. 3–44.

(1995). *Functionalism and Grammar*. Amsterdam: John Benjamins.

(2001). *Syntax*. 2 vols. Amsterdam: John Benjamins.

(2011). *Ute Reference Grammar*. Amsterdam: John Benjamins.

Givón, T. & Kawasha, B. (2006). Indiscrete grammatical relations: the Lunda passive. In: Tsunoda, T. & Kageyama, T., eds., *Voice and Grammatical Relations*. Amsterdam: John Benjamins, pp. 15–42.

Givón, T. & Yang, L. (1994). The rise of the English GET-passive. In: Fox, B. & Hopper, P., eds., *Voice: Form and Function*. Amsterdam: John Benjamins, pp. 119–149.

Golluscio, L. (2007). Morphological causatives and split intransitivity in Mapudungun. *International Journal of American Linguistics* 73.2: 209–238.

Good, J. (2007). Slouching toward deponency: A family of mismatches in the Bantu verb stem. In: Baerman, M., Corbett, G., Brown, D. & Hippisley, A., eds., *Deponency and Morphological Mismatches*. Oxford: Oxford University Press, pp. 203–230.

Graczyk, R. (2007). *A Grammar of Crow*. Lincoln, NE: University of Nebraska Press.

Green, G. (1974). *Semantics and Syntactic Irregularity*. Bloomington: Indiana University Press.

Grimes, C. E. (1991). The Buru language of eastern Indonesia. Ph.D. thesis. Australian National University.

Gropen, J., Pinker, S., Hollander, M., Goldberg, R. & Wilson, R. (1989). The learnability and acquisition of the dative alternation in English. *Language* 65.2: 203–257.

Guerssel, M. (1986). *On Berber Verbs of Change: A Study of Transitivity Alternations*. Cambridge, MA: MIT.

Guilfoyle, E., Hung, H. & Travis, L. (1992). Spec of IP and spec of VP: Two subjects in Austronesian languages. *Natural Language & Linguistic Theory* 10.3: 375–414.

Guillaume, A. & Rose, F. (2010). Sociative causative markers in South American languages: a possible areal feature. In: Franck, F., ed., *Essais de typologie et de linguistique générale. Mélanges offerts à Denis Creissels*. Lyon: ENS Éditions, pp. 383–402.

Gurevich, O. (2007). Steal me an apple: Version in Georgian. In: Hoyt, F., Seifert, N., Teodorescu, A. & White, J., eds., *Texas Linguistic Society IX: The Morphosyntax of Underrepresented Languages*. Stanford, CA: CSLI Publications, pp. 125–144.

Haider, H. (2010). *The Syntax of German*. Cambridge: Cambridge University Press.

Hale, K. (1972). Navajo linguistics. Ms., MIT.

    (1973). A note on subject-object inversion in Navajo. In: Kachru, B., ed., *Issues in Linguistics: Papers in Honor of Henry and Renée Kahane*. Chicago: University of Illinois Press, pp. 300–309.

Halle, M. & Hale, K. (1997). Chukchi transitive and antipassive constructions. Ms., MIT.

Haspelmath, M. (1987). *Transitivity Alternations of the Anticausative Type*. Cologne: Institut für Sprachwissenschaft der Universität zu Köln [Arbeitspapiere].

    (1990). The grammaticalization of passive morphology. *Studies in Language* 14.1: 25–72.

    (1993a). *A Grammar of Lezgian*. Berlin: Mouton de Gruyter.

    (1993b). More on the typology of inchoative/causative verb alternations. In: Comrie, B. & Polinsky, M., eds., *Causatives and Transitivity*. Amsterdam: John Benjamins, pp. 87–120.

    (1994). Review of *Grammatical Voice* by M. H. Klaiman. *Language* 70.1: 176–178.

    (1999). External possession in a European areal perspective. In: Payne, D. & Barshi, I., eds., *External Possession*. Amsterdam: John Benjamins, pp. 109–135.

    (2003). The geometry of grammatical meaning: Semantic maps and cross-linguistic comparison. In: Tomasello, M., ed., *The New Psychology of Language, Vol. 2*. Mahwah, NJ: Lawrence Erlbaum, pp. 211–242.

    (2007a). Further remarks on reciprocal constructions. In: Nedjalkov, V., ed., *Reciprocal Constructions*. Amsterdam: John Benjamins, pp. 2087–2115.

    (2007b). Pre-established categories don't exist: Consequences for language description and typology. *Linguistic Typology* 11.1: 119–132.

    (2007c). Ditransitive alignment splits and inverse alignment. *Functions of Language* 14.1: 79–102.

    (2011). On S, A, P, T, and R as comparative concepts for alignment typology. *Linguistic Typology* 15.3: 535–568.

Haspelmath, M., Calude, A., Spagnol, M., Narrog, H. & Bamyaci, E. (2014). Coding causal-noncausal verb alternations: A form-frequency correspondence explanation. *Journal of Linguistics* 50.3: 587–625.

Haspelmath, M. & Müller-Bardey, T. (2004). Valency change. In: Booij, G., Lehmann, C., Mugdan, J. & Skopeteas, S., eds., *Morphology: A Handbook on Inflection and Word Formation, Vol. 2*. Berlin: de Gruyter, pp. 1130–1145.

Haude, K. (2006). A grammar of Movima. Ph.D. dissertation, Radboud University Nijmegen.

    (2009). Hierarchical alignment in Movima. *International Journal of American Linguistics* 75.4: 513–532.

    (2010). The intransitive basis of Movima clause structure. In: Gildea, S. & Queixalós, F., eds., *Ergativity in Amazonia*. Amsterdam: John Benjamins, pp. 285–315.

(2014). Animacy and inverse in Movima: A corpus study. *Anthropological Linguistics* 56.3/4: 294–314.

Haude, K. & Zúñiga, F. (2016). Inverse and symmetrical voice: On languages with two transitive constructions. *Linguistics* 54.3: 443–481.

Haviland, J. (1979). Guugu Yimidhirr. In: Dixon, R. M. W. & Blake, B. J., eds., *The Handbook of Australian Languages*. Amsterdam: John Benjamins, pp. 26–180.

Heath, J. (1976). Antipassivization: a functional typology. *Proceedings of the Second Annual Meeting of the Berkeley Linguistics Society*. Berkeley: University of California, pp. 202–211.

(1999). *A grammar of Koyraboro (Koroboro) Senni: The Songhay of Gao, Mali*. Cologne: Rüdiger Köppe.

Heine, B. (2000). Polysemy involving reflexive and reciprocal markers in African languages. In: Frajzyngier, Z. & Curl, T., eds., *Reciprocals: Forms and Functions*. Amsterdam: John Benjamins, pp. 1–29.

Heine, B. & König, C. (2010). On the linear order of ditransitive objects. *Language Sciences* 32.1: 87–131.

Heine, B. & Miyashita, H. (2008). The intersection between reflexives and reciprocals: A grammaticalization perspective. In: König, E. & Gast, V., eds., *Reciprocals and Reflexives: Theoretical and Typological Explorations*. Berlin: Walter de Gruyter, pp. 169–224.

Hemmings, C. (2015). Kelabit voice: Philippine-type, Indonesian-type or something a bit different? *Transactions of the Philological Society* 113.3: 383–405.

(2016). The Kelabit language: Austronesian voice and syntactic typology. Ph.D. dissertation, SOAS, University of London.

Henderson, E. J. A. (1976). Vestiges of morphology in modern standard Khasi. In: Jenner, P. N., Thompson, L. C. & Starosta, S., eds., *Austroasiatic Studies*. Honolulu: University Press of Hawaii, pp. 477–522.

Hess, T. (1995). *Lushootseed Reader with Introductory Grammar, Vol. 1*. Missoula, MT: University of Montana.

Hetzron, R. (1969). *The Verbal System of Southern Agaw*. Berkeley: University of California Press.

Hewitt, G. (1989). *Abkhaz*. London: Croom Helm.

Hewitt, S. (2002). The impersonal in Breton. *Journal of Celtic Linguistics* 7: 1–39.

Hiirikoski, J. (2002). Transitive verbs of emotion in Finnish and English. In: Koskela, M. & Pilke, N., eds., *Erikoiskielet ja käännösteoria, VAKKI-symposiumi XXII* [Special Languages and Translation Theory, VAKKI Symposium XXII]. Vaasa: University of Vaasa, pp. 108–121.

Himmelmann, N. (2002). Voice in two northern Nulawesi languages. In: Wouk, F. & Ross, M., eds., *The History and Typology of Western Austronesian Voice Systems*. Canberra: Pacific Linguistics, pp. 123–142.

(2005). The Austronesian languages of Asia and Madagascar: Typological characteristics. In: Adelaar, A. & Himmelmann, N., eds., *The Austronesian Languages of Asia and Madagascar*. London: Routledge, pp. 110–181.

(2006). How to miss a paradigm or two: Multifunctional *ma-* in Tagalog. In: Ameka, F., Dench, A. & Evans, N., eds., *Catching Language: The Standing Challenge of Grammar Writing*. Berlin: Mouton de Gruyter, pp. 487–526.

(2008). Lexical categories and voice in Tagalog. In: Musgrave, S. & Austin, P., eds., *Voice and Grammatical Relations in Austronesian Languages*. Stanford, CA: CSLI Publications.

Hoffmann, C. (1963). *A Grammar of the Margi Language*. Oxford: Oxford University Press.

Hofling, C. A. (2011). *Mopan Maya-Spanish-English Dictionary*. Salt Lake City: The University of Utah Press.

Holvoet, A. (2015). Extended uses of morphological causatives in Latvian. In: Holvoet, A. & Nau, N., eds., *Voice and Argument Structure in Baltic*. Amsterdam: John Benjamins, pp. 147–177.

Hopper, P. & Thompson, S. (1980). Transitivity in grammar and discourse. *Language* 56.2: 251–299.

Huang, C.-T. J. (2002). Distributivity and reflexivity. In: Tang, S.-W. & Liu, C.-S. L., eds., *On the Formal Way to Chinese Languages*. Stanford: CSLI Publications, pp. 21–44.

Huang, C.-T. J. & Tang, C.-C. J. (1991). The local nature of the long-distance reflexive in Chinese. In: Koster, J. & Reuland, E., eds., *Long Distance Anaphora*. Cambridge: Cambridge University Press, pp. 263–282.

Iawata, S. (2008). *Locative Alternation: A Lexical-Constructional Approach*. Amsterdam: John Benjamins.

Ichihashi-Nakayama, K. (1996). The "applicative" in Hualapai: Its functions and meanings. *Cognitive Linguistics* 7.2: 227–239.

Iemmolo, G. (2011). Towards a typological study of differential object marking and differential object indexation. Ph.D. dissertation, Università degli Studi di Pavia.

Iwata, S. (2008). *Locative Alternation: A Lexical-Constructional approach*. Amsterdam: John Benjamins.

Jackendoff, R. (1990). *Semantic Structures*. Cambridge, MA: MIT Press.

Jacques, G. (2014). Denominal affixes as sources of antipassive markers in Japhug Rgyalrong. *Lingua* 138: 1–22.

Jacques, G. (forthcoming) Antipassive derivations in Sino-Tibetan/Trans-Himalayan and their sources. In: Janic, K. Witzlack-Makarevich, A. & Creissels, D., eds., *The Multifaceted Aspects of the Antipassive*. Amsterdam: John Benjamins.

Janic, K. (2010). On the reflexive-antipassive polysemy: Typological convergence from unrelated languages. *Proceedings of the 36th Annual Meeting of the Berkeley Linguistics Society*. Berkeley: Berkeley Linguistics Society, pp. 158–173.

Janic, K. (2016). *L'antipassif dans les langues accusatives*. Brussels: Peter Lang.

Janssen, T. A. J. M. (1997). Giving in Dutch: An intra-lexematical and inter-lexematical description. In: Newman, J., ed., *The Linguistics of Giving*. Amsterdam: John Benjamins, pp. 267–306.

Jaxontov, S. (1988). Resultative in Chinese. In: Nedjalkov, V., ed., *Typology of Resultative Constructions*. Amsterdam: John Benjamins, pp. 113–133.

Jelinek, E. & Demers, R. (1983). The agent hierarchy and voice in some Coast Salish languages. *International Journal of American Linguistics* 49.2: 167–185.

Jenny, M. (2010). Benefactive strategies in Thai. In: Zúñiga, F. & Kittilä, S., eds., *Benefactives and Malefactives: Typological Perspectives and Case Studies*. Amsterdam: John Benjamins, pp. 377–392.

Jeong, Y. (2007). *Applicatives: Structure and Interpretation from a Minimalist Perspective*. Amsterdam: John Benjamins.

Josephs, L. (1975). *Palauan Reference Grammar*. Honolulu: The University Press of Hawaii.

Kalectaca, M. (1978). *Lessons in Hopi*. Tucson: University of Arizona Press.

Kalinina, E., Kolomatskiy, D. & Subodina, A. (2006). Transitivity increase markers interacting with verb semantics: evidence from Uralic languages. In: Kulikov, L., Malchukov, A. & De Swart, P., eds., *Case, Valency and Transitivity*. Amsterdam: John Benjamins, pp. 441–463.

Kalmár, I. (1979). The antipassive and grammatical relations in Eskimo. In: Plank, F., ed., *Ergativity: Towards a Theory of Grammatical Relations*. New York: Academic Press, pp. 117–143.

Károly, S. (1982). Intransitive-transitive derivational suffixes in Hungarian. In: Kiefer, F., ed., *Hungarian Linguistics*. Amsterdam: John Benjamins, pp. 185–243.

Katagiri, M. (2005). Voice, ergativity, and transitivity in Tagalog and other Philippine languages: A typological perspective. In: Arka, I. W. & Ross, M., eds., *The Many Faces of Austronesian Voice Systems: Some New Empirical Studies*. Canberra: Pacific Linguistics, pp. 153–174.

Kaufman, D. (2009). Austronesian nominalism and its consequences: A Tagalog case study. *Theoretical Linguistics* 35.1: 1–49.

(2017). Lexical category and alignment in Austronesian. In: Coon, J., Massam, D. & Travis, L., eds., *The Oxford Handbook of Ergativity*. Oxford: Oxford University Press, pp. 589–628.

Kaufmann, I. (2007). Middle voice. *Lingua* 117: 1677–1714.

Kazenin, K. (1998). On patient demotion in Lak. In: Kulikov, L. & Vater, H., eds., *Typology of Verbal Categories*. Tübingen: Max Niemeyer Verlag, pp. 95–115.

(2001a). The passive voice. In: Haspelmath, M., König, E., Oesterreicher, W. & Raible, W., eds., *Language Typology and Language Universals: An International Handbook, Vol. 2*. Berlin: Walter de Gruyter, pp. 899–916.

(2001b). Verbal reflexives and the middle voice. In: Haspelmath, M., König, E., Oesterreicher, W. & Raible, W., eds., *Language Typology and Language Universals: An International Handbook, Vol. 2*. Berlin: Walter de Gruyter, pp. 916–927.

Keen, S. (1983). Yukulta. In: Dixon, R. M. W. & Blake, B., eds., *Handbook of Australian Languages 3*. Amsterdam: John Benjamins, pp. 190–304.

Keenan, E. (1985). Passive in the world's languages. In: Shopen, T., ed., *Language Typology and Syntactic Description, Vol I: Clause Structure*. Cambridge: Cambridge University Press, pp. 243–281.

Keenan, E. & Dryer, M. (2007). Passive in the world's languages. In: Shopen, T., ed., *Language Typology and Syntactic Description, Vol. I: Clause Structure*. Cambridge: Cambridge University Press, pp. 325–361.

Kemmer, S. (1993). *The Middle Voice*. Amsterdam: John Benjamins.

(1994). Middle voice, transitivity, and the elaboration of events. In: Fox, B. & Hopper, P., eds., *Voice: Form and Function*. Amsterdam: John Benjamins, pp. 179–228.

Keyser, S. J. & Roeper, T. (1984). On the middle and ergative constructions in English. *Linguistic Inquiry* 15.3: 381–416.

Kibrik, A. (1981). *Materialy k tipologii èrgativnosti: Bezhtinskij jazyk* [Materials For a Typology of Ergativity: The Bezhta Language]. Moscow: Institut russkogo jazyka AN SSSR.

(1996). Transitivity in lexicon and grammar. In: Kibrik, A. E. ed., *Godoberi*. Munich: Lincom Europa, pp. 107–146.

Kibrik, A., Kodzasov, S. V., Olovjannikova, I. P. & Samedov, D. S. (1977). *Opyt strukturnogo opisanija archinskogo jazyka* [Structural Description of the Archi Language]. 4 vols. Moscow: Izdatelstvo Moskovskogo Universiteta.

Kimenyi, A. (1980). *A Relational Grammar of Kinyarwanda*. Berkeley: University of California Press.

Kishimoto, H., Kageyama, T. & Sasaki, K. (2015). Valency classes in Japanese. In: Malchukov, A. & Comrie, B., eds., *Valency Classes in the World's Languages, Vol. 2: Case Studies from Austronesia, the Pacific, the Americas, and Theoretical Outlook*. Berlin: Mouton de Gruyter, pp. 765–805.

Kiss, K. (1998). Identificational focus versus information focus. *Language* 74.2: 245–273.

Kisseberth, C. & Abasheikh, M. (1974). A case of systematic avoidance of homonyms. *Studies in the Linguistic Sciences* 4: 107–124.

Kitano, H. (2006). Transitivity and pronominal clitic order in Kapampangan. *Studies in Philippine Languages and Cultures* 17: 88–97.

Kittilä, S. (2002). *Transitivity: Towards a Comprehensive Typology*. Turku: University of Turku.

(2005). Remarks on involuntary agent constructions. *Word* 56: 377–413.

(2006). The anomaly of the verb 'give' explained by its high (formal and semantic) transitivity. *Linguistics* 44.3: 569–612.

(2007). A typology of tritransitives: alignment types and motivations. *Linguistics* 45.3: 455–508.

(2009). Causative morphemes as non-valency increasing devices. *Folia Linguistica* 43.1: 67–94.

(2013). Causative morphemes as de-transitivizing mechanisms. What do non-canonical instances reveal about causation and causativization? *Folia Linguistica* 47.1: 113–138.

Kittilä, S. & Zúñiga, F. (2014). Recent developments and open questions in the field of semantic roles. In: Kittilä, S. & Zúñiga, F., eds., *Advances in Research on Semantic Roles. Studies in Language* 38.3: 437–462.

Kiyosawa, K. (2006). Applicatives in Salish languages. Ph.D. dissertation, Simon Fraser University.

Klaiman, M. H. (1988). Affectedness and control: A typology of voice systems. In: Shibatani, M., ed., *Passive and Voice*. Amsterdam: John Benjamins, pp. 25–83.

(1991). *Grammatical Voice*. Cambridge: Cambridge University Press.

Klamer, M. (1998). *Kambera*. Berlin: Mouton de Gruyter.

Kleinschmidt, S. P. (1851). *Grammatik der grönländischen Sprache, mit theilweisem einschluss des Labradordialects*. Berlin: G. Reimer.

Knott, J. (1995). The causative-passive correlation. In: Bennett, D., Bynon, T. & Hewitt, G., eds., *Subject, Voice, and Ergativity: Selected Essays*. London: School of Oriental and African Studies, University of London, pp. 53–59.

Koivisto, V. (1995). *Itämerensuomen refleksiivit* [Balto-Finnic Reflexives]. Helsinki: Suomalaisen Kirjallisuuden Seura.

Kok, M. (2016). Varjon kieliopillistuminen: *itse-saan* paradigman rakenne ja merkity-senkehitys itäisessä itämerensuomessa [Grammaticalization of shadow. The paradigm structure and the development of the meaning of the word *itse* 'self' in the eastern Balto-Finnic languages]. Ph.D. dissertation, University of Eastern Finland.

Kozinsky, I., Nedjalkov, V. & Polinskaja, M. (1988). Antipassive in Chukchee: Oblique object, object incorporation, zero object. In: Shibatani, M., ed., *Passive and Voice*. Amsterdam: John Benjamins, pp. 651–706.

Kozinsky, I. & Polinsky, M. (1993). Causee and patient in the causative of transitive: Coding conflict or doubling of grammatical relations. In: Comrie, B. & Polinsky, M., eds., *Causatives and Transitivity*. Amsterdam: John Benjamins, pp. 177–240.

König, E. (2001). Intensifiers and reflexive pronouns. In: Haspelmath, M., König, E., Oesterreicher, W. & Raible, W., eds., *Language Typology and Language Universals: An International Handbook, Vol. 1*. Berlin: Walter de Gruyter, pp. 747–760.

(2001). Internal and external possessors. In: Haspelmath, M., König, E., Oesterreicher, W. & Raible, W., eds., *Language Typology and Language Universals: An International Handbook, Vol. 2*. Berlin: Walter de Gruyter, pp. 970–978.

König, E. & Gast, V., eds. (2008). *Reciprocals and Reflexives: Theoretical and Typological Explorations*. Berlin: Mouton de Gruyter.

König, E. & Kokutani, S. (2006). Towards a typology of reciprocal constructions: Focus on German and Japanese. *Linguistics* 44.2: 271–302.

König, E. & Siemund, P. (with Töpper, S.). (2013). Intensifiers and reflexive pronouns. In: Dryer, M. & Haspelmath, M., eds., *The World Atlas of Language Structures Online*, Ch. 47. Leipzig: Max Planck Institute for Evolutionary Anthropology. Available online at wals.info/chapter/47, accessed on 2017-06-29.

König, E. & Vezzosi, L. (2002). Reziproke Konstruktionen im Deutschen. In: Yoshida, M., ed., *Grammatische Kategorien aus sprachhistorischer und typologischer Perspektive*. Munich: Iudicium Verlag, pp. 205–219.

Kroeber, P. (1999). *The Salish Language Family: Reconstructing Syntax*. Lincoln, NE: University of Nebraska Press.

(1993). *Phrase Structure and Grammatical Relations in Tagalog*. Stanford, CA: CSLI Publications.

(2005). *Analyzing Grammar*. Cambridge: Cambridge University Press.

Kroskrity. P. V. (1985). A holistic understanding of Arizona Tewa passives. *Language* 61.2: 306–328

Krüger, K. W. (1846). *Griechische Sprachlehre für Schulen*. Berlin: K. W. Krüger.

Kučanda, D. (1987). 'True' reflexives and pseudo-reflexives with particular reference to Serbo-Croatian. In: Van der Auwera, J. & Goossens, L., eds., *Ins and Outs of the Predication*. Dordrecht: Foris, pp. 77–92.

Kühner, R. (1904). [1834–1835] *Ausführliche Grammatik der griechischen Sprache ii: Satzlehre*. Revised by B. Gerth. Hannover: Hahn.

Kulikov, L. (2006). Passive and middle in Indo-European: Reconstructing the early Vedic passive paradigm. In: Abraham, W. & Leisiö, L., eds., *Passivization and Typology: Form and Function.* Amsterdam: John Benjamins, pp. 62–81.

   (2011a). Voice typology. In: Song, J. J., ed., *The Oxford Handbook of Linguistic Typology.* Oxford: Oxford University Press, pp. 368–398.

   (2011b). Passive to anticausative through impersonalization. The case of Vedic and Indo-European. In: Malchukov, A. & Siewierska, A., eds., *Impersonal Constructions: A Cross-Linguistic Perspective.* Amsterdam: John Benjamins, pp. 229–254.

Kurebito, T. (2012). An outline of valency-reducing operations in Chukchi. In: Nakamura, W. & Kikusawa, R., eds., *Objectivization and Subjectivization: A Typology of Voice Systems.* Osaka: National Museum of Ethnology, pp. 177–189.

Kuryłowicz, J. (1964). *The Inflectional Categories of Indo-European.* Heidelberg: Carl Winter.

Laitinen, L. (1995). Nollapersoona [Zero-person]. *Virittäjä* 99: 337–357.

Laka, I. (1993). Unergatives that assign ergative, unaccusatives that assign accusative. *MIT Working Papers in Linguistics* 18: 149–172.

Lakoff, R. (1971). Passive resistance. *Papers from the Seventh Regional Meeting, Chicago Linguistic Society.* Chicago: Chicago Linguistic Society, 149–162.

LaPolla, R. (2000). Valency-changing derivations in Dulong/Rawang. In: Dixon, R. M. W. & Aikhenvald, A., eds., *Changing Valency: Case Studies in Transitivity.* Cambridge: Cambridge University Press, pp. 282–311.

Larson, R. (1988). On the double object construction. *Linguistic Inquiry* 19: 33–91.

Laughren, M. (2002). Wanyi reflexive-reciprocal constructions. In: Allen, C., ed., *Proceedings of the 2001 Conference of the Australian Linguistic Society.* Available online at www.als.asn.au, accessed on 2017–07–10.

Lee, I.-Q. (1997). Dative constructions and case theory in Korean. Ph.D. dissertation, Simon Fraser University.

Lefebvre, C. & Muysken, P. (1988). *Mixed Categories: Nominalizations in Quechua.* Dordrecht: Kluwer Academic Publishers.

Lehmann, C. (2015a). Valency classes in Yucatec Maya. In: Malchukov, A. & Comrie, B., eds., *Valency Classes in the World's Languages, Vol. 2: Case Studies from Austronesia, the Pacific, the Americas, and Theoretical Outlook.* Berlin: Mouton de Gruyter, pp. 1407–1461.

   (2015b). Situation types, valency frames and operations. In: Malchukov, A. & Comrie, B., eds., *Valency Classes in the World's Languages, Vol. 2: Case Studies from Austronesia, the Pacific, the Americas, and Theoretical Outlook.* Berlin: Mouton de Gruyter, pp. 1547–1595.

Lehmann, C. & Verhoeven, E. (2006). Extraversive transitivization in Yucatec Maya and the nature of the applicative. In: Kulikov, L., Malchukov, A. & De Swart, P., eds., *Case, Valency and Transitivity.* Amsterdam: John Benjamins, pp. 465–493.

Leiss, E. (1992). *Die Verbalkategorien des Deutschen. Ein Beitrag zur Theorie der sprachlichen Kategorisierung.* Berlin: de Gruyter.

Leroy, J. (2003). Grammaire du mankon. Ph.D. dissertation, University of Paris 3.

Letuchiy, A. & Arkadiev, P. (forthcoming) Indirect antipassives in Circassian. In: Janic, K., Witzlack-Makarevich, A. & Creissels, D., eds., *The Multifaceted Aspects of the Antipassive*. Amsterdam: John Benjamins.

Levin, B. (1993). *English Verb Classes and Alternations: A Preliminary Investigation*. Chicago: University of Chicago Press.

(2015). Verb classes within and across languages. In: Malchukov, A. & Comrie, B., eds., *Valency Classes in the World's Languages, Vol. 2: Case Studies from Austronesia, the Pacific, the Americas, and Theoretical Outlook*. Berlin: Mouton de Gruyter, pp. 1627–1670.

Levin, B. & Rappaport Hovav, M. (1994). *Unaccusativity: At the Syntax-Lexical Semantics Interface*. Cambridge, MA: MIT Press.

(2005). *Argument Realization*. Cambridge: Cambridge University Press.

Levine, R. (1980). On the lexical origin of the Kwakwala passive. *International Journal of American Linguistics* 46.4: 240–258.

Levinson, S. (2011). Reciprocals in Yélî Dnye, the Papuan language of Rossel Island. In: Evans, N., Gaby, A., Levinson, S. C. & Majid, A., eds., *Reciprocals and Semantic Typology*. Amsterdam: John Benjamins, pp. 177–194.

Liao, H. (2004). Transitivity and ergativity in Formosan and Philippine Languages. Ph.D. Dissertation, University of Hawaii.

Lichtenberk, F. (1983). *A grammar of Manam*. Honolulu: The University of Hawai'i Press.

(1994). Reflexives and reciprocals. In: Asher, R. E., ed., *The Encyclopedia of Language and Linguistics*. Oxford: Pergamon Press, pp. 3504–3509.

Liver, R. (2014). Le romanche des Grisons. In: Klump, A., Kramer, J. & Willems, A., eds., *Manuel des langues romanes*. Berlin: de Gruyter, pp. 413–446.

Liu, M. (2000). Reciprocal marking with deictic verbs "come" and "go" in Mandarin. In: Frajzyngier, Z. & Curl, T., eds., *Reciprocals: Forms and Functions*. Amsterdam: John Benjamins, pp. 123–132.

Lopez, C. (1937). *Preliminary Study of Affixes in Tagalog*. Manila: Bureau of Print.

(1965). The Spanish overlay in Tagalog. *Lingua* 14: 467–504.

Lyons, J. (1968). *Introduction to Theoretical Linguistics*. Cambridge: Cambridge University Press.

Lyutikova, E. & Bonch-Osmolovskaya, A. (2002). What a causative construction can be used for? Paper presented at The Second International Conference on Construction Grammar (ICCG2), Helsinki, September 6–8.

MacDonald, L. (1990). *A Grammar of Tauya*. Berlin: Mouton de Gruyter.

MacKay, C. (1999). *A Grammar of Misantla Totonac*. Salt Lake City: University of Utah Press.

Maclachlan, A. (1996). Aspects of ergativity in Tagalog. Ph.D. dissertation, McGill University.

Maienborn, C. (2007). Das Zustandspassiv: Grammatische Einordnung, Bildungsbeschränkungen, Interpretationsspielraum. *Zeitschrift für Germanistische Linguistik* 35: 83–115.

Majid, A., Evans, N., Gaby, A. & Levinson, S. (2011). The semantics of reciprocal constructions across languages: An extensional approach. In: Evans, N., Gaby, A., Levinson, S. C. & Majid, A., eds., *Reciprocals and Semantic Typology*. Amsterdam: John Benjamins, pp. 29–60.

Malchukov, A. (1993). Adversative constructions in Even in relation to passive and permissive. In: Comrie, B. & Polinsky, M., eds., *Causatives and Transitivity*. Amsterdam: John Benjamins, pp. 369–384.

(2006). Transitivity parameters and transitivity alternations: Constraining co-variation. In: Kulikov, K., Malchukov, A. & De Swart, P., eds., *Studies on Case, Valency and Transitivity*. Amsterdam: John Benjamins, pp. 329–359.

(2016). "Ambivalent voice": Markedness effects in valency change. In: Kageyama, T. & Jacobsen, W., eds., *Transitivity and Valency Alternations*. Berlin: Mouton de Gruyter, pp. 389–422.

(2017). Markedness effects in applicative formation. In: Álvarez González, A. & Navarro, Í., eds., *Verb Valency Changes: Theoretical and Typological Perspectives*. Amsterdam: John Benjamins, pp. 3–29.

Malchukov, A. & Comrie, B., eds. (2015a). *Valency Classes in the World's Languages, Vol. 1: Introducing the Framework, and Case Studies from Africa and Eurasia*. Berlin: Mouton de Gruyter.

(2015b). *Valency Classes in the World's Languages, Vol. 2: Case Studies from Austronesia, the Pacific, the Americas, and Theoretical Outlook*. Berlin: Mouton de Gruyter.

Malchukov, A., Haspelmath, M. & Comrie, B., eds. (2010). *Studies in Ditransitive Constructions: A Comparative Handbook*. Berlin: Mouton de Gruyter.

Malchukov, A. & Ogawa, A. (2011). Towards a typology of impersonal constructions. A semantic map approach. In: Malchukov, A. & Siewierska, A., eds., *Impersonal Constructions: A Cross-Linguistic Perspective*. Amsterdam: John Benjamins, pp. 19–56.

Malchukov, A. & Siewierska, A., eds. (2011). *Impersonal Constructions: A Cross-Linguistic Perspective*. Amsterdam: John Benjamins.

Maldonado, R. (2000). Conceptual distance and transitivity increase in Spanish reflexives. In: Frajzyngier, Z. & Curl, T., eds., *Reflexives: Forms and Functions*. Amsterdam: John Benjamins, pp. 153–186.

Maldonado, R. & Nava, E. F. (2002). Tarascan causatives and event complexity. In: Shibatani, M., ed., *The Grammar of Causation and Interpersonal Manipulation*. Amsterdam: John Benjamins, pp. 157–195.

Manley, T. (1972). *Outline of Sre Structure*. Honolulu: University of Hawai'i Press.

Marantz, A. (1984). *On the Nature of Grammatical Relations*. Cambridge, MA: The MIT Press.

(1993). Implications of asymmetries in double object constructions. In: Mchombo, S., ed., *Theoretical Aspects of Bantu Grammar 1*. Stanford, CA: CSLI Publications, pp. 113–151.

Margetts, A. (1999). *Valence and Transitivity in Saliba, an Oceanic Language of Papua New Guinea*. Nijmegen: Max Planck Institute for Psycholinguistics.

(2008). Transitivity discord in some Oceanic languages. *Oceanic Linguistics* 47.1: 30–44.

(2011). Transitivity in Saliba-Logea. *Studies in Language* 35.3: 650–675.

Margetts, A. & Austin, P. (2007). Three-participant events in the languages of the world: towards a crosslinguistic typology. *Linguistics* 45.3: 393–451.

Marten, L., Kula, N. & Thwala Nhl. (2007). Parameters of morphosyntactic variation in Bantu. *Transactions of the Philological Society* 105.3: 253–338.

Marten, L. & Kula, N. (2012). Object marking and morphosyntactic variation in Bantu. *Southern African Linguistics and Applied Language Studies* 30.2: 237–253.

Masica, C. (1976). *Defining a Linguistic Area: South Asia*. Chicago IL: The University of Chicago Press.

Maslova, E. (2008). Reflexive encoding of reciprocity: Cross-linguistic and language internal variation. In: König, E. & Gast, V., eds., *Reciprocals and Reflexives: Theoretical and Typological Explorations*. Berlin: Mouton de Gruyter, pp. 225–258.

Maslova, E. & Nedjalkov, V. (2013). Reciprocal constructions. In: Dryer, M. & Haspelmath, M., eds., *The World Atlas of Language Structures Online*, Ch. 106. Leipzig: Max Planck Institute for Evolutionary Anthropology. Available online at wals.info/chapter/106, accessed on 2017–06–29.

Massam, D. (2001). Pseudo noun incorporation in Niuean. *Natural Language & Linguistic Theory* 19.1: 153–197.

(2009). Noun incorporation: Essentials and extensions. *Language and Linguistics Compass* 3.4: 1076–1096.

McCloskey, J. (2007). The grammar of autonomy in Irish. *Natural Language & Linguistic Theory* 25.4: 825–857.

McGinnis, M. (2005). UTAH at Merge: Evidence from multiple applicatives. *MIT Working Papers in Linguistics* 49: 183–200.

McGinnis, M. & Gerdts, D. (2004). A phase-theoretic analysis of Kinyarwanda multiple applicatives. In: Burelle, S. & Somesfalean, S., eds., *Proceedings of the 2003 Canadian Linguistic Association Annual Conference*. Montréal: Université du Québec, pp. 154–165.

McKaughan, H. P. (1958). *The Inflection and Syntax of Maranao Verbs*. Manila: Bureau of Printing.

Mchombo, S. (2004). *The Syntax of Chichewa*. Cambridge: Cambridge University Press.

Mel'čuk, I. A. (1993). The inflectional category of voice: towards a more rigorous definition. In: Comrie, B. & Polinsky, M., eds., *Causatives and Transitivity*. Amsterdam: John Benjamins, pp. 1–46.

(2006). *Aspects of the Theory of Morphology*. Edited by David Beck. Berlin: Walter de Gruyter.

Mel'čuk, I. A. & Xolodovič, A. A. (1970). K teorii grammatičeskogo zaloga [Towards a theory of grammatical voice]. *Narody Azii i Afriki* 4: 111–124.

Mettouchi, A. & Frajzyngier, Z. (2013). A previously unrecognized typological category: The state distinction in Kabyle (Berber). *Linguistic Typology* 17.1: 1–30.

Miestamo, M. (2014). Partitives and negation: A cross-linguistic survey. In: Luraghi, S. & Huumo, T., eds., *Partitive Cases and Related Categories*. Berlin: Mouton de Gruyter, pp. 63–86.

Miestamo, M.; Tamm, A. & Wagner-Nagy, B., eds. (2015). *Negation in Uralic Languages*. Amsterdam: John Benjamins.

Miller, M. (2014). A comparative look at the major voice oppositions in Sama-Bajaw languages and Indonesian/Malay. In: Arka, I. W. & Indrawati N. L. K. M., eds., *Argument Realisations and Related Constructions in Austronesian Languages*. Canberra: Asia-Pacific Linguistics, pp. 303–312.

Mithun, M. (1984). The evolution of noun incorporation. *Language* 60.4: 847–894.

(1994). The implications of ergativity for a Philippine voice system. In: Fox B. & Hopper P., eds., *Voice: Form and function*. Amsterdam: John Benjamins, pp. 247–277.

Miyaoka, O. (2012). *A Grammar of Central Alaskan Yupik (CAY)*. Berlin: Walter de Gruyter.

(2015). Valency classes in Central Alaskan Yupik, an Eskimoan language. In: Malchukov, A. & Comrie, B., eds., *Valency Classes in the World's Languages, Vol. 2: Case Studies from Austronesia, the Pacific, the Americas, and Theoretical Outlook*. Berlin: Mouton de Gruyter, pp. 1165–1204.

Mohanan, K. & Mohanan, T. (1998). Strong and weak projection: Lexical reflexives and reciprocals. In: Butt, M. & Geuder, W., eds., *The Projection of Arguments: Lexical and Compositional Factors*. Stanford, CA: CSLI Publications, pp. 165–194.

Morais-Barbosa, J., ed. (1967). *Estudos linguísticos crioulos. Reedição de artigos publicados no Boletim da Sociedade de Geografia de Lisboa*. Lisbon: Academia Internacional da Cultura Portuguesa.

Morris, W. (1999). Emergent grammatical relations: Subjecthood in Kapampangan. In: Hiraga, M., Sinha, C. & Wilcox, S., eds., *Cultural, Psychological and Typological Issues in Cognitive Linguistics: Selected Papers of the Bi-Annual ICLA Meeting in Albuquerque, July 1995*. Amsterdam: John Benjamins, pp. 299–311.

Mosel, U. (1991). Towards a typology of valency. In: Seiler, H. & Premper, W., eds., *Partizipation. Das sprachliche Erfassen von Sachverhalten*. Tübingen: Gunter Narr, pp. 240–251.

Mosel, U. & Hovdhaugen, E. (1992). *Samoan Reference Grammar*. Oslo: Scandinavian University Press.

Moyse-Faurie, C. (1983). *Le drehu, langue de Lifou (Iles Loyauté)*. Paris: Selaf.

Munro, P. (1983). When 'same' is not 'not different'. In: Haiman, J. & Munro, P., eds., *Switch Reference and Universal Grammar*. Amsterdam: John Benjamins, pp. 223–243.

Næss, Å. (2007). *Prototypical Transitivity*. Amsterdam: John Benjamins.

Nedjalkov, I. (1997). *Evenki*. London: Routledge.

Nedjalkov, V. (1988). Resultative, passive and perfect in German. In: Nedjalkov, V., ed., *Typology of Resultative Constructions*. Amsterdam: John Benjamins, pp. 411–432.

(2007a). Overview of the research. Definitions of terms, framework, and related issues. In: Nedjalkov, V., ed., *Reciprocal Constructions*. Amsterdam: John Benjamins, pp. 3–114.

(2007b). Polysemy of reciprocal markers. In: Nedjalkov, V., ed., *Reciprocal Constructions*. Amsterdam: John Benjamins, pp. 231–333.

ed. (2007c). *Reciprocal Constructions*. With the assistance of Emma Geniušienė and Zlatka Guentchéva. 5 vols. Amsterdam: John Benjamins.

Nedjalkov, V. & Jaxontov, S. (1988). The typology of resultative constructions. In: Nedjalkov, V., ed., *Typology of Resultative Constructions*. Amsterdam: John Benjamins, pp. 3–62.

Nedjalkov, I. & Nedjalkov, V. (1988). Stative, resultative, passive and perfect in Evenki. In: Nedjalkov, V., ed., *Typology of Resultative Constructions*. Amsterdam: John Benjamins, pp. 241–257.

(2007). Reciprocals, sociatives, comitatives, and assistives in Yakut. In: Nedjalkov, V., ed., *Reciprocal Constructions*. Amsterdam: John Benjamins, pp. 1095–1162.

Nedjalkov, V. & Otaina, G. A. (1988). Resultative and continuative in Nivkh. In: Nedjalkov, V., ed., *Typology of Resultative Constructions*. Amsterdam: John Benjamins, pp. 135–151.

Nedjalkov, V., Otaina, G. A. & Xolodovič, A. (1995). Morphological and lexical causatives in Nivkh. In: Bennett, D., Bynon, T. & Hewitt, G., eds., *Subject, Voice and Ergativity. Selected Essays*. London: University of London, pp. 60–80.

Nedjalkov, V. & Sil'nickij, G. (1973). The typology of morphological and lexical causatives. In: Kiefer, F., ed., *Trends in Soviet Theoretical Linguistics*. Dordrecht: Reidel, pp. 1–32.

Ngonyani, D. (2000). The constituent structure of Kindendeule applicatives. In: Carstens, V. & Parkinson, F., eds., *Advances in African Linguistics*. Trenton, NJ: Africa World Press, pp. 61–76.

Ngonyani, D. & Githinji, P. (2006). The asymmetric nature of Bantu applicative constructions. *Lingua* 116: 31–63.

Nichols, J. (1992). *Language Diversity in Space and Time*. Chicago: University of Chicago Press.

(1994a). Chechen. In: Smeets, R., ed., *The Indigenous Languages of the Caucasus, Vol. 4: Northeast Caucasian Languages*. Delmar, NY: Caravan Books, pp. 1–77.

(1994b). Ingush. In: Smeets, R., ed., *The Indigenous Languages of the Caucasus, Vol. 4: Northeast Caucasian Languages*. Delmar, NY: Caravan Books, pp. 79–145.

Nichols, J., Peterson, D. & Barnes, J. (2004). Transitivizing and detransitivizing languages. *Linguistic Typology* 8.2: 149–211.

Noonan, M. (1992). *A Grammar of Lango*. Berlin: Mouton de Gruyter.

Norwood, C. (2002). Voice and valency alternations in Karo Batak. In: Wouk, F. & Ross, M., eds., *The History and Typology of Western Austronesian Voice Systems*. Canberra: Pacific Linguistics, pp. 181–207.

Oehrle, R. (1976). The grammatical status of the English dative alternation. Ph.D. dissertation, MIT.

O'Herin, B. (2001). Abaza applicatives. *Language* 77.3: 477–493.

Oshima, D. (2005). Morphological vs. phonological contrastive topic marking. *Proceedings from the Annual Meeting of the Chicago Linguistic Society. Vol. 41. No. 1*. Chicago: Chicago Linguistic Society.

(2008). Semantic divergence of *-(r)are*: from a different perspective. In: Hudson, M. E., Sells, P. & Jun, S.-A., eds., *Japanese/Korean Linguistics, Vol. 13*. Stanford, CA: CSLI, pp. 309–320.

Otsuka, Y. (2006). Syntactic ergativity in Tongan. In: Johns, A., Massam, D. & Ndayiragije, J., eds., *Ergativity: Emerging Issues*. Dordrecht: Springer, pp. 79–107.

Oyharçabal, B. (2003). Lexical causatives and causative alternation in Basque. In: Oyharçabal, B., ed., *Inquiries into the Syntax-Lexicon Relations in Basque* [Supplements of ASJU XLVI], pp. 223–253.

Pacchiarotti, S. (2017). Bantu applicative construction types involving *-ɪd*: Form, functions, and diachrony. Ph.D. dissertation, University of Oregon.

Paperno, D. (2014). Grammatical sketch of Beng. *Mandenkan* 51 (Bulletin d'études linguistiques mandé 201). Available online at llacan.vjf.cnrs.fr/PDF/Manden kan51/51paper.pdf.

Pardeshi, P. (1998). A contrastive study of benefactive constructions in Japanese and Marathi. *Sekai no nihongo kyôiku* 8: 141–165.

Pastika, I. W. (1999). Voice selection in Balinese discourse. Ph.D. dissertation, Australian National University.

Pawley, A. (1973). Some problems in the Proto-Oceanic grammar. *Oceanic Linguistics* 12: 103–188.

Payne, D. & Barshi, I. (1999). External possession. What, where, how and why. In: Payne, D. & Barshi, I., eds., *External Possession*. Amsterdam: John Benjamins, pp. 3–29.

Payne, T. (1982). Role and reference related subject properties and ergativity in Yupik Eskimo and Tagalog. *Studies in Language* 6.1: 75–106.

(1997). *Describing Morphosyntax*. Cambridge: Cambridge University Press.

(2000). Towards a substantive typology of applicative constructions. Ms., University of Oregon.

Peterson, D. (2007). *Applicative Constructions*. Oxford: Oxford University Press.

Pinker, S. (1989). *Learnability and Cognition: The Acquisition of Argument Structure*. Cambridge, MA: MIT Press.

Polinsky, M., ed. (2012). Special issue of *Theoretical Linguistics* 38.1/2.

Polinsky, M. (2013a). Antipassive constructions. In: Dryer, M. & Haspelmath, M., eds., *The World Atlas of Language Structures Online*, Ch. 108. Leipzig: Max Planck Institute for Evolutionary Anthropology. Available online at wals.info/chapter/108, accessed on 2016–06–17.

(2013b). Applicative constructions. In: Dryer, M. & Haspelmath, M., eds., *The World Atlas of Language Structures Online*, Ch. 109. Leipzig: Max Planck Institute for Evolutionary Anthropology. Available online at wals.info/chap ter/109, accessed on 2016–06–17.

(2017). Antipassive. In: Coon, J., Massam, D. & Travis, L. D., eds., *The Oxford Handbook of Ergativity*. Oxford: Oxford University Press, pp. 308–331.

Prasithrathsint, A. (2003). A typological approach to the passive in Thai. In: *MANUSYA: Journal of Humanities, Special Issues 6: Thai from Linguistic Perspectives*. Bangkok: Chulalongkorn University, 61–17.

(2004). The adversative passive marker as a prominent areal feature of Southeast Asian languages. In: Burusphat, S., ed., *Eleventh Annual Meeting of Southeast Asian Linguistics Society 2001*. Tempe: Arizona State University, pp. 583–598.

Prost, A. (1956). *La langue soṅay et ses dialectes*. Dakar: IFAN.

Proulx, P. (1985). Proto-Algic II: Verbs. *International Journal of American Linguistics* 51.1: 59–93.

Pylkkänen, L. (2008). *Introducing Arguments*. Cambridge, MA: MIT Press.

Quick, P. (2002). A sketch of the primary transitive verbs in Pendau. In: Wouk, F. & Ross, M., eds., *The History and Typology of Western Austronesian Voice Systems*. Canberra: Pacific Linguistics, pp. 101–122.

(2005). Topic continuity, voice and word order in Pendau. In: Arka, I. W. & Ross, M., eds., *The Many Faces of Austronesian Voice Systems: Some New Empirical Studies*. Canberra: Pacific Linguistics, pp. 221–242.

Radetzky, P. & Smith, T. (2010). An areal and cross-linguistic study of benefactive and malefactive constructions. In: Zúñiga, F. & Kittilä, S., eds., *Benefactives and Malefactives: Typological Perspectives and Case Studies*. Amsterdam: John Benjamins, pp. 97–120.

Rappaport Hovav, M. & Levin, B. (2008). The English dative alternation: The case for verb sensitivity. *Journal of Linguistics* 44.1: 129–167.

Renck, G. (1975). *A Grammar of Yagaria*. Canberra: Australian National University.

Rennison, J. (1996). *Koromfe*. London: Routledge.

Rhodes, R. (1976). The morphosyntax of the Central Ojibwa verb. Ph.D. dissertation, University of Michigan.

(1985). *Eastern Ojibwa-Chippewa-Ottawa Dictionary*. New York: Mouton.

(1994). Valency inversion and thematic alignment in Ojibwe. *Proceedings of the Twentieth Annual Meeting of the Berkeley Linguistics Society*. Berkeley: University of California Press, pp. 431–446.

(2010). Relative root complement: a unique grammatical relation in Algonquian syntax. In: Wohlgemuth, J. & Cysouw, M., eds., *Rara & Rarissima: Documenting the Fringes of Linguistic Diversity*. Berlin: Walter de Gruyter, pp. 305–324.

Rice, K. (2000). Voice and valency in the Athapaskan family. In: Dixon, R. M. W. & Aikhenvald, A., eds., *Changing Valency: Case Studies in Transitivity*. Cambridge: Cambridge University Press, pp. 173–235.

Riesberg, S. (2014a). Passive actors are not adjuncts: Consequences for the distinction between symmetrical and asymmetrical voice alternations. In: Arka, I. W. & Indrawati, N. L. K. M., eds., *Argument Realisations and Related Constructions in Austronesian Languages*. Canberra: Asia-Pacific Linguistics, pp. 281–302.

(2014b). *Symmetrical Voice and Linking in Western Austronesian Languages*. Boston: Mouton de Gruyter.

Rigsby, B. & Rude, N. (1996). Sketch of Sahaptin, a Sahaptian language. In: Goddard, I., ed., *Handbook of North American Indians, Vol. 17: Languages*. Washington: Smithsonian Institution, pp. 666–692.

Rijksbaron, A. (1984). *The Syntax and Semantics of the Verb in Classical Greek*. Amsterdam: Gieben.

Rincón, A. del. (1595). *Arte mexicana compuesta por el padre Antonio del Rincón de la Compañía de Jesús*. Mexico City, DF: Oficina Tipográfica de la Secretaría de Fomento.

Rissman, L. (2013). Event participant representations and the instrumental role: A cross-linguistic study. Ph.D. dissertation, Johns Hopkins University.

Roberts, I. (2005). *Principles and Parameters in a VSO Language: A Case Study in Welsh*. Oxford: Oxford University Press.

Robinson, S. (2011). Split intransitivity in Rotokas, a Papuan language of Bougainville. Ph.D. thesis, Radboud University Nijmegen.

Rosen, C. (1990). Rethinking Southern Tiwa: The geometry of a triple-agreement language. *Language* 66.4: 669–713.

Rosen, S. T. (1989). Two types of noun incorporation. *Language* 65.2: 294–317.

Rosenblum, D. (2013). Passive constructions in Kwa'kwala. Survey report, Survey of California and Other Indian Languages, University of California at Berkeley.

Available online at escholarship.org/uc/item/4mk0c2dm.pdf, accessed on 2017–07–25.

Ross, M. (2002). The history and transitivity of western Austronesian voice and voice-marking. In: Wouk, F. & Ross, M., eds., *The History and Typology of Western Austronesian Voice Systems*. Canberra: Pacific Linguistics, pp. 17–62.

Rozwadowska, B. (1989). Are thematic relations discrete? In: Corrigan, R., Eckman F. & Noonan, M., eds., *Linguistic Categorization*. Amsterdam: John Benjamins, pp. 115–130.

Rubino, C. (1997). A reference grammar of Ilocano. Ph.D. dissertation, University of California at Santa Barbara.

   (2005). Iloko. In: Adelaar, A. & Himmelmann, N., eds., *The Austronesian Languages of Asia and Madagascar*. Abingdon: Routledge, pp. 326–349.

Rude, N. (1988). Ergative, passive and antipassive in Nez Perce. In: Shibatani, M., ed., *Passive and Voice*. Amsterdam: Benjamins: pp. 547–560.

   (1997a). On the history of nominal case in Sahaptian. *International Journal of American Linguistics* 63.1: 113–143.

   (1997b). Dative shifting and double objects in Sahaptin. In: Givón, T., ed., *Grammatical Relations. A Functionalist Perspective*. Amsterdam: John Benjamins: pp. 323–349.

Russell, J. (1985). Swahili quasi-passives: The question of context. In: Goyvaerts, D., ed., *African Linguistics: Essays in Memory of M. W. K. Semikenke*. Amsterdam: John Benjamins: pp. 477–490.

Russell, L., Genee, I., Van Lier, E. & Zúñiga, F. (2012). Referential hierarchies in three-participant constructions in Blackfoot: the effects of animacy, person, and specificity. *Linguistic Discovery* 10.3.

Sadock, J. (1986). Some notes on noun incorporation. *Language* 62.1: 19–31.

Salas, A. (2006). *El mapuche o araucano. Fonología, gramática y antología de cuentos*. 2nd, revised edition. Santiago: Centro de Estudios Públicos.

Saltarelli, M. (1988). *Basque*. London: Routledge.

Sandoval, M. & Jelinek, E. (1989). The *bi-* construction and pronominal arguments in Apachean. In: Cook, E.-D. & Rice, K., eds., *Athabaskan Linguistics: Current Perspectives on a Language Family*. Berlin: Mouton, pp. 335–77.

Sansò, A. (2006). 'Agent defocusing' revisited. Passive and impersonal constructions in some European languages. In: Abraham, W. & Leisiö, L., eds., *Passivization and Typology: Form and Function*. Amsterdam: John Benjamins, pp. 232–273.

   (2017). Where do antipassive constructions come from? *Diachronica* 34.2: 175–218.

Sapir, E. (1911). The problem of noun incorporation in American languages. *American Anthropologist* 13.2: 250–282.

Schachter, P. (1977). Reference-related and role-related properties of subjects. In: Cole, P. & Sadock, J., eds., *Syntax and Semantics 8: Grammatical Relations*. New York: Academic Press, pp. 279–306.

   (1996). The subject in Tagalog: Still none of the above. *UCLA Occasional Papers in Linguistics* 15.

Schachter, P. & Reid, L. (2009). Tagalog. In: Comrie, B., ed., *The World's Major Languages*. 2nd edition. London: Routledge, pp. 833–855.

Schäfer, F. (2008). *The Syntax of (Anti-)Causatives: External Arguments in Change-of-State Contexts*. Amsterdam: John Benjamins.

(2009). The causative alternation. *Language and Linguistics Compass* 3.2: 641–681.

Schiefer, E. (1983). *Überlegungen zur Tauglichkeit des Passivbegriffs und bisheriger Passivuntersuchungen: mit besonderer Berücksichtigung finnisch-ugrischer Sprachen*. Wiesbaden: Harrassowitz.

Schikowski, R. (2013). Object-conditioned differential marking in Chintang and Nepali. Ph.D. dissertation, University of Zurich.

Schladt, M. (2000). The typology and grammaticalization of reflexives. In: Frajzyngier, Z. & Walker, T., eds., *Reflexives, Forms and Functions*. Amsterdam: John Benjamins, pp. 103–124.

Schröder, H. (2015). Alignment systems and passive-antipassive distribution in Nilotic languages. *The University of Nairobi Journal of Language and Linguistics* 4: 42–81.

Schulze, W. (1997). *Tsakhur*. Munich: Lincom Europa.

Seidl, A. & Dimitriadis, A. (2003). Statives and reciprocal morphology in Swahili. In: Zribi-Hertz, A. & Sauzet, P., eds., *Typologie des langues d'Afrique et universaux de la grammaire, Vol. 1*. Paris: L'Harmattan, pp. 239–284.

Seiler, W. (1978). The modalis case in Inupiat. *Working Papers of the Summer Institute of Linguistics* 22: 71–85.

Seiter, W. J. (1980). *Studies in Niuean Syntax*. New York: Garland Publishing.

Seržant, I. (2016). External possession and constructions that may have it. *Sprachtypologie und Universalienforschung* 69.1: 131–169.

Shibatani, M. (1973). A linguistic study of causative constructions. Ph.D. dissertation, University of California, Berkeley.

(1976). The grammar of causative constructions: A conspectus. In: Shibatani, M., ed., *Syntax and Semantics, Vol. 6: The Grammar of Causative Constructions*. New York: Academic Press, pp. 1–40.

(1985). Passives and related constructions: A prototype analysis. *Language* 61.4: 821–848.

(1988). Introduction. In: Shibatani, M., ed., *Passive and Voice*, 1–8. Amsterdam: John Benjamins.

(1996). Applicatives and benefactives: A cognitive account. In Shibatani, M. & Thompson, S., eds., *Grammatical Constructions: Their Form and Meaning*. Oxford: Clarendon Press, pp. 155–194.

(1998). Voice parameters. In: Kulikov, L. & Vater, H., eds., *Typology of Verbal Categories*. Tübingen: Niemeyer, pp. 117–138.

(2000). Issues in transitivity and voice: Japanese perspective. *Bulletin of the Faculty of Letters, University of Kobe* 27: 523–586.

(2004). Voice. In: Booij, G., Lehmann, C. & Mugdan, J., eds., *Morphology: A Handbook on Inflection and Word Formation*. Berlin: de Gruyter, pp. 1145–1165.

(2006). On the conceptual framework for voice phenomena. *Linguistics* 44.2: 217–269.

Shibatani, M. & Artawa, K. (2015). Valency classes in Balinese. In: Malchukov, A. & Comrie, B., eds., *Valency Classes in the World's Languages*. Berlin: Mouton de Gruyter, pp. 857–920.

Shibatani, M. & Pardeshi, P. (2002). The causative continuum. In: Shibatani, M., ed., *The Grammar of Causation and Interpersonal Manipulation*. Amsterdam: John Benjamins, pp. 85–126.

Shibatani, M., ed., (2002). *The Grammar of Causation and Interpersonal Manipulation*. Amsterdam: John Benjamins.

Shopen, T. & Konaré, M. (1970). Sonrai causatives and passives: transformational versus lexical derivations for propositional heads. *Studies in African Linguistics* 1: 211–254.

Siewierska, A. (2008). Introduction – Impersonalization: An agent-based vs. a subject-based perspective. *Transactions of the Philological Society* 106.2: 115–137.

(2013). Passive constructions. In: Dryer, M. & Haspelmath, M., eds., *The World Atlas of Language Structures Online*, Ch. 107. Leipzig: Max Planck Institute for Evolutionary Anthropology. Available online at wals.info/chapter/107, accessed on 2016–06–17.

Silverstein, M. (1972). Chinook Jargon: language contact and the problem of multilevel generative systems, I. *Language* 48.2: 378–406.

(1976). Hierarchy of features and ergativity. In: Dixon, R. M. W., ed., *Grammatical Categories in Australian Languages*. Canberra: Australian National University, pp. 112–171.

Simons, G. F. & Fennig C. D., eds., (2017). *Ethnologue: Languages of the World*, 20th edition. Dallas, Texas: SIL International. Available online at www.ethnologue.com.

Simpson, J. H. (1983). Aspects of Warlpiri morphology and syntax. Ph.D. dissertation, MIT.

Skorik, P. (1948). *Očerk po syntaksisu čukotskogo jazyka: inkorporatsija* [Outline of Chukchi Syntax: Incorporation]. Leningrad: Učpedgiz.

(1968). Čukotskij jazyk [The Chukchi language]. In: Vinogradov, V.V. et al. eds., *Jazyki nadorov SSSR, Vol. 5* [Languages of the Peoples of the U.S.S.R.]. Leningrad: Nauka.

(1977). *Grammatika čukotskogo jazyka 2: Glagol, narečie, služebnye slova* [*Grammar of the Chuckchi Language 2: Verb, Adverb, Function Words*]. Leningrad: Nauka.

Smeets, I. (2008). *A Grammar of Mapuche*. Berlin: Walter de Gruyter.

Smith-Stark, T. (1978). The Mayan antipassive: Some facts and fictions. In: England, N., ed., *Papers in Mayan Linguistics*. Columbia, MI: University of Missouri, pp. 169–187.

Smyth, D. (2002). *Thai: An Essential Grammar*. London: Routledge.

Smyth, H. W. (1974). [1920] *Greek Grammar*. Revised by G. M. Messing. Cambridge, MA: Harvard University Press.

Sneddon, J. N. (1996). *Indonesian: A Comprehensive Grammar*. London: Routledge.

(2006). *Colloquial Jakartan Indonesian*. Canberra: Pacific Linguistics.

Song, J. J. (1996). *Causatives and Causation: A Universal-Typological Perspective*. London: Longman.

(2001). *Linguistic Typology. Morphology and Syntax*. Harlow: Pearson Education Limited.

(2005a). Periphrastic causative constructions. In: Haspelmath, M., Dryer, M. S., Gil, D. & Comrie, B. eds., *The World Atlas of Language Structures*. Oxford: Oxford University Press, pp. 446–449.

(2005b). Nonperiphrastic causative constructions. In: Haspelmath, M., Dryer, M. S., Gil, D. & Comrie, B. eds., *The World Atlas of Language Structures*. Oxford: Oxford University Press, pp. 450–453.

(2008a). Periphrastic causative constructions. In: Haspelmath, M., Dryer, M. S., Gil, D. & Comrie, B. eds., *The World Atlas of Language Structures Online*. http://wals.info/chapter/110.

(2008b). Nonperiphrastic causative constructions. In: Haspelmath, M., Dryer, M. S., Gil, D. & Comrie, B. eds., *The World Atlas of Language Structures Online*. http://wals.info/chapter/111.

Sperlich, W. (1993). Serial verb constructions in Namakir of Central Vanuatu. *Oceanic Linguistics* 32.1: 95–110.

Spreng, B. (2005). Third person arguments in Inuktitut. In: Armoskaite, S. & Thompson, J., eds., *Workshop on the Structure and Constituency of the Languages of the Americas*. Vancouver: University of British Columbia, pp. 215–225.

(2010). On the conditions for antipassives. *Language and Linguistics Compass* 4.7: 556–575.

Stiebels, B. (2006). Agent focus in Mayan languages. *Natural Language & Linguistic Theory* 24.2.: 501–570.

Sugita, H. (1973). Semitransitive verbs and object incorporation in Micronesian languages. *Oceanic Linguistics* 12.1/2: 393–416.

Sun, T.-S. J. (1998). Nominal morphology in Caodeng rGyalrong. *The Bulletin of the Institute of History and Philology, Academica Sinica* 69.1: 103–149.

Svantesson, J.-O. (1983). *Kammu Phonology and Morphology*. Lund: University of Lund.

Tamura, S. (2000). *The Ainu Language*. Tokyo: Sanseido.

Tatevosov, S. (2011). Detelicization and argument suppression: Evidence from Godoberi. *Linguistics* 49.1: 135–174.

Teng, S. F.-C. (2005). Grammatical relations in Puyuma. In: Arka, I. W. & Ross, M., eds., *The Many Faces of Austronesian Voice Systems: Some New Empirical Studies*. Canberra: Pacific Linguistics, pp. 137–152.

Terrill, A. (1997). The development of antipassive constructions in Australian languages. *Australian Journal of Linguistics* 17.1: 71–88.

Tesnière, L. (1959). *Eléments de syntaxe structurale*. Paris: Klincksieck.

Thomas, D. M. (1969). Chrau affixes. *Mon-Khmer Studies* 3: 90–107.

Thompson, C. (1994). Passive and inverse constructions. In: Givón, T., ed., *Voice and Inversion*. Amsterdam: John Benjamins, pp. 47–63.

(1996). The history and function of the *yi-/bi-* alternation in Athabaskan. In: Jelinek, E., ed., *Athabaskan Language Studies: Essays in Honor of Robert Young*. Albuquerque: University of New Mexico Press, pp. 81–100.

Toyota, J. (2008). *Diachronic Change in the English Passive*. Basingstoke: Palgrave Macmillan.

Trask, R. L. (1992). *A Dictionary of Grammatical Terms in Linguistics*. London: Routledge.

Tsujimura, N. (1996). *An Introduction to Japanese Linguistics*. Oxford: Blackwell.

Tsuboi, E. (2010). Malefactivity in Japanese. In: Zúñiga, F. & Kittilä, S., eds., *Benefactives and Malefactives. Typological Perspectives and Case Studies*. Amsterdam: John Benjamins, pp. 419–436.

Tsunoda, T. (1988). Antipassive in Warrungu and other Australian languages. In: Shibatani, M., ed., *Passive and Voice*. Amsterdam: John Benjamins, pp. 595–649.

Tucker, A. & Bryan, M. (1966). *Linguistic Analyses. The Non-Bantu Languages of North-Eastern Africa*. London: Oxford University Press.

Ura, H. (1996). Multiple feature-checking: A theory of grammatical function splitting. Ph.D. dissertation, MIT.

Valenzuela, P. (2002). Causativization and transitivity in Shipibo-Konibo. In: Shibatani, M. ed., *The Grammar of Causation and Interpersonal Manipulation*. Amsterdam: John Benjamins, pp. 417–483.

Valijärvi, R.-L. & Kahn, L. (2017). *North Sámi: An Essential Grammar*. Abingdon: Routledge.

Vamarasi, M. K. (1999). *Grammatical Relations in Bahasa Indonesia*. Canberra: Pacific Linguistics.

Van de Kerke, S. (1998). Verb formation in Leko: Causatives, reflexives and reciprocals. In: Kulikov, L. & Vater, H., eds., *Typology of verbal categories. Papers presented to Vladimir Nedjalkov on the occasion of his 70th birthday*. Tübingen: Max Niemeyer Verlag.

Van de Visser, M. (2006). *The Marked Status of Ergativity*. Utrecht: LOT Publications.

Van der Voort, H. (2004). *Kwaza*. Berlin: Mouton de Gruyter.

Van Valin, R. & LaPolla, R. (1997). *Syntax: Structure, Meaning, and Function*. Cambridge: Cambridge University Press.

Vázquez Soto, V. (2002). Some constraints on Cora causative constructions. In: Shibatani, M., ed., *The Grammar of Causation and Interpersonal Manipulation*. Amsterdam: John Benjamins, pp. 197–244.

Velázquez-Castillo, M. (1996). *The Grammar of Possession: Inalienability, Incorporation and Possessor Ascension in Guaraní*. Amsterdam: John Benjamins.

(2002). Grammatical relations in active systems: The case of Guaraní. *Functions of Language* 9.2: 133–167.

Veraart, F. (1996). On the distribution of Dutch reflexives. M.A. thesis, MIT.

Vichit-Vadakan, R. (1976). The concept of inadvertence in Thai periphrastic causative constructions. In: Shibatani, M., ed., *Syntax and Semantics 6: The Grammar of Causative Constructions*. New York: Academic Press, pp. 459–476.

Vidal, A. (2008). Affectedness and viewpoint in Pilagá (Guaykuruan): a semantically aligned case-marking system. In: Donohue, M. & Wichmann, S., eds., *The Typology of Semantic Alignment*. Oxford: Oxford University Press, pp. 412–431.

Washio, R. (1992). When causatives mean passive: A cross-linguistic perspective. *Journal of East Asian Linguistics* 2.1: 45–90.

Watanabe, H. (2015). Valency classes in Sliammon Salish. In: Malchukov, A. & Comrie, B., eds., *Valency Classes in the World's Languages*. Berlin: Mouton de Gruyter, pp. 1293–1338.

Weir, E. M. H. (1986). Footprints of yesterday's syntax: Diachronic development of certain verb prefixes in an OSV language (Nadëb). *Lingua* 68.4: 291–316.

Williamson, K. (1965). *A Grammar of the Kolukuma Dialect of Ijo*. Cambridge: Cambridge University Press.

Willie, M. (1991). Navajo pronouns and obviation. Ph.D. dissertation, University of Arizona, Tucson.

(2000). The inverse voice and possessive *yi-/bi-* in Navajo. *International Journal of American Linguistics* 66.3: 360–382.

Wolfenden, S. (1929). *Outlines of Tibeto-Burman Linguistic Morphology: with special references to the prefixes, infixes and suffixes of classical Tibetan and the languages of the Kachin, Bodo, Nâgâ, Kuki-Chin and Burma groups*. London: Royal Asiatic Society.

Wolff, J. (1972). *A Dictionary of Cebuano Visayan*. 2 vols. Ithaca, NY: Southeast Asia Program, Cornell University.

(1996). The development of the passive verb with pronominal prefix in western Austronesian languages. In: Nothofer, B., ed., *Reconstruction, Classification, Description: Festschrift in Honor of Isidore Dyen*. Hamburg: Abera, pp. 15–40.

Woodbury, A. (1977). Greenlandic Eskimo, ergativity, and Relational Grammar. In: Cole, P. & Sadock, J. (eds.), *Syntax and Semantics, Vol. 8: Grammatical Relations*. New York: Academic Press, pp. 307–336.

Woodcock, E. C. (1959). *A New Latin Syntax*. Cambridge, MA: Harvard University Press.

Wouk, F. & Ross M., eds., (2002). *The History and Typology of Western Austronesian Voice Systems*. Canberra: Pacific Linguistics.

Yap, F. H. & Iwasaki, Sh. (2007). The emergence of 'give' passives in East and Southeast Asian languages. In: Alves, M., Sidwell, P. & Gil, D., eds., *SEALS VIII: Papers from the 8th Annual Meeting of the Southeast Asian Linguistics Society (1998)*. Canberra: Pacific Linguistics, pp. 193–208.

Young, R. W. (2000). *The Navajo Verb System: An Overview*. Albuquerque: The University of New Mexico Press.

Zavala, R. (2011). Reciprocal constructions in Olutec. In: Evans, N., Gaby, A., Levinson, S. C. & Majid, A., eds., *Reciprocals and Semantic Typology*. Amsterdam: John Benjamins, pp. 265–276.

Zúñiga, F. (2006a). *Mapudungun: el habla mapuche*. Santiago: Centro de Estudios Públicos.

(2006b). *Deixis and Alignment: Inverse systems in indigenous languages of the Americas*. Amsterdam: John Benjamins.

(2010). La marca diferencial del objeto en mapudungún. *Lingüística* 24: 141–164.

(2014). An exploration of the diachrony of Mapudungun valency-changing operations. Ms., University of Bern.

(2016). Selected semitransitive constructions in Algonquian. In: Janic, K. & Nau, N., eds., *Valency-Changing Operations Within and Across Languages*, thematic issue of *Lingua Posnaniensis* 58.2.

(2017). Mapudungun. In: Fortescue, M.; Mithun, M. & Evans, N., eds., *The Oxford Handbook of Polysynthesis*. Oxford: Oxford University Press, pp. 696–712.

Zúñiga, F. & Fernández, B. (forthcoming). Basque antipassives revisited. In: Janic, K., Witzlack-Makarevich, A. & Creissels, D., eds., *The Multifaceted Aspects of the Antipassive*. Amsterdam: John Benjamins.

Zúñiga, F. & Herdeg, A. (2010). A closer look at Mapudungun inversion and differential object marking. Paper read at the Workshop on Referential Hierarchy Effects on the Morphosyntax of Verbal Arguments, University of Leipzig, August 28–29.

Zwart, J.-W. (1997). Rethinking subject agreement in Swahili. Paper read at the 28th Annual Meeting of the North East Linguistic Society, University of Toronto, October 24.

Author Index

Abraham, Werner, 85
Aikhenvald, Alexandra, 15, 105, 174, 207
Aissen, Judith, 108, 135, 145
Aldridge, Edith, 104, 126–127
Alsina, Àlex, 17, 19, 64
Amberber, Mengistu, 33, 39, 52, 60
Apollonius Dyscolus, 2
Aristotle, 2
Arka, I Wayan, 9, 120–121, 130, 132–134, 143, 188, 194
Austin, Peter K., 13, 19, 24, 29, 32–33, 55, 58, 61–62, 65–66, 69, 75, 107, 214, 220, 234–236, 240

Barber, Elizabeth J. W., 171
Beck, David, 31, 57
Bickel, Balthasar, 4, 113, 205
Blust, Robert, 133
Bobaljik, Jonathan D., 110
Bossong, Georg, 3, 108
Branigan, Phil, 110
Brown, Dunstan, 7

Clayre, Beatrice, 128, 130
Comrie, Bernard, 4, 10, 15, 90, 181, 229, 251
Cooreman, Ann, 8, 113, 125–126
Creissels, Denis, 27, 62, 85, 178, 222
Croft, William, 6, 10, 133, 172, 191–192, 246, 253
Curl, Traci, 151

Demers, Richard A., 145
Dionysius Thrax, 2, 83, 168
Dixon, R. M. W., 4, 15, 26–27, 32, 34, 37, 39–40, 46, 101, 103, 105, 107, 126, 135, 138–139, 174, 178, 207
Dowty, David, 46
Dryer, Matthew S., 4, 8, 84, 92–94, 97, 102, 208
Duranti, Alessandro, 46

Eriksen, Pål, 19, 33
Evans, Nicholas, 151, 162–163, 165, 167

Faltz, Leonard, 151, 155
Fauconnier, Stefanie, 3, 46, 203
Fernández, Beatriz, 101, 107

Foley, William, 90, 122, 127, 222
Frajzyngier, Zygmunt, 151, 182

Gaenszle, Martin, 113
Gast, Volker, 151
Geniušienė, Emma, 70–71, 172, 230
Gerdts, Donna B., 65, 104, 116–117, 176
Gerstner-Link, Claudia, 24
Gildea, Spike, 73, 147, 224, 240
Givón, T., 8–9, 18, 85, 90, 100, 147, 151, 172, 195, 220

Hale, Ken, 109, 147, 222
Halle, Morris, 109
Haspelmath, Martin, 4, 6, 8, 10, 41, 45, 49, 51, 68, 70, 72, 90–91, 98, 105, 151, 173, 180–181, 184, 192, 197, 220–226, 239–241
Haude, Katharina, 135, 140–141
Heine, Bernd, 191, 230, 232
Himmelmann, Nikolaus P., 120–123, 125, 133–134
Hopper, Paul J., 3, 18, 200
Hukari, Thomas E., 104, 116–117, 176

Iemmolo, Giorgio, 3, 109

Janic, Katarzyna, 103, 105, 240, 248
Jaxontov, Sergei, 44–45
Jelinek, Eloise, 145, 147
Jenny, Mathias, 221

Kahn, Lily, 73
Kaufman, Daniel, 123, 220
Kaufmann, Ingrid, 173
Kazenin, Konstantin, 90, 92, 97, 102, 155, 171
Keenan, Edward, 41, 84, 92–94, 97, 102, 241
Kemmer, Suzanne, 172–173
Kittilä, Seppo, 6, 18, 20–21, 24, 33, 46, 66, 199, 203, 226, 241, 253
Kiyosawa, Kaoru, 65
Klaiman, Miriam H., 8–10, 13, 122, 143–144, 147, 149, 151, 173–174, 246–247, 252
Kokutani, Shigehiro, 162
König, Ekkehard, 151, 157, 162, 184, 191, 232
Koontz-Garboden, Andrew, 51

Language Index

Subject Index

affectedness, 3, 8–9, 18–19, 22, 37, 61, 68, 112, 114, 134, 173, 177, 185, 192–193, 200, 226, 246
agency, *See* agentivity
agent focus construction, 110
agentivity, 3, 8–9, 18–19, 21, 25, 46, 61, 100, 131, 140, 158, 200–203, 226, 235, 240–241
alternation
  agent-patient diathesis, 194
  antipassive-like, 189
  benefactive, 183
  causative, 178, 181
  conative, *See* alternation, antipassive-like
  dative, 191
  external possession, 184
  instrumental, 187, 193
  locative, 193
  passive-like, 188
  P-removing/installing, 186
  preposition drop, 186
animacy, 3, 9, 35, 38–39, 46–48, 50, 52, 80, 93–94, 108–109, 114, 116, 135, 140, 142, 144, 147, 158, 173, 191–192, 195, 202–204, 209–210, 213, 215, 240, 246, 249
animate, *See* animacy
antipassive
  adjunct-P, 105
  direct vs. indirect, 106
  lexicalized, 108
  lexically constrained, 70, 107
  non-promotional, 104
  patientless, 72, 105–106, 115
  potential, 115
  spurious, 109–110
  suppressing, *See* antipassive, patientless
antireflexive, 20
applicative
  comprehensive, 68, 186
  direct vs. nondirect, 58
  dynamic vs. nondynamic, 57
  high vs. low, 64
  oblique, 13, 58
  periphrasis, 62
  relational vs. redirective, 65
  remapping, 57, 65
  symmetric vs. asymmetric, 63

atransitive, *See* transitivity
attitude holder, 160
avalent, 12, 33, 73, 79–80
  definition, 3

backgrounding, 8, 90, 99, 113, 172, 241, 245
benefactive, 58, 62, 66–67, 69, 78, 183–185, 191, 222, 233–234, 237
  autobenefactive, 151, 173, 176, 237, 242
  ego-benefactive, 176
Benefactive Voice, 76
beneficiary, 53–54, 56–57, 59, 64, 74, 76, 78, 81, 97, 125, 129–130, 184, 237
bivalent (definition), 3

causation
  agent-related, 18–20, 37
  direct vs. indirect, 25, 33–34, 36–37
  sociative, 34
causative-reflexive, 151, 169–171, 174, 176–177, 226, 237, 241–242
causativization
  agentive, 21, 249
  covert, 20, 25
  detransitivizing, 20, 23, 25
comitative, 56, 66–67, 70, 76, 164
control, 18, 23, 37, 39, 46, 51, 100, 125, 173–174, 235, 246
conversive, 88
Conveyance Voice, 97, 124

definite, *See* definiteness
definiteness, 3, 24, 30, 70, 72, 94, 106, 109, 112, 116, 126, 134, 178, 190, 192, 202, 206, 213, 223–224, 227–228, 241
deponents, 170–171, 173, 252
detransitive, *See* transitivity
differential object marking, 3, 101, 108
direct-inverse, 89, 137, 142–143, 148–149, 247, 252
ditransitive, *See* transitivity
duplex
  diathesis, 153
  voice, 11, 154–155, 162–163, 176
durative, *See* durativity